CHINATOWN, HONOLULU

Chinatown, Honolulu

PLACE, RACE, AND EMPIRE

Nancy E. Riley

Columbia University Press
New York

Columbia University Press
Publishers Since 1893
New York   Chichester, West Sussex
cup.columbia.edu

Copyright © 2024 Columbia University Press

All rights reserved

Library of Congress Cataloging-in-Publication Data
Names: Riley, Nancy E., 1955– author.
Title: Chinatown, Honolulu : place, race, and empire / Nancy E. Riley.
Description: New York : Columbia University Press, [2024] | Includes bibliographical references and index.
Identifiers: LCCN 2023053210 | ISBN 9780231196789 (hardback) | ISBN 9780231196796 (trade paperback) | ISBN 9780231551823 (ebook)
Subjects: LCSH: Chinatown (Honolulu, Hawaii)—History. | Honolulu (Hawaii)—Race relations—History. | Chinese Americans—Hawaii—Honolulu—History. | Chinese Americans—Hawaii—Honolulu—Social conditions.
Classification: LCC DU629.H7 R56 2024 | DDC 996.9/31004951—dc23/eng/20240130
LC record available at https://lccn.loc.gov/2023053210

Printed and bound by CPI Group (UK) Ltd, Croydon, CR0 4YY

Cover design: Noah Arlow
Cover image: Doug Young, *Coke and Peanuts*, watercolor.

CONTENTS

ACKNOWLEDGMENTS vii

NOTES ON TERMINOLOGY ix

Introduction: Race and Place in the Empire 1

Chapter One
Setting the Stage: Chinese Experience Before 1900 37

Chapter Two
1900 to 1930: Destruction of Chinatown
and the (Re)building of a Chinese American Community 71

Chapter Three
World War II Comes to Hawai'i: The 1930s Through 1945 102

Chapter Four
Statehood Amid Cold War Politics 135

Chapter Five
Reconstructing Chinatown for a New Era 160

Chapter Six
Chinatown Today: Confluence of Past and Present 185

NOTES 219

BIBLIOGRAPHY 247

INDEX 263

ACKNOWLEDGMENTS

Hawai'i is the place I would nearly always rather be. I treasure my time there, and miss it when I am away. I probably would have loved it had I no friends in the Islands. Butin fact, my friends have made my time in Hawai'i even better. I should thank lots of people, but here let me single out Phyllis Tabusa, Elisa Johnston, Val Wong, Randy Wong, Andy Mason, Janet Mason, Gretchen Alther. For all their support; good food; advice on places, people, and ideas; their knowledge; and their aloha. Pearl Chang Johnson helped me envision what it was like to grow up Chinese in Hawai'i, and talking with her was always fun. I take all the responsibility for any errors in this book, but these folks all made it much better than it would have been.

Thanks to the East-West Center, which has several times provided me office space, library access, and colleagues.

I have used libraries and archives extensively, sometimes with a clear sense of what I was looking for but often not knowing what I might find or whether it might help me. In those times especially, archivists and librarians were incredibly helpful—their knowledge of their collections (and beyond) and their ability to make sense of the sometimes unclear requests or goals of patrons like me is amazing. I will always be grateful for their help and deep knowledge. Thanks to Sherman Seki at the Romanzo Adams Social Research Laboratory archives; the folks at the Hawaiian and Pacific Collection at Hamilton Library at the University of Hawai'i, Mānoa (and especially Jodie Mattos, Dore Minatodani, and Eleanor Kleiber); and staff at Hawai'i State Archives. Doug Chong and others at the Hawai'i Chinese History Center were also welcoming and helpful to me.

viii

ACKNOWLEDGMENTS

Other scholars have given me time, patience, wonderful ideas, including arguments that sometimes challenge my own and forced me to work harder and think better. For their insights, I thank Jon Okamura, Chris Yano, Dean Saranillio, John Rosa, and the late Nancy Lewis. I also acknowledge that whatever their efforts, any errors of scholarship and judgment are my own.

In this work, I have depended heavily on the scholarship and research of others, and while I cite them throughout this volume, I would like to further acknowledge the enormous and extensive contributions they have made to understandings of Hawai'i. Much of this work is not published in regular outlets but hides in archives and elsewhere. It was with pleasure and a real sense of gratitude that I learned so much from these scholars who were active before me.

Columbia University Press has been a most friendly home for this book, and I thank Eric Schwartz for his support all the way through. I am grateful for the reading and suggestions of the anonymous readers of this manuscript.

Sara Dickey remains my favorite reader of my work, someone who helps me find my way through complicated arguments or terrible writing.

My colleagues at Bowdoin have kept Asian American studies, politics, and perspectives always on the agenda. It has been a privilege to work with Belinda Kong, Connie Chiang, Shruti Devgan, and Shu-chin Tsui. Dharni Vasudevan will always be a good friend and important touchstone. I am lucky to have found a home in Bowdoin's sociology department, and I thank my departmental colleagues: Ingrid Nelson, Oyman Basaran, Theo Greene, Shruti Devgan, Hakim Zainiddinov, and Marcos Lopez. Without the help of Lori Brackett, I would never have been able to do what I have, here or in any other part of my work.

I interviewed a number of people during my research. These respondents include community leaders and heads of organization but many others as well. I thank everyone who was willing to talk to me and allowed me to see Hawai'i and Chinatown through their eyes.

A special mahalo to Elisa Johnston, who was always willing to listen to and comment on my mental wanderings and ready to join me on my actual wanderings around Chinatown, too. And thanks always to Bob, for everything.

NOTES ON TERMINOLOGY

In Hawai'i, *Hawaiian* refers not to those who live in Hawai'i but to Native Hawaiians, also known as Kānaka Maoli. I use *Hawaiian* in that manner.

In Hawai'i, people rarely identify as or even speak of "Asian Americans." Jonathan Okamura has written a useful piece on this issue: "Why There Are No Asian Americans in Hawai'i."[1] Following local convention, I refer to Chinese residents of Hawai'i—including those with American citizenship—not as "Chinese Americans" but as "Chinese." I use the same convention for other ethnic groups such as Japanese and Filipinos.

Haole is the term used in Hawai'i for white people. In this volume, *haole* refers to white people living in the Islands. I distinguish white individuals living in and from the continental United States by using *white* to describe them.

CHINATOWN, HONOLULU

INTRODUCTION

Race and Place in the Empire

In the early morning hours, Chinatown begins to awaken as vendors start their days. The fish market, where wholesale buyers snag the best fish caught in Pacific waters, is especially lively. Chinatown's proximity to the harbor makes the market seem well placed even though many of the fish are caught in waters far from Chinatown. As the morning develops, office workers are seen on the streets patronizing Chinatown businesses to gather breakfast food and drink, which they can carry to their offices a few blocks away. In Chinatown's parking garages, some cars hold office workers catching a few more minutes of sleep; getting to the area early allows them access to inexpensive parking, and they often stay in their cars until they need to be at work. They then walk to the tall buildings nearby, to the financial companies, the trading firms, and the government offices within. By midmorning, most businesses are open, and people from all parts of Honolulu come in to shop at the open markets. The produce in Chinatown is known to be fresh, varied, and less expensive than at most other places. Lei shops in the area bring in regular traffic throughout the day; everyone knows the best lei are to be found in Chinatown. Lunchtime brings more office workers in to grab a quick and inexpensive bite to eat. There might be a few tourists, often obvious because of their clear unfamiliarity with the area, the food offerings, or even where to find parking. Throughout the day, the clan and village associations welcome members,

INTRODUCTION

often older Chinese who like the familiar places and people. After schools let out, children might arrive to attend classes that teach lion dancing or kung fu; some of these children are Chinese, but many are not. Mun Lun School, the oldest Chinese language school in the Islands, gets underway after the regular school day ends. The evening brings a very different crowd as younger Honolulu residents come in to eat at upscale restaurants—many of them serving what might be called contemporary Pacific food—or to poke into the art galleries. But the sidewalks grow quieter as the evening progresses, and soon Chinatown seems less open to visitors. It is in these hours that Honolulu's homeless people settle into corners, doorways, and small spaces, catching sleep until the next day comes around. The area is often described as "gritty" or even dangerous, and for many it retains that character. But Chinatown is also deeply integrated into Honolulu society. That it acts as a place for so many activities and attracts people from all backgrounds suggests its multiple connections to contemporary Honolulu life: "The real Chinatown in Hawai'i is not a physical place. To the people of Chinese ancestry, it is a collective memory. There is a geographic area ewa of [i.e., west of] Honolulu's Central Business District which is referred to as 'Chinatown.' However the real Chinatown is a metaphor that has been assimilated into the genetic and cultural fabric of the Hawaiian people."[1]

Nayan Shah has described Chinatown "as the conflation of race and place."[2] That brief description captures key elements of the meaning of Chinatown in Honolulu and addresses the central arguments of this book. Honolulu's Chinatown shares some characteristics with other Chinatowns in other places. But the specific context of any Chinatown also matters, and Honolulu's Chinatown reflects its unique context and history. Thus, the focus of this volume on Chinese in Hawai'i requires situating these experiences and processes in the setting of Hawai'i. Two overarching frameworks ground this analysis.

The first framework argues that, because context is important to the meaning of any Chinatown, to understand the meaning of Honolulu's Chinatown necessarily requires attention to structures and processes that have shaped Hawai'i society more generally, including racial construction, labor history, relations between the United States and Hawai'i, Hawai'i's role in U.S. empire building, and the role of race in that process. Most Chinese first came to Hawai'i as laborers on sugar plantations, part of the first wave of laborers of various nationalities that made up the plantation labor

INTRODUCTION

force and that has shaped Hawai'i's social and racial landscape ever since. The sugar industry dominated Hawai'i for over a century; that industry's economics and politics were also an important connection between Hawai'i and the United States. Hawai'i was also important to the United States as a site for empire building, acting as a military outpost and a stepping stone to Asia and the Pacific. Important, too, was Hawai'i's role in the process of racial construction in the United States more generally, as Hawai'i's racial difference was used to shore up U.S. claims of global dominance during the Cold War. In the story of Chinese in Hawai'i and Honolulu's Chinatown, we see how race and place are linked to empire.

The second, related, framework recognizes that Honolulu's Chinatown highlights the settler colonial history of Hawai'i and the role of the United States, haole, Chinese, Native Hawaiians, and others in that process. Alongside the story of Chinese success in Hawai'i has been the story of Native Hawaiians, who over those same years experienced loss of land, decimation of communities and nation, and threats to their very survival. Both groups—and all others in Hawai'i—have navigated their success, future, and survival against the background of colonialism and white supremacy. The role of race is key here; Hawai'i is (another) example of the power of whiteness and the way that whiteness is not simply about white bodies: "Whiteness is 'more about the discursive practices that because of colonialism and neocolonialism, privilege and sustain the global dominance of white imperial subjects and European worldviews than about specific white individuals . . . [W]e must situate and evaluate postcolonial whiteness within the 'interlocking axes of power, spatial location, and history.'"[3] As I will discuss in later chapters, Hawaiian leaders made the best choices available given the difficult circumstances in which a colonial society left them. Chinese also moved into Hawai'i society with constraints and obstacles on many sides; by many standards, Chinese achieved enormous success in their efforts. I will argue that while Chinese were not the principal organizers of these large-scale processes, their rise and experience were intimately tied to settler colonialism. Indeed, an understanding of how race has been brought into American narratives, ideology, and empire must take into account the settler colonialist processes in that history, as well as how settler colonialism continues to shape racial politics today. The pathways and choices that Chinese had available to them were constrained by the organization and power structures of the society in which they lived. But at the same time, their experiences and their routes—the channels they used and the channels they created—helped to shape contemporary Hawai'i.

Chinese success—and particularly the narrative of that success—is rooted in an ideology of neoliberal multiculturalism that undergirds the U.S. empire and the role of race within it. At first glance, Chinese success in Hawai'i might suggest American racial tolerance and the country's interest in bringing all groups into a racial plurality. But a closer examination reveals the complicated process of "inclusion," differences in the racial hierarchy and white supremacist framework, and how that difference is excluded in these processes, even under the guise of multiculturalism. Different groups are allowed into the polity in different ways, for different purposes, and with different outcomes. The story of Chinese in Hawai'i, we will see, allowed an American narrative of inclusion partly for the purposes of empire building and capitalist development. These processes help to explain how Chinese and other Asian Americans have been tagged with the "model minority" label and highlight the connection between that discourse and race-making within empire building and settler colonialism.

In Chinatown, we see physical, concrete traces of these processes. Like all Chinatowns, Honolulu's Chinatown was constructed around race. In many places, including Honolulu, Chinese immigrants were widely seen as especially alien and thus dangerous to the surrounding community. In its early years, Chinatown was a mostly segregated community, often targeted by haole but also valued by Chinese as a safe harbor that offered some protection from difficult interactions with others in Honolulu. Later, Chinatown took on different meanings, as we will see throughout this volume. In Chinatown, we can trace the ways Chinese moved from newly arrived plantation laborers to a mostly segregated community through to their successful establishment into Honolulu society. We will see that, as Chinatown highlights the role of racialized consumption, it also marks the pathway of Chinese into a host society and the achievement of social citizenship. Because Hawai'i's relationship to the United States throughout these years was the backdrop to and a major player in the place of Chinese in Hawai'i, Chinatown also reflects Hawai'i's place in racial politics in the United States. The complicated history of race in Hawai'i means that Honolulu's Chinatown has both mirrored and diverged from Chinatowns in other places.

If Chinatown "preserves and displays the cultural legacy of racial-ethnic ancestry so that new generations can look back and comprehend with better insight the trajectory of their posterity,"[4] then Chinatown's place in Hawai'i society mirrors the process and manner in which race has been brought into the empire—partially, unequally—to shore up that empire, often in explicit partnership with Chinese themselves. In this book, I examine Chinatown—what it represents, preserves, and celebrates, as well as what it covers up or disappears—over the course of two centuries, investigating how its meaning and composition have changed over the years, always against a backdrop of local politics and geopolitics.

Thus, the themes that organize the volume are all visible from the perspective of Chinatown. A Chinatown lens not only provides a way to examine the experience and place of Chinese in Hawai'i but also allows a larger view of racial politics in Hawai'i and in the United States. As Gregory Bourassa argues, "Central to this process is how, under the pretense of diversity and multiculturalism, capitalism has managed to remain exclusive while finding nourishment through the lexicon of inclusion: the proliferation of diversity rhetoric in institutions, the widespread adoption of multiculturalism as state policy, the insidious rise of neoliberal multiculturalism as a form of governance, and the enlisting of 'diversity' and 'multiculturalism' into the framework of neoliberalism."[5]

In this introduction, for each of the book's central themes, I review existing literature and theory and briefly discuss Hawai'i's perspective to foreground my analyses in later chapters. As with most complex social issues, meaning develops through context. A thorough understanding of Honolulu's Chinatown and Chinese experience in Hawai'i underscores the importance of context in discussions of place or identity. Not all Chinatowns are the same, and what it means to be Chinese changes across place and time. Thus, I will be linking Chinatown with political, economic, global, and local contexts at every turn. We will see not only that the meanings of Chinatown have changed over time but also that those meanings vary among different groups. A Chinese perspective on Chinese experience in Hawai'i will be different from any other perspective—whether from haole, other Asians in Hawai'i, Native Hawaiians, Asians or non-Asians living in the continental United States. The shifting ground of how Chinese experience is interpreted and the lack of a single bird's-eye view of these issues remind us of the complexities and contradictions of any social phenomenon. Still, drawing from the various perspectives available gives us a more complete understanding.

INTRODUCTION

WHAT'S IN A NAME?
SPACE, PLACE, ETHNIC ENCLAVE, GHETTO

Scholars, activists, residents, and others have described Chinatowns across the world in many ways. Each includes, in some form, the concept of an ethnic area, an area that takes on different meanings depending on the observer, the place, and the historical time—underscoring the complexities of any Chinatown.

Cultural geographers distinguish space from place in a way that is useful when thinking about a geographical area. Space is something abstract, without any substantial meaning—a location that has no social connections. Place is space that has meaning. Meaning incorporates the ways that people use, think about, avoid, or pass through a space. Places come to resonate with people, and people are attracted to or discouraged from spending time in a place. Their activities within a place are shaped by the meanings attached to it. A sacred place—such as a temple or an area in a forest—is likely to guide the activities that people feel they can, should, or should not perform there, even if they are not believers in the meanings behind the sacred designation of the place. According to David Wilson, "Spaces . . . function as 'realities' that help to infuse narrations of people, places and processes with meaning . . . [P]eople and processes [are] made 'known' by the spaces they operate in, the spaces they create, the spaces that create them."[6]

Thus, though people shape places, place also has a role in shaping human behavior. Thomas Gieryn argues that place is "an agentic player . . . a force with detectable and independent effects on social life."[7] He describes the relationship between people and place as interactive, with place and people working together to create the meaning of a space. Particularly relevant to thinking about a place like Chinatown is Gieryn's assertion that "place sustains difference and hierarchy both by routinizing daily rounds in ways that exclude and segregate categories of people, and by embodying in visible and tangible ways the cultural meanings variously ascribed to them."[8]

Gieryn's arguments are helpful in making sense of the debates about whether Chinatowns are ethnic enclaves or ghettos, reminding us that which term seems most appropriate is usually not about the physical space itself but rather connected to the assumptions that go with each term. *Ghetto* is often used—in popular and some scholarly work—to emphasize the involuntary nature of the residential segregation of a racial, ethnic, or religious group.[9]

INTRODUCTION

Others use *ghetto* to mark an area of extreme poverty. And some believe that *ghetto* encompasses both race and class characteristics—and the ways that, in many places including the United States, racial and class inequality are deeply connected. *Enclave*, on the other hand, is less often assumed to be the result of forced segregation. Yoonmee Chang sees this debate differently, pointing out that the usual practice of labeling Chinatowns "ethnic enclaves" rather than "ghettos" makes invisible the involuntary nature of these sites' construction and obscures the reality that segregation has been imposed on Chinese by the mainstream society. The phrase *ethnic enclave* suggests that the segregation was chosen by the residents themselves. *Ghetto*, Chang argues, would make it more obvious that Chinatowns have been indeed structurally imposed sites of racial inequality.[10]

But, of course, even without physical borders or codified laws regarding where a group may or may not reside, it is often unclear whether residential segregation is forced or voluntary. "Constrained choice" may better describe the process of racial or ethnic segregation—choice limited by constraints that come from long-standing discrimination across a variety of social institutions, from schooling to law to real estate. Indeed, more important than the label used to describe an area is that the segregation is the spatial result of upstream processes. In that vein, Chaddha and Wilson argue that instead of disagreeing about what a ghetto is or is not, we should focus on "ghettoization": "the underlying and interrelated processes that produce and maintain ghetto areas."[11]

This volume is focused more on the social processes that defined, challenged, and maintained Chinatown than on a discussion of whether it was and is a ghetto or an ethnic enclave. As we will see, Chinatowns both constrained where Chinese were allowed to live and provided them with a safe haven. I discuss Chinatown as both an ethnic enclave and as a site of racial and class difference in more detail in chapter 5.

More important than a discussion of how we name a segregated space is a recognition that Chinatown is as much an idea as a physical place where Chinese live. Chinatowns are a product of the racialization processes that have occurred in many societies. Racialization—"the process by which attributes such as skin color, language, birthplace, and cultural practices are given social significance as markers of distinction"[12]—marks each Chinatown as a place of Chinese people and gives meaning to the place and the group. Thus, Chinatowns have long been "a spatial expression of forms

INTRODUCTION

of exclusion."[13] Key to the meaning of that physical space is the place of Chinese in North America. Being Chinese has a meaning that incorporates notions of difference, East versus West, and orientalism, as well as the power of the mainstream, white majority to define, characterize, and govern marginalized groups. Related to this meaning, then, is how for some, particularly outsiders and tourists, Chinatown can be interpreted as an essentialized place rather than a local place with a specific history and meaning. Visitors may visit, perceive, and consume a Chinatown not with an understanding of its local meaning but with an assumption that it reflects some generalized idea or image of China or "Chinatown."[14] In such cases, where a Chinatown is located—in New York, Honolulu, or Manila—is less significant than the assumptions that visitors bring to their Chinatown visits—assumptions about China, Chinese, and Chinatowns in general, which have contributed to the way that Chinatown has become a metaphor for larger processes and meanings.[15]

CHINATOWN'S HISTORICAL CONSTRUCTIONS

Chinatowns have long functioned as both sites of forced segregation and refuges to an often-marginalized Chinese community, usually at the same time. In the early years of immigration from China, Chinatowns were most often sites of racial segregation, the result of prohibitions about where some groups were allowed to reside.[16] For example, in San Francisco, Chinese were long restricted in where they were permitted to live. In 1892, federal courts upheld restrictions on renting housing to Chinese outside Chinatown, restrictions that were in place until 1947.[17] Chinese segregation in the United States is reflected in data from the 1920 census that show that 41 percent of the total population of Chinese in the United States lived in Chinatowns or "Chinese quarters" in eight cities (San Francisco, New York, Oakland, Chicago, Los Angeles, Seattle, Boston, and Portland, Oregon). The rest of the Chinese population lived in small towns or rural areas,[18] often working in mines, in logging, at lumber sites, or on the railroads; building corrals; erecting stone walls; or working as servants in white households.[19]

Chinese segregation was intertwined with how Chinese were subjected to discrimination, whether through residency restrictions or other institutional practices such as school segregation or discriminatory hiring practices; they also regularly endured everyday acts of harassment and violence.[20] Reflecting how race and place are mutually constructed, Chinatowns and Chinese were subject to similar negative assumptions about danger and foreignness. As Kay Anderson argues about Vancouver's Chinatown, "Citizens seemed to believe that the Chinese district was a natural outcome of the 'herd instinct' of the 'clannish Chinese' with their 'habit of huddling' in limited quarters of their own, directly opposed to our conceptions of civilized progress, morality and hygiene."[21]

One of the most significant and powerful discourses about Chinatowns came from a public health perspective that viewed these areas not only as foreign but also as sites of danger and disease. Throughout history, in many societies, foreigners were often suspected of carrying disease.[22] The United States began screening people for disease and ill health at its borders in the late nineteenth century and turned away an increasing number of immigrants for medical reasons: only 2 percent of immigrants who were rejected in 1898 were rejected for medical reasons, but that percentage increased to 57 percent in 1913 and to 69 percent by 1915.[23] That change reflected not a rise in the number of ill immigrants but a shift toward border officials identifying "chronic, mental, or moral conditions, such as feeblemindedness, constitutional psychopathic inferiority or hookworm" as the basis for rejection.[24] Increasingly, immigrants were seen as threatening the physical, social, and moral health of the nation.[25] Asians were turned away at U.S. borders for health reasons at rates far higher than other groups. Chinese were seen as essentially and completely foreign; in 1908, the *New York Times* described them as "the most foreign of our foreigners."[26] It is not surprising, then, that Chinese immigrants were regularly depicted as disease carriers. Chinatown was similarly a target of concern, often described as a site—and the source—of disease. Such constructions were supported by the belief that disease was caused by filth and dirt (rather than bacteria or viruses). Chinatowns were often run-down and crowded and thus easily associated with disease. But Chinatowns were seen as unsanitary not because of some environmental or social reason but because of something innate to the Chinese themselves. As Nayan Shah argues about San Francisco's Chinatown, "The discourse of health and hygiene played a formidable role in cultural definitions of racial difference and the racial character of living conditions. . . . Public health officials took the prevailing languages of anti-Chinese antipathy and reshaped them into justifiable medical aversion. Popular observations about filth and overcrowding were enfolded into

INTRODUCTION

medical conceptions of epidemic disease, health risk, and sanitary danger and then recycled back into popular discourse."[27] Further, citizens, health officials, and government leaders argued that Chinatown and Chinese were a danger to the rest of the population. The poor sanitary and moral habits of Chinese, it was argued, put the entire population of a city at risk, whether because of disease, prostitution, or opium use.

Also important in these discussions was the assumption that Chinatown marked a boundary not only between Chinese and non-Chinese, or even East and West, but also between uncivilized and civilized. Just as Chinese were considered "always foreign," Chinatown was considered a foreign land in the midst of a Western city. Visits by outsiders were regularly depicted as adventures into a foreign and uncivilized land: "For many white tourists, Chinatown satisfied not only their curiosity about the unfamiliar but also their need to rediscover their superiority. For them Chinatown stood as a site of comparison: one between progress and stagnation, between vices and morality, between dirtiness and hygiene, and between paganism and Christianity."[28] Barbara Berglund argues that these tourist "adventures" helped to define white America: "Whereas natural wonders and places of historical significance allowed tourists to define who they were and what they were a part of, the various peoples that became part of the tourist terrain—Mormons, Native Americans, Mexicans, and Chinese—were generally displayed and consumed in such a way as to reinforce their differences from and inferiority to the white tourists who gazed upon them."[29] This notion helps to explain why San Francisco's Chinatown was attractive to tourists, even amid strong anti-Chinese sentiments and actions.[30]

Such attitudes and the discourses around them also reflect an Orientalist belief that justified a perceived need for city officials to control Chinatown and Chinese for their own good and the good of a city's entire population: "In that sense, Chinatown was more than a cultural construct of European imagining; it was a political projection through which a divisive system of racial classification was being structured and reproduced."[31] Further, in arguing that the bad, backward, dangerous, and disreputable places were confined to one (racially inscribed) place, whites could imagine that the rest of the city contained no such elements and was thoroughly moral, clean, safe, and modern.[32]

Amy Sueyoshi argues that in San Francisco at the turn of the twentieth century, whites used their assessment of the foreignness of Chinese and

INTRODUCTION

Japanese residents to understand their own anxieties about issues of race and sexuality; it was less threatening to watch and judge the behavior of Asian residents than to examine their own transgressions of racial or gender norms, even though such norms were undergoing shifts at the time.[33] Thus, the place and perception of Chinatowns across North America and in other parts of the world reflected the deep prejudice that existed toward Chinese, especially in terms of their perceived foreignness and connection to disease. Forced segregation was a way that whites could attempt to prevent these traits from "infecting" the rest of a city.

Although Chinatowns arose from segregationist policies and discriminatory practices, for Chinese, these areas also provided residents with a community and were seen as a refuge,[34] a safe haven from racial discrimination and harassment.[35] Chinatown was home, where Chinese could find friends, speak a familiar language, read newspapers that provided news of both home and their current place of residence, and maintain connections to family and home villages in China. Chinatowns also had social clubs and organizations, which were usually organized around clans or geographical ties, such as home villages or districts; the Sam Yap Company, for example, represented immigrants from a group of districts in Guangdong Province in Southern China. North American Chinatowns were more likely than those in Europe or Australia to have associations that structured services in the community.[36] These associations provided an especially important source of support, a sense of belonging, and often a connection to home for Chinese residents.

Partly for these reasons, in many places, Chinese residents actively protected the place of Chinatown, often against powerful forces that wanted to remove or at least move the community.[37] Chinese residents often resisted the negative perceptions of Chinatowns, instead arguing that they were often sites of cultural and social strength that existed in the midst of and as bulwarks against racism. In that spirit, Yong Chen wrote about the Chinatown in nineteenth-century San Francisco, at the time home to the largest Chinese American community: "The Chinese community that started to take shape in the 1850s was no impoverished ghetto; rather it demonstrated significant economic strength. Its dynamic economy was another source of its vitality and helps to explain its longevity."[38] Chen argues that that longevity "most clearly underscores its [Chinatown's] defiance of anti-Chinese forces that persistently tried but failed to eradicate or dislocate this large and visible Chinese community from the heart of the city."[39]

INTRODUCTION

In many places, as Chinese became more settled, they built social institutions such as schools, hospitals, and community organizations within Chinatowns. These developments not only provided the community with needed services but also went some way in convincing Chinese and non-Chinese alike that Chinese deserved a place in the broader society, allowing them to become "recognizable citizens in a nation that denied the Chinese the privileges and possibilities of full participation in society."[40] Chinese struggles in San Francisco schools reflected how Chinese had tried to use the American system to gain acceptance. When Chinese children were not allowed to attend public school, some parents sued for their admittance, leading to a California Supreme Court decision that upheld the right of Chinese children to attend school. However, that ruling led to the establishment of race-segregated schools.[41] In the face of such treatment, Chinese often built parallel institutions to meet their community's needs. In 1900, Chinese community leaders in San Francisco opened a hospital, the Tung Wah Dispensary, in Chinatown, which was staffed by both Chinese and non-Chinese professionals.[42] The hospital provided the Chinese community access to medical care, which was regularly denied in San Francisco at the time. The hospital was also touted by Chinese community leaders for its modern, Western approaches to illness and health.[43] Seeking a different kind of access to services and institutions, some Chinese managed to move out of Chinatown despite laws enforcing residential segregation. But in California, Chinese were effectively barred from living outside segregated areas, especially after the passage of the Alien Land Act in 1913, which made illegal land ownership by "aliens ineligible for U.S. citizenship" (read: those Asians born outside the United States). It was only after the repeal of the Exclusion Act in 1943 and the invalidation of the Alien Land Act in 1952 that Chinese and other Asian Americans began to settle in any numbers outside racially segregated areas in many parts of North America.

CHINATOWN TODAY

Most Chinatowns have undergone changes in recent decades that reflect transformations in their cities and shifts in the place of Chinese in the wider society. Just as Chinatowns in the past differed by location, Chinatowns have changed in different ways, functioning for different purposes. Some continue to be sites of first settlement for new immigrants, havens

INTRODUCTION

for new arrivals that provide resources for adjustment to the new country in the form of newcomer clubs, immigrant employment assistance, language training, or real estate services. Some serve employment purposes, helping to organize and distribute labor to Chinese businesses in the area.[44] Many are places of "cultural maintenance"[45] and sites of Chinese schools and cultural events and festivals. Many, of course, provide for the needs of Chinese residents in the form of grocery stores, restaurants, and small retail stores.

An important development in recent decades is the newly created "satellite Chinatowns," often arising some distance from the original community. After the change in immigration laws in 1965, a new Chinatown in Flushing, Queens (New York), grew and flourished separate from the original one in Lower Manhattan.[46] The Chinese immigrants who settled there tended to be better educated, of a higher socioeconomic status, and more likely to move with their families than were earlier Chinese immigrants; Queens provided these new immigrants with housing and a place to establish new businesses. "Ethnoburbs"—suburban clusters of businesses and people of a minority ethnic group—are also numerous in places like Southern California. Monterey Park, not far from Los Angeles, is a classic example of the suburbanization of minority ethnic groups, most of whom previously resided in urban areas.[47] Monterey Park's population has shifted from being almost completely white in the 1950s to being composed of several ethnic groups, including Latinos, Japanese Americans, and Chinese Americans today. By 2000, whites made up only 7 percent of Monterey Park's population; two-thirds of the population were Asian American (Japanese and Chinese), and just under a third were Latino.[48] The Chinese there were mostly from Taiwan, rather than from Southern China as had been true in many urban Chinese communities, and a large percentage were professionals. With the development of Monterey Park into a majority-Asian community came similar changes in nearby communities as more Asian immigrants and Asian Americans settled in the region.[49] The rise in numbers of Asian immigrants brought in new businesses and services owned and run by members of these communities, as well as other businesses that catered to the communities.

These changes in the residential patterns of Chinese—both long-settled immigrants and their children, as well as newly arrived immigrants—reflect several key changes. In most places, Chinese no longer live in segregated communities but have moved into the middle class and into neighborhoods and communities that once were off limits.[50] And many

INTRODUCTION

newly arrived Chinese immigrants in the United States do not settle in Chinatowns at all but take up first residence in suburbs. These immigrants are often well educated, and many are professionals.

These changes in residential patterns point to changes in Chinatowns themselves and a shift in the strong connections between ethnicity and place that were part of Chinatowns in the past. Indeed, in many places now, Chinatown is no longer a separate community with its own culture and networks; rather, many residents are not Chinese. That most Chinese in a city live outside Chinatown is itself significant and can influence the character and meaning of Chinatown.

Nevertheless, Chinatown retains importance. Chinese have often continued to embrace Chinatowns as places of community, consumption, political organizing, resource building, resistance, and historical remembrance.[51] Indeed, the predicted disappearance of Chinatowns[52] never occurred, underscoring that Chinatown remains meaningful and valued. And even though they have undergone significant changes, contemporary Chinatowns retain some of their historical legacy. As we will see, Chinatowns have also been targets of destruction by city governments looking to erect "modern" buildings and institutions in their stead, from new shopping areas to sports arenas.[53] Residents and others connected to Chinatowns in many cities have fought such redevelopment projects with varying degrees of success.[54]

The Role of Consumption

For most of their existence, Chinatowns have been places of consumption. Thus, a central factor in the changing meanings of Chinatown is the different form consumption has taken in different historical eras.

For many years, Chinatown was a place to obtain goods made in China, goods that Chinese immigrants might miss from home, or goods that provide a sense of connection to China. Along with Chinese goods, Chinese stores have also offered domestically produced items. This remains the case today, even though Chinese retailers and merchandizers are no longer confined to Chinatown in most cities. Chinatown's restaurants have also long provided low-cost meals to workers in the city. In recent decades, the kinds of restaurants and their clientele have shifted to appeal to new customers—especially non-Chinese middle- and upper-class diners. Today, most Chinatowns are dominated by businesses that

INTRODUCTION

provide services. Service businesses such as beauty and hair parlors and nail salons have proliferated,[55] reflecting changes in consumption patterns across society and illustrating another way that consumption connects Chinatowns with people living beyond their borders.

As we will see, the importance of consumption to Chinatown reflects how consumerism is central to most current societies and how that consumption is racialized. For non-Chinese, Chinatown has been and continues to be a place where non-Chinese consume Chinese things and services. Indeed, with urban areas having developed into places of and having built their economies on consumption, Chinatowns are often seen as potentially valuable to cities. Such ethnic spaces and their energy can help revive cities, increase commercial traffic in areas where manufacturing or other businesses have departed,[56] and even become a destination for visitors. Indeed, Chinatowns can help sell a particular version of a city as a site of diversity, excitement, and the new. Many Chinatowns have gone from being seen as foreign and dangerous to being hailed as exotic and hip. In the new version, Chinatowns can be seen as a form of racial commodification, where "outsiders have exploited Chinatown's non-Whiteness by commodifying its racial identity to derive economic value."[57] Other scholars point out, "In our globalizing world—where local difference and place identity are increasingly important—heritage and cultural diversity have become crucial components of post-industrial societies."[58] In these new constructions, Chinatowns are physical evidence for a continuing discourse—a powerful Orientalist discourse—that sees Chinese as outsiders, even though they have become middle-class citizens in many societies. As commodities in the contemporary social scene, Chinatowns are still depicted as different, with Orientalized street signs, building designs, and stores, still a bit of foreign land within the domestic city. These changes reflect urban development and how cities have refashioned themselves into destinations for investment, tourism, consumption, and new residence. Cities are now routinely "branded," a process that turns whole cities or communities within them "into identifiable local products."[59]

Chinese themselves are not immune from promoting these discourses and often capitalize on selling ethnic difference, participating in what might be seen as "purposeful Orientalizing,"[60] or "strategic self-orientalizing,"[61] as Peter Li and Eva Xiaoling Li argue has happened in Vancouver: "Such an enclave facilitates the success of ethnic businesses by increasing the

INTRODUCTION

visibility of ethnic goods and services. A high public profile is important for tourist-type businesses such as Chinese restaurants and gift shops, which rely heavily on the successful marketing of oriental cuisine and cultural exotica to tourists and white customers. At the same time, the concentration of many Chinese restaurants, ethnic grocery stores and ethnic retail stores provides convenience and choices to customers from the growing Chinese community inside and outside of Chinatown."[62]

By selling a version of Chinatown that aligns with a non-Chinese vision and by participating in racial capitalism in their own way, Chinese might achieve goals that range from making a profit to promoting the city to preventing the declaration of Chinatown as a ghetto that should be razed to make room for "modern" businesses. In these ways, Chinese and Chinatowns have continued to be reimagined within old discourses of foreign, different, and separate.

The examination of Chinatown in Sydney, Australia, by Kay Anderson and colleagues adds important layers to the understanding of the place and meaning of Chinatowns today, illuminating how Sydney's Chinatown is productive and influential in that city.[63] They argue that transnationalism, the increasing influence of China as a world power, connections between Australia and Asia, and the changed position of Chinese in Sydney and Australia are key factors in the changing place of Sydney's Chinatown. Chinatown can no longer be seen as fixed, separate, and unchanging but must be recognized as fluid, hybrid, adapting, and influential in Sydney's future. Most importantly in this new era, they argue, the boundaries that have been key to defining Chinatown—between East and West, past and present, foreign and domestic—are no longer so easily distinguishable but rather interwoven and entangled. Recognizing those changes and entanglements allows us to see Chinatown as a place that helps disrupt the way that concepts of difference and normative are viewed in a society. This new Chinatown, Anderson and her coauthors argue, provides a lens such that "it might be possible to envisage a future in which difference is no longer 'other' to a mainstream, but inherent to the very fabric of an evolving metropolitan culture."[64]

Chinatowns are also places of celebration. Most offer celebrations around key holidays such as New Year or Autumn Festival. These celebrations bring together Chinese communities in the area and invite in outsiders, all in a spirit that serves to recognize the community and often the

INTRODUCTION

continuing importance of Chinese ethnicity. However, even though we can recognize the significance of these celebrations, it is also important to ask what (else) is being celebrated by these gatherings and in this place. I will explore these questions throughout this volume.

CHINESE: ALIENS, MODEL MINORITY, CHANGE-MAKERS

As a built environment with embedded social meanings, Chinatown's place and meaning have undergone changes that reflect the shifting place of and attitudes toward Chinese in Western societies and how, despite those shifts, some assumptions remain. In the early decades of Chinese immigration to North America, Chinese were seen as ultimate foreigners, alien and threatening to white society. Much of the anti-Chinese legislation around immigration and other processes reflected white anxieties over a potential change in the United States as a white American nation.[65] Those earlier images changed in seemingly remarkable ways such that Chinese Americans—and some other Asian Americans—came to be depicted as "model minorities." In recent years, as we have moved toward an "Asian era" or a "Pacific century," Chinese have sometimes been seen as potential change-makers, central players in new multicultural, transnational societies. Importantly, throughout the last two centuries, Chinese have been depicted simultaneously as threatening to other Americans and as worthy of admiration. Similarly, Chinatowns have maintained a contradictory image as both sites of danger and threat and alluring places of exotic wonder.

Seen as "the yellow peril," Chinese immigrants from the mid-nineteenth to the early twentieth centuries were depicted as the most foreign of foreigners, even in places like the United States where immigration was at peak levels. The perception that Chinese immigrants were incompatible with Western culture came from a Western model of Asia in which Asia "stands in opposition to the world we know and the laws that govern it, and thus was beyond and outside the realm of order and sensibility."[66] As such, Chinese were seen as dangerous—particularly likely to spread disease—and needing to be controlled, both in numbers permitted to enter the United States and in where they lived once in the country. A virulent anti-Chinese movement arose from these sentiments. Chinatowns were targeted during these times and were subject to "a broader-based national ideology reconstituting American cities as white, English-speaking, and racially unified."[67]

INTRODUCTION

The segregation of Chinese in Chinatowns was seen as a way to control this yellow peril, again bringing people, place, and race together. Assumptions about Chinatowns also applied to Chinese people—who were considered dangerous in their extreme difference from American culture and society.

In more recent decades, Chinese have not necessarily been seen in the same ways, but old assumptions persist. Chinese are often assumed to be "foreigners," even if they are fifth-generation Americans. And although not seen as diseased in the same way they once were, the ways that U.S. Chinatowns and Chinese Americans were avoided during the SARS epidemic in 2003[68] suggests that the assumption of being innately diseased still follows Chinese today. Many long-standing and still-present fears that Chinese are alien, diseased, and dangerous arose again during the COVID-19 pandemic, during which Chinese were harassed, threatened, verbally and physically attacked, and blamed for the pandemic.[69]

Since the 1950s, Asian Americans, particularly Chinese Americans, have also been held up as "model minorities." Presumed to be more successful than other minority groups because of a combination of innate abilities (e.g., the "math gene"), hard work, and a willingness to keep their heads down and not complain, in this way Asian Americans have been held up as an example of doing the right things to get ahead in U.S. society.[70] Consumption plays a role here: because of the role of consumption in modern industrial societies like the United States, Asian Americans' proper consumption—the houses they buy, the education they attain, the careers they choose—has enabled them to attain at least partial social citizenship in the United States, even though they continue to be viewed as outsiders. Chinatown's place as a site of consumption, then, marks this achievement, celebrating that Chinese know how to buy and sell and how to interact with non-Chinese in proper—market—ways.

As we will see, there is much wrong and misleading about the model-minority stereotype, but it is important to recognize that the concept of the model minority is related to the concept of the yellow peril. As Gary Okihiro has argued, "The Asian work ethic, family values, self-help, culture and religiosity, and intermarriage—all elements of the model minority— can also be read as components of the yellow peril. The yellow peril and the model minority are not poles, denoting opposite representations along a single line, but in fact form a circular relationship that moves in either direction. . . . Moving in one direction along the circle, the model minority

INTRODUCTION

mitigates the alleged danger of the yellow peril, whereas reversing direction, the model minority, if taken too far, can become the yellow peril."[71]

Today, although Chinese Americans (and other Asian Americans) are still regularly assumed to be foreigners, their exoticism is seen as enticing and attractive and has become an element of "racial capitalism," a notion tied to the use of multiculturalism for neoliberal aims. In this model, a constructed exoticism is at the heart of a fascination for Chinese people and things, whether that involves white men's sexual and romantic fantasies about Asian women, an interest in bringing Asian fashion to the West, or many people's interest in eating food that is different from their own cuisines. That fascination, combined with an increasingly consumptive society, has refashioned Chinese and Chinatown as sites of consumption because they continue to symbolize difference. Cities try to distinguish themselves by highlighting their ethnic neighborhoods; thus, Chinatowns can contribute to an area's attractiveness to outsiders, and a visit might be seen as a safe exotic experience. Volkan Aytar and Jan Rath have described the "diversity difference" of Chinatowns: "In our globalizing world—where local difference and place identity are increasingly important—heritage and cultural diversity have become crucial components of post-industrial societies."[72] Here, racial diversity is absorbed by white society and used to further its capitalist goals.

As global power has shifted in recent decades and as Asia and the Pacific take on new dominance in economic, cultural, and political spheres, cities and countries are eager to use Chinese, other Asians, and Chinatowns to strengthen their ties to Asia. In Sydney, for example, where most envision a future shaped by and interwoven with that of Asia and particularly China, Chinese can be seen as productive in helping Australia retain a global position and a successful integration with Asia's increasing influence.[73] Such a perspective moves away from seeing Chinese and Chinese communities as passive or reacting to their treatment by white majorities. Rather, it focuses on diasporic Chinese communities as active players in creating a new society and a new world, one that is transnational and fluid.[74]

That Chinatowns remain speaks to the continuing need for such communities and institutions for elements of the Chinese community, particularly for new arrivals to the city and older Chinese who have spent much of their lives involved in Chinatown. But the fluctuations in and different meanings of Chinatown also speak to how Chinese continue to be seen

INTRODUCTION

in contradictory ways. Chinatowns are reminders of how Chinese are still seen as separate from the rest of a city's and country's population—forever foreign, even after being in a country for decades and through many generations. Kay Anderson describes how in British Columbia by the 1930s, white settlers had developed more positive ideas about Chinese than they had held at first and began to draw on "western romantic conceptions of 'Orientals' and their ancient and opulent civilization"[75] in their imagining of the Chinese. But, she argues, although that conceptualization made the lives of Chinese easier, it also represented an enduring process of racial categorization. The perception of Chinese as a model minority contains similar contradictory images and assumptions. The term "model minority" consists of a positive characteristic alongside a word that suggests that Chinese are still seen as a part of—but apart from—the rest of a country's population. The meaning, place, and continuity of Chinatowns reflect the changing and contradictory attitudes and beliefs that whites have had about Chinese over the last two centuries.

CHINESE IN HAWAI'I AND HONOLULU'S CHINATOWN

Chinatown in Honolulu has been shaped by some of the same changes and influences experienced by many other Chinatowns, but it has been uniquely shaped by how Chinese moved into Hawai'i society.

As in other places, Chinese faced discrimination in Hawai'i; for that reason, Chinatown was both a symbol of discrimination and a place of refuge for the Chinese community. Around the turn of the twentieth century, Chinatown ("the Chinese district," as it was known then) began to develop as Chinese moved away from the plantations. When their contracts ended, they had few resources; Chinatown provided a community of shelter, aid, and familiarity. There were no formal laws against their living elsewhere, but widespread anti-Chinese sentiment deterred such settlement. As was true elsewhere, Chinatown in Honolulu was seen as a dirty, diseased place and was often the target of health officials; they and the haole population they represented often worried that Chinatown and its residents would pollute the city, whether through disease or immoral habits. Julia Katz makes an important argument that worries and regulations around opium use among Hawai'i's Chinese were less about the dangers of opium and more about constructing the Chinese population as needing to be controlled:

INTRODUCTION

"The strategies and institutions devised for its regulation doubled as the architecture of exclusion of the Chinese themselves. In the name of drug regulation, white citizens demanded intensified policing of Chinatown and Chinese social space."[76]

In the early decades of the twentieth century, Chinese began to move out of Chinatown, first to nearby areas and then farther into greater Honolulu. That movement reflects both the entry of Chinese into the middle class and the increasing acceptance of Chinese as legitimate members of Hawai'i society; changes in Chinese residence coincided with occupational and educational advancement. Today, Chinese are seen as successful members of Hawai'i society. It is their relatively high incomes that are often cited as evidence: in 2000, 44.9 percent of Chinese earned yearly salaries of more than $60,000, compared to the state average of 37.4 percent. However, at the same time, 14 percent of Chinese earned below $14,999, above the state average of 12 percent; it is actually in the working- and lower-middle-class strata that Chinese are not well represented (37.3 percent earned between $15,000 and $54,999, compared to the state average of 50.6 percent).[77]

As we trace the pathway of Chinese in Hawai'i, we will hear echoes of the model-minority discourse, although the discourse of the Islands differs from that of the continental United States. With relatively few African Americans in Hawai'i, less emphasis was placed on which groups were *not* models, and more was placed on how Chinese success reflected their hard work and proper consumption. That it was their financial success that was often highlighted speaks to how model-minority language is embedded in and actually bolsters a multicultural neoliberal framework and how that framework is connected to global capitalism. The perception of Chinese as the embodiment of a model-minority opportunity argues for seeing acceptance and success as available to all, irrespective of race and ethnicity, as long as people take the proper steps. The distance that Chinese had come is evident in that by the 1930s, many with financial resources had moved out of Chinatown, and the area was no longer where most Chinese lived. Nonetheless, Chinatown has remained a place of community for Chinese residents, is well traveled by both Chinese and non-Chinese residents, and is sometimes an attraction for visitors to the Islands.

As is true elsewhere, consumption plays an important role in Honolulu's Chinatown. It has shaped the physical area with its shops and markets. It was also vital to how Chinese immigrants, their children and their

INTRODUCTION

grandchildren found ways to survive and sometimes thrive by participating in that economy, selling the goods and services needed by Hawai'i residents, Chinese and non-Chinese alike. As was the case in most Chinatowns, early Chinese groups in Hawai'i were mostly single men and looked to services in Chinatown to provide what family members might have provided in other places. Offerings such as barbers, laundry services, and restaurants made Chinatown convenient. To Hawai'i's Chinese, Chinatown is a frequent destination for buying Chinese goods and foods, and weekend trips to Chinatown's markets are a regular event for many Chinese in Honolulu. Many Chinese also participate in Chinatown celebrations, such as those around New Year and the Narcissus Festival, and find community there—many surname societies retain offices in the area. It is also where Chinese culture is taught—through lion-dancing organizations and Chinese language schools like the Mun Lun School, which first opened in 1911 and continues to offer after-school programs for children. Some of these events and activities may be particularly attractive and important to new immigrants from China, but even third, fourth and older generations of Chinese see Chinatown as important. For many Chinese, "the real Chinatown in Hawai'i is not [only] a physical place. To [them], it is a collective memory,"[78] thus retaining both practical and symbolic value.

For non-Chinese, Chinatown has been and continues to be a place to buy Chinese goods and services, usually provided by Chinese people. In different historical eras, such consumption took different forms. In the late nineteenth and early twentieth centuries, Chinese provided goods and services that were in demand by a growing population in Hawai'i, everything from farmed produce to restaurant meals. Whereas Chinatown simply provided Chinese a practical way to acquire daily necessities, goods and services were also sold as distinctly Chinese for non-Chinese, who consumed such things partly because they were different. Thus, that consumption, and the exchanges around it, signaled both an acceptance and a declaration of difference. Tourists and non-Chinese were often attracted to material goods that reflected—or seemed to reflect—a culture very different from their own and looked for opportunities to participate in "other cultures" through consumption. In the 1940s, for example, George Shaheen, a local designer, sold "Chinese embroidered pajamas" to tourists, a type of outfit described in a tourist magazine as featuring "gorgeous Chinese dragons that add to its distinction and exclusiveness."[79] An article in the same

INTRODUCTION

magazine makes clear that Chinatown was attractive to outsiders for its exotic sights, sounds, and tastes:

> The flavor of the Orient that permeates sections of Hawaii always intrigues the visitors. Portions of downtown Honolulu, where there are Oriental temples, teeming markets, lei sellers, and street vendors with wares balanced on long poles, provide endless material for camera fans. . . . Most tourists are adventurous in the matter of new eating experiences and are anxious to dip their fingers into a bowl of poi, try chopsticks, eat saimin, and experiment with shave ice . . . if they have the opportunity of attending a luau or a Chinese or Japanese banquet, they consider their holiday an assured success.[80]

Indeed, such consumption was a type of cultural capital for some whites, who could claim exposure to an exotic place by purchasing its goods and eating its food. This participation in Chinese culture was also welcomed by Hawaiʻi's (haole) leaders because it was seen as a way of taming and controlling the foreign, a safe way of bringing a foreign culture into the white community.[81]

As described in chapter 3, during World War II, soldiers on leave or R&R went to Chinatown to buy the services of prostitutes as the area had developed the reputation of being a red-light district. Prostitution is no longer part of Chinatown, but the element of danger remains part of its allure today. Regularly described as "gritty," even in positive travel reviews,[82] the dangers—today, but especially in the past—are clearly meant to add a layer of interest for outsiders and even some locals. As one tourist blogger has written, "Yes, it's a little gritty and there are definitely more beautiful areas of Oahu to explore. But Chinatown has history, diversity, award-winning restaurants and overall a really cool vibe if you are looking for something different than the common tourist spots."[83]

But for most locals, Chinatown is simply part of the city. Government workers in nearby areas walk over for lunch. Residents of all ethnicities visit to buy vegetables, fish, and meat at prices lower than those found in regular grocery stores. And in recent years, non-Chinese businesses such as art galleries and small retail stores have started bringing customers in to browse and shop. Nevertheless, Chinatown represents difference; it is a space that marks its difference through consumption—for Chinese, non-Chinese locals, and tourists. Chinese may take pride in the achievements

INTRODUCTION

of Chinatown and in the distance their community has traveled, from plantation laborers to successful community members. But Chinatown also reflects the ways that ethnicity is still relevant in Hawai'i and in the United States. In addition, seeing Chinatown as an achievement emphasizes the role of consumption in Chinatown and that consumption is a marker of achievement more broadly.

While there are many similarities between Chinatowns in Honolulu and other places, Honolulu's Chinatown is unique, underscoring the importance of context for each Chinatown. Bringing Hawai'i into larger conversations about race and colonialism requires paying careful attention to both similarities and differences between Honolulu's Chinatown and those in other places, including other parts of the United States.[84] Although its relationship with the United States shaped the Islands, Hawai'i's history is not solely American history.[85] As we consider how place and race are brought together in Chinatown, understanding the meaning of Chinatown requires us to ponder the ideologies, structures, frameworks, and histories that have contributed to the construction, maintenance, and interpretations of Chinatown and Hawai'i more generally.

CONTEXT MATTERS

A close examination of Honolulu's Chinatown underscores that context matters. Despite the many similarities among Chinatowns across the globe, there are also differences that come from their individual locations, histories, and politics. The place of Chinese in the larger society, the dominance of the surrounding white communities, and the makeup of the Chinese communities or other communities associated with Chinatown all uniquely shape each Chinatown and impressions of that space. Most American Chinatowns in the late nineteenth century reflected the strong anti-Chinese sentiments of the day. At that time, Chinatown in San Francisco was seen as a site of "dens, density, and the labyrinth," and suggested that some viewed those living there as nearly inhuman.[86] In New York around the same time, the media depicted Chinatown "as primarily a site of opium smoking, gambling, violence, and little else,"[87] with some articles accusing Chinese as being so depraved that they regularly ate rats.[88] Along with those shared anti-Chinese sentiments were differences in how Chinese fared in different places. For example, even though they faced discrimination and legal

INTRODUCTION

restrictions, Chinese in some western American towns in the nineteenth century also found white neighbors willing to collaborate with them to meet the needs of those living in the area.[89]

Today, we continue to see similarities and differences across Chinatowns. Ching Lan Pang's work on two contemporary Chinatowns in Belgium—those of Antwerp and Brussels—underscores that even in one country and in the same era, Chinatowns take on unique characters that depend on the history of migration, who settles where, and the expectations of the surrounding communities. Partly because the area was settled by Chinese from different places, the Chinatown in Brussels did not develop the local Chinese associations that formed in Antwerp's Chinatown. And the proximity of the Brussels Chinatown to a popular shopping area also influenced its shape. The Brussels Chinatown is seen as a hip, trendy area that invites non-Chinese to shop there, whereas Antwerp's Chinatown primarily attracts only Chinese shoppers.[90]

Anderson and colleagues' argument that the importance of Sydney's Chinatown's transnationalist connections draws attention to its context. Transnationalism connects the diasporic Chinese communities across the world, but those connections are particularly important in Sydney, which has one of the world's highest proportions of a population born outside the country. Most importantly, Australia's future, they argue, is tied to Asia's, and China's rising global power has influenced the place of Chinese and Chinatown in Sydney. As Sydney is Australia's leading center for international business and finance, its connections with Asia and specifically with China are particularly key to that city: "Chinatown is constitutive of, rather than exception to, Sydney as a global city on the edge of the Asia-Pacific region."[91]

Honolulu's Chinatown has undergone some of the same processes, but its unusual position in the Pacific and its relationship with the United States have made it unlike most other Chinatowns, not only complicating those shared events but also resulting in unique influences in Honolulu. Honolulu's Chinatown is situated in the Pacific, in a society in which whites dominate but have never been the numerical majority, and in a place where U.S. empire building has been a dominant feature of the social, political, and economic landscapes. Its location—in that space and among those processes—has been integral to its development and meaning. As the place of Chinese in Hawai'i has shifted and as new groups have arrived, Chinatown's politics and goals have likewise changed. Hawai'i's racial composition has led to

INTRODUCTION

racial politics and processes that were constructed differently in Honolulu from those in other places. The East–West divide, for example, is not as clear as it is elsewhere. The role of Chinese in Hawai'i society has similarly been influenced by Hawai'i's racial politics; although Chinese faced discrimination in Hawai'i, by some measures they may have experienced greater acceptance than Chinese in other places as Hawai'i underwent rapid social change. Nevertheless, through all that change, Chinatown has remained an important area of Honolulu to Chinese and non-Chinese alike.

Chinatown's meaning has varied in different eras and for different groups of people; with Chinatown as a constructed (and now a preserved and protected) space, those meanings have sometimes been explicit and other times assumed, suggested, or inferred. The importance of the district beyond Chinese residents was most evident as Hawai'i and Honolulu worked to make Chinatown a national historic district in the early 1970s. In their testimony and reports, city and state officials argued that Chinatown was beneficial to the city and state; in a state where tourism is the biggest industry, Honolulu lends itself to efforts to market Chinatown as a draw for tourists. In recent decades, as Honolulu has sought changes in its footprint and profile, Chinatown has also come under threat, and various groups and individuals have stepped up to protect Chinatown from destruction. In the process, the value and meaning of Chinatown have been assessed and debated, allowing insight into how connections between place and race are understood by Honolulu residents.

The longer, larger history and experience of Chinese, Asian Americans, race, and racism in the United States and in other societies reinforce how Chinatowns reflect Chinese and Asian American experience. Hawai'i's particular history reflects Hawai'i's role in the U.S. empire and the role of race in empire building. As mentioned, two processes have been especially important in shaping Chinese experience in Hawai'i and thus the meaning of Chinatown there. The first involves the relationship between Hawai'i and the United States and Hawai'i's position in the process of U.S. empire building. That process included the U.S. imperialist moves of the late nineteenth and early twentieth centuries that resulted in takeovers across the globe, including of Hawai'i, the Philippines, and Guam. The second process involves the first arrival of Chinese to Hawai'i amid the settler colonial takeover of the Islands, as whites settled in Hawai'i and seized power there and over the next decades.

INTRODUCTION

Hawai'i came to be increasingly valuable to the United States, as is most evident in the way that the Americans occupied, seized, and annexed Hawai'i. Those moves solidified American control over Hawai'i, and the Islands continued to be central to U.S. wars and other American involvement in the Pacific. The Japanese attack on Hawai'i, the U.S. response, and events surrounding U.S. involvement in World War II—in the United States and elsewhere—shaped how Chinese—as an Asian group that was not Japanese—were seen and how they could move in Hawai'i society at the time. Later, Hawai'i was also affected by U.S. involvement in the Korean War and especially the Vietnam War. In addition to the ways that U.S. entanglements in Asia reflected racial constructions and contributed to racial politics and hierarchies within the United States, those wars also brought more traffic through Hawai'i. During World War II, an estimated one million U.S. military personnel passed through Hawai'i for either short periods of R&R and training or longer periods of training, and deployment.[92] Encounters between local residents and military personnel shaped both groups, with residents learning more about American politics and ways of life, and military personnel experiencing a society that Beth Bailey and David Farber characterize as "the first strange place,"[93] one with a racial makeup and organization far different from any most Black and white soldiers were used to. During the Korean War and especially during the Vietnam War, many soldiers spent time in Hawai'i for training and R&R. In wartime, Chinatown was a destination for many visiting soldiers, then considered a red-light district at the service of American military personnel.

The Pacific and Asia wars positioned Hawai'i between the United States and Asia, increasing Hawai'i's value as a U.S. territory, which would provide ballast to U.S. claims and interest in the Pacific and in Asia. Pearl Harbor, first acquired in 1887, was strategically important to American interests in Asia, as the Japanese attack in 1941 highlighted. But it was not only its geographic position that convinced the United States that Hawai'i was important for the country's forays into Asia. That a large percentage of the population was ethnically Asian was often considered part of Hawai'i's value as well. For example, during the Vietnam War, the training of new soldiers often took place in Hawai'i, which was seen as similar enough to Vietnam—because of its terrain and its people—that it would provide a good substitute for in-country training.[94]

INTRODUCTION

Debates over Hawai'i's statehood are evidence that Hawai'i became even more important to the United States during the Cold War era as the United States vied for alliances with countries in the Third World. Until that time—when Asians and Native Hawaiians made up 70 percent of the population—Hawai'i's racial composition was considered threatening; many Americans opposed statehood because they doubted that Asians could ever be "real" or loyal Americans. But Cold War politics changed the narrative of Hawai'i. As the USSR used U.S. racial inequalities and unrest to argue that the American system should not attract Third World alliances, the United States began to position Hawai'i in a new light. Its racial difference came to be seen as a strength, one that could be strategically important to U.S. geopolitical goals. By giving Hawai'i statehood, the United States hoped to win hearts and minds in the Third World by demonstrating its racial tolerance, shifting attention away from the growing U.S. civil rights movement, and insisting that the acceptance and success of Asians in Hawai'i was evidence of the United States allowing and encouraging anyone of any skin color to find success in its democracy.

Model Minorities in Hawai'i

It was during the Cold War era that Hawai'i's racial politics, and U.S. involvement in them, came to shape U.S. racial politics in ways that have reverberated ever since. In Hawai'i, the term "model minority" may be heard less often than on the continent, but it is nevertheless the basis of a powerful framework that underlies many racialized practices and assumptions. In the similarities and differences in the term's use in Hawaii and the continental United States, we see the shadow of American influence on most aspects of life in Hawai'i over the last 150 years. One of the biggest differences derives from the relatively small Black population in Hawai'i. In Hawai'i, the model-minority discourse is not used to highlight the failure of Black people to achieve success, as is true in the continental United States, although other ethnic groups—Filipinos, Pacific Islanders, and sometimes Native Hawaiians—are sometimes compared unfavorably with Chinese and Japanese groups in terms of their economic or educational success. But the wider influence of this discourse is seen in its use in an American way of measuring success. In the American view, success comes—or should come—from individuals putting in hard work, making

INTRODUCTION

the right economic decisions, and not complaining about any roadblocks they face. In this way, Asian success is seen—or touted as—and participated in as a defense of a neoliberal capitalist system. As we will see, the model-minority framework not only shaped the process of Chinese struggling to find their place in Hawai'i society and how they came to assess those struggles, but it also helped to define Hawai'i's value and use to the United States.

Chinese and Japanese in Hawai'i were lauded as examples of success and were seen as demonstrating that hard work and sacrifice without complaint and the tolerance of the society around them were the recipe for that success. In this story, the efforts and sacrifices of Hawai'i's Japanese American soldiers during World War II were evidence of their loyalty to the United States. For Chinese, it was their economic success in the face of many hurdles that was celebrated. In this way, we see Hawai'i's own engagement with model-minority construction, with characteristics such as Asians' belief in the American system, their proper consumption, their willingness to make sacrifices for the country, and their avoidance of causing trouble emphasized as the way to succeed in the United States.

Indeed, Hawai'i began to be described as a model of U.S. racial harmony, with John F. Kennedy arguing in 1963 that Hawai'i demonstrates "how the American people can live more happily and more securely together" and that Hawai'i "represents all that we are and all that we hope to be."[95] Out of the Cold War years came support for a multiculturalism that bolstered a white neoliberal system in which nonwhites are granted access to the system but only on white, neoliberal terms, rewarding those who show faith in a consumerist, capitalist system that supports a racial hierarchy that keeps whites at the top. This framework led to an increased acceptance of the status quo systems of racialization and economics and a reduced effort to challenge the structures that had created that racialized, unequal society to begin with.

A key influence on the experience of Chinese in Hawai'i and in Honolulu's Chinatown was the position of Chinese in a settler colonial society, including their relationships with other groups in the Islands and how Chinese experiences and relationships were shaped by U.S. colonialism and empire building. The historical record shows that Chinese began their successful push into Hawai'i society just as Native Hawaiians were experiencing decline. It was a time when haole were taking increasing control of Hawai'i,

INTRODUCTION

amassing political and economic power and imposing a white American framework on all aspects of Hawai'i society. As we will see, both the fates of various groups and how they interacted with one other were tied to that rising haole control. For Native Hawaiians, this was an era of great loss: Hawaiians lost land rights after land was privatized in 1850; they lost their nation with the U.S. seizure of Hawai'i in 1893 and its annexation in 1898; they lost their language and many aspects of their culture under haole rule, which forbade these cultural practices in schools and public places; and they experienced a steep population decline because of foreign-introduced diseases. These losses have reverberated into the present.[96]

Chinese were not in a position to influence the decisions, legislation, or actions that were changing Hawai'i but nevertheless found ways to ride the waves of these changes to their advantage. We will see that some of the negotiations they made were with Native Hawaiian communities; there were both cooperation and tension between Native Hawaiians and Chinese throughout the nineteenth and early twentieth centuries, which contributed to the direction and outcomes of Chinese efforts. For example, the cooperation between Chinese and Kānaka in rural areas both allowed Chinese to develop successful business ventures and permitted Hawaiians to survive in the face of adversity. But some Hawaiians also saw Chinese migrants as a threat to their own tenuous place in the developing society and worked to restrict Chinese immigration.

Hitching their own success to the haole framework was probably the best choice that Chinese could make, given the control haole had over all aspects of Hawai'i society and the ways that modernity is racialized across the world, connecting "notions of morality, continuous progress and liberal thought" with whiteness.[97] Efforts to change or dismantle that system were not likely to be effective. But accepting that framework also allowed Chinese to take advantage of the difficulties and losses of the Hawaiians: Chinese were able to buy land and find work with less competition than would have been the case had the Hawaiian community been able to offer stronger resistance to white invasion. Similarly, World War II gave Chinese opportunities—land purchases, job opportunities—that likely would have been unavailable except for the discrimination that Japanese experienced during that era.

Chinese experience in Hawai'i must thus be understood in terms of how Chinese migrants and their descendants were positioned and positioned

INTRODUCTION

themselves relative to other groups. Important in this process was how haole treated groups differently and the underlying reasons for that. During much of the nineteenth and early twentieth centuries, haole were more likely to find an Asian presence more threatening than a Hawaiian one; subsequently, Asians faced targeted discrimination from haole in schooling, work, and where they lived. Haole saw Hawaiians as more controllable; that such a large percentage had converted to Christianity and had been eager to gain literacy as encouraged by early haole settlers probably contributed to these haole perceptions. But it was also true that haole had successfully taken over the Hawaiian government and society, which they perceived as evidence that the indigenous population could be silenced or eliminated altogether, a process that Patrick Wolfe has argued is an element of settler colonialism.[98] Tellingly, during the Cold War era, when Hawai'i's racial difference began to be touted as a strength and a model for the United States, discussion centered on Asians, and Hawaiians were left out of the conversation altogether. At that time, narratives often focused on the economic success of Chinese and how Japanese had shown loyalty during World War II. Highlighting Asian success in this way had a dual purpose: it promoted the notion of American racial tolerance, and it effectively erased the nation's colonial history by inviting select groups into the white hierarchy. To admit and celebrate Hawaiians would require the United States to face, acknowledge, and explain its seizure of Hawai'i for its imperialist and geopolitical goals.

Chinatown embodies these processes and political maneuvers: not only can it be used to sell Hawai'i's safe exoticism, but it can also be seen as a physical manifestation of tolerance of racial difference and the outcome of Asian success in the United States. According to Jan Lin, "The ethnic heritage sector preserves and displays the cultural legacy of racial-ethnic ancestry so that new generations can look back and comprehend with better insight the trajectory of their posterity."[99] Given that, we must ask what it is that Chinatown preserves and celebrates, as well as what is missing or obfuscated. As I discuss throughout this volume, the Chinatown narrative illustrates a model-minority story of hard work, American loyalty, and a tolerant society leading to economic success. It celebrates the achievements of Chinese, who rose from the bottom to the top of social and economic hierarchies. The Chinese story represented in Chinatown—and even Chinatown's existence—allows for the argument that Hawai'i is a special place

INTRODUCTION

where this achievement—the ascent of a marginalized, nonwhite group— can be realized. From that conclusion follows the belief that we can build a pluralistic society out of the different histories and experiences of immigrant groups.

This narrative invites scrutiny, however. Hawai'i is not the racial paradise it is sometimes sold as. Many Chinese immigrants did succeed in gaining a toehold in the Islands, and subsequent generations did become successful in Hawai'i's business and professional life. Chinatown's very proximity to Honolulu's Central Business District, with its towers full of international businesses, points to how important consumption and economic achievement are to this version of success. In the American focus on Asian success, Chinatown celebrates both capitalist accumulation and a multicultural neoliberal model. But other Chinese immigrants did not do as well. Chinatown's existence and achievements thus implicitly point to an underlying argument about "good" and "bad" Asians, about how those Chinese who behaved properly and made the right choices—especially economic ones—succeeded while others did not do as well.

Also missing in the Chinatown success narrative are the very different struggles of other groups, including Hawaiians and Filipinos, whose histories point to the complicated racial politics that continue to shape Hawai'i.[100] It is not surprising that those stories do not have the same physical representation as the success story of some Chinese. These absences return us to constructions of model minorities, and to "good" and "bad" Asians in general, and how achievement has been or could and should be accomplished by any group in Hawai'i or in the United States more broadly. Thus, we can see that the civil rights movement and racial unrest in the wider United States have also contributed to the history of Hawai'i and to how the experiences of some groups there have been interpreted. Constructs of the model minority and of "good" and "bad" Asians have been implicitly or explicitly part of the racial narratives of the United States and of Hawai'i. Those constructs have been used throughout history to encourage particular pathways and discourage others and have in turn been used to explain why some Asians in the United States—and in Hawai'i specifically—have found a place for themselves while others have not. It is a narrative that also disappears the history of settler colonialism and the experience of Native Hawaiians and renders U.S. involvement in Hawai'i benevolent.[101] Those stories—missing and present—can also be seen in Chinatown.

INTRODUCTION

In this volume, I contend that Chinese experience—especially the success found by Chinese—was particular to the setting and time. As the first contract laborers and the first to leave the plantations to seek other kinds of work, Chinese had certain advantages despite experiencing discrimination and obstacles because of their race. In addition, Chinese experience—what was gained and lost as Chinese found acceptance into Hawai'i society—raises issues of the construction of a model minority: what such a construction does and who or what it omits. Chinese experience also prompts a careful thinking of pluralistic societies, of how difference is absorbed, celebrated, or discouraged in such societies. Hawai'i challenges us to think differently—avoiding such binaries as East versus West, us versus them, and global versus local—and address the fluidity, contradictions, and complexities of race.

In the process of acknowledging the complications of race, it is important to note Hawai'i's unusual status. It is a place that has absorbed difference differently from other places and one that often defies commonly accepted understandings of race. Hawai'i's experience encourages us to consider what difference means and how difference is accepted in a society. What about an immigrant group gets preserved in a new place? Is it something more (values or norms, for example) or something less (say, food or lion dances) that remains? And how does difference—and even acceptance—translate into power? In ways similar to and different from what occurred in other places, the entry of Chinese into various aspects of Hawai'i social life was often shaped by expectations about what it meant to be Chinese, how a proper citizen should act, and which pathways to success were celebrated or questioned. As they worked to establish themselves in schools, the business world, and social life generally, Chinese were expected to act "like Americans" (whatever that meant) but at the same time were seen as "always Chinese." We will see that Chinese themselves struggled to be enough "not Chinese" while retaining their Chineseness, which they considered vital to their identity and their sense of their place in the world.

Chinatown remains important to Honolulu and to Hawai'i. How Chinatown has been developed, preserved, celebrated, and fought over brings the experience of Chinese and other nonwhite ethnic groups into plain and explicit sight. Chinatown represents the achievements, discrimination, and difference that Chinese represent in Hawai'i society. As a place, Chinatown

INTRODUCTION

delineates that difference and underscores the meaning of ethnic difference to various groups with stakes in Hawaiʻi: Chinese and non-Chinese locals, Native Hawaiians, state and city officials, tourists and visitors, and Americans more generally. Chinatown—its meaning and importance—reflects the ways that ethnicity is still relevant in Hawaiʻi. Difference is important: race and ethnicity organize American society, and that is true in Hawaiʻi even though its racial politics and outcomes are different from those in the continental United States. The settler colonial imprint has also heavily influenced and been influenced by Hawaiʻi's racial politics, politics that include the attempted erasure of Native Hawaiians and that have shaped the meaning of Chinatown. Hawaiʻi's racial history and politics allow new perspectives on these issues, and Honolulu's Chinatown provides a window into many complex and important questions. In this way, Hawaiʻi's story, and the story of Chinese there, is etched onto the landscape of Chinatown, providing evidence that "built places give material form to the ineffable or invisible, providing a durable legible architectural aide-memoire."[102]

METHODOLOGY

This book is built on data and evidence of many kinds. It is not an ethnography of Chinatown, although I do use ethnographic methods. I spent hundreds of hours in Chinatown observing and talking to people in the area. In addition, I conducted formal interviews with fifteen individuals; some of those interviews lasted an hour or so, whereas others went on for many hours over the course of months. I chose to talk to each respondent because of their knowledge of Chinese in Hawaiʻi or Chinatown. I lso conducted informal, generally shorter, interviews with about twenty people who I thought could help me understand some aspects of these processes. I interviewed tourists in Chinatown, restaurant owners and workers in the area, people who frequent Chinatown, and Chinese residents who avoid the area, among others. I supplemented my methods with secondary data released from Hawaiʻi government offices and agencies and some from scholars. An important part of my evidence comes from archives as I sought to understand the history of Chinatown and race in Hawaiʻi. I spent long stretches in archives in Hawaiʻi, particularly those of the University of Hawaiʻi's Asia and Pacific Collections at Hamilton Library and the Romanzo Adams Social Research Laboratory. The latter is a collection of student and

INTRODUCTION

faculty papers collected over fifty years (from the 1920s through the 1970s) that contain observations of family and community relations throughout Hawai'i. I also used the Hawai'i State Archives and the collections at the Hawai'i Chinese History Center in Chinatown, Honolulu. I read both published and unpublished personal and family memoirs. Because one of my main goals was to put the history and experience of Chinatown into the larger context of Hawai'i and the United States, I relied on the research and writings of dozens of scholars, often drawing on unpublished work (housed in libraries or archives in Hawai'i). These scholars—published and unpublished—have done extraordinary work, allowing me to consider many perspectives and arguments.

THE STRUCTURE OF THE BOOK

This volume is generally organized chronologically. Looking at key historical times allows us to situate Chinese experience within the important historical, political, and racial contexts that shaped it. I focus on six key historical periods, chosen because of what was happening to Chinese in Hawai'i at the time or because of the events (in Hawai'i, the United States, or the world more broadly) surrounding Chinese. Chapter 1 examines the important nineteenth-century era, a time when Chinese were beginning to leave the sugar plantations after their contracts expired. This was an era of virulent anti-Chinese sentiment in California (where some 80 percent of Chinese in the United States lived). It was also a time of great change in Hawai'i, a period of active American imperialism; during these years, the United States overthrew the Hawaiian Kingdom, put Americans in charge of the Islands, and annexed Hawai'i to the United States. These contexts—in the United States and in Hawai'i—were key to the experience of Chinese. Chapter 2 focuses on the years from 1900 through the 1930s. That time began with great trauma when Chinatown was burned to the ground in 1900 by the Board of Health in an attempt to contain a bubonic plague epidemic. The later years of this era were a time when Chinese were establishing themselves in Hawai'i society and beginning to move into the middle class. Chapter 3, covering the 1930s and 1940s, covers the continued movement of Chinese into the middle class. One example of that shift was the increasing involvement of Chinese in public health, a great departure from the vilification of Chinese and the destruction of

INTRODUCTION

Chinatown in 1900, and their increasing positions of power and influence in the Board of Health. The key event of that era was, of course, U.S. entry into World War II. During those years, Hawai'i served as the "first strange place" for many white Americans who had their first experience of a multiethnic society there. At that time, Chinese experience was different from that of the Islands' Japanese, who were haunted by Japan's attack on Pearl Harbor and under suspicion by the U.S. government as potential "enemies within." Chapter 4 focuses on the Cold War years. It was during this era that Hawai'i played a pivotal role both in U.S. empire building and in the construction of race to meet state goals, a time when the notion of a model minority took hold. Debates over U.S. statehood illuminated the racial politics within Hawai'i and between the United States and Hawai'i. Chapter 5 focuses on the post-statehood decades, the 1960s through the 1980s, when state and city officials fought to preserve Chinatown against the surge in urban renewal projects that threatened to destroy it. Eventually Honolulu received national historic landmark status for the area. These efforts make clear the value of Chinatown and the Chinese experience to Hawai'i more generally. Not coincidentally, these efforts were underway as the civil rights movement and racial unrest in the United States took center stage and forced more attention onto America's long and troubled racial history. The events and debates throughout these decades also foreshadowed the construction of neoliberal multiculturalism as a model for incorporating racial and other differences into the white landscape. In chapter 6, I examine contemporary Chinatown in light of the historical processes and politics that have shaped it. Chinatown continues to be important to many in Honolulu although gentrification has changed the look and customer base of the area. At the same time, Chinatown retains some of its old value and allure. In this final chapter, comparisons among ethnic groups in Hawai'i make clear that continuing racial and ethnic inequalities belie any claim to Hawai'i as an ethnic or racial paradise. I argue that Chinatown's position and value reflect the history of Chinese in Hawai'i, as well as the history, politics, colonialism, racialization, and racism that have been ongoing forces in the Islands.

Chapter One

SETTING THE STAGE

Chinese Experience Before 1900

The last decades of the nineteenth century were significant years in Hawai'i for many reasons. Most importantly, it was during these years that Americans—who had been increasing their domination over the Islands' government and processes over the past decades—took complete control over the Kingdom of Hawai'i, seizing control in 1893 and then annexing Hawai'i to the United States in 1898.

Chinese experienced many changes during this time, and the events that led to or came from these changes reverberated for years in the Chinese community and beyond. From this period, we can trace the historical roots of their later success as they shifted from contracted plantation laborers to other types of workers in rural communities and then to successful, well-established members of Honolulu society. As Chinese were the first contracted plantation laborers and the first to rise from the plantations to become integrated into Hawai'i society, their path anticipated those of later groups such as Japanese and Filipinos: brought in for labor and then, once contracts had ended, moving into the larger Hawai'i society despite facing widespread discrimination and formal restrictions. But no group's history was exactly like any other. Chinese made their way into the wider community at a particular time in Hawai'i history, at a time of enormous change. In many ways, there was more room for them to do so than later groups had. At that time, the middle class was not yet established; so, not only did Chinese begin to enter the middle class, but they actually created it. We can see the importance of that creation when we compare Hawai'i with the United States: in 1884, three-quarters of Hawai'i's entire workforce was in unskilled labor, compared to 31 percent in the United States.[1] This suggests that, at the time, there were virtually only two classes in Hawai'i: the elite haole at the top and everyone else below. Chinese, then, opened up the class hierarchy, inserting themselves and making room for a middle class.

Hawai'i's racial landscape was fluid and sometimes unpredictable. Chinese came to the Islands as outsiders, and in the decades after they first came in any numbers, their acceptance and status varied, often depending on events and who was evaluating their behavior and value to Hawai'i society. In how they were received, welcomed, discriminated against, and seen as assets, we see the complicated ways that race operated in a settler colonial society. The early welcome Chinese laborers received because of their contributions on the plantations changed to alarm as they left the plantations at the end of their contracts and began to settle in Honolulu. Haole in particular, raised concerns about whether Chinese were a threat in the Islands, especially now that they were no longer under the control of plantation owners and bosses. Between Chinese and other groups, especially Native Hawaiians, were tensions and hostility but also cooperation as each vied for acceptance, success, and survival in an increasingly haole-dominated system. The discrimination and hardship that Chinese faced during the last decades of the nineteenth century helped generate events in the Chinese community in the early decades of the twentieth century. The hurdles they faced contributed to their vision of their ability to succeed in Hawai'i; in particular, they worked to join haole society, relying on education, occupational status, and language to make it possible.

Key to Chinese experience and strategy was the changing relationship between Hawai'i and the United States, driven by the increasing role that white settlers were playing in shaping the Islands' future. The enormous changes occurring to Native Hawaiians as a result of American imperialism was central to this process. Chinese negotiated in a context in which Hawaiian control and power were waning and American power was increasing. The Chinese community was thus a "a diasporic community striving to manifest rights in a colonial context,"[2] and we can see in this early era that how Chinese were perceived by haole leaders and by

SETTING THE STAGE

Hawaiians foreshadowed the politics of later Hawai'i society and the role of the various ethnic and racial groups in it.

Chinatown was starting to take shape during these years, reflecting many of the tumultuous events occurring in Hawai'i and in the Chinese community in particular. It was during these years that, in spite of their rural backgrounds, Chinese became increasingly located in Honolulu. Chinatown played a key role in the migration and transition of Chinese who were moving off the plantations and out of rural areas into the city. Chinese continued to face strong and growing discrimination and restriction during this time. Thus, Chinatown was simultaneously a haven from discrimination and a physical place that reflected Chinese exclusion in Hawai'i. In this chapter, I trace the changes in Chinese lives in Hawai'i in these early years, the reasons behind those shifts, and the role of Chinatown in those changes, and I suggest how those events would reverberate in later decades.

PLANTATION TIME

While some Chinese came to Hawai'i for other purposes, most initially came as laborers recruited for work on the sugar and pineapple plantations. Scholars have estimated that between 1852 and 1899, some 56,720 Chinese came to Hawai'i to work on the plantations.[3]

The first group of Chinese were brought to Hawai'i to work on the sugar plantations as contracted laborers in 1852 as haole business leaders began to establish the sugar industry and lacked laborers to work the growing plantations. Over the next decades, Chinese were regularly recruited from southern China, peaking in 1896.[4] Chinese were hired through several channels. In the beginning, plantation owners hired recruiters who traveled to China, hired men, and returned to Hawai'i with contracted laborers promised to various owners. Recruitment also occurred through other institutions, such as Christian missions. Basel missionaries (based in Switzerland), for example, brought a group of Hakka Chinese Christians to work on a Kohala plantation in the 1870s.[5] After the earliest years, some Chinese in Hawai'i also became involved in recruitment.[6] Chinese recruiters were more likely to recruit those who were already in their circle of contacts, such as family members and fellow villagers. The ties that existed before migration would translate into tight-knit communities in Honolulu.

SETTING THE STAGE

Plantation life was difficult. Early immigrants were usually on five-year contracts, but these contracts were shortened to three years during the later years of Chinese labor recruitment.[7] Nearly all of Hawai'i's early labor recruits were men, meaning that plantation life was organized not around family, as it might have been in China, but around the rules of the plantation and the pace of work in the cane fields. Men, who were usually single, were housed in large groups, often in one room; workers were thus in constant contact with others. But because most plantations housed different ethnic groups separately, and because the plantation camps were isolated from the rest of Island life, most of the contact Chinese had with others was with other Chinese laborers. There was little to do during off hours and little means to do anything outside the plantation. Some plantation owners were more considerate of Chinese workers' needs and desires (providing enough rice to eat, for example), so life varied for Chinese workers depending on where they lived and worked.

Plantation work was hard, highly routinized, and regimented and was often done in hot, difficult conditions. Many of the tasks associated with sugar growing were grueling and sometimes dangerous. One of the most tedious and truly backbreaking tasks was hoeing weeds. As described by Karen Lee, "Workers had to 'hoe hoe hoe . . . for four hours in a straight line and no talking,' said a laborer. They stopped only to sharpen the blades and then walked to the next lot. . . . As they hoed, they were not permitted to stand up straight and ease the pain in their shoulders and backs. After a week of 'hoe hana,' many of the workers felt as if they had been 'kicked and beaten all over,' their bodies 'tight' and their backs 'aching from stooping and working' at one thing for so long without a say or without fun mixed in."[8] Hole-hole, the stripping of dead leaves from the cane, was particularly hard; laborers contended with insects and the sharp, needle-like cane leaves. Harvesting cane was also exhausting work, involving wrestling with cane stalks and the clouds of dust raised in the process.[9] All of this took place over long hours, at low pay, and with a luna's constant oversight (lunas acted as the immediate supervisors of plantation workers), meaning that the men were generally eager to leave plantation life. When their contracts were finished and when the debt of transport and recruitment was paid—usually after five years—most Chinese workers left plantation work.

Leaving the plantations soon became an enormous issue in Hawai'i. Plantation owners wanted their Chinese laborers to stay; they needed the

SETTING THE STAGE

labor, and Chinese were seen as good workers. Commentators often compared their work habits favorably with those of Hawaiians. The president of the Royal Hawaiian Agricultural Society, speaking early in the process of recruiting Chinese laborers, proclaimed, "The Chinese brought here in the Thetis [ship] have proved themselves quiet, able and willing men, and I have little doubt, judging from our short experience, that we shall find Coolie labor [sic] to be far more certain, systematic, and economical than that of the natives. They are prompt at the call of the bell, steady in their work, quick to learn, and when well fed will accomplish more and in a better manner than any other class of operatives we have."[10] With the regular turnover of Chinese laborers, plantation owners were continually recruiting new labor.

OFF THE PLANTATIONS

The population of Chinese plantation workers declined quickly. In 1882, Chinese made up about half of all plantations laborers; by 1894, because of Chinese leaving this work and the recruitment of Japanese workers, Chinese made up only 13 percent of the plantation labor force (2,784 Chinese workers out of 21,294 plantation workers).[11] Some returned to China— estimated to compose about half of the Chinese laborers in the later years of the nineteenth century[12]—but many stayed in Hawai'i, finding new work and societal roles.

Chinese and Hawaiians in Rural Hawai'i

Of those who stayed in Hawai'i, some Chinese, especially initially, moved to rural areas away from the plantations on O'ahu and other islands. In 1884, for example, 80 percent of Chinese in Hawai'i were involved in rural work, but fewer than half (six thousand) were working on sugar plantations, having branched out into other work.[13] Such moves made sense given the rural backgrounds of most Chinese migrants, but it was not an easy move because it was difficult for Chinese to purchase land. They faced restrictions because they were not citizens and because, newly released from low plantation wages, "they were capital-poor."[14]

But Chinese found ways to get a toehold in rural Hawai'i. Because of the low initial investment needed, many began peddling small wares; they could buy small amounts of goods and sell them throughout rural areas. Some were able to set up small rural stores that catered to local residents and travelers. This work served more than one purpose; in addition to earning an income, they also made contact with Hawaiians who lived in these rural communities "for companionship, credit, labor, and land."[15] Indeed, the alliances made between Chinese and Native Hawaiians in rural Hawaiʻi communities were an important phase of Chinese settlement in the Islands. As we will see, some Hawaiians opposed the migration of Chinese to Hawaiʻi, especially those in urban areas, and that sentiment was fanned by haole efforts. There may have been some wariness of new Chinese settlers in rural areas as well, but there is also evidence that Native Hawaiians collaborated with Chinese to the betterment of both groups.

The context for this cooperation was the destruction of Hawaiian communities. Hawaiians were facing severe population decline; many communities did not have the labor power needed to work the land, and they did not have the resources (capital or labor) to develop or even maintain their existing enterprises. For rural Hawaiians, Chinese migrants could be useful; Chinese peddlers and stores made it possible to buy goods that might not otherwise be available outside urban areas. And Chinese could fill the labor gaps in Hawaiian communities. Hawaiians could lease their land to Chinese, who would then develop taro or rice crops. Further, Hawaiians and Chinese might decide to work together to develop a business. Julia Katz has argued for seeing rural enterprises such as fishponds or poi factories not as being "taken over" by Chinese (as some describe it) but as "joint ventures engineered and managed by diasporic networks of labor and capital along with indigenous knowledge and resources."[16] Many Hawaiians developed business and personal relationships with Chinese; Native Hawaiian women were central in these cooperative strategies. Some Hawaiian women married Chinese men and began raising children.[17] Others formed business and social ties that they drew on to survive and thrive. In these partnerships, Hawaiian women owned the land and had local knowledge of land and techniques, while Chinese men contributed their own resources, especially labor networks and capital. The cooperation of local and foreign residents allowed many Hawaiians to sustain their enterprises without succumbing to the increasing pressures of the global capitalist market. Through "intimate and economic transactions between indigenous Hawaiians and migrant Chinese,"[18] Hawaiians, especially Kānaka women, were able

SETTING THE STAGE

to maintain or develop agricultural holdings and businesses. At the same time, these arrangements gave landless Chinese migrants opportunities beyond the plantations, more autonomy, investment opportunities, and a pathway toward economic growth.

Recognizing these moments and sites of cooperation between Native Hawaiians and Chinese and the benefits these alliances brought to each group is important for many reasons. It allows us a fuller picture of how different groups in the Islands interacted, in both positive and negative ways. It also allows us to understand the trajectory of Chinese during the latter half of the nineteenth century and the early twentieth century, a time when most Chinese had few resources to advance their own or their community's standing. What Chinese brought to their rural enterprises with the Hawaiians reflected the value of their networks. Chinese merchants were ready and willing to invest capital in these small family businesses, and kin and village networks regularly provided the necessary labor. In this way, "Chinese found opportunities through sociofinancial networks that translated intimacy and friendship into real financial capital."[19] These networks also provided a visible and reliable pathway for newcomers to the Islands to reach their economic and social goals.

The interactions and exchanges between Hawaiians and Chinese were some of the first steps in a process that tied the fate and future of Chinese to that of Hawaiians and were how both groups became part of the haole-created settler colonial system. As we will see, haole regularly discouraged these interactions, seeing them as a potential threat to their own control of the Islands. The sites of cooperation between Native Hawaiians and Chinese also underscore the ways that these two groups have been differently placed in the process of settler colonialism. When they found ways to cooperate, both Hawaiians and Chinese could benefit. But just as often, Native Hawaiians and Chinese were seen, depicted, and themselves assumed to be in competition as they struggled to break through the barriers of a white-dominated society. As Katz argues, the stereotypes of Chinese as conniving, stealthy, and inherently business oriented and of Hawaiians as incompetent "fetishize racial difference and descend from colonial thinking about native and migrant labor [and] continue to stand in for historical explanations of divergent outcomes among communities under colonialization."[20] The conflicting aspects of the relationship between Chinese and Native Hawaiians—including wariness, cooperation, resistance, and alliance—can be understood as the result of how the lives and futures of both groups were strongly shaped by haole dominance in the Islands. Each group had to navigate a sometimes confusing racial landscape. For Chinese, the second half of the nineteenth century was full of uncertainty as they tried to find a route into acceptance in the white-dominated system and began to find traction up the class ladder. For Native Hawaiians, these decades were particularly devastating as they lost their livelihoods, their land, and their country and suffered severe population decline. Neither group had power relative to that of haole and their different positions and experiences made an alliance both necessary and difficult.

Rice

One of the most important industries that Chinese moved into from the plantations was rice growing. Hawai'i soil and climate was conducive to this crop, and many Chinese had experience growing rice in China. Key factors in the growth of Hawai'i's rice industry were the availability of land in the late nineteenth century and the reasons for that availability. Many rice fields were planted on land previously devoted to growing taro; with the decimation of Hawaiian communities through disease and colonialist politics, many of these fields were unused. In many cases, Hawaiians were able to lease the land to Chinese, allowing them to earn some income from the Chinese rice industry. As the rice industry expanded, previously unused land was also brought into cultivation. Harvested rice was sold in Honolulu and later in California, as the growing Chinese communities in Hawai'i and California provided increasing demand. These rice farms were financed mostly from within the Chinese community; many started very small, enabled by money borrowed from friends and other community members. Labor was recruited from former plantation workers and later directly from China. By the end of the nineteenth century, there were around five hundred rice farms; a few were large-scale operations, but most were small, consisting of between one and thirty acres, and most of those were closer to the smaller end of that range.[21] The growth of rice farming continued into the twentieth century, even after Hawai'i's annexation to the United States in 1898. But within the next decade, these farms decreased in number and production, the central reason for which was the labor shortage created by restrictions on immigration from China after 1898 when

SETTING THE STAGE

Hawai'i became subject to the U.S. Chinese Exclusion Act of 1882. The Chinese community appealed to the new government to permit more laborers to immigrate, but nothing came of such appeals.[22]

In the rise and fall of the rice industry, we see how the United States and haole settlers in Hawai'i shaped Island politics and society around racial stratification in ways that would hold for many decades to come. Chinese were brought to Hawai'i to work on the plantations, which they subsequently left to look for a new and better life. Rice provided just such an opportunity, giving them access to a way of life they had had in their own country. Their migration from the plantations provided the necessary labor, experience, and market to make the rice industry successful. But Hawai'i's recent history was key to the growth of rice as well; there was room for the rice industry to expand because of the devastation experienced by Hawaiians and their communities at the hands of haole settlers. Hawaiians no longer had enough labor power to work their own fields and saw leasing their land to Chinese as a way to sustain some of their old life. For a couple decades, Chinese and Hawaiians coexisted in rural areas, often cooperating around work in rice, taro, and other crops. But Chinese rice production could not be sustained. Just as haole leaders had altered Native Hawaiian communities through their policies and interactions, the laws and restrictions they passed—especially immigration laws that curtailed labor recruitment—struck fatal blows to the rice industry, making it impossible for Chinese to maintain their farms or industry. After the United States annexed Hawai'i, rice production in Hawai'i also began to face enormous competition from American growers in the southern United States. The growth of the sugar industry—propelled by haole elites—also helped elbow out rice farmers. The decline in the rice industry, in turn, helped fuel the exit of Chinese from Hawai'i's rural areas and into Honolulu and set Chinese on a pathway into Hawai'i society very different from the one they had been on.

We can trace the different influences on Chinese and Native Hawaiian communities under white colonial influence in the Waipahu area of O'ahu.[23] The earliest Chinese settlers in the area were former plantation workers whose contracts had ended. They sought opportunities in Waipahu for several reasons. The land was good for growing crops, and fresh water was available through wells. In addition, tracts of land previously farmed by Hawaiians were lying fallow as that population declined. Chinese reclaimed former taro fields, using them to grow taro or converting them to rice. Rice growing in Waipahu followed a pattern of growth and decline similar to that seen across Hawai'i. The first rice farm in Waipahu was established in 1875. The number of rice farms grew in the 1880s and 1890s, reached a peak in 1900, and began to decline about ten years later; they were completely gone by 1930. As rice declined in the Waipahu area, Chinese began taking up new jobs, especially in providing area residents with goods and services. When the O'ahu Sugar Plantation was established in 1897, Chinese took on new roles in the community. While some new Chinese immigrants worked the plantation fields, longer-established residents developed the land into farms that provided fresh produce, chickens, and eggs for plantation workers and their families. Others set up restaurants and small businesses that catered to all types of residents, from single male plantation workers to plantation administrators. They opened stores, bakeries, and coffee shops. During those years, the Waipahu Chinese community flourished and diversified, becoming one of the largest Chinese communities in Hawai'i. In the early decades of the twentieth century, most businesses in the area were run by Chinese.

What happened in Waipahu is an example of how Chinese in Hawai'i worked hard to establish their community and were savvy about setting up businesses that the community needed, finding niches that led them to achieve success. The sugar industry was tightly controlled by a small group of haole,[24] and Chinese would not be able to break into that part of the economy. Instead, they filled in around the sugar industry, developing new businesses that supported the industry and its workers. Chinese were successful partly because they watched for opportunities and moved quickly to pursue them. They also were able to draw on a strong and widespread network of kin and friends that helped them at several points, such as setting up new businesses and providing labor.

But the ways that the Chinese community and its businesses grew in the Waipahu area also reflect the loss that Hawaiians were experiencing across the Islands. As one observer wrote, "But for the Chinese, Ewa [District, including Waiawa, Waipio, and Waipahu areas] would be indeed a desolate place. The natives seem to have disappeared from the face of the land. But the ... [Chinese] have entered in most emphatically to possess the land and their rice fields stretch in every direction. . . . Towards evening we reached Honouliuli where the whole valley is leased to rice planters."[25] Some have argued that Chinese activity in the area benefited all: "Initially, Chinese may have posed a threat to the Hawaiian community when they took over the management of so many fishponds. Yet in their industrious pursuit of the industry, they not only worked toward improving the environment by reclaiming low swamp areas for fishponds, but repaired and renovated existing ancient fishponds, providing communities with seafood commodities at reasonable prices."[26] And there is some truth that Hawaiians benefited from Chinese presence. But another way to read Chinese success in building not only a thriving community but also many strong businesses that catered to local residents' needs is that this was one step for this newly arrived ethnic group in working their way into the settler society. Indeed, some Hawaiians saw Chinese as a threat to their own survival and filed complaints with the Hawaiian government that Chinese were invading their fishing grounds.[27] Ultimately, Native Hawaiians and Chinese were left to find their own ways to survive—often competing with each other in a place where haole control was dominant and near total.

Honolulu-Bound

While some Chinese were seeking work in rural areas, many more were moving to cities; between 1890 and 1920, the percentage of Chinese workers living in rural Hawai'i declined from 80 percent to 45 percent. As we will see, the largest majority of the urban population lived in Honolulu, an early sign of how urban the Chinese population in Hawai'i would soon become. Honolulu was an attractive destination for Chinese for many reasons, even for those living in larger, successful communities like Waipahu. For one, the best schools, and sometimes the only schooling, was available in Honolulu, and most Chinese communities viewed education as the best pathway to a successful future. Zane Kee Fook, for example, tells the story of his family, who lived on the Big Island, near Hilo. Kee Fook was born in 1899, one of twelve children. In spite of Hilo's being the second-largest Chinese community, educational opportunities were limited. For Kee Fook's parents, sending their children to the best schools meant sending them to Honolulu, at least for the higher grades.[28] Indeed, some Honolulu schools, such as the Mills Institute (later to become Mid-Pacific Institute), catered to just this population: Chinese immigrant families throughout the Islands eager to place their children in good schools.

SETTING THE STAGE

Perhaps the most important influence on this large-scale movement to Honolulu came from the difficulty that Chinese had in making a successful living in rural areas. While rice cultivation had succeeded for some years, that success waned, especially because of U.S. restrictions on the Chinese community. Because restrictions prevented most Chinese from becoming citizens, most could not purchase land, making their investments in farming tenuous.[29] As Chinese immigration became increasingly restricted, Chinese farmers had no source of labor for their farms, and, as the Chinese population growth slowed, so too did the demand for rice. After the rice industry collapsed, Chinese were increasingly focused on education as the means of rising in Hawai'i society: "For the children of former contract workers, education rather than homesteading held the promise of autonomy, offering an alternative to the precariousness of rural production in a plantation colony where sugar inflated the cost of land and exclusion laws terminated the circulation of inexpensive kindred labor."[30]

The Chinese population in Honolulu grew steadily from the time of Chinese arrival in Hawai'i. As early as 1866, there were 370 Chinese residents in Honolulu, out of a total population of 13,521.[31] As Table 1.1 shows, by 1890, nearly a third of all Chinese were living in Honolulu, where they made up 19 percent of the city's population. By 1930, because of the arrival of other groups, Chinese made up a smaller proportion of Honolulu's population, but by that year, Chinese had become a largely Honolulu-based community, with 71 percent of the Chinese community living in Honolulu. And Chinese have mostly remained in Honolulu since those years. In 1970, for example, while 58 percent of the Islands' total population lived in Honolulu, 93 percent of the Islands' Chinese population were Honolulu residents.[32]

As we will see, it was the movement of Chinese into urban areas, especially Honolulu, that particularly alarmed both haole and some Hawaiians.

TABLE 1.1
Chinese in Honolulu, 1890–1930

	1890	1900	1930
Percentage of Chinese in Hawai'i living in Honolulu	29	35	71
Chinese as a percentage of the Honolulu population	19	23	14

Source: Clarence Glick, *Sojourners and Settlers: Chinese Migrants in Hawaii.* Honolulu: University of Hawai'i Press, 1980, 128–132.

SETTING THE STAGE

Whatever haole acceptance of or appreciation for Chinese as plantation laborers had existed quickly vanished when Chinese became urban residents and moved into new areas of work.

CLIMBING THE SOCIAL AND ECONOMIC LADDERS

The late nineteenth century saw the beginnings of Chinese class mobility. In the economy and in education, Chinese were finding and taking advantage of new opportunities and making a place for themselves. From the last two decades of the 1800s, we can see the trajectory of Hawai'i's Chinese and the ways they would become successful across many occupational sectors in the Islands, going on to accumulate capital, businesses, land, and status.

Chinese were able to find a niche in Honolulu's economy for several reasons. First, there were new opportunities in the late 1800s as Hawai'i's population and economy were growing, creating a corresponding growth in demand for goods and services. Second was the kind of competition Chinese faced in this area of the economy. Some in Honolulu protested that Chinese were taking jobs from others, both haole and Hawaiians. But relative to what was happening in places like San Francisco, Chinese faced less resistance from white working-class laborers, as there were fewer working-class white people in Hawai'i in the late nineteenth and early twentieth centuries. Native Hawaiians might have been the most serious competition to Chinese ownership of retail businesses. But the Hawaiian community had been devastated by haole settlers through the introduction of diseases that killed many Hawaiians and the haole takeover of the Kingdom of Hawai'i. There was some complaint and resentment from Hawaiians on these issues, who "saw their field invaded and their profits threatened by the cheap labor of the Chinese."[33] But little was done to change what became an inexorable increase in Chinese ownership of most retail businesses, especially in Honolulu.

The structure and nature of the Chinese community contributed to Chinese success in starting these businesses. The community was tight-knit. Chinatown—in its stores or even on the street—provided a space for constant and productive residential, social, and work interactions, making it easier to get new businesses off the ground. As in rural areas, urban Chinese developed effective social and financial networks. Chinese regularly formed huis (groups), which enabled individuals to acquire small amounts of capital that could be used to start small businesses. In other situations, Chinese who had already achieved some success were willing to invest in newcomers, further strengthening the Chinese community. Leading Chinese merchants also began to collaborate with haole and sometimes received loans and other forms of assistance from them.[34] These early ties across racial groups set the stage for cooperation between some Chinese and haole later on but also foreshadowed divisions in the Chinese community between the less and more successful. Overall, what we see is the beginning of a transition in Honolulu, and in rural enterprises, in which many Chinese "climbed up from plantations into independent or cooperative production. The structure of these sociofinancial networks, which encouraged young men to prove themselves through humbling and rigorous labor and rewarded the stalwart with credit and opportunity, provided the major cultural mechanism for the stunning mobility of Chinese migrants. These economic maneuvers . . . translated kinship and friendship into real financial capital."[35]

Schooling

Schooling was an important step for Chinese in Hawai'i; their involvement with the institution of education in Hawai'i reflects and foregrounds efforts and strategies to move away from plantation labor and take up other positions in Hawai'i society, especially as rural work and opportunity dried up. It was in and through the public schools that Chinese truly began their push into Hawai'i's middle class.

As Chinese were leaving the plantations in the late nineteenth century, schooling in Hawai'i was expanding rapidly. Even before Chinese began to arrive as plantation workers, the Hawaiian government had begun to require schooling for some children, started funding schools, and made English the official school language. In 1896, schooling was made compulsory for children aged six to fifteen years; while not rigorously enforced initially, schooling-related laws and regulations were evidence of the importance of education in the Kingdom and (later) Territory of Hawai'i.

Chinese entered schooling gradually toward the end of the nineteenth century. Two factors contributed to the slower pace in those early years. First, the early Chinese community consisted mostly of single men, and it

SETTING THE STAGE

was only as Chinese men married and had children that Chinese school enrollment was even possible. Second, school enrollment increased only once Chinese started to settle in urban areas; not many schools were available in rural areas, and even fewer were available to plantation families.[36] Early schools for Chinese children were often run by missionaries and churches. The first school for Chinese, the Bethel Mission School, was established in Honolulu's Chinatown in 1869, and several more mission-run schools were established in the following decades. Chinese children also began entering public schools. There were eighty-five Chinese pupils in public schools in 1890, but that number increased by 500 percent to 1,289 by 1900[37] and continued to grow over the next several decades.

During the years of the late nineteenth and early twentieth centuries, the system of public education grew rapidly. New schools were established throughout the Islands, especially in urban areas and in Honolulu in particular. For example, between 1895 and 1920, across the territory, there were only four high schools and one normal school (focused on training future teachers), but over the next twenty-five years, those numbers grew to twenty-one high schools, twenty-nine intermediate schools, and four vocational schools.[38]

For all involved, schooling was seen as an effective means of socialization into American culture. The importance of Americanizing the population—and the connection of that process to race—was pointed out by Thomas Gibson, a deputy superintendent of Hawai'i schools, who argued in 1920, "We must Americanize the rising Oriental generation or be submerged by it."[39] As one scholar points out, "the Americanized curriculum . . . force[d] students to speak standard English, as opposed to their native languages, and stressed industriousness, morality, and the doctrine of being a passive, consenting citizenry."[40]

As more Chinese men married and had children, education became an important goal for many families. Most early Chinese immigrants were uneducated[41] and wanted their children to receive the education they had not. They encouraged their children to take schooling seriously and excel in their academics. At the same time, Chinese parents often were torn between thinking of education as the means to their children's success and as a threat to their children's knowledge of and connection to their own culture and history. To some extent, the ways that success was measured in the schools mirrored Chinese parents' ideas of success. In one study conducted in the late 1980s, Chinese students were asked what their parents (first-generation immigrants) thought of as success. Their answers included "get the highest education possible," "being employed and respectful," "have a good position in society," "get a good job," and "earn a good income."[42] These goals paralleled those of Hawai'i's schools. But success for Chinese would have to be defined on haole terms, and parents knew that would mean a potential loss of connection to Chinese culture for their children.

One solution, Chinese community leaders and parents hoped, was Chinese language schools, the first of which was established in Hawai'i in the 1870s.[43] The schools became more organized in the 1890s and grew in number across Hawai'i throughout the 1890s. They operated as a complement to the mainstream education that children received and were usually run for a couple hours after regular school each day and on Saturday mornings. Children were taught Chinese language as well as Chinese history and culture. Teachings were rarely political, but Chinese leaders and educators hoped that through this exposure to China and Chinese culture, children would come to understand and value Chinese principles and values and thus develop strong and long-lasting ties to China and to the Chinese community in Hawai'i. Enrollment in these schools increased steadily until World War II at which point the U.S. government outlawed all language schools, arguing that they were dangerous to the U.S. war mission.

Whether in Chinese language, public, or private schools, Chinese began to make visible the value they put on education. Parents increasingly prioritized their children's education and made decisions about where they lived and about financial investments based on a belief that education would allow their children to attain a middle-class life. Schools were also key sites for the influence and control of haole settlers over Hawai'i society, with emphasis placed on American values and ways of life and Christianity. Early missionaries and their children saw schooling as the way to "Americanize"—and Christianize—a population the vast majority of which was neither white, nor American, nor Christian.[44] Despite opposition from planters who argued that schooling would mean that immigrants would not want to work as plantation laborers, the missionary force won out, and schools and universal enrollment were supported by the government. And the Chinese community subscribed to these ideas, recognizing the value of education in Hawai'i and doing all they could to get their children into and through the best schools. Thus, Hawai'i's schools in many ways met their original goals and purposes. As we will see in chapter 2, the influences affecting schooling would continue and grow stronger in the early twentieth century. As education is a major socializing agent in a society, schooling became an important step by which the immigrant Chinese population not only earned their ticket to a middle class life but also came to accept a middle-class life that was defined by white Christian American values.

RELIGION AND LAND IN THE SHIFTING HAWAIIAN LANDSCAPE

Chinese were beginning to establish themselves in a site that was deeply engaged in settler colonial practices, one where white people were seizing increasing control over all aspects of life and imposing an interrelated set of white, Christian, and capitalist practices that would shape the trajectory of Hawai'i long into the future.

We have seen that the socialization that Chinese received strongly reflected white and Christian values and perspectives. The power of those perspectives came from the presumed assumptions that a modern society was one that valued Christianity, Western ideologies, and capitalism and that only by accepting and adopting those values could an individual, community, or territory come to be seen as legitimate. Even though Chinese were more resistant to Christian conversion than were Native Hawaiians, many of the most powerful and successful Chinese did become Christians, underscoring the importance of religion in shaping Hawai'i and its economy during the late nineteenth and early twentieth centuries in ways that continue to reverberate today.

During these and later years, land ownership was crucial to the development of racial inequality in Hawai'i. Land had always been precious in Hawai'i. Among Native Hawaiians, land and community were tightly bonded: "Hawaiian understanding of human life and social organization . . . [was based on] using and giving, rather than possessing . . . land."[45] These beliefs shaped how Hawaiians lived on the land and related to one another:

SETTING THE STAGE

"Extending over many generations, these relationships between families residing in the same ahupuaʻa (the traditional Hawaiian subdivision of land) were strong. Interdependence and reliance on one another created a societal bond that ensured that people of all ranks worked together for the common good of all."[46]

That organization and connection to the land was shattered with the 1848 Mahele division of land and the 1850 Kuleana Act, which privatized all land. Hawaiian leaders supported these measures under the recommendation of haole advisers, who argued that land reform would benefit Native Hawaiian communities. Hawaiian leaders may have been skeptical of haole intentions, but they also hoped that privatization would protect their communities: if Hawaiians could secure land rights, doing so might slow the ongoing aggression of haole settlers and prevent them from acquiring the land they were seeking. But the new system only deepened haole power, and the result was "the aggressive accumulation of property by foreigners, the formalization of native elite claims to land resources, and the widespread dispossession of commoners."[47] Most Hawaiians were unable to acquire rights to land; they lacked the funds needed for such purchases, and they were unfamiliar with this new, capitalist approach to land use. The changes in the relationship between people and the land undermined the basis of Hawaiian communities, making "it impossible for commoners to subsist on the land without participating in the market economy, either through produce sales, cash cropping, or wage labor."[48] Competition, not cooperation, became the law of the land.

These changes in land ownership influenced everyone in Hawaiʻi, including Chinese. Privatization of land—which occurred before the arrival of the first Chinese plantation laborers—gave second- and third-generation Chinese a pathway to success. Once they began to accumulate capital, they began to buy land. While their land purchases never rivaled the enormous tracts of land seized by early haole plantation owners, Chinese purchases of house lots and smaller parcels nevertheless would form the basis of capital accumulation and propel their future success. Chinese land purchases thus contrasted sharply with the land losses experienced by Hawaiians at the same time: Chinese were able to capitalize on the imposed land system that caused Hawaiian dispossession. Most importantly, these mid-nineteenth-century changes in land ownership further embedded Hawaiʻi in a Western, white, capitalist economic system.

THE ESTABLISHMENT AND GROWTH
OF CHINATOWN, HONOLULU

In these early decades of the twentieth century, most Chinese lived in or near the area of the city that later came to be known as Chinatown; a small number of Chinese lived in other parts of the city, but many of these likely worked as domestic servants in haole homes.[49] The "Chinese quarter," as it was known, was a low-lying area just west of the present central business district, near the harbor. Because it was prone to flooding, it was not considered good land and for that reason was available for Chinese settlement. Its location was a spatial reflection of the ongoing and developing racial politics of the era: "Originally, Hawaiians had occupied the more pleasant areas within the city. But as the number of Caucasian residents increased, they pushed the Hawaiians to the less desirable parts of Honolulu and the more attractive areas were soon occupied by Caucasians. The Chinese, on the other hand, moved into the least expensive areas close to the sea. This placed the Hawaiians in the middle; and, as the Chinese population expanded, Hawaiians were squeezed out to the edges of the city or into small pockets within Chinatown."[50]

The late nineteenth century was a time of strong anti-Chinese sentiment and action, and while no formal laws kept Chinese from settling in other parts of Honolulu, many more informal but effective barriers existed. From its early days, the Chinese quarter had a diverse range of businesses, many catering to the Chinese population but also offering goods and services beyond it. In 1882, one haole minister observed, "If you will ride slowly through the Chinese quarter with your eyes open, you will go to your home with food for thought. You will find watchmakers, and jewelers' shops, tin-shops, shoe shops, tailor shops, saddle and harness shops, furniture shops, cabinet shops and bakeries all run by Chinese with Chinese workmen. You can find anywhere from a stove, or a shovel down through drugs, groceries, notions and whatnots."[51]

Indeed, in Honolulu during this period, as we observe the jobs Chinese took and the businesses they opened, we can see the beginning of the Chinese movement into increasingly higher-status occupations and socioeconomic classes. They began to open small businesses and services, many of which catered explicitly and primarily to Chinese, mostly single men. Restaurants thus took the place of family meals, providing public spaces for interactions with fellow Chinese. Stores and businesses were also able to provide Chinese goods and services unavailable outside Chinatown. But Chinese stores—even those located in the Chinatown area—also increasingly catered to others, particularly Hawaiians. Chinese quickly moved into retail businesses; by 1884, Chinese had come to own most of the retail businesses and restaurants in Honolulu.[52] By 1896, Chinese operated 118 general merchandise stores and thirty-five grocery stores in Honolulu, seventy-two of which were in Chinatown. To get a sense of Chinese dominance in this area of the economy, according to the 1890 census, there were 1,833 merchants and traders in Hawai'i, and 776 (about two-thirds) of these were Chinese.[53] Chinese found success by filling in where haole were not present and where Native Hawaiians were largely absent.

Several Chinese stores in Chinatown were seen as community centers, places where members of the community could gather to exchange news and check in with one another. A student researcher at the University of Hawai'i described such a store that her grandfather operated in the late nineteenth century: "Besides general retailing . . . [it] served as a post office, a part-time bank and a social center for the Chinese immigrants who came to work on the plantations."[54] Her grandfather, as a respected community leader, mediated disputes in the community and provided loans to community members. Indeed, stores' role as banks was very important to the community, as it meant access to credit and money that could be invested in new businesses. It was also a social and financial link between Chinese residents and their family members in China, providing a way to send remittances back home.[55] With banks unavailable to most Chinese at this time, many in the community used Chinese stores as depositories for their savings, trusting store owners to keep their money safe; these stores were thus precursors to later Chinese-owned banks, offering financial support and providing community members with ways to invest and develop new businesses. Chinese stores also offered places for newly arriving or traveling Chinese to spend a few nights or find employment leads. Another student researcher described the social contact her uncle's store in Chinatown provided: "For many . . . the store represented not only a shopping center but also a place of social contact with old friends. They often sat on the round wooden chairs situated in various areas of the store and engaged in informal, friendly, intimate discussions generally relating events occurring within their families."[56] Thus, at a time when other places were inaccessible to Chinese, these stores functioned as important social institutions that strengthened ties in the community.

As their businesses proliferated, Chinese were able to invest more and more. The first Chinese bank, the Chinese American Bank, opened in 1916, and other Chinese banks opened in the 1920s and 1930s.[57] These banks provided some of the services that had earlier been provided by Chinese stores. Some new businesses offered the same goods and services as those owned and operated by haole, giving the Chinese community better access to a wider variety of things and services. The tight-knit community that had developed as a reaction to immigrant loneliness and haole mistreatment transitioned into a strength for the Chinese: a resource for developing businesses.

In addition to providing for the needs of the Chinese community, many businesses also sought clientele outside the community; in a growing society, with increasingly global connections, there was a growing demand for the kinds of goods and services Chinese could provide, from transportation to baked goods to barbering. Chinatown shops eventually began to attract non-Chinese customers: "Gradually, through the medium of trade, the Chinese increased their contacts with other racial groups in the Islands, and became more a part of the wider community than they had been as laborers."[58] These growing connections developed even though Chinatown continued to be seen as an insular and foreign community.

Chinatown and Disease

Indeed, Chinatown became the space that represented the dangers of Chinese immigrants. Haole writers regularly expressed concerns about the potential contamination that Chinese and Chinatown brought to Honolulu. These concerns mirrored the rhetoric seen across the world: a belief that Chinese carried diseases and would infect a city, threatening the health and lives of white people. Writing about reactions to San Francisco's Chinatown in the late nineteenth century, one scholar notes, "Medical discourse reproduced the configuration of its streets and alleyways, perceptions of filth and crowding, and the bodies resident within Chinatown as pathological.... Each process of pathologization—that is, of Chinatown and of the bodies resident within it—would have been incomplete, and in retrospect incompletely understood, without the other."[59] Because many believed that Chinese were likely to spread disease, laws were enacted to contain the population in one area and restrict their movement.

While most of the media stories connecting Chinese, Chinatown, and disease in Hawai'i came from haole writers, some Hawaiians were also wary of Chinese in Honolulu. As one writer explained at the turn of the twentieth century, "Public-spirited Hawaiians protested against their [Chinese] vices, as a corrupting element in the body politic. Artisans complained that their competition was lowering wages and the standard of living. But the menace to public health involved in importing shiploads of Orientals was perhaps the argument that told most heavily against them."[60] For Hawaiians, it was the spread of leprosy—which was widely (and likely incorrectly) attributed to Chinese—that made these arguments most relevant. Leprosy had arrived in Hawai'i in the nineteenth century, and it was Native Hawaiians and their communities who had been most affected by the disease—and by an official policy of exiling those diagnosed with leprosy to the island of Moloka'i for life, destroying families and communities in the process.

Hawaiians' concern about the arrival of new diseases was a legitimate one; the Hawaiian population had been decimated by the new diseases—smallpox, gonorrhea, syphilis, measles, and others—brought in by new settlers. Leprosy—with its required exile—was devastating to Hawaiian communities. But the origin of these newly introduced diseases was more likely white settlers than Chinese immigrants. It should come as no surprise that haole contributed to the rhetoric that blamed Chinese. An 1865 piece in the *Pacific Commercial Advertiser* asserted, "There is very little doubt that the leprosy was brought here originally by the coolies [*sic*] imported in [1850]."[61]

That Chinese were blamed for the spread of disease was consistent with the treatment of Chinese in many places well beyond Hawai'i. The disease argument was powerful because the stigma of disease was likely to last longer than any connected to perceived economic or social dangers: "Whereas an improved economy and increasing jobs eventually eased the hostilities of the working class toward the Chinese, the stigmas of disease and filth ascribed to Chinatown lodged firmly among the upper classes and proved harder to erase."[62] We will see in the next chapter that the suggested association of Chinese with disease shaped the future of Chinese experience in Hawai'i, both in the actions of haole leaders toward Chinatown

SETTING THE STAGE

and in how it likely encouraged second- and third-generation immigrants to seek careers in medicine and public health. But until then, a belief in the connection between Chinese and disease reflected the larger anti-Chinese sentiment of many in Hawai'i.

ANTI-CHINESE DISCRIMINATION AND RESTRICTIONS

While praised as good plantation workers, Chinese were strongly criticized once they moved to other areas of Hawai'i, and it was in the cities that Chinese met the strongest resistance and faced the most severe harassment and discrimination. Haole feared that once Chinese left the plantations and were no longer under the control of their employers, they presented economic, social, and political threats. One haole leader complained in 1869, "It is hard . . . to keep the coolies to their contracts, and when their terms have expired what becomes of them? . . . The Chinese are pagans; they won't be Christianized; they won't re-engage to labor, but are turned loose on the country, with all their vices."[63] A government official made clear that Chinese were perceived as a threat to white rule, arguing, "Unless adequate measures are adopted, Oriental civilization will extinguish, and be substituted for, the Anglo-Saxon civilization of this country. . . . It is the desire that the Chinese should remain on the plantations and not engage in those other employments which must be the means of support of those of Anglo-Saxon civilization, if such are to remain here."[64]

Even though—and because—Chinese were moving up in Hawai'i's social and economic circles, they faced discrimination and restriction. Much of the anti-Chinese sentiment and many of the negative actions against Chinese came from haole communities. Discrimination took several forms. The media regularly portrayed Chinese as subordinate, less important, dangerous, or needing to be removed. Newspapers published articles that criticized Chinese, and while these articles were penned by individuals, they reflected a general feeling among haole. Newspapers were highly influential in shaping public opinion. And they played an important role in the effort to convince the public of the dangers of Chinese. One of the major newspapers of the time, the *Pacific Commercial Advertiser*, was key to the connection among the media, the public, and government policies. Its owner, Walter Murray Gibson, was also a member of the colonial government. He used the newspaper to stir up and encourage anti-Chinese attitudes in Hawai'i, reporting news, rumors, and sentiments unfavorable to Chinese. For example, in 1881, Gibson wrote a pamphlet that warned Native Hawaiians of the dangers of Chinese to the Hawaiian community and suggested that they avoid Chinese doctors.[65] This pamphlet also served as a haole attempt to keep Hawaiian and Chinese communities separate and opposed to each another. As a powerful player in the government, Gibson also worked to pass anti-Chinese legislation.[66]

Many in Hawai'i feared that Chinese would be able to undercut white rule because of their seeming ability to do any kind of work, for inhumanly long hours, and at the very lowest wages[67]; indeed, by the 1880s, Chinese were competing more successfully with haole than was any other ethnic group.[68] These stereotypes contributed to the perception of Chinese as wholly different from other people, since these qualities were seen as typical not of humans but of alien beings. As one scholar characterizes the motivations behind the attacks on Chinese,

> In the Malthusian terms of the late nineteenth century, which reframed life as a racialized bid for survival, Chinese were described as a uniquely competitive race, not because they had evolved through virtue and civilization into a higher form of life, but because they had adapted to suffering. They survived by virtue of their lower life form, their willingness to feed from the bottom, their ability to cheat and skimp. Where the European went with his torch of enlightenment, to bestow the gifts of knowledge and progress upon lesser creatures, the Chinese lurked in the shadows, eager to siphon even the humblest of dregs of wealth back into his celestial kingdom.[69]

By 1870, more organized and active anti-Chinese work was underway. As plantation owners tried to find solutions to their labor needs, public meetings and discussions took place weighing the pros and cons of importing more Chinese workers. It was in the course of these discussions that a decision was made to bring in more workers from other countries, particularly Japan, Korea, and the Philippines. Assuming that these groups would not get along with one another, plantation owners hoped that by bringing in workers from different countries, they could prevent workers from gaining too strong or united a voice in Island or labor politics.

Throughout this time, Native Hawaiian opinion on Chinese immigration was mixed. We have seen that in rural areas, many Hawaiians cooperated

SETTING THE STAGE

with Chinese to maintain or develop farms and other enterprises. But others, particularly those in Honolulu, saw Chinese as an economic threat. Some Hawaiians were concerned about the domination of Chinese in retail businesses in Honolulu, arguing that Hawaiians were unable to compete.[70] To draw attention to their concerns, Hawaiians organized public meetings to discuss the issue of Chinese migration. At one such meeting in 1869 at the Kaumakapili Church, Hawaiians drafted a plea to the government to limit Chinese immigration.[71] At times, Hawaiians spoke out more strongly against Chinese immigration than did white people. For example, as haole plantation owners were expanding their industry in the 1880s, they sought more workers from China, but Hawaiians felt that Chinese threatened their own place in the Islands. In 1886, the Hawai'i government, influenced partly by Hawaiians who opposed further Chinese immigration, passed several laws restricting Chinese immigration.[72]

In addition to immigration laws, the Hawai'i government passed laws restricting Chinese within Hawai'i. A law passed in 1857 supposedly to encourage employment among Chinese in reality was used to curtail Chinese from loitering and roaming the streets: police officers were given the discretion to arrest any Chinese who was wandering in Honolulu "under suspicious circumstances."[73] Later, to address more significant concerns about Chinese taking employment off the plantations, workers' contracts in the 1890s did not allow a migrant to remain in Hawai'i unless he was working in agriculture or domestic service.[74] Again, there was some support for further restrictions on the part of Hawaiians. But as haole gained more and more power in Hawai'i, the restrictions and regulations were established mostly by the haole elite.

In the midst of this anti-Chinese fervor, Chinatown came to be seen not only as foreign, dangerous, and unhealthy but also increasingly as a threat to innocent Honolulu residents. One haole writer described the dangers of the area this way: "This once innocent Hawaiian people are now the victors [victims?] of John Chinaman. They are enticed into dens of debauchery, dens of deception, dens of corruption, dens of infamy, dens of gambling, dens of contagion, dens of opium, dens within dens, dens adjoining dens, dens encircling dens, and lastly, dens, the most filthy that the human power can conceive of."[75]

In public meetings to discuss Chinese immigrants and immigration, many Hawaiians expressed concerns about Chinatown, arguing that it reflected the inability of Chinese to assimilate: Chinese stayed in one area of the city, associated only with one another, and spoke only Chinese.[76] There was a certain irony to these arguments because one of the central reasons Chinese were located in Chinatown, in a segregated area, was that they were often not allowed to live in other parts of the city. And these concerns were expressed despite Chinese shop owners and businesses increasingly providing services beyond the Chinese community.

Even in these early years, we can see the beginnings of the rhetoric around "good" and "bad" Asians. In an 1869 letter to "the citizens of Honolulu," Chinese merchants tried to use class distinctions among Chinese to ease tensions and reduce the hostility toward the Chinese community. They spoke out against a "lower-class" Chinese group: "We heartily oppose the introduction of coolies here under that system. Some of the Chinese coolies are very bad men and criminals. We know our countrymen better than anyone else, and we believe that a much better class of men for plantation and other kinds of work can be procured from China by some arrangement for the encouragement of free immigration."[77]

Important to the Hawaiian perception of Chinese were the efforts of haole leaders to discourage cooperation between Hawaiians and Chinese. Haole racism and hostility toward Chinese is clear in their writings, speeches, meetings, petitions to the government, and legal actions. They spoke about Chinese as ultimately foreign, clannish, dishonest, and uncontrollable. But in how haole pitted groups against each other, we can see how racialization and racism were also part of the process of empire building. Haole treated Hawaiians and Chinese as distinct groups with different needs and uses and requiring different kinds of control.

Through the second half of the nineteenth century, haole leaders wrote and spoke of the dangers that Chinese posed to Native Hawaiians. One editorial argued that Chinese who had left the plantations should be sent back to China and "not be let among us to drive away our mechanics and small traders and to pollute the Hawaiian race by their presence."[78] Another writer, in an 1882 editorial in *The Friend*, wrote, "The Chinese are a persistent race; the Hawaiians are evanescent. The former have the very qualities which the latter most lack—industry, providence, economy, subtlety— all the money-making and money-saving virtues are with the Chinese. Idleness, carelessness, generosity, simplicity, all the money-losing qualities are with the Hawaiian. Everywhere the Chinaman is quietly, peaceably, smilingly but persistently displacing the Hawaiian. Nothing is more absolutely sure, which is not already an accomplished fact, than this: That as a laborer, small farmer, shopkeeper and tradesman the Chinaman will crowd the native Hawaiian to the wall, and will take his place."[79] In their writings and speeches, haole made clear both their interest in keeping these two groups apart and their different perceptions of Native Hawaiians (as needing governing) and Chinese (as threatening). The view of Ida Pope, a haole educator of Native Hawaiian girls, reflected the general haole sentiment about Hawaiians: "To her, Native Hawaiians were a dark-skinned, primitive, child-like race unable to take care of themselves. She perceived their cultural beliefs and their conceptions of motherhood and womanhood as backward, ancient, and uncivilized. Such ideas and practices, she believed, represented obstacles to civilization that needed to be eliminated and replaced with middle-class American ideals if Native girls and their people were to survive modernity."[80] Coloniality influenced how haole perceived Chinese and Native Hawaiians as a danger or needing saving, and both views were connected to strategies to strengthen and maintain white domination of Hawai'i.

A framing in which Chinese were depicted as dangerous and Hawaiians as victims perpetuated myths that Hawaiians were childlike and in need of haole governance and that Chinese were aiming to disrupt and overturn the white dominance of society. At the same time, haole defense of Hawaiians was meant to keep these two groups—Hawaiian and Chinese—from cooperating, since doing so might threaten haole place and dominance.[81] According to Julia Katz, "That these two irrational—and often illegible— groups appeared to collaborate so fluently posed its own problem for protocolonial governance and the imagined destiny of Hawai'i. Each group would have to be rationalized and assimilated to the haole colonial vision of Hawai'i separately: while Hawaiians were to be proselytized, tutored, and groomed for positions within the nation according to the dictates of paternalism and white settler colonialism, Chinese were to be immobilized, criminalized, and segregated as guest-workers and outsiders within a growing regime of exclusion."[82]

Haole were also motivated to encourage anti-Chinese sentiment among Hawaiians because of their own worries that the United States would be disinclined to support the Territory if it saw Asians as having too much power or influence. At the time, haole worried about whether the United States would renew the Reciprocity Treaty of 1875, a free-trade agreement between Hawai'i and the United States. An editorial in the *Advertiser* claimed, "If the United States were to find these benefits being granted to a 'non-assimilating race' that was causing difficulties in places like California, it 'may pause about extending our treaty beyond the time prescribed.'"[83]

Some Native Hawaiians opposed Chinese immigration, and some were worried that the movement of Chinese off the plantations would threaten the place of Hawaiians. But it is unclear how much, if any, anti-Chinese sentiment among Native Hawaiians derived from the haole fearmongering. In speeches, newspaper articles, meetings, and attempts at legislation, haole raised alarm and concern regularly, often under the guise of wanting to protect Hawaiian communities. The *Pacific Commercial Advertiser* was unabashedly anti-Chinese and frequently carried stories about the dangers of Chinese. As one scholar put it, "There can be little doubt that highly emotional and sensational newspaper articles did much to convince many residents of the Kingdom that all Chinese smoked opium and were a threat to the Kingdom, and in particular a threat to the health and well-being of the unfortunate and uninformed native Hawaiian."[84] Whatever concerns Hawaiians had about Chinese immigrants, haole provoked these negative sentiments further through their own rhetoric and publications. The different fates that awaited Chinese and Hawaiians would become further apparent during the process of annexation.

HAWAI'I'S ANNEXATION TO THE UNITED STATES

With the U.S. seizure and overthrow of the Hawaiian Kingdom in 1893 and its annexation in 1898, Chinese faced new difficulties. Violence against Chinese in Hawai'i increased, with more direct attacks made on the Chinese community. Some were small and likely carried out by individuals, but others involved groups of haole, some perhaps authorized by those in power. One such attack took place in the Mānoa area of Honolulu in 1898 when about a hundred U.S. soldiers destroyed the market gardens of Chinese residents, tearing up fruit trees, flowers, and more. Another attack took place in Chinatown, where soldiers destroyed shops and businesses in the district. These attacks seemed fueled by a belief that the increasing presence and success of Chinese in the business community were a threat

SETTING THE STAGE

to haole dominance.[85] But they were also the result of the increasing exclusion of Chinese in the new society.

At the time of annexation, Asians were the only ethnic groups completely excluded from enfranchisement. In spite of petitions from the Chinese and Japanese communities, all Chinese and Japanese were disenfranchised, including those who had been citizens of the Hawaiian Kingdom. In addition, Hawai'i was subject to the rules of the U.S. Chinese Exclusion Act, which further restricted the movement of Chinese into Hawai'i. Annexation was a watershed moment for the Chinese community, as the discrimination and exclusion they had faced for decades was enacted into law. In response, they used a variety of means to push back, including forming opposition groups, taking direct action against unjust treatment, and writing letters, petitions, and pleas to government officials and committees. In these, they pointed to the significant contributions they had made to Hawai'i and how they had been part of Hawai'i's success and movement toward a modern age. In their petition to the government, they argued that they were "orderly, law-abiding, industrious, and materially add to the wealth and value of the country"[86] and had "done much to foster and ensure the commercial and industrial resources of the Hawaiian Islands."[87] In their efforts, we can see how they were drawn to and adopted the language and frameworks of white settler colonialism, including what—many years later—would be referred to as model-minority status and achievement: they asserted their right of place and inclusion based on their economic contributions, highlighted their successful merchants, and, in comparisons made between themselves and Native Hawaiians, argued that Chinese were more productive and better contributors to Hawai'i's goals and future. At times, they were quite pointed in their view of themselves in comparison to haole. Ho Fong, a prominent Chinese community member, wrote in an 1888 editorial in the *Pacific Commercial Advertiser*,

Most of my countrymen, in fact, are thrifty and determined men, whose perseverance was not a bit different to American or European, and on arriving here strived to better themselves. . . . They proceeded to work and to learn the trades, arts, and resources of the country, and being frugal, and I venture to say, honest in their dealings, very soon made a good mark for themselves, They did and still do well for themselves, and have placed both goods, clothes, and shoes, etc. at a reasonable and fair figure for all the community. But alas, by doing this unequivocal good, they invited and obtained the hatred and jealousy of the whole Haole race. They built themselves up out of but little, keeping to their business, by sobriety, temperance and hard work. Which sir, is the race on the Islands that can compete with my countrymen for all these virtues?

They came here to work[;] their tact and assiduity and constancy soon bring the desired reward because their knowledge is good and their conduct better than most Haoles. They in general succeed, and because these workers don't throw money and idle hours away, they become the envy of those in the trade who do[;] I mean the other Haole tradesmen of the same kind. I ask, Sir, why should my prosperous, industrious, and persevering countrymen be treated to envy and maliciousness?[88]

The tenor of these arguments would foreground later efforts and rhetoric as Chinese struggled to be accepted as part of Hawai'i society. While they were unsuccessful in gaining acceptance at the time of annexation, in the way they shaped their arguments, they showed that they had begun to figure out the currency of the Territory, where a racialized, Western-style economy ruled most aspects of Island life. They would continue to pursue acceptance into the haole-created society over many decades. And though cooperation between Chinese and Native Hawaiians had been fundamental to Chinese success in rural areas, the strategies adopted by Chinese would result in increasing distance from the efforts of Native Hawaiians to sustain their own communities.

In the midst of the chaos, exclusion, disenfranchisement, racism, and colonialism that ran through most of Hawai'i during these decades of the end of the nineteenth century, we can see how the Chinese community and Chinatown would take shape against a backdrop of white settler colonialist maneuvers, one that pitted Native Hawaiians and immigrant groups against one another, with different ethnic and racial groups having different relationships with the increasingly dominant white population of the Islands. In the early and challenging years of Chinese immigration, Chinatown provided a safe place, one that Chinese immigrants could count on to offer some protection from the forces in Honolulu that made their lives difficult. As Chinese moved from the plantations to rural areas and then to Honolulu, the Chinese community was able to give early immigrants the means—small as they were at first—to work their way into the broader Hawai'i society.

SETTING THE STAGE

COMPARISON WITH SAN FRANCISCO

While anti-Chinese sentiment was sometimes strong and violent in Hawai'i in the second half of the nineteenth century, even a brief comparison of Chinese experiences in Hawai'i and California can help us contextualize the situation in Hawai'i and see how key elements in the experience of Chinese there were unique to the setting and era. California, too, was experiencing rapid growth in its population and economy, and Chinese contributed in some similar ways there, providing services to their own and surrounding communities. As is clear from media reports at the time describing violent acts against Chinese and restrictions on where Chinese could live and go to school, the racism against Chinese was strong, deep, and active in California, especially in the San Francisco area, at that time home to the largest Chinese American community. But in California, there was also a growing white working class who resented Chinese involvement in the economy. Californians—both government officials and the general public—worked hard to exclude Chinese from regular society. The 1882 Chinese Exclusion Act is the best known of the restrictive immigration legislation from these times, but Congress passed a further ten pieces of legislation in the dozen or so years after 1882 that further tightened exclusionary measures. California's anti-Chinese sentiment was key to this legislation being enacted.[89]

In addition to being seen as an economic threat, California Chinese were said to be violating not only race norms but also gender norms; in California, as in Hawai'i, males greatly outnumbered females in the immigrant population and in Chinese communities; in 1900, women made up only 5 percent of Chinese in the United States. Restrictive immigration laws played a large role in that gender ratio. The Page Act of 1875 was directed at female Chinese migrants; presuming that all female Chinese migrants were prostitutes, California officials simply forbade women entry to California. In addition, Chinese were not permitted to marry non-Chinese. Together, these two laws meant that Chinese men who came to the United States would not easily find a spouse there and were effectively forced to remain single. Because of these restrictions, Chinese were forced to live what was considered a gender-deviant life, contributing to the continuing negative rhetoric and assumptions about Chinese: "Since Chinese workers were perceived as bachelors without family obligations, the notion of the 'coolie' standard was invested with fears about a socially disordered world of unemployed men, women prostitutes, and working families ripped apart by vice, poverty, and disease. The vigorous diatribes against 'Chinese coolies' emphasized the irreconcilable differences between the putatively unfree, racially inferior, and alien Chinese workers and the free, independent, white producer-citizens. In labor rhetoric the presence of the Chinese antagonized American workers and contaminated their aspirations for prosperity, democratic citizenship and family life."[90]

White Californians did not want Chinese women to immigrate; they believed that being married in the United States might make it less likely that men would eventually return to China, and it might be harder to get Chinese men to agree to long hours and low wages if they had family responsibilities nearby. But at the same time, these restrictions deepened white concerns about Chinese: the inability of Chinese to have families and their living outside that key social institution were central factors in their being seen as alien, as not belonging.

While there was a larger percentage of women in the Chinese community in Hawai'i, they still made up only 13.5 percent of that population in 1900,[91] and that unbalanced sex ratio was of concern in Hawai'i as well. Most Chinese men did not have Chinese wives in Hawai'i; for many years, it was only the wealthiest Chinese men who did.[92]

But Hawai'i officials approached the issue of Chinese women differently from those in California. In Hawai'i, plantation owners and government officials wanted women to migrate with men; they believed that if women accompanied men, Chinese were more likely to stay on the plantations and to work hard. Chinese women might also be employable to do plantation work. Missionaries argued that women would be a civilizing influence on the Chinese community; one wrote, "No surer safeguard can be erected against the thousand possible ills which may arise from the indiscriminate herding together of thousands of men! Let the sweet and gentle influence of the mother, the wife, the sister, and the daughter be brought to bear upon the large and yearly increasing company of Chinese in our midst, and we shall soon see a change wrought, such as police regulations cannot produce."[93]

Indeed, many Hakka Chinese, who were often Christian converts, came to the Islands with their families.[94] It was the presumed positive influence of women that was behind the immigration practices through which Hawai'i's leaders permitted and even encouraged the immigration of Chinese women, particularly as wives. During the last decades of the nineteenth century, several measures were passed to encourage or require those recruiting laborers from China to include women, wives, and families; recruiters were also sometimes paid more for women than men.[95] When Chinese immigration was restricted in the 1880s, Chinese women and children were exempt from these restrictions and permitted to travel with their husbands or alone. Because of these interventions, the percentage of women in the Chinese population increased by 167 percent between 1866 and 1878.[96] Another important difference between Hawai'i and California was that Hawai'i permitted Chinese men to marry outside their community, and many married Hawaiian women. By 1900, some 1,500 Chinese men were married to or living with Hawaiian women and raising families.[97] While still male-dominated, Chinese communities in Hawai'i were much more likely than those in California to house families, making them seem much less threatening to haole than bachelor communities.

Even though Chinese in both Hawai'i and California experienced discrimination, their experiences differed in important ways. The lives of Chinese in California were much more constrained and restricted in most arenas, from housing to schooling to marriage. The influence of the white working class in California was key in this process, as was the hope of California leaders that by restricting immigration, Chinese communities would not be able to build a normal life and would be more inclined to return to China. In this situation, the Chinese had no way to counter the negative images and actions that were a constant part of their lives. In Hawai'i, rules about housing, schooling, and marriage were not as harsh, which allowed Chinese a narrow route to changing their position. They were not completely restricted in how they went about opening new businesses, and Chinese children were allowed into public schools. And under the rules governing the immigration of women, they were at least permitted a way to meet haole standards of family and gender norms.

These early years set the stage for much of what would come in the following decades. As we will see in the next chapter, anti-Chinese sentiment would become particularly focused on Chinatown in the early decades of the twentieth century. But again, the place of Chinatown in Honolulu and in its Chinese community took on a different tenor from that of Chinatowns and Chinese communities in places like San Francisco because of the unique racial politics in Hawai'i. Whereas in San Francisco, Chinese remained segregated in Chinatown and isolated from the rest of the city, Chinese in Hawai'i were beginning to rework the meaning of Chinatown. Sometimes that repositioning was forced on the Chinese, as happened when Chinatown was destroyed during the 1900 fire. But even so, there was more opportunity to imagine a Chinese community beyond Chinatown than in other places. At the same time, the relationship between Hawai'i and the United States established a particularly racialized context that inevitably shaped the Chinese community, as it shaped all ethnic and racial groups in Hawai'i. Chinese would make their way into the greater Hawai'i community against a background of settler colonialist politics and a difficult and fluid relationship with the United States. As they negotiated their way forward, those politics played a significant role in Chinese efforts and in the acceptance of their place in Hawai'i society by surrounding communities.

Chapter Two

1900 TO 1930: DESTRUCTION OF CHINATOWN AND THE (RE)BUILDING OF A CHINESE AMERICAN COMMUNITY

The decades following the turn of the last century represent some of the most important in the history of Chinese in Hawai'i. It was during this period that Chinese found ways to combat the discrimination and mistreatment they had experienced. While discrimination did not disappear, Chinese began to use strategies and processes—as individuals and as members of a community—to forge a place for themselves in Hawai'i society. This period opens with one of the most enduring devastations experienced by the Chinese community, the 1900 fire that destroyed most of Honolulu's Chinatown. By the end of this period, 1930, just under a decade before the beginning of World War II, we find Chinese moving into the middle class, taking up an accepted place in wider Honolulu society. In between the two signposts of the 1900 Chinatown fire and the onset of World War II, the Chinese community changed in significant ways. In earlier decades, Chinese were settling into Hawai'i society and beginning a process of social mobility. In the beginning of the twentieth century, we see these processes more fully underway. It was a time when Hawai'i-born Chinese came of age, having been socialized in schools, workplaces, churches, and communities as citizens of Hawai'i—and America. Their expectations—of themselves and of Hawai'i—differed from those of their parents.

1900 TO 1930: DESTRUCTION OF CHINATOWN

The Chinese and the Chinese community came out of the 1900 fire substantially changed. At the time, partly because they were seen as outsiders, Chinese were more likely to keep to themselves and their community as much as possible. More obvious class differences were also developing, with many Chinese continuing to work as laborers, earning low salaries, while others entered schools, graduated from university, sought education in the continental United States, and took on high-status jobs, earning salaries that allowed them to purchase homes or land. They looked for acceptance into spaces previously occupied only by haole or looked for exclusive spaces for themselves that reflected their newfound social class standing. By the end of this period, Chinese, especially the younger generation, became more visible and audible, working to make a place for themselves, sometimes in the face of hostility. In the process, Chinese began to use the system around them—a white American system established and controlled by haole—and found ways to use American processes and laws to help their community.

The processes underway both within the Chinese community and throughout Hawai'i society also reflected and sparked new distance between Chinese and Native Hawaiians. During these years, Hawaiians faced further devastation to their communities and survival. The routes taken by the Chinese and Hawaiian communities further embedded each in the white settler colonial framework, and established the different relationship to that framework that has been maintained since. Chinese began to work toward inclusion, whereas Native Hawaiians were only further away from reclaiming their sovereignty, land, and nation. In a different way, the tensions between and the overlapping interests of Chinese and Japanese in Hawai'i at the time foregrounded what would happen during World War II and in the decades afterward.

What took place at the time established Chinese success in future decades; some in the Chinese community—especially the elite merchant class—began to attempt to align themselves with haole community leaders and politicians, and those efforts contributed to the growing gap between the goals of Native Hawaiian and Chinese communities. In addition—and relatedly—it is at this time that we see the early musings of a model-minority construction, a discourse about "deserving" and "not-deserving" minority and immigrant groups, according to a standard derived from white middle-class society. In the class differences among Chinese in

1900 TO 1930: DESTRUCTION OF CHINATOWN

Hawai'i, we also see the forerunner of the discourse of "good" and "bad" Asians that has continued to haunt Asian American communities. In fact, it is a counternarrative to the model-minority discourse, especially as it delineates groups of Asians who follow the model from those who do not.

The Chinese community faced obstacles in achieving their goals, however. In particular, the Chinatown fire was a defining moment for Chinese in Hawai'i. It forced Chinese residents out of Chinatown and into new communities. But it was also symbolic: it made clear the place and standing of Chinese and Chinatown in the larger Honolulu community and reminded Chinese of the power of health officials to shape the lives of ordinary people. It suggested a need for change, both for individuals and for the Chinese community as a whole, a need for a new kind of community, one that was not strictly based on place but that could connect Chinese across the Islands while maintaining a connection with China. The new community would be both inward and outward looking, providing protection to its members while encouraging engagement with non-Chinese neighbors.

The changes that took place over the first few decades of the twentieth century also argue for Chinatown's place in Honolulu as a commemorative site, Not necessarily only as a place of daily living, but as a symbolically important place that is recognized as such by both Chinese and non-Chinese citizens. Chinese see Chinatown as a reflection of all that the community has endured and a symbol of its success in surviving many difficulties; others see it as a representation of Hawai'i's tolerance of difference and a way to project an image of Hawai'i as a racial paradise. Chinatown connects past discrimination to future success of the Chinese community in Hawai'i. Chinatown anchors these transition years, a place of continued discrimination and actions against Chinese, but also a way to understand how events such as the Chinatown fire propel Chinese into a future trajectory.

HAWAI'I IN 1900

Hawai'i was undergoing enormous change at the turn of the twentieth century. The political arena had been tumultuous, causing chaos and uncertainty. Most significantly, the United States had annexed Hawai'i in 1898; that move followed earlier actions by haole to seize control of Hawai'i. In 1887, the white community had engineered a new constitution, forcing

1900 TO 1930: DESTRUCTION OF CHINATOWN

King Kalākaua to sign a document stripping the monarch of his power and transferring it to the legislature, a body by then controlled by Americans. The King's Cabinet was also replaced by powerful white people. Connecting voting rights to land ownership and income gave Americans voting rights and excluded most Hawaiians. Asians were completely disenfranchised.

Thus, annexation in 1898 arose from earlier events and processes, including the creation of the 1887 Constitution of the Hawaiian Kingdom. Although the United States had had significant influence in the Islands before annexation, the 1893 takeover and 1898 annexation signaled the complete dismantling of the Hawaiian Kingdom by haole and the construction of a new Hawai'i, with new laws and regulations.[1] During the early years of the twentieth century, Americans solidified their economic and political control over the Islands and began to petition for the Islands' formal inclusion in the United States. The United States also added to its acquisition of Hawai'i's lands, mostly for military purposes. The United States acquired control of Pearl Harbor in 1887, around the time of the Bayonet Constitution, and built further military encampments throughout the early twentieth century. Fort Shafter was established as an army base in 1907, for example, and Wheeler Army Airfield was constructed in 1922. The establishment of these bases is further evidence of the military and strategic importance of Hawai'i to the United States. Because many of these events were interwoven with race and ethnicity—from who would rule Hawai'i to who would be included and excluded in the new society that was being constructed—Chinese were directly or indirectly involved in many of them.

After annexation, the people of Hawai'i lived under U.S. law, including, importantly, immigration law. That meant the Chinese Exclusion Act of 1882 was firmly in place. In 1907, the Gentlemen's Agreement between the United States and Japan curtailed Japanese immigration, again significantly affecting Hawai'i. Not only did this mean a reduction in immigrants (although some merchants and other elites continued to be allowed entry), but it was also a concrete manifestation of anti-Chinese and anti-Japanese sentiment. For Hawai'i in 1900, where more than half the population was Asian,[2] immigration law was particularly meaningful as it was used as a way to designate elements of the population as included or excluded and meant the establishment of a regime that made race and ethnicity a central pillar of its rule.

1900 TO 1930: DESTRUCTION OF CHINATOWN

The first years after annexation were significant in setting a racialized economy in motion, one that developed in the shadows of the United States and its imperialist history and future. Haole increased their land ownership; in 1856, haole owned 5 percent of all land in Hawai'i; by 1896, that figure was 57 percent and by 1911 was 76 percent.[3] Land ownership was connected to the way that the Hawai'i economy was increasingly dominated by sugar; the sugar oligarchs, mostly the children and grandchildren of the original haole missionaries, held a monopoly over nearly all sectors of the economy, including transportation, shipping, and banking. The sugar oligarchy "created an industrialized environment that began a process of remaking nearly all of the island environments. Institutional changes in political authority, economic organization, and land use policies resulted from industrial sugar's invasion of the landscape."[4] But Julia Katz reminds us that even though sugar and its stewards (wealthy haole settlers) ruled Hawai'i ("with an iron fist, tolerating opposition from neither competitors nor the labor force."[5]), there were other important sectors of the economy and society. For example, as we saw in the last chapter, Chinese were active in rural areas, developing and working on rice farms or working cooperatively with Native Hawaiians in other enterprises such as fishponds and taro fields. However, during the first decades of the twentieth century, most of Hawai'i society and, perhaps most importantly, the future of the Islands were strongly influenced by a small group of elite white individuals who had settled in and colonized the Islands. According to Noel Kent, "Those presenting a challenge to the existing power structure were crushed without hesitation."[6]

Chinese were thus trying to make their way—and finding ways to survive—in an economy and social landscape that were not only dominated by white people but also isolated from the colonial center (i.e., the United States). At the same time, Hawai'i was increasingly becoming involved in global politics. Chinese were one of several ethnic groups navigating this landscape. Japanese were, too, but a larger proportion of Japanese were working on the plantations. Those who had left plantation work were beginning to make inroads into the middle class, as the Chinese had, but at a much slower pace. Filipinos were fairly new to Hawai'i, and most worked on the plantations. Hawaiians were particularly hard hit at this time, having lost almost everything: their land, most of their population, their economic center, their political power, and their nation. Even their culture was being scorned by those in power.

1900 TO 1930: DESTRUCTION OF CHINATOWN

In 1900, Honolulu was a burgeoning town, with an expanding economy and increasing connections beyond Hawai'i. Its population had grown from 13,521 in 1866 to 20,487 in 1884 to 39,306 by 1900.[7] Chinese, who were steadily moving from plantations and rural areas to Honolulu, made up 23 percent of the Honolulu population in 1890.[8] The Chinese population made up 16.7 percent of the total population in the Islands at the time, but 35 percent of the total Chinese population lived in Honolulu, a figure that would grow to 71 percent by 1930.[9] Chinatown was home to many Chinese residents of Honolulu. But not all Chinese lived in Chinatown, nor was Chinatown exclusively Chinese. In 1884, 65 percent of Chinese in Honolulu were living in Chinatown; another 10 percent lived in the nearby business district, and a sixth of the population lived in the primarily haole districts, likely working as servants in haole households.[10] By 1900, only 44 percent of those living in Chinatown were Chinese. Residents also included Hawaiians, part Hawaiians, and Japanese.

ANTI-CHINESE SENTIMENT AND ACTION IN HAWAI'I: THE ROLE OF PUBLIC HEALTH

Anti-Chinese sentiment and actions may not have been as virulent and violent in Hawai'i as in California, but Hawai'i's Chinese did face explicit discrimination in the early twentieth century. As one scholar has stated, "The difference in racial climate between Hawaii and the west coast was one of degree rather than kind. White supremacy was assumed among European Americans in both places."[11] Chinese endured verbal and physical attacks on the streets and in other public places in Honolulu and faced discrimination in schooling, housing, and employment. Most discrimination was not formalized in law but occurred informally in all areas of life. In addition, and connected to these acts of racism, the haole media kept up its anti-Chinese campaign, often commenting on how unsanitary Chinese were and comparing Chinese to dogs.[12] Laws preventing Chinese from testifying in Territorial courts and Chinese disenfranchisement are further evidence of the position of the Chinese community in the Islands during the early Territorial years.[13]

Health was one of the most significant areas of concern about Chinese immigrants in both the continental United States and in Hawai'i. Indeed, one of the most obvious similarities between Honolulu and San

Francisco was that Chinese were seen as disease carriers; concerns about health caused some of the most significant disruptions to Chinese communities, including in Honolulu. The construction of Chinese as disease carriers epitomized the position of Chinese in Western societies; they were regularly viewed as foreign invaders, living outside "normal" standards of civilization. Issues of health and sanitation targeted Chinese residents and Chinese communities as dangers to any modernizing city.

Some health concerns arose from racist ideas about racial difference. Seen as the most foreign of foreign settlers in the United States, Chinese ways were so poorly understood that assumptions were made that Chinese were not only unknown but unknowable and dangerous. The construction of Chineseness as diseased and contagious fit well in the discourses of the era. The late nineteenth century saw rising immigration to the United States as well as increasing acceptance of the germ theory of disease as public health officials came to understand that disease was spread through microorganisms. With that understanding came new efforts to control disease spread, often through the control of people.[14] But not all groups were seen as equally likely to have or to spread disease. Eugenics theories also had strong adherents at this time, and, combined with new understandings of disease, were used to target some groups as more likely to harbor disease than others. In the United States, it was immigrants who were most often blamed for disease and disease outbreaks, and within that group, it was those from southern and eastern Europe, Mexico, and Asia who were singled out as needing to be controlled.[15] Another element of the connection between disease and immigrants at this time was that many American cities were trying to assert themselves as modern, attractive places for living, investment, or travel. Disease and illness were associated with backwardness and a lack of modern sensibilities. These discourses were racialized so that immigrants and non-whites in general were often public health targets.[16] In many localities, Chinese became "medical scapegoats,"[17] blamed for any of a society's ills.

In many areas where immigrants resided, including in Chinatowns, rates of disease and death were often higher than in other areas. But rather than attributing these rates to the discrimination experienced by these populations in the form of lack of access to adequate housing, food, and other aspects of basic care, white people regularly blamed the residents themselves for a lack of interest in good health. Chinatowns, in particular, were seen as places of "hygienic lassitude and moral bankruptcy."[18] In San Francisco, while the city pushed for cleaner streets and a better, more modern image, it also ignored Chinatown's public health and civic needs. The city did not clean the streets and public areas of Chinatown as it did the rest of the city.[19] Buildings in Chinatown were often rundown and dilapidated; because they rarely owned the buildings they lived and worked in, Chinese residents were dependent on often-absent white owners for building upkeep and sanitation. However, Chinese were usually blamed for building conditions, with many white people suggesting that Chinese preferred to live in such conditions. Indeed, Chinese were seen as nonhuman, living among and like animals, whether those were rats or cattle.[20] Because of their poverty and restrictions prohibiting them from living in most areas of San Francisco, Chinese lived in a Chinatown that was crowded and densely populated, with residents forced to share buildings—and rooms—with many others.

Concerns about Honolulu's Chinatown were similar to those in San Francisco, but there were also some differences. First, San Francisco's Chinatown was the largest Chinese American community,[21] making that space both more and less connected to the rest of San Francisco. Its size—and the size of the Chinese population there—meant that Chinese could conduct most of their activities—including eating, shopping, banking, and working—within the bounds of Chinatown. That segregation kept Chinese from interacting with other San Francisco residents and may have provided greater protection against racially motivated verbal and physical attacks.[22] But at the same time, the size of Chinatown and the Chinese population were seen as a menace to the rest of the city, difficult to ignore and a constant reminder that difference was seen as dangerous. In Honolulu, Chinatown occupied a smaller area, although because it was near the harbor, it was visible and central to the city. Another major difference was that Chinese made up a larger proportion of the Honolulu population: 23 percent, compared to less than 1 percent in San Francisco. Again, this fact both hurt and helped Chinese in their interactions with haole. That there were more Chinese than haole (and many more Asians than haole when Japanese and Filipinos are included) was seen as a threat to white authority and power. But because of their relative numbers, Chinese played a more vital, integrative role in Honolulu than in other cities. They provided for many of the city's basic needs, including labor, small stores selling daily necessities, fish markets, and restaurants. Because of that, it was much more difficult to contain Chinese within—or for Chinese to keep themselves to—a single ethnic district.

Nevertheless, Hawai'i was no exception to the racist views of Chinese and Chinatowns seen in most places. In Honolulu, too, haole saw Chinese as dirty and diseased and considered Chinatown to be a danger to the rest of the city. Chinese and Chinatown were regularly blamed for establishing and spreading infectious diseases. One newspaper editorial fumed that "Chinese . . . seem to make dirt and filth primary conditions of their existence . . . [they] are the greatest and most inveterate offenders against sanitary laws."[23] As in San Francisco, such commentary ignored the fact that the sanitary conditions of Chinatown were primarily the result of the lack of public services in the area, as noted by an 1882 report from the Hawai'i Board of Health: "At present, the premises in the centre of these blocks have no way of removing their rubbish and filth."[24] Chinese were blamed for many disease outbreaks in the city and Territory, including smallpox[25] and leprosy. Leprosy was called *mai pake* ["Chinese disease"] in Hawai'i, reflecting the widely held—but never substantiated—belief that the disease had originated in China. Evidence suggests that most disease outbreaks were actually caused when Westerners first settled among Hawaiians, who had had no exposure and thus had no immunity to the diseases the new settlers brought with them. According to O. A. Bushnell, it was the first European arrivals who brought "microbiological mayhem" to Hawai'i, exposing the population to syphilis, gonorrhea, tuberculosis, streptococcal infections, and common viruses.[26] Later trading routes through Hawai'i brought smallpox, leprosy, measles, mumps, influenza, and cholera.[27] Paralleling what was happening in the continental United States, Hawai'i began to screen immigrants for disease and set up a quarantine station in Honolulu. And as in other places, Chinese were targeted in these efforts.[28]

Chinatown was at the center of this attention to and concern about disease. Even though the germ theory was beginning to take hold in public health circles, most people continued to believe that disease arose from dirt and filth. Honolulu's Chinatown was run down and marshy: "This area consisted of low-lying land, subject to damage from floods, and was least desirable of the residential areas located close to the central business district. . . . The area, about one-fifth of a square mile in size, was used partly for commercial purposes but principally for residence. (It came later to include the largest and worst 'tenement district' of the city)."[29] It was near the harbor and thus was exposed to the comings and goings of the ships and crews passing through Honolulu. According to James Mohr, "Chinatown was regarded as Honolulu's worst slum and as a generally unhealthy area. It received only a meager flow of fresh water from the hills above the city, yet parts of Chinatown near sea level remained mucky and stagnant year around. Sanitary inspections by the Board of Health reveal[ed] overflowing cesspools, privies disgorging their contents, garbage rotting almost everywhere, and alleys impassable due to large piles of refuse."[30]

There was disagreement about who was to blame for these conditions, with blame placed on residents, owners, on-site property managers, and absentee landlords, depending on the observer. Significantly, after a large fire in the area in 1886, Chinatown was rebuilt without a safe water supply or sewage system.[31] The poor physical condition of Chinatown made it easy to link disease with race. Clifford Wood, the president of the Hawai'i Board of Health in 1900 made the link explicit: "Plague lives and breeds in this filth and when it got into Chinatown, it found its natural habitat."[32]

The ways that Chinese immigrants and Chinatowns were associated with disease provide key insights into the place of Chinese vis-à-vis Americans and how concepts of disease and health were used in the construction of race. This construction shows that race was scripted as biological, as being about bodies—race was not considered a social construction. When Chinese bodies are assumed to be intrinsically diseased and capable of infecting surrounding communities, there is an inevitability, a danger, and a permanence to the perceived differences of Chinese. Such perceived differences helped to rationalize the treatment of Chinese, including surveillance of communities and segregation from white communities: "More than any other discursive tactic, the pathologization of the Chinese body enabled intervention into that body and an intensified governance of its social functions."[33] While Chinese immigrants were considered economic threats in many places where they settled, competing with white people for jobs and positions, it was still possible that economic and social conditions could change and that a place in the community could be made for Chinese. In contrast, racial difference that is scripted onto the body is less easily changed or accommodated, even when social or economic conditions shift.[34] Bad health was considered an "immutable racial difference."[35] This construction labels Chinese as subhuman, or

1900 TO 1930: DESTRUCTION OF CHINATOWN

alternately human, and makes it easier to perceive Chinese as a "yellow peril." Because of the danger it was believed Chinese posed to surrounding communities, authorities and others felt justified in intervening in Chinese communities, regulating life in Chinatown, and constraining Chinese movement and interactions.

Here, then, is how the government regulates space and bodies in racialized ways, insisting on white middle-class norms as the standard to be achieved. Such interventions were "animated by the relentless comparison of the Chinese to so-called normative practices, most clearly evidenced by the practices of the white middle class. . . . The production of these norms relied upon the recognition and reproduction of social differences. In the United States, race was perceived as the most immutable difference that could be used to distinguish population subsets and that could also be easily finessed into the public health hierarchy of the normative and the aberrant."[36]

As diverse as the experiences of Chinese were across the United States and throughout the world, they were seen everywhere through a lens of health and disease. In many places, health, disease, racism, and immigration were all aspects of the treatment of Chinese; with Chinese seen as less than human, dangerous to others, and unlikely ever to assimilate (read: ever to be *allowed* to assimilate), immigration restrictions were a natural outcome. In Honolulu, immigration restrictions were important not only in their effect on Chinese residents who were unable to travel or bring family members to Hawai'i but also in their manifestation of how Chinese were viewed by haole and Hawaiians. In Honolulu, haole feared Chinese would bring disease and death to the city and treated Chinese and Chinatown accordingly. While no formal restrictions barred Chinese from living where they chose, informal restrictions meant that most Chinese had to live in segregated areas. Racist attitudes, treatment, and restrictions came together during the bubonic plague outbreak of 1899–1900 and the subsequent Chinatown fire of 1900. No event has been more important, devastating, or meaningful to the Chinese position in Hawai'i.

THE CHINATOWN FIRE

Throughout the last decades of the nineteenth century, people in Hawai'i attributed many epidemics to Chinese racial differences or to the poor conditions in which they lived. In the 1880s, several ships carrying Chinese passengers experienced smallpox outbreaks, killing several passengers.[37] A smallpox outbreak in Honolulu in 1881 killed about five hundred residents,[38] and in 1895, a cholera epidemic in the city killed eighty-five people.[39] These outbreaks were attributed to the Chinese community, although, as mentioned, it was most often Westerners who brought the diseases that decimated the Hawaiian population.

When the first cases of bubonic plague were identified in Chinatown in 1899, few expressed surprise. Bubonic plague had arisen in Asia in the 1860s and had become a global pandemic by the 1890s. While its origins in south-central China might be considered the impetus for its racialization and its connection to Asia, the racialization of disease had begun long before this outbreak. In Honolulu, that bubonic plague was first discovered in Chinatown should have come as no surprise not because of something about Chinese bodies but because of the location of Chinatown.

Honolulu was a busy port city, with ships arriving from and departing to countries across the Pacific and sites in the continental United States such as San Francisco and Los Angeles. Chinatown was located very close to the city's ports. That meant that along with exposure to travelers who might harbor a disease, Chinatown's residents were exposed to other things that came in on the ships, most notably rats. At the time, the medical world knew that bubonic plague was caused by bacteria, but they did not yet understand the key role of rats (and the fleas they carried) in spreading the disease.[40] We now know that it was the combination of Chinatown's proximity to the harbor, the presence of rats in the area (on board and then departing ships once they had docked), and the rat infestations in Chinatown itself that contributed to the spread of plague. Today, precautions are taken to prevent rats moving from ship to shore, but no such measures were in place then.

At the time, however, the transmission of the disease to humans—from bacteria to rats to fleas and then to humans—was unknown. That the first cases of plague showed up in Chinatown was attributed to the assumed association of Chinese people and Chinese areas with disease. Because Chinatown was run down, it was a good breeding ground for rats. In addition, it was a densely populated and segregated area, with few outsiders venturing in, which left the area unmonitored, and often unnoticed, during citywide announcements or emergencies. As we have seen, most important to the link between Chinese and disease was the deep resentment toward and wariness of Chinese by many in Hawai'i.

1900 TO 1930: DESTRUCTION OF CHINATOWN

Christian rhetoric also influenced the construction of Chinese and Chinatown. Hawai'i was strongly influenced by foreign missionaries who first arrived in the 1820s and whose goal was the conversion of the population to Christianity.[41] They were very successful among Native Hawaiians, first bringing the *ali'i* (chiefs) into the religion and then extending their reach to the commoners (*maka'āinana*). Missionaries established schools for Hawaiians where they promoted literacy. The Chinese were less quick to adopt Christianity and were perceived as a challenge to the Christian haole: "The Chinese with their supposed filth and disease, their 'degenerate' habits, and the stigma of the 'coolie' label, frightened a society with a missionary worldview that strove for purity as the only means of attaining a higher state of religious well-being. These Puritan fears helped to fuel an anti-Chinese movement that was a rational response to a competing worldview."[42] Part of the Christian critique of Chinatown was that uncleanliness and bad habits led to disease.

As important as the identification of the first cases of plague in Chinatown (and Honolulu) was the handling of the disease (both individual cases and the overall approach), which would have significant repercussions for years to come. How should the Board of Health (BOH) handle the outbreak? Such an epidemic could have many impacts: the disease could spread throughout the city, infecting and killing many people, and it could have an effect on the economy, damaging Honolulu's reputation as a safe city to invest in or travel to. Decisions made by the BOH and others reflected those concerns. But they were based on racialized assumptions about disease and health.

Great mistrust existed between the Chinese community and the BOH. Behind it was the continual racialization of all aspects of Chinese residents' lives, from their work to their marriage practices to their health outcomes. A few years before the 1899 plague outbreak, a cholera outbreak incurred what Chinese saw as a heavy-handed response from the BOH and very poor treatment on the part of medical authorities. The outbreak was contained, but only after eighty-five people had died[43] and after lives and businesses in Chinatown had been severely interrupted. The Chinese population and Chinatown were treated differently—more harshly—than the rest of the population because the outbreak was attributed to the Chinese community. Most Chinese avoided contact with haole doctors and the BOH if at all possible. Unsurprisingly, that mistrust would prove harmful. Rather than

1900 TO 1930: DESTRUCTION OF CHINATOWN

seeking help, Chinese residents often hid ill friends or family members, increasing the possibility of disease spread. Chinese resistance also put pressure on the BOH to find a way to intervene with the Chinese community effectively.

Once it was clear that there was an outbreak of bubonic plague, the BOH was given emergency powers to contain the disease. Three BOH physicians—all haole men (two originally from the continental United States and one who had grown up in Hawai'i and trained in the continental United States) were put in charge of the government response. They faced enormous pressure from the government and population to contain the epidemic but also significant resistance from the Chinese community, where the disease was first identified.[44] The doctors used a number of tactics with varying degrees of intrusiveness to deal with the outbreak. They conducted building inspections and performed medical exams of people suspected of having the disease. They also imposed several quarantines, stopping most movement between islands and within Honolulu. But the quarantines were enforced more stringently for Chinese compared with other groups. Chinatown itself was strictly quarantined. When more cases of plague were discovered in Chinatown, the BOH doctors extended the length and scope of the quarantines there. The quarantines caused enormous disruption to the city and to the Territory, affecting shipping between the islands and to and from Hawai'i. But Chinese businesses were especially hard hit; the quarantines brought Chinatown businesses to a halt, and Chinese merchants and workers were left unemployed and without any income.[45]

The BOH managed cases differently depending on several factors. With the first cases appearing in Chinatown, it seemed to make sense to quarantine Chinatown, which affected Chinese, Japanese, and Hawaiians living and working there more than haole who were less likely to live, work, or shop in the area. But race played the biggest role; there was an underlying belief that haole were less likely to get ill than were others. And quarantine was less strictly enforced for haole residents of Honolulu.[46] In addition, plague cases among haole were treated much less harshly than Chinese. For example, haole with plague were often allowed to remain at home, whereas Chinese homes were usually burned if plague was found there.[47]

Meanwhile, many in the haole community felt that the BOH doctors were not doing enough to prevent the spread of disease and argued that

1900 TO 1930: DESTRUCTION OF CHINATOWN

more needed to be done to protect the city and Territory. The BOH doctors in charge thus made the decision to perform a controlled burning of places where cases of plague had been found—although not where plague had been identified in the haole community. Many were unhappy with this approach, including Chinese who did not want to have to evacuate buildings or areas of the city. But some of the biggest resistance to a controlled burn came from haole who argued that Chinatown should be completely destroyed because it was a significant site of disease outbreak and thus threatened the city. Supporters of this approach included powerful people in Honolulu, including those in the Honolulu Chamber of Commerce.[48] Even after cases were found outside Chinatown and among haole, the assumption remained that it was Chinatown and the Chinese who were at the heart of the epidemic.

In spite of such pressure, the BOH physicians decided on controlled burning only where specific cases had been found, and they attempted to minimize the extent of the fires. However, disaster struck in early 1900, when one controlled fire got out of hand because of unexpected winds and ended up burning Chinatown to the ground, leaving only five gutted buildings standing. As the fire raged, Chinatown residents were initially prevented from escaping the area, held back by the BOH's cordon sanitaire (in this case, a blockade meant to prevent people from leaving an area, and spreading disease outside Chinatown) and by white vigilantes.

As the newspaper *The Friend* reported at the time, "Several hundred citizens were at once armed with improvised clubs such as pick-handles, to assist the military and police."[49] By the time most residents finally escaped, most of Chinatown—twenty-five city blocks—was destroyed, causing huge losses to the Chinese community. No one died, but nearly four thousand people were displaced, rounded up, and placed in quarantine camps in other parts of the city. Businesses were destroyed and communities torn apart. Most residents had fled without possessions. It was not only Chinese residents who were affected, however: less than half (1,780) of those displaced were Chinese; the rest were Japanese, Hawaiians, and others who likewise were left homeless and with businesses destroyed.[50] Many refugees from the fire were treated poorly in the quarantine camps. After Chinese women were forced to strip publicly to enable health officers to inspect them, Chinese leaders argued for fire refugees to be treated more respectfully.

1900 TO 1930: DESTRUCTION OF CHINATOWN

All evidence suggests that the fire was not intentionally set to destroy Chinatown. But many—if not most—Chinese believed it was a deliberate attack on their community, an attempt to rid Honolulu of Chinese or at least reopen Honolulu more quickly at the expense of the Chinese community.[51] What cannot be disputed is that Chinese community members were not included in decisions made regarding the epidemic and its control; that they felt powerless to shape their own futures is understandable. Chinese living in Hawai'i had long felt beleaguered and under attack. They had been stripped of their rights as citizens of the Territory. They had faced constant discrimination and restrictions because of their ethnicity. They were seen as a threat to the haole and Hawaiian populations. During this and earlier epidemics, they had been treated much more severely than haole, with little respect or concern shown for their livelihoods or safety. As Julia Katz argues, "The persistent rumors around the Chinatown fire indexed a profound sense of persecution in the wake of annexation. Rumors like these offer a synthesis of vernacular wisdom and sense, and given the physical, legal, political, and economic attacks on Chinese—by men in American military uniform, restrictive immigration policies, and discriminatory legislative proposals—it was logical for Chinese communities to extrapolate from the explicit desire for their exclusion a deliberate effort to remove them when an opportunity presented itself."[52]

Indeed, the Chinatown fire was the most visible and most influential of a series of incidents that continually demonstrated to Chinese that they had not been accepted as true citizens of Hawai'i. Their lack of inclusion in the 1887 constitution and the 1898 annexation, underscored that Chinese were deliberately, carefully, and explicitly being disenfranchised from the new Territory, leaving them without the privileges or security of citizenship.

Immediately after the fire, people disagreed about what to do with the Chinatown area. Chinese owned very little of the land or buildings that had housed them and their businesses—in 1900, only 12 percent of Chinese residents owned their homes[53]—so they would not be the ones to decide how to rebuild the area. Many in Honolulu hoped that the fire would mean the end of Chinatown. But there was enough impetus on the part of others that it did get redeveloped; owners and landlords were interested in continuing their investment in the area and were strong proponents of redevelopment. Chinatown was thus rebuilt in its former location. The BOH put in place new regulations there and in other parts of Honolulu

1900 TO 1930: DESTRUCTION OF CHINATOWN

meant to improve sanitary conditions, including requiring more ventilation in buildings, better drainage, regular garbage removal by the city, and the building of a sewer system.[54] One challenge was funding the rebuilding. Insurance companies balked because of the government's role in the fire and destruction.[55] Now that Hawai'i was a U.S. territory, many believed funding should be the responsibility of the federal government.

Many Chinese wanted their old familiar area back, but within the community were competing priorities. The various perspectives on the fire and subsequent rebuilding reflected ongoing and developing differences and disagreements within the Chinese community. The community was diverse, and class differences were particularly salient in many disagreements. Residents who had endured the refugee camps felt that they had been most severely affected and thus deserved compensation, both for the hardship they endured in the camps and for their business losses. These individuals tended to be single men from the bottom of the class ladder, many of them day laborers who worked as stevedores, house servants, or laborers in manufacturing. They often resisted haole contact and saw the actions of the elite or professional Chinese as selling out to haole and as ethnic betrayal.

But Chinese who lived outside Chinatown were also affected by the fire and also had strong opinions about the rebuilding. This group included members of the new Chinese middle class who were employed as professionals, entrepreneurs, newspaper writers, law clerks in haole law offices, and skilled tradesmen. These were the Chinese who had started to move into new economic and occupational roles and were beginning to see value in using American legal and economic structures to their community's advantage.[56] Some of the most vocal were the relatively few but powerful merchants and managers, many of whom did not live in Chinatown, were more likely to have resources and connections outside the area, and more likely to side with haole leaders about what should happen to Chinatown. Although few in number, they had a great deal of influence in what route the community took. In fact, the first cases of bubonic plague were reported to the BOH by two Chinese doctors who believed that working with haole authorities was the best course of action. The laborers, on the other hand, who had disagreed with Chinese community leaders about how the community should deal with the epidemic and the haole public health officials who were in charge, continued to be wary of haole officials.

1900 TO 1930: DESTRUCTION OF CHINATOWN

The fire made clear that even though only about half of Honolulu's Chinese had lived in Chinatown and many Chinese stores were located outside Chinatown,[57] the area anchored the entire Chinese community, no matter where they lived or worked. After the fire, Chinese had to decide how to rebuild their community and what their relationship should be with other groups. In many ways, 1900 was a watershed year for most Chinese in the Territory, not only because of the physical destruction but also because the public health crisis highlighted tensions between different groups of Chinese in Hawai'i that had existed for decades.

Disagreement about the best way forward continued after the fire. Single male laborers were the ones most likely to return to Chinatown after its rebuilding, but they continued to be wary of haole mistreatment. However, they also felt that the elite Chinese did not represent their interests. Those at the top and those with newly claimed middle-class status saw value in cooperating with the haole population and were more willing to conform to haole standards and expectations; they were also more eager to leave Chinatown, at least as a place of residence, seeing vulnerability there. But they, too, resented the outcomes of the fire, believing they had not been fairly compensated for their losses—by the U.S. government or by the Chinese community associations who had worked on the issue.[58]

Thus, the Chinatown fire and the events of its aftermath were significant both in shaping the Chinese community and in highlighting how differences within the community were handled. It was in the first decades of the twentieth century that Chinese began to find a place for themselves in the wider community of Honolulu and in the Territory. Their new-found toeholds into haole society and their subsequent achievements were integral not only to the fate of the Chinese community but also to Hawai'i as a whole. It is not the only story to be told of the Chinese in Hawai'i, but it is an important one.

THE RISE OF A CHINESE MIDDLE CLASS

One of the most important developments in the Chinese community during the early decades of the twentieth century was the rise of the middle class; in the last chapter, we saw the beginnings of those changes before 1900. We can see the continued movement of Chinese into higher socio-economic classes by looking at middle-class markers. At the time, Chinese

1900 TO 1930: DESTRUCTION OF CHINATOWN

were increasingly represented in schools and higher-status occupations, and they were moving into new neighborhoods, often after purchasing land and homes. Importantly, some of the opportunities that Chinese were able to take advantage of came at the expense of other groups. Most notable is that many opportunities arose as the Native Hawaiian community lost power, land, and population—losses that were initiated by haole settlers and their descendants. But Chinese benefited from them, even if inadvertently. These losses created gaps that, combined with the needs of a growing Hawai'i population, gave Chinese space to grow their community and move in new directions.

The Chinatown fire of 1900 displaced many Chinese in the area, and some began to move away from Chinatown. As noted, not all of Honolulu's Chinese residents were living in the Chinatown area at the time; even in 1884, only 65 percent of Honolulu's Chinese were living in the area.[59] But the fire, and the subsequent lack of available housing in the area for many years, provided further impetus to the process of Chinese looking to live elsewhere in the city and beginning to integrate into new neighborhoods.

Where Chinese moved was the result of a combination of influences, including the informal rules and resistance of haole that prevented Chinese from living in certain areas.[60] Chinese began to move from one segregated area, in and around Chinatown, to other areas that were still ethnically segregated but more desirable. Some moved to existing neighborhoods farther from Chinatown as Honolulu's boundaries expanded from the central districts. A new Chinese-dominated neighborhood grew in Kaimuki, an area a few miles east of Chinatown, and the Bingham Tract area was regularly referred to as "Chinese Hollywood" because in the 1930s, it housed mostly middle-class and professional Chinese families.[61] In other cases, because of informal restrictions, it was often just easier for Chinese to buy newly marketed land as it became available for sale in areas where there were no haole residents and few, if any, housing structures.

How this land became available is significant. Chinese were able to purchase newly privatized and marketed land because of the 1848 Māhele land division and the 1850 Kuleana Act, which, as we saw in chapter 1, utterly transformed Hawai'i's landscape. Those measures privatized all land and resulted in thousands of Hawaiians losing their access to land. Hawaiians were unable to buy the land they had lived on for generations, some of which new haole owners put up for sale just as Chinese were looking for ways to increase their own stake in the Territory. In some areas, Chinese made up most of an area's residents. In the Makiki area of Honolulu, for example, Chinese both bought houses from former homeowners, who were haole, and erected new homes on recently subdivided lots. Throughout the 1920s, 1930s, and 1940s, this area, particularly Makiki Heights, became dominated by Chinese residents[62] and remains so today.

Moving out of Chinatown to other areas of Honolulu often meant living in safer, better-kept neighborhoods. The area in and around Chinatown was run down, congested, and subject to industrial pollution, all of which negatively affected the health of residents.[63] Absentee (mostly haole) landlords were not attentive to the needs of the Chinese community, and the area had few resources for families. New neighborhoods meant access to better resources for children in particular, especially better public schools. Indeed, it was because of an increasing number of families with children that some of this movement out of Chinatown occurred. These families had needs and interests beyond those of the population of single men that made up much of Chinatown, such as schools. And families may have seemed less threatening than single men to their non-Chinese neighbors as they sought new neighborhoods and residences.

At the same time, Chinese were also making their way into the Territory's schools. The passing of a law mandating free public education for all in the mid-eighteenth century meant that Chinese had access to the Territory's schools and did not need to rely on the mission schools that first settlers attended. As most of the early Chinese immigrants to Hawai'i were single men, there were not many Chinese children to attend schools. But as the number of families and children grew, Chinese began to enter Island schools. As we saw in chapter 1, the number of Chinese students increased fairly quickly, and they soon achieved a very high representation of the student population. Even though immigrants themselves were not well educated and often not literate, they strove to put and keep their children in the public schools. Table 2.1 shows the distribution of students of various ethnicities in public schools in 1930. Once begun, Chinese enrollment in schools increased steadily and rapidly, and their enrollment numbers were soon higher than their representation in the population and higher than for other groups.

By 1935, more than 91 percent of Chinese children between the ages of 10 and 14 years were attending school,[64] a higher proportion than found in

1900 TO 1930: DESTRUCTION OF CHINATOWN

TABLE 2.1
Number and ratio of students of different ethnicities in elementary and high school in Hawai'i, 1930

Ethnicity	Number in elementary school	Number in high school	Total number, aged 15–19 years	Number in high school for every 1,000 students in school age group
Hawaiian	3,187	146	2,198	66.42
Portuguese	5,456	361	3,427	105.34
Chinese	5,187	1,091	2,572	424.18
Japanese	33,152	3,241	13,167	246.15

Source: Sylvianne Fei-Ai Li, "A History of the Education of the Chinese in Hawaii" (Master's thesis, Oberlin College, 1940), 42.

any other group.[65] This widespread school attendance came about partly because of haole efforts to educate nonwhite children. But although Asian students were not banned from school, as was true in California, the goal of Hawai'i's education system was not about "providing space for all present nationalities to teach their own languages, values, and cultures. Instead, haole intended to mold nonwhite schoolchildren into English-speaking patriotic workers who would continue to serve the economic interests of the islands' white establishment."[66] Indeed, by 1896, all instruction was in English. Some haole business leaders were concerned about how education might change the racial hierarchy. They attempted to discourage educational aspirations, particularly among the children of plantation workers, whom they encouraged to stay in low-level agricultural work. In part to discourage attendance in the higher grades, the Territory legislature passed a bill in 1933 requiring tuition for high school students and fees for textbooks.[67] But Japanese and Chinese parents overcame those obstacles and encouraged their children to stay in school and train for higher-level careers. Chinese students were well represented in all grades, exceeding their representation in the Territory's population, and they were more likely to stay in school through the upper grades than were students from other ethnic groups.[68] For example, in 1919, Chinese students numbered 250, making up 32.4 percent of the student body at Honolulu's largest high school, McKinley High School, even though they comprised only 9.2 percent of the Territory's population.[69] By 1929, they had also become visible at the university level; that year, nearly 20 percent of students at the University of Hawai'i were ethnic Chinese, twice their representation in the Territorial population.[70]

1900 TO 1930: DESTRUCTION OF CHINATOWN

School introduced second- and third-generation Chinese to new ideas, ones espoused by Americans. Students at McKinley High School studied American revolutionary heroes, learned about individualism, and grew to understand the expectations of and opportunities offered by an American system; in that way, they were socialized into the American way of life. The following 1935 education bulletin describing the desired function of a school cafeteria:

> The function of the cafeteria is directed towards better standards of living, gradual and natural adjustment to American social usages. Improvement in health habits, consciousness of the importance of home and community sanitation, etc. "Through the lunch service, when properly and completely carried on, the child of foreign parentage has opportunity for constant practice of simple customs and ordinary social procedure so important in the everyday future of the child." . . . The cafeteria is financed partly by the territory and partly by the proceeds of the cafeteria. Lunch costs five cents and consists "of a substantial main dish, preferably with meat or fish flavor in small quantities, a starchy vegetable, a green succulent vegetable, . . . a whole slice of bread and butter, and the addition of an occasional fruit or sweet." There is served at mid-mornings a one-cent lunch which consists of either milk or chocolate for children who are undernourished.[71]

The author concludes, "The public school system of Hawaii with its Americanization program in the schools show the schools can in a few decades produce a very considerable degree of cultural uniformity and a common political loyalty."[72]

In addition, Christianity was infused into school curricula, particularly in the private schools, most of which had been established by churches or missionary orders. But even the public schools had a heavy flavor of American Christianity. That was not surprising; as discussed in the previous chapter, Christian principles—with their connection to capitalism, race, and gender—were embedded in most practices and institutions in Hawai'i[73] and became foundational characteristics of the developing society. American Christian values, expectations, and principles would guide Chinese in their new places in Hawai'i society.

Although schools socialized Chinese students into the American way of life, they also exposed them to Hawai'i society different from the one they were experiencing: "America, described as a democratic society full of opportunity and reward, contrasted sharply with the social system in Hawaii, especially that experienced by the plantation children."[74] Most directly, education launched Chinese into the middle and, later, the professional classes. Most of the first Chinese immigrants were laborers, with little education and with experience only of agricultural work. But the next generation went to school and began to pursue other vocations. They moved from laboring, unskilled work to semiskilled work and then to occupations that required skill and training, such as clerical work and, later, professional and managerial occupations. By 1890, only 11.6 percent of Chinese were employed in agricultural labor, but most (76.8 percent) worked in unskilled jobs[75]; only 10 percent worked in professional or management jobs. However, those figures changed rapidly. By 1920, about a third of employed Chinese were employed in professional or managerial work, and that percentage increased to 50 percent by 1930. By that year, only 4.4 percent of working Chinese were employed in agricultural labor, 13.1 percent were working as domestic servants, and 26.6 percent were employed in unskilled labor.[76] Chinese were quickly moving into the higher-status jobs in Honolulu. By 1930, Chinese made up 11.8 percent of Hawai'i's physicians, 26.8 percent of its dentists, and 5.2 percent of its lawyers,[77] proportions that would only grow over the next decades. These changes in occupational status shifted the rhetoric about the perceived threat posed by Chinese. In earlier years, it was working-class laborers, particularly Native Hawaiians, who were seen as threatened by Chinese migrants. As Chinese moved into higher-status jobs, haole worried that the Chinese elite might elbow their way into haole occupational and class territory.[78]

The Chinese community addressed haole resistance in a number of ways, especially by building a parallel system that supported their developing interests and desire to attain higher-status positions. Beginning in 1916, several Chinese banks opened,[79] permitting a formal way for Chinese community members to save, invest, and borrow funds. Data show that Chinese residents were, in fact, saving at an increasing rate throughout the first decades of the twentieth century, doubling their per capita savings from $13.25 to $27.37 per year in just the years between 1910 and 1915. By 1928, their per capita savings had risen to $186.69, demonstrating a rate of saving that had outpaced all other non-haole ethnic groups, for most by a significant amount.[80]

1900 TO 1930: DESTRUCTION OF CHINATOWN

Gradually, Chinese businesses and firms became increasingly tied to the wider Honolulu public. As we saw in chapter 1, at first their businesses catered mostly to other Chinese, selling goods and services that the immigrant population needed. But as that early generation was replaced by Chinese who had been born or raised in Hawai'i, Chinese businesses began to meet the demands of other communities in areas such as laundry, tailoring, and taxi services.[81] They often started small and expanded as their connections deepened. The next phase of business growth, in the 1920s and 1930s, involved the development of large corporations controlled by Hawai'i-born Chinese, some of whose investments and board members came from beyond the Chinese community and sometimes included subsidiary corporations.[82] It was at this point that Chinese economic success began to be noticeable—and noticed.

During these years, members of the Chinese community also began to form various social organizations. Some arose from continuing concern for and connections with China and were political in nature. But many were simply social clubs that permitted networking within the community. Some had a specific focus, such as the Chinese Student Alliance, which was formed in the 1920s. The most powerful organization was probably the Chinese Civic Association, which included Chinese of many ages, generations, and occupations. These organizations were important in the development and extension of Chinese influence in Hawai'i. Membership was sought after and considered necessary not only because of the positive impact they had on the Chinese community but also because Chinese were not allowed in haole-dominated clubs such as the Oahu Country Club, the Outrigger Canoe Club, and the Pacific Club.[83] For example, the United Club of Kohala, a Chinese club on the Big Island, opened in 1922 with a statement by the soon-to-be president, Choy Zane, who argued for "the need and purpose of . . . the club." He argued that "we, individually, do not have recognition from other races, but . . . if we form a club and work for the betterment of our race, we will not only be recognized but also respected . . . by those outside of the Chinese race."[84] Chinese newspapers were also important, giving the Chinese community its own version of local and world events.

Through these actions, early entrepreneurs and community leaders developed strategies through and around the discrimination that kept them from top positions in haole-controlled organizations. By developing and investing in their own businesses and corporations, these early businesspeople not only found success for themselves but also forged a path forward for younger Chinese. In addition, these ventures allowed for the accumulation of wealth that was then reinvested in new businesses and firms. Chinese were often criticized for their "insular" ways, and it is likely that some saw these developments—Chinese-owned banks, businesses, and newspapers, as well as mentors and role models available through Chinese social clubs—as reflecting such insularity. But we can also see how they were a response to haole discrimination and marginalization. As one early writer argued, antagonism from haole "forced the Chinese to seek mutual protection and status within their own 'Chinatown' community."[85] Success in these endeavors was not limited to the Chinese community, however; many Chinese organizations began to bring in non-Chinese not only as clients and customers but also as board members, thus encouraging integration among ethnic groups. It is important to note that this integration was the result of a marginalized group having achieved enough traction in the economy to make it happen, in its own way and to its own benefit.

Certainly, not all Chinese were achieving success in Honolulu during the first few decades of the twentieth century. During these years, the major differences within the Chinese community were no longer between the Punti and Hakka groups but between generations and socioeconomic classes. In Hawai'i in 1938, there were 24,087 Hawai'i-born Chinese compared with just 4,283 Chinese who had been born in China.[86] These groups often overlapped—most Chinese had not received an education in China, and education was seen as the ticket out of low-paying jobs for second- and third-generation immigrants. However, where the rising Chinese middle class were looking to haole and U.S. models of how to conduct their lives, others were much less connected to or interested in mimicking haole ways. Thus, some Chinese continued to live in poor circumstances (many in Chinatown) and labor at low wages in low-status jobs. Many were wary of even trying to find acceptance in the haole-dominated society, doubtful that the discrimination and poor treatment would end. Some were distrustful not only of haole but of other Chinese who seemed to welcome connections to and integration into haole life. But as the proportion of second- and third-generation Chinese grew—by 1930, 72.5 percent of Chinese in Hawai'i had been born in Hawai'i[87]—immigrants made up an increasingly smaller proportion and were much less visible than younger Chinese who were pushing for change, including in their relationship with the haole community.

The higher-class Chinese were a small group—in 1930, only 5 percent of Chinese men were in professional occupations—but a very vocal part

1900 TO 1930: DESTRUCTION OF CHINATOWN

of the Chinese community. Many favored the "Americanization" of the Chinese community, encouraging their neighbors and young Chinese to work with haole and to adopt haole ways. They argued that by doing so, they would face less discrimination and haole would be more likely to recognize Chinese success.[88] T. F. Farm, for example, gave a lecture (later published in the *Hawaii Chinese Journal*, whose mission was to report on pro-American values and activities in the Chinese community) arguing that the hard work of Chinese had contributed to Hawai'i's success and that "it was 'industrious Chinese work ethics that had redeemed the lands which have been in disuse for a number of years.' . . . [Chinese] did not sit back and wait for help; but they rolled up their sleeves and went to work."[89]

The *Hawaii Chinese Journal*—where this speech was published—provided an important voice for the Americanization efforts of the elite of Chinese society. The journal's audience was the Chinese educated middle class, and it regularly reported on the accomplishments of Chinese professionals and published editorials on such things as how to display and show respect for the American flag.[90] However, it ignored other elements of Chinese society, particularly Chinese restaurant owners, whom they saw as "too Chinese" and "perpetuat[ing] an image that went against the program of the Chinese Americanizers."[91] Notably, in 1930, Chinese represented nearly a third of all restaurant owners. But elite Chinese saw these community members as "undermining the assimilation process. . . . They practiced traditional Chinese beliefs, spoke pidgin-english, and worked non-professional or service oriented jobs."[92]

The visibility and messaging of the Chinese elite were key because it is this group around whom stereotypes and assumptions began to be molded; here, we see the first inklings of the concept of the model minority and the rhetoric around "good" versus "bad" Asians that remain elements of Asian American discourse today. In the early twentieth century, designations of "good" and "bad" were often connected to whether or not a Chinese community member had achieved the visible markers of middle-class haole life. Importantly, however, the Americanization movement was double-edged. While it encouraged some Chinese to follow haole ways, it also taught Chinese how to use American institutions and practices to counter the mistreatment they faced and to achieve a better position for themselves in society.[93]

1900 TO 1930: DESTRUCTION OF CHINATOWN

INTERRACIAL AND INTERETHNIC RELATIONS

The differences, similarities, tensions, and alliances among Hawai'i's racial and ethnic groups during these years foretold the shape of the relationships and the varying access to power and resources of these groups for many decades. By the middle of the twentieth century, the paths of Chinese and Native Hawaiians continued to diverge in important ways, whereas those of Chinese and Japanese took on similar characteristics, despite tensions and political disagreements between them.

The increasing division between Chinese and Native Hawaiians can be attributed to the different experiences of these groups. After decades of haole interference and discrimination, Hawaiians were focused not on moving into the middle class but on struggling for basic survival. Chinese and other Asians saw their path forward differently from Hawaiians, and haole leaders similarly treated these groups differently. Celebrating Chinese success as Chinese stepped into higher-status roles and positions allowed haole to masquerade as welcoming to all nonwhite racial and ethnic groups. And, as we will see in later chapters, this pretense helped to shore up a particular—and inaccurate—narrative of multicultural acceptance. But Chinese also saw an advantage to this narrative. We can understand this process as the beginning of the partial admittance of a minority group into white society. Some Chinese were offered what the race scholar Lani Guinier has labeled a "racial bribe,"[94] defined as "a strategy that invites specific racial or ethnic groups to advance . . . [and] to secure high status for individual group members within [an] existing" racial hierarchy.[95] That offer seemed to hold out the best chance of acceptance into and success in haole-dominated Hawai'i society. Many Chinese believed that only by adopting haole ways could Chinese find success. Given the enormous power of haole—not only in economics and politics but also in the ideology and structures of the new Hawai'i—that belief was not easily challenged. In comparing the plights of Hawaiians and Chinese, we again see the beginnings of the model-minority framework, with Chinese celebrated for and celebrating their rising status and what got them there (hard work, attempting to blend in, and not complaining) and Hawaiians' reluctance to change cited as the reason for their community's failures.

By keeping our eye on both Chinese and Native Hawaiians, we can also see just how dominant American values and ideologies were in Hawai'i in the early twentieth century. American assumptions were encoded into Māhele and later laws, promoting a belief that land is (or should be) based on market relations. Foremost among the Americans ideas promoted at the time was individualism, with its attendant "individual concepts of the self—self-improvement, individual ownership—and the privatization of land use."[96] These ideas were far from the notion of reciprocity that organized Native Hawaiian communities.[97] But many Chinese leaders subscribed to the new system, promoting definitions of individual success that closely mirrored those of haole and, in turn, helped to buttress haole settler ideological dominance in the Islands and further alienate Native Hawaiians.

Lessons and a glimpse of future interethnic relations can also be found in the interactions between Chinese and Japanese during the early years of the twentieth century. Tensions between the two groups were often tied to what was happening in Asia, especially as Japan became more aggressive in its determination to build its empire. Japan's seizure of Manchuria in northeast China in 1931 was a signal of Japan's intent toward China. The Chinese diaspora, including those in Hawai'i, responded with renewed nationalism and efforts to support their home country. Tensions were somewhat muted in Hawai'i but still existed. A student researcher who polled Chinese students enrolled at the University of Hawai'i in 1937 found that even though these "are college students [who] have mingled with all types of peoples in social gatherings and schools," there is a "definite . . . existence of a racial prejudice in the selection of a marriage mate." Nearly all reported reluctance to marry outside the Chinese community, some saying they would rather "be an old maid or remain a batchelor [sic]" and others saying that they "would never consider going out with any boy" of another race or ethnicity.[98] Other research provides evidence that even in neighborhoods of mixed ethnicity, each group kept mostly to itself. One observer noted that in Bingham Tract, children of different ethnicities might play together but were unlikely to be invited into one another's homes. This observer also saw that interactions between Japanese and neighbors of other ethnicities were even less friendly: "The Japanese is an outgroup as far as the rest of the neighborhood is concerned. This may be due to the fact that they are relatively newcomers. . . . The Japanese make no effort to be congenial and the Chinese reciprocate this attitude."[99] While we don't know all the reasons for the continuing mistrust of some Chinese toward other groups, it is reasonable to assume that it involved both a strong preference for their own community (which helps to explain reluctance to mix with other groups, including Koreans, Hawaiians, and haole) and the influence of events taking place in Asia, which affected Chinese–Japanese relations in Hawai'i. The local Chinese press in Hawai'i kept the community abreast of what was happening in Asia and solicited funds and other support for China in its efforts to slow Japan's aggression.[100] By the time both countries were fully engaged in the Sino-Japanese War of 1937, these efforts were widespread, and many in Hawai'i's Chinese community were deeply involved.

Haole contributed to Japanese-Chinese hostility in several ways. On plantations, Chinese and Japanese communities were housed separately; planters believed such separation would keep the groups from engaging in labor organizing. In addition, haole elite regularly pitted Chinese and Japanese against each other. At various times, planters argued that either Chinese or Japanese laborers were preferred over the other group. Japanese were originally brought to Hawai'i because they were seen to be better workers than were Chinese. But after Japanese immigrant numbers began to rise, plantation owners began to petition to allow Chinese immigration to resume. In one 1921 petition to the U.S. Congress, Walter Dillingham, representing Hawai'i's planters, argued that Japanese workers were becoming "increasingly . . . arrogant, insolent, domineering, and truculent"[101] and that Chinese workers would be less likely to seek better working conditions or higher pay, as Japanese plantation workers were doing.

As Japan gained strength and territory in Asia, and as the United States became increasingly watchful and concerned with developments in Asia, haole leaders in Hawai'i more often drew on security rhetoric to make the case for finding ways around the Chinese Exclusion Act to once again allow Chinese immigration. They were unsuccessful, but the argument that Japanese living in the United States—including nisei (second-generation Japanese born in the United States)—were risks to the country's security was widely accepted. Chinese and Japanese sometimes saw themselves in competition with each other. Their progress and success in achieving higher status in Hawai'i society was not a zero-sum game, but it might have seemed that way to both groups, with one group's success meaning a loss for the other. Certainly, World War II affected the Japanese and Chinese communities in very different ways. At the same time, there were reasons for reduced tensions between Chinese and Japanese in Hawai'i, particularly after the end of the war. As each community settled into the local environment, second- and

1900 TO 1930: DESTRUCTION OF CHINATOWN

third-generation Chinese and Japanese increasingly saw themselves as American and were generally less engaged with happenings in Asia than were their parents and grandparents. Importantly, both groups were trying to make their way into Hawai'i's haole-dominated society. The common experiences of Chinese and Japanese communities—of discrimination and working toward economic success and social acceptance—allowed the two groups to begin the work of mutual respect and acceptance. As we will see in the next chapter, the years before World War II set the stage for what happened in Hawai'i during the 1940s and 1950s.

THE CHANGING PLACE OF CHINATOWN

In the stages of the growth and development of the Chinese community in Hawai'i, we can see Chinatown in a new light. Rather than a segregated area of marginalized people unaccepted by others as equal participants in society, Chinatown was becoming much more fluid. Not all members of the community agreed on what Chinatown meant or should mean. It continued to be a site of Chinese businesses and services, a place for Chinese residents to get the things they needed. But it also represented the tensions that existed within the Chinese community. How were they to make Chinatown into both a Chinese place supporting a Chinese community and part of an American city? The Chinese elite who were working toward the Americanization of the Chinese community had to find their way through this question, and in the face of some Chinese opposition to American ways. Wealthier Chinese—who often lived outside Chinatown— wanted to find ways to make Chinatown "seem less . . . closed and clannish and [Chinese seem less wanting] . . . to mingle only with their own kind."[102] One solution was to emphasize the exoticism of Chinatown by inviting outsiders into the area and developing it as a tourist attraction. In that spirit, Wo Fat Restaurant reopened in 1938. While it had been in existence for decades, the restaurant was now housed in a new three-story building designed in a "Chinese style" that would anchor Chinatown for decades. Careful attention was paid to the restaurant's layout, its bar, and its roof garden. The new restaurant could seat up to one thousand people. The goal of this project was to invite in "Americans of all races as well as the local born Chinese."[103] And Wo Fat was able to draw a large crowd from well outside the Chinese community. Famous visitors to Hawai'i, including

1900 TO 1930: DESTRUCTION OF CHINATOWN

Frank Sinatra and Jacqueline Kennedy, made stops at the restaurant.[104] But even though such businesses connected the area to other parts of the city, the role of Chinatown for the Chinese community did not disappear. Rather, Chinatown was envisioned as also an area that allowed Chinese to develop the kinds of resources that could be sling-shotted into the larger society. Not as "lesser-than" businesses and firms but as increasingly powerful institutions that incorporated many smaller businesses and efforts as well as ones that drew in leaders from other ethnic groups. Many successful Chinese businesses got their start in Chinatown. With financial help from wealthier Chinese businesses, Ching Sing Wo opened his furniture store in a building on King Street in 1911.[105] His business grew until it became the largest furniture business in the Islands, C. S. Wo. Chinatown thus became a source of pride in Chinese accomplishments. As Leonard Wong writes, "This wavering between preservation, acceptance and denial of the Chinatown culture demonstrates the continuous struggle for the Chinese in their ongoing desire to be recognized as Americans."[106]

Despite their many successes, Chinese continued to face discrimination in Hawai'i in the early years of the twentieth century. Although they were more and more often working alongside haole and others in higher-status occupations, they were not mingling socially with haole.[107] At the time, Chinese—even second- and third-generation immigrants—remained a mostly segregated group, separate most notably from haole, with whom they had begun to share occupational and educational status. For those reasons, Chinatown remained a necessary and vital place, helping to maintain not only connections but also resources that would enable continued financial and other successes. The Chinese community had survived a fire that wiped out their space in Honolulu, but they resisted calls that would have meant the end of Chinatown. Instead, Chinatown began to take on a new and different shape, one that represented the changing nature and status of Chinese residents. What has been said about San Francisco's Chinatown pertains to Honolulu's as well: "Racial prejudice affected but never totally dictated the lives of the immigrants. Chinatown's longevity most clearly underscores its defiance of anti-Chinese forces that persistently tried but failed to eradicate or dislocate this large and visible Chinese community from the heart of the city."[108]

Chapter Three

WORLD WAR II COMES TO HAWAI'I

The 1930s Through 1945

After the transformative years of the early twentieth century and the key events of that era, including the 1900 Chinatown fire, the next significant period, the 1930s and 1940s, was about strengthening the Chinese community and the place of Chinese in the larger Hawai'i community. This period ends in 1945, at the end World War II, in which Hawai'i played a central role. The 1930s saw Chinese moving steadily into a middle class that in many ways they were creating themselves. This change was possible in part because of generational shifts in the Chinese community, with the second generation of Chinese immigrants coming of age. American citizens educated in public schools, they saw themselves as deserving a place in American society and worked toward achieving that. The first and second generations were also accumulating resources and assets, which they used to open and expand businesses, buy land, establishing a physical and economic presence in Hawai'i, particularly in Honolulu.

Equally important to the Chinese rise were the events that occurred in Hawai'i during those years, events that handicapped other groups in various ways, consequently creating an easier passage for Chinese. While all residents of Hawai'i experienced hardships related to the war and the military occupation of Hawai'i, some groups faced more difficulty than others, particularly Japanese, who were seen as potential enemies. But the dominance of the U.S. military presence was as important to Native Hawaiians,

WORLD WAR II COMES TO HAWAI'I

who saw their hold on their land slipping further away; the processes that initiated that loss (discussed in chapter 2) only intensified during the war and were difficult to recover from once the war was over. For example, after the Japanese attack on Pearl Harbor on December 7, 1941, the U.S. military seized Kaho'olawe, an island sacred to Hawaiians, for use as a bombing target and continued to hold the island until 2003. That kind of attack on Hawaiian land reverberated deeply, especially for a community whose connection to the land is central to cultural survival.

As Chinese moved out of Chinatown (though maintaining strong ties to the area), Chinatown began to take on a new tenor, with changes occurring in residents and visitors alike. Non-Chinese residents became an increasingly large presence in the area; in 1920, 53 percent of Chinatown's residents were Chinese. But by 1930, that number had dropped to 47 percent, with Japanese accounting for 36.5 percent and Hawaiians, Filipinos, and other groups making up the remainder.[1] Chinese businesses still predominated in the 1930s, but new businesses owned by non-Chinese began to take root, bringing new customers into the area. With the buildup toward war with Japan and an increasingly large U.S. military presence in the Islands, prostitution began to play a role in shaping Chinatown—and attitudes toward the area.

World War II was a watershed event for Hawai'i; it put Hawai'i on the U.S. and global maps in key ways. As we have seen, Hawai'i was an important military outpost well before the Japanese attack on Pearl Harbor in 1941; after the United States took over Pearl Harbor in 1887, it became a central port for the U.S. Navy and greatly increased Hawai'i's value to the United States. It also made Hawai'i both a strategic site and a vulnerable target. Not everyone in the United States knew how involved the U.S. military was in Hawai'i, but with the attack on Pearl Harbor, Hawai'i was in the headlines. Immediately, Hawai'i's place in the United States came into question, with many viewing it as part of the country but not with the status of a state.

Beyond the explicit military consequences of the Pearl Harbor attack and the entry of the Unites States into the war, Hawai'i experienced rapid and far-reaching changes during these years, changes that resonated for decades afterward. Issues of race were central to all that happened and to all that continued or changed. In 1940, no single ethnic group made up a majority in Hawai'i, and most of the population were not white. The war changed Hawai'i's population and residents' interactions with the people around them. The military buildup—which began before December 1941 but was stepped up after the attack on Pearl Harbor—meant that Hawai'i was now experiencing new demographic shifts and new interactions among different groups. Hundreds of thousands of troops passed through or were stationed in Hawai'i during the war.[2] Most notably, with the military's arrival, haole in Hawai'i now included a sizable proportion of white working-class individuals, a marked contrast to earlier eras when most haole were of the elite or ruling class. The newness of these interactions went both ways. Hawai'i residents began to get used to seeing white people who were not necessarily highly educated, wealthy, or powerful. And many of these white individuals had never before encountered a demographic mix like that which existed and functioned in Hawai'i, where nonwhite people occupied all strata of society and together made up the majority of the population.

Central to the story of prewar and wartime Hawai'i is the place of Japanese at the time. With Japan now an enemy nation, Japanese in Hawai'i came under further scrutiny and faced even more discrimination than they had previously. As we saw in chapter 2, anti-Japanese sentiment had been strong even before the war, arising and being sustained for a variety of reasons; some of that discrimination came from events outside the Territory, especially as Japan gained strength in Asia and the Pacific. But events and developments within Hawai'i also contributed to discrimination against the Japanese. That was true during the war as well; while some of the discriminatory rules and regulations affecting Japanese in Hawai'i (and others) came from the federal government, Hawai'i's Japanese also faced increasing discrimination from within the Territory.

Although it continues to be important to keep in sight the situation and experiences of Native Hawaiians, during these war years, it was comparisons of Japanese and Chinese wartime experiences that best illuminate the place of Chinese in Hawai'i and in the United States at the time. As in an earlier era, when haole treatment of Hawaiians and Hawaiian communities created openings for Chinese to improve their prospects, the anti-Japanese actions of the 1920s through the 1940s also created opportunities for Chinese. As before, Chinese were able to take advantage of opportunities created by the woes of others. These years were marked by Chinese success in many social spheres.

WORLD WAR II COMES TO HAWAI'I

HAWAI'I IN THE BUILDUP TO AND DURING WORLD WAR II

The attack on Pearl Harbor clarified the strategic role that Hawai'i had and would continue to play in U.S. global strategies. But as Daniel Immerwahr points out, at the start of the war, it was not yet clear that Americans would see Hawai'i as part of the United States. A territory at the time, Hawai'i was a part but not really a part of the United States. Nevertheless, President Franklin Roosevelt wanted to make clear that the attack on Pearl Harbor was an attack not just on the Territory of Hawai'i but also on the United States; of note, he changed the initial wording of his announcement from "the island of Oahu" to "the American island of Oahu."[3] Indeed, the ships that were attacked were vital parts of the U.S. Navy. And the president made clear that "very many American lives" had been lost.[4] Following the U.S. entry into the war and Roosevelt's framing of the Pearl Harbor attack as an attack on the United States, Hawai'i became more visible and more accepted as part of the United States. However, it was argued that Hawai'i had a "problem": three-quarters of the population of the Territory were not white. At the time of war with Japan, this issue—specifically, the 40 percent of the population that was ethnic Japanese—was of great concern to American citizens and government officials alike. Hawai'i's Japanese community was thus critical to the connection between Hawai'i and the United States. Japanese were the largest single ethnic group in Hawai'i, they made up the vast majority of Hawai'i's workforce, and their homeland was a nation at war with the United States. Most importantly, they were a non-European, nonwhite group that white Americans had been deeply suspicious of and discriminatory toward for decades.

Because of the central role of Japanese in Hawai'i and white American attitudes toward Japanese, martial law was declared in Hawai'i soon after the attack on Pearl Harbor and was in place for three years, well beyond the immediate or substantial threat of another Japanese attack. Martial law did not reflect concerns about Japan's aggression; it was about controlling the Japanese population in Hawai'i. As one scholar has written, "Resolving the 'Japanese question,' then, soon became the single most important issue for wartime Hawai'i."[5] Again, worries about Hawai'i's Japanese population did not start in 1941; rather, anti-Japanese discourse had existed both in the continental United States and in Hawai'i for many years. The anti-Japanese discourse grew out of the changing situation of Japanese in Hawai'i.

They constituted a large and growing ethnic group. A sizable number were issei (those born in Japan) who were not permitted to become U.S. citizens. But at the same time, white people feared the growing number of nisei (American-born Japanese) because they had greater access to resources and privileges, including land ownership and voting rights. In addition, Japanese had been rising into the middle class using available public resources, especially public schools. They were leaving the plantations and taking up new jobs and occupations that moved them closer to middle class life. Whereas Japanese workers had made up 73.5 percent of plantation workers in 1902, they made up only 18.8 percent by 1932.[6] Plantation owners saw Japanese as a threat not only because they refused to stay on the plantations but also because many Japanese plantation workers had been involved in several labor strikes during the 1920s and 1930s. That Japanese laborers would organize and strike suggested a determination to find ways to achieve a better position in their new home. Another area of concern was Japanese language schools, which were widely defended by the Japanese community. Most nisei school children attended these schools after their regular school day in the public schools, and Japanese families relied on them to teach Japanese language and culture to their American-born children. But some in Hawai'i saw the schools as evidence of how tied to "their own culture" Japanese were and questioned whether they could be seen as "truly American." Haole elite wondered aloud if the increasing presence and status of Japanese would mean the demise of white leadership in the Islands and worked to prevent Japanese from assuming positions of authority. At issue was "the durable Japanese presence and determination to share in the promise of America."[7]

The Pearl Harbor attack brought haole concerns into sharp focus but added another: Japanese were no longer just "alien" and an economic threat; now, many Americans believed, they were also dangerous and a security risk to the nation. Especially in the early years of U.S. involvement in the war, much discussion took place about whether Japanese should be moved to incarceration camps, as was happening on the West Coast of the continental United States. But Japanese made up 40 percent of the population in Hawai'i and a significant part of most sectors of the labor force: 95 percent of the skilled labor force,[8] half of all craftspeople, three-quarters of all domestic workers, half of all small farmers and fishers, and more than half of all car mechanics.[9] Incarcerating all Japanese would not only be logistically difficult but would also mean the collapse of the local economy. In addition, some community leaders had long been working to support interethnic unity, looking for ways that Hawai'i might endure just the kind of attack it did experience. Because of Hawai'i's unique ethnic composition, which included both Japanese and immigrants who came from lands that were currently under Japanese occupation or experiencing Japanese aggression, these community leaders were aware of the sensitive and potentially explosive nature of some interethnic relations. Many of Hawai'i's leaders thus argued for policies for Hawai'i different from those being enacted on the West Coast. For example, when the War Department ordered that all ethnic Japanese civilians be terminated from employment with the military in 1942, Hawai'i's military governor, Delos Emmons, pushed back, pointing out that Hawai'i's Japanese made up 80 percent of construction workers, and no work—for the military or otherwise—could be done without them. The War Department rescinded the order.[10]

Although only a relatively small proportion of Hawai'i's Japanese population was incarcerated, Japanese in Hawai'i had trouble accessing the war economy. It was especially difficult for issei, but nisei (Japanese American citizens) also experienced many hardships. After the attack on Pearl Harbor, Japanese residents were removed from some geographic areas near military bases and strategically important installations such as railroads. Issei were not allowed to work in military jobs, gather in groups of ten or more (even for religious reasons) crippling social organizations and connections, Nor were they permitted to leave their homes during blackout periods (which were longer than curfews). They also had no access to Japanese language news, as all foreign language newspapers and media were banned.[11] Many lost their jobs and their homes early in the war. Nisei were not always subject to such strict restrictions, but their lives, too, were significantly affected. They were allowed to take some military jobs (although they had to wear large black badges at all times, singling them out for added attention),[12] but they faced a great deal of discrimination in military-based jobs. Pearl Harbor Shipyard, for example, "blatantly discriminated against Japanese Americans in its hiring practices, always putting them at the bottom of the list."[13] Compared with Chinese or Koreans in the Islands, Japanese were more likely to be employed by contractors working with the military or federal government rather than directly by the military or government.[14] Outside the military, ethnic Japanese, regardless of their citizenship status, faced discrimination and harassment. Employers, government officials, and other Hawai'i residents regarded Japanese with wariness and worse. It is not surprising, then, that Japanese living in wartime Hawai'i lived with "an extreme degree of fear."[15]

During the war, all of Hawai'i's residents experienced shortages and hardship. Because the Islands were under martial law for most of the war, activities were restricted, and various curfews and blackouts were put in place. Many stores and restaurants closed permanently because of shortages or government regulations.[16] Newspapers and mail were censored, and courts changed the way they processed cases. Many schools, parks, and other public spaces were used for war activities such as bomb shelters, housing for troops, and hospitals.[17] Thus, the residents of Hawai'i were reminded of the war daily. Many in Hawai'i were also involved in the war effort. Some enlisted in the military, although Japanese Americans were not permitted to do so until later in the war. Chinese from Hawai'i enlisted, many serving in the Asia and China theaters. Other Chinese participated in Hawai'i through organizations such as the Hawai'i Defense Volunteers, a mostly Chinese militia group of about eight hundred individuals who aided regular military personnel in the Islands. This group was one of several (some Japanese, some ethnically mixed) whose work was allied to the regular military.

Some citizens lamented the effect of the war and the influx of new people on the old ways of both Japanese and Chinese communities. Many practices within Chinese households were affected; with shipments from China stopped, Chinese in Hawai'i no longer had access to certain foodstuffs or other goods they regularly received from China and were thus forced to adopt other foods into their diets. Ceremonies around holidays were curtailed or eliminated. In addition, greater restrictions were enforced on many practices that relied on non-English language sources. Radio shows no longer broadcast programs in Chinese, and language schools were outlawed. One wartime researcher worried that "Americanization programs, the influence of the ever increasing number of Mainland arrivals in Hawaii, together with a form of patriotic pressure, have forced a large number of common Chinese practices to one side. . . . Many of these displacements are not temporary wartime events but rather . . . they are permanent changes, changes that will tend gradually to reduce Oriental mannerisms and customs to a minimum, if it did not eliminate them entirely."[18]

WORLD WAR II COMES TO HAWAI'I

The war also brought about interactions between groups who previously had had little contact, such as service personnel and civilian workers from the continental United States and the local population, and such experiences affected both groups. Before the war, most haole in Hawai'i were from elite groups, with high economic and political standing. White visitors to Hawai'i were similarly from upper-class backgrounds, and most tourists at that time were wealthy. In contrast, American service personnel and civilian workers were from different socioeconomic backgrounds from these earlier groups. Living among white people from different classes contributed to a breakdown of long-standing assumptions about the connections between race and class.[19]

And for many Americans who went to Hawai'i to support the war effort either in or connected to the military, or in another capacity, such as teaching, Hawai'i was an unusual place, for many the "first strange place."[20] Unlike most of the places these Americans came from, Hawai'i had a multiethnic population, about two-thirds of which was not white but Asian or Pacific Islander. In addition, although haole were dominant, many nonwhite residents held positions of authority and responsibility. One sailor made clear just how unusual Hawai'i was to white Americans who had grown up on the Continent: "This is a strange land and they keep telling me I am in the US, but from the time I walked off the ship, I have doubted it."[21] Some Hawai'i residents tried to keep their distance from military personnel, seeing their presence as intrusive. But others reached out and invited the young people to their homes for dinners or gatherings, hoping to ease their homesickness.[22]

One scholar described the "bewildering variety of Army, Navy, Marine Corps and Coast Guard units [that] came and went," noting that the increase in just the number of army soldiers alone—from 43,000 in December 1941 to 135,000 six months later—is testament to the enormous numbers of military personnel in Hawai'i during the war.[23] Thousands of service members—nearly all of them white American men—spent time in Hawai'i during the war years; many passed through Hawai'i on their way to or from Pacific or Asia battle sites or spent a short time in Hawai'i on R&R. But others stayed longer, supporting the war while stationed in Hawai'i. Nonmilitary employees supporting the war effort were also present, including those in clerical work, engineering or construction work, and unskilled workers such as truck drivers and miners. Those who spent lengthy time in the Islands—both military and non-military—were able to see even more of Hawai'i and had more interaction with the local population. They might meet and date local women, or get to know local families.

Despite the inconveniences and hardships brought by the war, many in Hawai'i experienced financial gains from the booming war economy by finding new, often higher-paying work opportunities.[24] Because of the labor shortage, more women began working, thus bringing more income into their families. Even Japanese experienced an improvement in their financial situation: "Although they did not share in economic gains to the same extent as Caucasians, the majority of the Nikkei were better off financially in 1945 than they had been in 1941."[25] But other groups made faster and broader gains. Certainly, haole elite maintained dominant social and economic positions; they had developed relationships with the U.S. military before the war that continued throughout wartime. Those relationships helped to shape labor regulations that were kept in place during martial law and made it easier for plantation owners to keep workers on the plantations.[26] The economic and social positions of Chinese also improved; they continued to rise rapidly into the middle class partly because they were making further inroads into education and the workforce and, as we will see, because they were often accepted more than Japanese by both Americans and Hawai'i haole. Young people of all backgrounds found some financial independence from their parents and families through the available jobs and relatively high pay that the war economy offered, giving them a newfound confidence of their place in Hawai'i society. As one researcher wrote at the time, "The call to defense work is a stimulating experience for the young men. The demand for workers seems to be unlimited, and here, for the first time, they appear to be indispensable. Thus they acquire a new valuation of themselves, a new sense of self esteem. . . . [Before] they were part of the traditional family group and their contribution was shared within the group. Now their employment is individualized and their attitudes likewise have become individualized."[27]

Such opportunities began to shape the younger generations in new ways; while they helped to convince them that they deserved an equal place in the social order, they also provided another kind of exposure to a market economy based on individual—not collective—interests, goals, and desires.

For Hawaiians, World War II was a time of continued subjugation, although many engaged in the war effort. Some two thousand Hawaiians

WORLD WAR II COMES TO HAWAI'I

served in the military, along with those of mixed Hawaiian and other ethnicities. At home, too, Hawaiians engaged in military work. In the early war years, they made up the largest proportion of National Guard troops, partly because Japanese were not permitted to serve in these roles.[28] However, the role of the military in Hawai'i—which would continue long after the end of the war—had a profound effect on Hawaiian communities and lives. The military shaped the economy and labor market across the Islands. But even more important was the land loss that Hawaiians experienced. According to Kyle Kajihiro, "The military expropriated and occupied the richest and most strategic locations, including important religious sites, fishing, farming, hunting, and gathering areas."[29] While the military presence in Hawai'i affected all who lived there and nearly every aspect of social life, Native Hawaiians were more substantially affected than others because of the loss of land. Military lands included a large proportion of "ceded lands," which were former national and Crown lands belonging to the Kingdom of Hawai'i that had been taken illegally by the United States in 1898.[30] The legacy of 1898 continues to be felt: today, more than half of the military-controlled lands in Hawai'i are former government and Crown lands of the Hawaiian nation.[31] It was during World War II that the military began to use the island of Kaho'olawe—considered sacred land by Hawaiians—as a bombing target. Though promising to return it after the war ended, the military continued bombing there until 1990. It was only in 2003 that the military ceded the island back to Hawai'i. The buildup of the U.S. military in Hawai'i during World War II has caused Hawai'i to become one of the most densely militarized U.S.-controlled areas in the world.

CHINATOWN

During the 1930s and 1940s, Chinatown underwent changes that reflected both the change in Chinese residents' status and the enormous impact of the war on Hawai'i in general. As we saw in chapter 2, before this period, Chinese had begun leaving the area to reside elsewhere. By 1940, Chinese made up less than half of Chinatown's residents.[32] However, despite the fact that most Chinese no longer lived there, Chinatown remained important to Hawai'i's Chinese community. Indeed, Chinese continued to shop in Chinatown markets and attend community meetings there. And most Chinese associations (those organized by surname or hometown) were headquartered in the area. But once Chinatown was no longer the only place where Chinese lived, it experienced changes as Hawaiians and Japanese also began to open businesses there.

The war brought other changes to Chinatown, primarily in terms of who visited. Writing in 1950, Gwenfread Allen remarked that "Hotel Street became one of the most famous thoroughfares in the Pacific and River Street was its close second. Along one mile of Hotel Street and its intersecting streets was a honky-tonk town of cheap attractions for the hordes of fun-hungry visitors."[33] During wartime, Chinatown became best known as a red-light district and was frequented by American servicemen seeking prostitutes. Because men often had to wait in line for a prostitute, the area was regularly full of white servicemen. But Chinatown was also frequented by many people for many reasons:

> Hotel Street during the war was a rush of reeking fish markets, overflowing tattoo parlors, dinging pinball games, sing-songing concessionaires and pushing, shouting, elbowing men in uniform and out. Men stood in lines everywhere, for everything. The district had been crowded before the war swelled Hawaii's population but during the war Hotel Steet pulsed with money, sex, and occasional violence. . . . In every nook and cranny of the district, men and women set up stands to sell watches, jewelry, popcorn, postcards, keepsakes. Some worked the street full-time; others, part-time. They came to catch some of the free-flowing money. Most of them were Chinese; it was Chinatown, after all. With few exceptions, every person on the street selling or posing or hawking wares and services to the haoles from the mainland was of pure or mixed Chinese, Japanese, Puerto Rican, Hawaiian, Portuguese, or Filipino descent.[34]

During the wartime years, Chinatown was full of bars, saloons, cheap restaurants, and souvenir stores. Two of the most recognizable Chinatown locations today were established then. The building on Hotel Street that now houses Smith's Union Bar was erected in 1904 and for many years held small shops that sold wares such as jewelry or clothing. For a while, in the 1920s, it was a shooting gallery.[35] It became Smith's Union Bar in 1939 and has since remained so. During the war, sailors frequented the establishment, but today it draws a crowd from across Honolulu. Perhaps even more famous was Club Hubba Hubba, a former café that took on

WORLD WAR II COMES TO HAWAI'I

this name in 1946. Even though the club was established after the war, it is reminiscent of Honolulu's wartime years partly because the phrase "hubba hubba" was made famous at that time by a number of events, including Bob Hope's USO tours to entertain troops, the 1945 movie *Doll Face*, and the presence of servicemen.[36] In the 1950s, the club was well known for its dance and burlesque shows. It closed in 1996, but its sign—fully restored in 2010[37]—remains a Chinatown landmark today.

During the war years, Chinatown was perhaps best known as a red-light district. Even though the prostitutes were nearly all white women, most from San Francisco,[38] Chinatown was negatively branded because of the activity that took place there. It continued to be seen as exotic and immoral, both dangerous and attractive, much as it had been before the war. But wartime attention—especially the prostitution that brought in military men—made the area even more disreputable. The rhetoric around Chinatown, including the general condemnation of the area and and its being considered off limits to "decent people," strengthened during the chaotic war years. The presence of American military personnel in Chinatown complicated the relationship between Chinese residents of Chinatown and those who lived outside the area, and it underscored the importance for some in the community of distancing themselves from earlier racial discourses that lumped all Asians—or even all Chinese—together and labeled them as foreign and untrustworthy. That white visitors and service personnel could not or would not distinguish among Asians contributed to the unease of local Chinese.

If place helps to create racial meaning,[39] then Chinatown's latest chapter cast a pall over Chinese status in Hawai'i. It is thus easy to see that the continuing connection between Chinese and a Chinatown full of vice and immorality made some Chinese even more determined to find a way out of the area into a more acceptable middle-class haole community. As we saw in chapter 2, the Chinese community in Hawai'i had stabilized over the first decades of the twentieth century; with more families, more children, a deeper connection to public schools, and a stronger presence in the urban community, many Chinese had already begun to move into the middle class. The changes seen in Chinatown during the war years further encouraged moves away from Chinatown; in the process, those who had left Chinatown were more likely to be seen as "good" Chinese—because they had found financial success in a haole-dominated society—whereas

WORLD WAR II COMES TO HAWAI'I

those who remained in Chinatown were more likely to be depicted as "bad"—poorer—Chinese. These characterizations and groupings of class and education differences within the Chinese community would continue to shape the relationship of all Chinese to Chinatown. During these years, Chinatown took on new meanings and new assumptions. Because of Chinatown's role during the war, resuming its old ways became difficult, and the area would have to be resurrected and recreated after the war.

CHINESE MOVEMENT INTO THE MIDDLE CLASS

Many Chinese in Hawai'i were doing very well during the 1930s, 1940s, and 1950s. One scholar has remarked on this history, "World War II in the 1940s saw the rise of a most unusual generation of Chinese who had gone to high school in the 1920s. In their thirties when the war started, these Chinese were to gain spectacular fame in business and politics. Their lives are individually dazzling and collectively fortuitous."[40] While such fame and fortune by no means came to all in the Chinese community during these years, it is true that in nearly all areas of social and economic life, Chinese were staking a larger and larger claim in Honolulu and moving up occupational, economic, and social ladders. As we saw in chapter 2, Chinese children were increasingly involved in the Islands' schools, with most Chinese children attending school. By 1940, Chinese school attendance for those aged five to twenty-four years was 70.6 percent, higher than for any other group and higher than the average of 58 percent for the Territory.[41] And Chinese children were staying in school longer;[42] by 1947, among public school students, Chinese were more likely than those of any other ethnic group to graduate from high school. College enrollment and graduation were also on the rise; in the 1930s, Chinese students continued to make up a significant proportion of the enrollment at the University of Hawai'i,[43] and they also started to travel to the continental United States to attend university.

Chinese were even making inroads into the English Standard Schools, a system established in 1924 that restricted admission to children whose "proper" English (read: not pidgin, the local language that arose among plantation laborers) met haole standards. These schools—which had more resources, better teachers, and higher English standards than regular public schools—were a way to allow racial segregation of haole and non-haole

WORLD WAR II COMES TO HAWAI'I

children without being completely explicit in intention. By 1937, there were ten such schools, covering elementary through high school grades. Until about the onset of World War II, enrollment at these schools comprised mostly haole students. At the time, haole children made up half the Standard School population but only 2.5 percent of regular public schools. But those proportions changed as Japanese and Chinese students began passing the required language exam and enrolled in English Standard Schools. By 1947, there were more Japanese than haole students enrolled in these schools. However, relative to their numbers in the general population, Japanese were still underrepresented. Chinese children, on the other hand, began to enter these schools at high rates, and by the late 1930s and 1940s, their representation there outpaced their representation in the general population.[44] Many Chinese parents worked hard to prepare their children to gain admission to English Standard Schools. And in spite of the fact that in many Chinese households, parents did not speak English well, some parents did not permit their children to speak anything but "proper" English at home, hoping they would develop the English language skills needed to pass the language test[45] to gain entry into these top schools. English Standard Schools maintained their status as elite, highly select public schools throughout their existence from 1924 to 1960; only a small proportion of all students—from a low of 2 percent in 1925 to a high of 9 percent in 1947 were able to attend these schools. Because most Chinese (and Japanese) were effectively prevented from attending most private schools (during these years, Punahou Academy, for example, maintained a quota of 10 percent for Chinese and Japanese students),[46] English Standard Schools played an important role in springboarding Chinese into higher-status positions in Hawai'i.

Chinese involvement in education and their success in the public school system were the main basis for their movement into new occupations. This process, begun in the first decades of the twentieth century, continued apace through the 1930s and accelerated during the war years. In 1910, around 48 percent of Chinese worked in jobs classified as "laborer" (the bottom of the occupational hierarchy), and less than 1 percent were classified as professional (the top of the hierarchy). But those numbers changed over the next decades. By 1930, the percentage of Chinese in the laborer category had dropped to 24.4 percent, and 3 percent were professionals. By 1950, 5.3 percent were laborers and 10.7 percent were professionals.

Those figures continued their trajectories over the next two decades so that by 1960, the percentage of Chinese in professional jobs (16.6 percent) was close to that of haole (17.9 percent).[47] Chinese were also steadily moving into the middle class. In 1940, for example, close to 60 percent of male workers were in what were labeled "preferred classes," which included not only professional workers (who made up 5.7 percent of all Chinese men in the labor force) but also proprietary (14.7 percent), clerical (28.7 percent), and skilled (10.2 percent) workers.[48] This upward mobility demonstrates that Chinese were developing a stronger influence in Honolulu life and, as their areas of work and numbers of businesses expanded, gaining more contact with people of other ethnic groups.

Incomes rose in parallel with occupational advances. In 1938, Chinese earned considerably less than haole. Where haole salaried workers earned an average of $137.91 per month, Chinese earned an average of $90.56.[49] But this was still more than any other non-white group in the Islands was earning. By 1949, the median annual income of Chinese workers was $2,964, the highest of any group in the Islands, including haole, who earned an average of $2,856 annually.[50] It is true that some of that convergence between the white and Chinese communities came from the influx of working-class white people into Hawai'i, who made considerably less than elite haole. But these data also reflect the increasing earning power of Chinese.

Not surprisingly, Chinese also began to accumulate financial assets. Territory records show a steady increase in savings deposits made by Chinese through these decades. Per capita deposits totaled about $59 annually in 1920 but had risen to $150.76 by 1930; while savings declined during the Depression era, they began rising again by the end of the 1930s.[51] The increase in savings reflected not only a rise in Chinese income but also, as the proportion of first-generation immigrants declined and the proportion of second-generation immigrants rose, a decrease in the amount of money being sent to family in China.[52] Noting this change, as well as a difference in savings behavior between ethnic groups, one early scholar remarked, "During the early period, the Chinese . . . sen[t] their savings to the Orient, while the Portuguese who were later immigrants had no such disposition and so had larger savings in 1910. But the Chinese soon acquired more wealth than the Portuguese and correspondingly increased their bank deposits."[53]

One of the most notable areas in which Chinese gained entry and became successful is land acquisition. As noted in chapter 2, a major factor

WORLD WAR II COMES TO HAWAI'I

in this process was the continuing loss of land for Native Hawaiians after the privatization of land in the mid nineteenth century. In addition to not having the resources to acquire land as it came up for sale, Hawaiians incurred further losses because of the military presence in Hawai'i. As mentioned in chapter 2, even before annexation, the U.S. government had seized large parcels of land, and it continued to acquire land throughout the decades after annexation. Land acquisition was also central to the process of the United States building an increasingly large and permanent military presence in Hawai'i. Hawaiians—for whom access to, respect for, and relationship to the land are vital to cultural survival—were the group most affected by the U.S. land grab.

Chinese were not involved with the actions of the U.S. government, but they were able to take advantage of the increasing privatization of land and the resulting land sales. Chinese were especially involved in buying land because of the movement of Chinese out of Chinatown and surrounding districts into more settled, wealthier districts of Honolulu. In many areas of the city—Mānoa Valley, Upper Nu'uanu Valley, Black Point, and Pacific Heights, among others—haole maintained informally organized but strongly segregated neighborhoods.[54] But Chinese were able to enter other areas, ones with better schools, larger lots, and safer neighborhoods than in Chinatown; statistics show that because of building conditions, overcrowding, and environmental pollution, those who lived closest to the city's center, the location of Chinatown, experienced higher rates of disease, death, and hospitalizations than those who lived farther out,[55] so there were many motivations for Chinese to live elsewhere.

During the 1920s, so many Chinese moved to Bingham Tract, an area several miles east of Chinatown, that it became known as "Chinese Hollywood" even though the area and its housing were modest by the standards of the time.[56] Still, this neighborhood stood out. One student researcher, a young Chinese American woman, writing in 1950 described the residents as full of pride and the area as attractive to many:

> The homes and lands here have always had a high value[;] therefore they were naturally inhabited by moderate and large income Chinese families and Chinese merchants. However, since World War II, when all people earned a great deal of money, the homes have been in great demand by other racial groups especially the Japanese. . . . Each house is located on a lot of about

fifty by a hundred feet. Since most of the people own the houses they live in[,] great care is taken to see that the whole house is kept clean and that the trees and lawn are nicely trimmed. Another factor contributing to the consciousness of the appearance of their homes is the pride which the people possess of their community. It is a community of high standards and high land values to which the people try to live up.[57]

In many cases, newly available land allowed Chinese to buy in areas not previously settled by any other immigrant group; these lands were often sold by haole who had purchased them after the 1850 Māhele land division. In the later years of the war, for example, Chinese were able to proffer ready cash and were the highest bidders for newly available and highly desirable land in Tantalus, an area that included the hills above Mānoa.[58] Likewise, by 1948, about a quarter of the residents of the newly settled Ālewa Heights district were Chinese.[59]

Looking at the history of one residence can give us a sense of how some elite Chinese were able to move to such areas. In 2011, a successful application was made to designate a house in the Ālewa Heights area, the Hung Lum Chun Residence, a historic property on the Hawai'i State Register of Historic Places.[60] The application outlines the history of the house and its importance to the Chinese community. The lot was first made available by the state government as one of a group of residential lots in 1905; the area was considered highly desirable because of its proximity to downtown Honolulu and its scenic views. The first people to live on this lot were Min Hin Li and his wife, Minnie, who moved there in 1929. Li was a prominent doctor and the son of two physicians, Khan Fai Li and Tai Heong Kong Li, who had immigrated from China and participated in helping control the bubonic plague outbreak in 1900. The Lis sold the property in 1942 to Hung Lum Chun. He and his wife, Elsie, lived there until their deaths in 2003 (Hung Lum) and 2007 (Elsie). Chun was an important businessperson, following in the footsteps of his father, Quon Chun, who had founded C. Q. Yee Hop, one of the largest Chinese businesses in Hawai'i. When he retired in 1953, Hung Lum and his brothers took over and expanded the business. Hung Lum was important in the Chinese community because of his business success and because of his involvement in the local community. Along with the residence's unique architecture, it was the history of its two first owners, Li and Chun, and their importance to the history of Chinese in

WORLD WAR II COMES TO HAWAI'I

the Islands that decided the argument for designating the house a historic property. We can also read the history of elite Chinese in this house's history and significance, as it was the wealthy Chinese who were able to buy homes in some of the most exclusive residential neighborhoods.

While movement to wealthy areas was only possible for elite Chinese, the movement of Chinese into Bingham Tract reflects how Chinese as a community were moving into new areas of the city, either renting or owning smaller properties. By 1940, Chinese generally comprised low percentages, often less than 5 percent, of the poorest districts in Honolulu (home to those earning a median annual income of less than $2,000). While the proportion of Chinese in the most desirable districts (home to those with a median annual income of more than $4,900) was usually less than 10 percent, much movement was made into the middle-income districts.[61] It is clear that during these years, Chinese were choosing to invest their growing savings and assets in land and housing. And Chinese were not only investing in land but also building larger and more luxurious homes. Whereas in 1930, the mean per capita property value of Chinese-owned homes was $5,049—well behind that of the haole average of $9,102—by 1940, these values were much more similar, though also much lower because of the Depression, at $3,226 for Chinese and $4,037 for haole. (The home value for all other ethnic groups was much lower in both years.)[62] Chinese homes also had more luxuries than those of others, including haole; for example, a higher proportion of Chinese homes had bathtubs and showers.[63]

At the same time, many Chinese were unable to buy expensive land or homes, or any housing at all. These Chinese, who rented throughout the city, were more likely to live in poorer neighborhoods and much less likely than haole renters to own any appliances or fixtures considered luxurious.[64] We see in this bifurcation of the Chinese community a continuation from the decades before 1940. As we saw in chapter 2, Chinese elites urged the community to "Americanize," while others resisted such changes. Several themes of this era would resonate long after. One is class division and the notion that some Chinese were able to consume "properly" and even extensively, buying large homes in desirable communities with sought-after amenities like schools. Others were not so well positioned, and as we have seen, those who succeeded (according to haole standards) often wrote and spoke disparagingly of those who had not. In such rhetoric, we see a deepening of the constructs of "good" versus "bad" Asians and of the model minority. "Model minorities" were those who achieved success through hard work and consumed "properly" by amassing material wealth and consuming material goods.

Reasons for Chinese Success

There were many reasons Chinese found success in Hawai'i, especially during the first several decades of the twentieth century. First, the second and third generations of Chinese were completing school and entering the labor market. These individuals had grown up in Hawai'i, spoke English as a first language, and had advantages that the first generation was not privy to, especially access to schooling.

But those achievements did not necessarily come easily or without resistance mounted by haole who continued to see Asians as a threat to their own position. We have seen that Chinese had faced discrimination and segregation in Hawai'i since they first arrived in the mid-nineteenth century, and that continued into the mid-twentieth century. Research done by a student at the University of Hawai'i in 1935 traced the career trajectories of all Chinese members of the 1928 graduating class, "the first class in which there is a large enough proportion of Chinese to show definite trends."[65] He found that all nineteen Chinese graduates (out of a total graduating class of eighty-four students) went on to work in professional capacities, although their income was not always high. But the study also found that most believed that their "opportunities for further advancement are slim. . . . Even though vacancies should occur above them, they would in all probability not be promoted but . . . haoles would be hired to take the positions. They believe that although they had equal or superior ability to fellow employe[e]s of the haole group, they would not receive equal treatment in promotions."[66]

Similar opinions were expressed a few years later; in a survey of students at the University of Hawai'i and seniors at Punahou School, many respondents wrote about the perceived privilege of haole: "The haoles are definitely the ones who get all the breaks. They aren't any better," wrote one Chinese woman student. Another wrote, "We still are not given equal rights. The Chinese are not considered equal to the whites here."[67] Chinese felt they received unequal treatment even in the distribution of regular

WORLD WAR II COMES TO HAWAI'I

household amenities; in another study, one Chinese respondent insisted that the delay she was experiencing in getting a phone line was because of her race: "I've had an application in for a telephone for almost two years. All haoles have phones."[68]

Partly because of actual or perceived discrimination, Chinese had developed an almost parallel economy that addressed their own needs, and in this era, that system paid off. Because they needed access to cash and loans but could not count on haole-run establishments for these needs, they founded their own banks. The first Chinese bank in Hawai'i, the Chinese American Bank, opened in 1916, and others soon followed, including the Honolulu Trust Company in 1921, the Liberty Bank in 1922, and the American Security Bank in 1935.[69] Studies have shown that such ethnic banks provide ready loans and funding for business startups, thus helping to fuel and sustain the efforts of entrepreneurs of nondominant ethnicity and strengthen the financial base of ethnic communities.[70] Because Chinese were not allowed into social clubs like the Outrigger Club or the Elks, they organized their own social and commercial clubs, such as the Chinese Civic Association and the American-Chinese Club, formed by Chinese professionals and businesspeople. The networks established through such clubs proved powerful and effective, sometimes to the point of upsetting others in Honolulu. In the following description of Chinese *huis* (groups) by a white American writer, we can see the concerns of whites and haole about the use of such networks in the midst of a booming war economy:

> The hui became a financial institution to reckon with, as the Chinese took over real estate, fine homes, businesses, anything [available for sale]. . . . 'Hui' . . . means a group or meeting. . . . Over the telephone, a live-wire hui promoter such as Chin Ho or Ruddy Tongg, can raise a half million dollars in an hour, with nothing on paper. . . . The actual switch of wealth into the hands of Asiatics is less important than the surge of confidence bordering on cockiness these deals have sparked in the Asiatic element of Hawaii's population.[71]

But a student researcher writing about *huis* argued that such groups were "actually a western-influenced thing," not found in China, that arose because of "the hostile attitude of other racial groups" in Hawai'i.[72] The researcher goes on to argue, "Therefore their establishment in Hawaii is the first sign of their conformity to the values of the host society."[73]

Indeed, Ruddy Tongg's decision to start a new airline was very much about the place of Chinese in Hawai'i—what it was and what Chinese wanted it to be. Tongg started Trans-Pacific Airlines in 1946 (later changed to Aloha Airlines) after experiencing racist treatment by Hawaiian Airlines, the only airline in Hawai'i at the time. For example, he was repeatedly forced to give up his seat on many interisland flights to haole. Hawaiian Airlines was owned by haole and for many years had a policy of not hiring any Asian employees as pilots or flight attendants or to work the counter.[74] He decided to create an airline that would offer an alternative model, welcoming passengers and employees of all races and ethnicities. The airline had broad support among ordinary people and Chinese investors alike. "During the tough early days, employees nursed the company along by working without pay and often waited to cash their paychecks until the airline had enough money in the bank," writes Mike Gordon.[75] Although strongly opposed by the haole owners of Hawaiian Airlines, Tongg's airline—with the help of other Chinese investors and under the leadership of the powerful and skilled Chinese businessperson, Hung Wo Ching—soon became the second largest airline in Hawai'i and was nicknamed "the People's Airline" because of its insistence that all were welcome. The airline maintained a significant presence in the Islands until it ceased operations in 2008.

The parallel Chinese economy arose and was effective for several reasons. First, the Chinese community used its own ties effectively to garner the resources it needed to reach individual and community goals. But as research by Robert Man War Lee suggests, equally as important was the continuing discrimination that Chinese (and other non-haole) faced in Hawai'i's haole-dominated business world. As a student researcher wrote about the time before the war, "Chinese are oriented to the American culture and social order, yet when they seek a place as members of the dominant group, they are not recognized. Race discriminations may not be open, yet the subtle types define just as clearly the conception the American has of the Chinese."[76] Chinese might have been able to receive a good education, but "that did not necessarily mean there was room at the top."[77] In interviews with top haole businesspeople, Lawrence Fuchs learned that these haole leaders were wary of appointing non-haole to top positions.

WORLD WAR II COMES TO HAWAI'I

They insisted that it was "not because of racial discrimination" but because there were not many such candidates who were "articulate, knowledgeable about mainland business conditions and rich in mainland financial and business contacts."[78] In addition, they reported worrying that non-haole would not be able to supervise haole well enough and that white business-people from the continental United States would not want to do business with them. Another student researcher interviewed Chinese working in various fields in 1946, including labor, skilled work, and management. She repeatedly heard stories of a ceiling "beyond which non-haoles cannot go," and her respondents repeatedly stated a belief that "no haole can work under a non-haole." This writer argued that while the war changed some things, many stayed the same, and that after the war, most non-haole returned to positions where there was no future for them.[79] One of her respondents asserted, "You know you're at your ceiling when you stay in the same job and a haole keeps going on above you." Given this kind of discrimination and lack of opportunity, the decision of Chinese to pursue success using their own parallel system made sense.

The shifting economy was another important influence on Chinese achieving economic success. As we saw in chapters 1 and 2, in the early twentieth century, Hawai'i's economy was developing in ways that allowed Chinese opportunities in a variety of fields. This development continued through the 1920s and 1930s, despite the hardship caused by the Depression, and into the 1940s. During these years, the Native Hawaiian community continued to experience significant challenges as the effects of population decline and alienation from land and power continued to take a toll; Hawaiians, therefore, were rarely competitors with Chinese in the job or housing markets. The war resulted in rapid economic growth in Hawai'i around industries and services for the war effort, and most people ended up better off economically after the war than they had been before. Despite the discrimination Chinese faced in the immediate postwar years, they began to move into higher positions. One study focused on socioeconomic mobility during the 1940s found that although haole retained control in high-prestige professions, Chinese representation was two and half times higher than expected, higher than that of Japanese at the time and much higher than that of Filipinos.[80]

But one of the most important reasons for Chinese success during the years immediately before and during the war is that they were *not* Japanese.

I will discuss this issue in greater detail later, but here, it is important to note that while the experience of the Hawaiians makes the best comparison to illuminate the experience of Chinese success in the late nineteenth and early twentieth centuries, it is a comparison with the Japanese that best highlights Chinese success in the 1930s and 1940s. During these years, anti-Japanese sentiment and action were rampant. As another Asian group, Chinese were seen as a "better alternative." Perhaps most relevant is that during the war years, Japanese were barred from some jobs. For example, first-generation Japanese immigrants—those who were born in Japan and denied U.S. citizenship—were not permitted to work at any military job. But even Japanese Americans were not hired into many jobs, as people in Hawai'i—both those who had come from the continental US as well as local people—grew wary of or actually antagonistic toward ethnic Japanese, sometimes seeing them as potential enemies. With Japanese restricted in where they were able to work, Chinese were able to seize new opportunities. As one observer of the war years economy described, "New wealth produced some startling economic changes. Nobody knows how much, but a good share of it found its way into the hands of the astute Chinese, third and fourth generation Americans, who had the foresight to start buying property, particularly in Honolulu, early in the war, when the haoles, or whites, were timidly selling."[81]

Chinese in Medicine, Dentistry, and Public Health

An illustration of how important these decades were to the changing place of Chinese in Hawai'i society comes from the story of how Chinese moved into the fields of medicine, dentistry, and public health. Chinese came to dominate these fields, taking up positions at levels well beyond their representation in the population. How that came about reflects their experience in Hawai'i and key events in that history. During the early years of the twentieth century, new discoveries—everything from germ theory to improvements in microscopes and other technology—contributed to the large changes medicine and public health were undergoing. The germ theory—the understanding that pathogens (viruses or bacteria, for example) cause illness—gave health officials and practitioners more effective tools to combat and prevent disease. That advance led to important public health interventions such as potable water, effective sewage systems, and safe food handling, all of which helped to reduce disease transmission. But Chinese—in Honolulu and other places—had a particular reason to be interested in medicine and public health. As noted in chapter 1, they had long been vilified as being unclean and spreaders of disease. The racism they experienced at the hands of public health officials, particularly during the bubonic plague outbreak of 1899–1900 (as described in chapter 2), made clear just how powerful heath officials were and how their interventions shaped communities. Chinese learned that they would need to take responsibility for the health needs of their community. Medicine became a way not only to provide necessary care to their community, care that many felt was not available from haole doctors, but also to enter the larger, haole-dominated community. Further, medicine was a way to make contact with many ethnic groups, and a medical degree gave an individual status, respect, and, sometimes, a good income.

Chinese in Hawai'i began to enter the fields of medicine, dentistry, and public health in the early years of the twentieth century. The first Chinese doctors to practice medicine in Hawai'i were Kong Tai Heong and Li Khai Fat, a wife and husband team who had trained in Hong Kong and come to Hawai'i as young adults. Others also traveled this route—training in Asia and then moving to Hawai'i to practice (or try to practice) medicine. But there were only a small handful of such first-generation immigrant doctors; it was the second and third generations of Chinese immigrants who really paved a pathway into medicine for the Chinese community.

By 1930, Chinese made up 12.5 percent of all doctors in Hawai'i and 27 percent of dentists; by 1940, those figures were 15 percent and 18 percent, respectively, and by 1949, they had increased to 22 percent and 23 percent, respectively.[82] Just how significant their involvement was in these fields is underscored by the fact that Chinese made up only between 6 and 7 percent of the total population, and three-fifths of employed Chinese men were immigrants.[83] Acquiring a medical degree at this time was not easy. The accomplishments of Chinese in this area were especially notable because until 1965, when the University of Hawai'i opened its medical school, Chinese had to gain acceptance into, find funding for, and travel to universities in the continental United States for medical training. During some of those years, some schools barred the entry of Chinese, and none made it easy for to apply, gain acceptance, and travel from Hawai'i—not yet a U.S. state—to attend school. In public health, training also took place in schools on the U.S. continent until 1965, when the School of Public Health opened at the University of Hawai'i.

But in spite of the difficulties in doing so and in addition to their over-representation in medicine and dentistry, Chinese also began to take up jobs in public health. They began to make inroads into the Hawai'i Board of Health in the 1930s[84] and then moved into increasingly prominent positions. Although the Board of Health remained heavily haole through the early 1950s, Chinese were nevertheless well represented there. They held key posts in public health in 1951, including the directorships of Health Education, Sanitary Engineering, Food and Drugs, Mosquito Control, Housing, Mental Hygiene, and Local Health Services.[85] By 1953, the Chinese American physician Richard K. C. Lee became the first Chinese director of a U.S. Territorial health office, and when Hawai'i became a state, he became the first Chinese director of a state health department.[86]

The movement of Chinese into medicine, dentistry, and public health was important for many reasons. First, it is evidence of how Chinese used access to public schooling to find a solid place in the community and to establish a pathway for themselves not just into the middle class but into the highest professional circles. Second, the importance of medicine and public health—and the power that officials in those fields had—was abundantly clear to the Chinese community, who were regularly targeted as being unclean and spreaders of disease. In five decades, Chinese went from being victims and targets of the Board of Health to being in charge. And third, medicine was an acceptable and well-regarded field; entering the most powerful sectors of the economy—those controlled by the sugar barons—was nearly impossible. But medicine was a respectable alternative and thus opened a door into the social and economic worlds of Hawai'i that haole had kept locked for more than a century.

EARLY MODEL-MINORITY CONSTRUCTIONS

In the efforts the Chinese were making, we can see the beginnings of the model-minority framework. That discourse is evident even though the actual use of the phrase; "model minority" has been less used in Hawai'i than in the continental United States. Nevertheless, the framing of Chinese success and the relative positions of Hawai'i's various ethnic and racial groups mirror the model-minority language. The framework began to take

WORLD WAR II COMES TO HAWAI'I

shape in many ways. First, Chinese achievement could be interpreted as the embodiment of the argument that hard work brings success. Though they arrived as plantation workers, Chinese had shown that by working hard, a group could find success in Hawai'i, even in the face of restrictions and racial discrimination. Connected to this telling of Chinese history was how that success—that economic success—bolstered other arguments. At several key moments—most notably at times when the United States was considering or making changes in its relationship with Hawai'i—Chinese argued that their economic success and contributions should be the basis of acceptance as equal citizens: "It was their investment in the land—their infusion of labor, capital, and enterprise—that grounded their claims to belonging."[87] Tying claims for social and political citizenship explicitly to economic success was the beginning of a narrative of evaluating the deserving and undeserving that has been perpetuated ever since: economic success was, is, and should be the basis of citizenship, both political and social. These distinctions—more or less successful, more or less deserving, and more or less accepted—could be found within the Chinese community and were the basis of divisions among Chinese. The divides hinged most clearly on class and generation, with second- and third-generation Chinese more likely than the first generation to have achieved American markers of success in education and work.

There were geographical divisions, too, with Chinese living in Chinatown more likely to be less educated than those who had moved out. Those who were able to move to other parts of the city—because they had the financial means or because they were better integrated into the larger Honolulu society—did so. The professional and merchant elite encouraged young people to follow the path of the ones seen as successful, who were most often those who had gotten an education and taken up professional careers.[88]

The timing of the establishment of these distinctions within the Chinese community and the discourse around them were also key. The 1930s and 1940s pitted Chinese against Japanese and in that comparison, Chinese were more clearly the "good" Asians, since Japanese in Hawai'i were connected to a wartime enemy. Even though there were never any incidents of sabotage or enemy collaboration on the part of Japanese in Hawai'i, they remained under suspicion throughout the war. But in addition to their potential ties to Japan, Hawai'i's Japanese were seen as less a model group than Chinese for other reasons, and these sentiments had been expressed long before Hawai'i's involvement in the war. As anti-Japanese sentiment grew, Chinese came to be seen as a more acceptable group.[89] First were simple numbers: there were more Japanese in Hawai'i than any other ethnic group, and those numbers were threatening to the haole elite and their power in local politics. In addition, Japanese were leaving the plantations and moving into other communities. This was exactly the concern about Chinese decades earlier, but there were more Japanese, and they were seen to be crowding out others. Even Japanese success in new fields was seen as problematic. During these decades, Chinese were outpacing Japanese in educational and occupational achievement—mostly because they had arrived in Hawai'i, and Honolulu, earlier—but because they were a smaller group, these achievements were not seen to be as threatening as those of the more numerous Japanese.

Japanese were also seen as threatening because they were forming families. Japanese men were more likely than Chinese men to be married, and they usually married Japanese women. At the time, Japanese had the lowest rates of marrying outside one's ethnic group than any other group; in 1941, 96 percent of Japanese American grooms and 91 percent of Japanese American brides married other Japanese Americans.[90] To some, that suggested insularity; but much more significantly, this meant the beginning of a new American-born Japanese generation who could vote and own land and who were legally American citizens. Throughout the decades around the war, it was the second-generation, and later the third-generation, Japanese who were seen as the biggest threat to the status quo of haole control.

One of the most significant pieces of the construction of "good" and "bad" Asians, and of what makes a group a "model," was how the group reacted to their treatment, and here, Japanese were contrasted with Chinese and found wanting. Whereas there were few instances of Chinese publicly or collectively protesting their situation or treatment, Japanese and Filipinos had organized labor strikes to protest against the poor treatment of plantation workers. Japanese not only spoke out against the status quo, but they also joined together with other groups and struck at the plantations, demanding higher wages and better conditions. As one historian has described Japanese action, "From the first wildcat strike in 1885, the immigrant Japanese worker had shown an inclination to stand up and be counted. The result was a long stream of protests, confrontations, work stoppages, and wildcat strikes.

WORLD WAR II COMES TO HAWAI'I

Eventually, these rolled into the mass strike of 1909."[91] Labor action had a long history in the United States, and Japanese were employing an American strategy to change their situation, just as the Chinese had used other institutions, such as education, to change theirs. But importantly, in contrast to the labor strikes, Chinese actions were aimed at becoming part of the system, not changing it. Joining rather than overthrowing or even changing the status quo was much more acceptable to haole elite. Indeed, when viewed in this light, Chinese efforts can be read as bolstering the status quo, strengthening the existing—haole-controlled—social organization.

Chinese reactions in Hawai'i paralleled what occurred in other places. In San Francisco, where Chinese endured deep discrimination, they did not often directly challenge the laws, including the Exclusion Act: "This is in part because Chinese Americans did not choose protest as their main strategy for fighting discrimination. Rather, for the most part they resorted to moral persuasion and to emphasizing Sino-American friendship. . . . [In] 1943 the [San Francisco] Chinese Times published an article about how to deal with discrimination, . . . suggest[ing] being humble and praiseful."[92] Evidence of a similar approach in Hawai'i included not only that Chinese did not involve themselves in labor strikes but also that they married out of their community at a higher rate than Japanese, suggesting to haole that they wanted to assimilate into the wider society. That many Chinese converted to Christianity while Japanese did not was also a notable contrast and provided more support for the view of Chinese as less threatening than Japanese. Even as early as 1907, a reporter for the New York Post, visiting Hawai'i with a U.S. congressional delegation, wrote, "The Chinese are much better liked than the Japanese in Hawaii, because they have shown themselves much more susceptible to the genius of American institutions."[93] Indeed, Chinese used arguments that they led lives like those of haole to insist on fuller inclusion in Hawai'i society. In a congressional hearing discussing whether the Chinese Exclusion Act should be repealed, a Chinese doctor from Hawai'i made a case for inclusion, pointing to the success of Chinese in the Islands and how "professional men have come forth from the rank and file of sons of former plantation laborers, and are today surgeons, physicians, dentists, lawyers, architects, and experts in Government agricultural experiment stations."[94] He argued that "Chinese had become entwined into the fabric of everyday life in Hawai'i as leaders and stalwarts of the economy."[95] It was in such efforts to become part of the system that we can see how Chinese actions contributed to and reinforced a settler colonial system and discourse. While alternative directions would be hard to sustain in a situation where haole were so dominant, that Chinese used the framework of the settler colonial society to argue for inclusion was significant: they argued that they deserved better treatment because they were economically successful, had risen from poor backgrounds into professional sectors of the economy, and lived "American" lives. Here again, we can recognize a claim to acceptance because of model-minority achievements.

The Pearl Harbor attack and the entry of the United States into the war brought all of these issues into sharp relief. Beth Bailey and David Farber have argued that the attack on Pearl Harbor and the U.S. reaction to it made Hawai'i more American than it had ever been. But Hawai'i's large Asian population continued to make many Americans wonder just how American it really was. The large Japanese population in the Islands was worrisome and created a tension between a desire—a need—to claim Hawai'i as American soil and the simultaneous concern about of a group of American citizens who looked like the enemy. In this context, Chinese could play the role of a "safe" group of Asians, allowing for Asians to be characterized as a group that was not threatening to the American way, in Hawai'i or the United States. In this process of a non-white group becoming increasingly accepted into haole-dominated power structures, the role of empire in Hawai'i—which created the system—is also effectively erased. American intervention gets recast as benevolent, as creating opportunity for minority groups to rise, thrive, and succeed; the United States was no longer viewed as erasing ethnic or racial groups or holding them hostage. And by lauding the achievements of Chinese and including them in the American community, discrimination against Japanese was more easily justified. Americans and locals in Hawai'i could claim to be accepting of nonwhite groups, provided they were the "right" kind of nonwhite groups. And so a model minority was born.

LEGACIES OF THE WAR YEARS

The wartime years saw continuing tensions among ethnic and racial groups. While some publicly declared social relations to be harmonious, many others were willing to point out the role of race and ethnicity in social and economic life. Chinese and Japanese workers spoke out about the unequal treatment they received, especially in opportunities for promotion. One researcher at the time compiled statistics from the Bureau of Labor to show that non-haole were earning considerably less than haole in all areas, including government and mercantile work, arguing that "even a casual observation of local attitudes indicates that there is, in the popular mind, at least, a marked conflict between what is and what is supposed to be as far as equality of opportunity in Hawaii is concerned."[96] And however much discrimination Chinese faced, other groups faced even more. One survey of social mobility showed that while Chinese had three times their representation in the fields of medicine and dentistry in the 1940s, Filipinos, Native Hawaiians, and Puerto Ricans were poorly represented in all professional occupations.[97]

Hawai'i remained a race-segregated society into and beyond the 1940s. Neighborhoods continued to be fairly segregated. Groups rarely mixed socially. As reported by student researchers and others, many were wary of interacting with those of other groups. One haole student researcher explained, "None of my close friends has been non-white. This is, in general, the pattern for most haoles—while we are friendly with the non-whites, we are never intimate with them; for that matter, neither group desires it and neither questions it." He went on to assert that if he did try to associate with non-haole, "I know as do my friends that we would be rejected by our own groups if we did so. . . . We would [be failing] to live up to our idea of ourselves as part of the 'superior' group."[98]

And not all Chinese were eager for intergroup interactions either; many young Chinese were strongly encouraged to date only Chinese and expected strong disapproval if they dated or married outside their own group. In interviews with student researchers, some Chinese spoke disparagingly of other groups, especially Native Hawaiians and Filipinos.[99]

During the 1940s, Hawai'i was thus a place where the influence of race and ethnicity continued earlier patterns. Most nonwhite groups faced discrimination in daily life and in their jobs, and some struggled for fair treatment more than others. One student researcher pointed to the more subtle ways that racism existed as part of daily life: "Published statements derogatory to the Orientals in urban occupations have become less frequent, it is true . . . but opposition to their advances has correspondingly stiffened in certain quarters. [In spite of] the racial etiquette of Hawaii, which does not admit public approval of racial discrimination . . . the color bar to free competition in the upper economic and social levels is drawn—less rigorously but probably no less painfully—by the informal 'understandings' within certain fields."[100]

The racialization of social processes contributed to the wariness that many had about interacting outside their own communities. But as things were shifting, and as more non-haole were rising into the middle class, we also see that discourse and constructions of which minority groups are more acceptable than others became more deeply embedded into the larger American racial system. Even the later success found by Japanese traveled along the early pathway used by Chinese to achieve success. While before and throughout most of the war, Japanese were considered a threat, they, too, later became part of the model minority, by hewing to an acceptable American pathway: they joined the military and fought—as Americans—for their country. Their heroic actions—and their silence on their poor treatment in the military—convinced Americans that they too should be considered "good" Asians. This process deepened the narrative of acceptable minority groups and how they handled adversity: "'Rather than succumbing to fatalism or racial bitterness,' Japanese Americans poured their energies into positive futures for their children, believing that 'if one worked hard, then material, social, and spiritual well-being would be possible for the coming generation.'"[101]

Those who reached the status of being acceptable gained new entry points into the status quo and had more reasons to accept a "racial bribe."[102] During the war years in Hawai'i, Chinese were able to take advantage of their position. Just as the destruction of the Hawaiian community in the late nineteenth century was not directly attributable to the Chinese but did allow them more room to be successful, during the war years, Chinese did not create the situation that favored their advance—they lacked the power to be the major players in discrimination of Japanese and the pervasive anti-Japanese sentiment. Nevertheless, during these years, Chinese were able to move into higher-level jobs and to buy land and establish businesses that increased their economic power in the Islands.

Most importantly, these actions and the distinctions that were made among groups strengthened a narrative that has grown in power ever since, one about how a group is evaluated and what kind of actions—and nonactions—come to be acknowledged, encouraged, discouraged, and

WORLD WAR II COMES TO HAWAI'I

celebrated. In this narrative we see all the elements of model-minority construction, although couched in the context of Hawai'i, where less emphasis was placed on the nonmodel groups (particularly African Americans) and more was placed on how a group could achieve acceptance and success. Such a construction was embraced not only by haole who were most powerful but also by the minority groups themselves as they tried to envision a path to success in the world they found themselves in. The tensions and goals that had been playing out in Chinatown would do so for years to come.

Hawai'i's role in World War II was significant for all those in Hawai'i, and for those in the United States. As we will see, the experiences, events, and ideology of World War II have continued to shape social life in Hawai'i and the relationship between the United States and Hawai'i.

By the end of the war, most Americans saw Hawai'i as part of the United States. The framing of the Pearl Harbor attack as an attack on Americans and America set the stage for that. But also important was that millions of Americans had been to Hawai'i during the war. Their experiences in Hawai'i were significant, as were the tales of Hawai'i they brought back to family, friends, and neighbors in the continental United States. The war opened a wider door to U.S. military presence in the Islands as the military acquired lands, established permanent bases, and settled into its permanent place in the economy. Thus, the military came to play a wider role in Island life, shifting the racial composition of the population, and influencing Island power balances as well as the relationship between Hawai'i and the United States. Hawai'i retained and even strengthened its place as a strategic outpost of American empire and military might.

However, while the U.S. government was now firmly committed to keeping Hawai'i in its orbit, it still had to deal with Hawai'i's "race problem." Americans might have come to accept Hawai'i as part of the United States, but many still did not believe that a territory where most of the population was not white could really be an equal part of the nation. As we will see, rhetoric about Hawai'i's racial composition began to shift during the Cold War years as Asian Americans and their experience during and after the war came to take on an important role. The developing civil rights movement and efforts to tackle racism in the United States took on added significance as the United States entered the tense Cold War years and worked to position itself against the Soviet Union. The experience of Japanese during the war—from incarceration to discrimination to widespread enlistment in the army—added more weight to the narrative of "good" and "bad" Asians, of how minority or marginalized groups can be expected to act in the face of discrimination. This rhetoric formed the basis of a rising belief in a model minority. As we will see in the next chapter, Hawai'i and its racial composition and politics came to play a significant role in the Cold War era and, in the process, shaped much of the American racial discourse, and had a strong influence on the development of racial politics in the United States more generally.

Chapter Four

STATEHOOD AMID COLD WAR POLITICS

World War II ushered in a new era in Hawai'i, as it did in many places across the world. The most important changes had roots in Hawai'i's racial history. As the power of the haole elite declined, as more working-class white people settled in the Islands, and as Japanese and Chinese in Hawai'i began to grow into more powerful political and economic forces, what was once a clear and immutable racial hierarchy, with haole elite at the top, was severely shaken. Sugar's dominance shifted, and tourism began to take on its future role as the center of Hawai'i's economy. These changes in Hawai'i took place as the United States increased its global power and developed a wider and deeper military presence across the world. Hawai'i, viewed as a bridge to Asia, saw an increase in U.S. military presence via U.S. military land acquisition and economic dominance. All of this happened against a backdrop of ongoing Cold War tensions between the United States and the USSR as the two countries competed for military dominance and for the hearts and minds of peoples in the Global South. In these geopolitical struggles, Hawai'i took on further importance to the United States and became a tool in its strategy to convince newly independent nations to align with the United States against the Soviet Union. Key to this strategy was Hawai'i's racial composition and its racial frameworks, which the United States touted as evidence of American tolerance and acceptance of racial difference. With the increase in Hawai'i's value to the United States came renewed calls for statehood—a way to bring Hawai'i safely and visibly into the United States. Not coincidentally, statehood was part of a process that held up Asian Americans and their success as model minorities as one way to counter the increasingly louder voices of those pointing to the racism that shaped social, economic, and political life in the United States. This was also an era when neoliberal ideology began to take hold in the United States and other parts of the world. Multiculturalism and the role of marginalized groups began to be imagined as part of a neoliberal strategy and as the best way to bring differences into the United States. In this construction, Hawai'i was a useful canvas. Through these processes and the discourses that emerged from them, the history of U.S. empire building in Hawai'i and the experience of Native Hawaiians dropped out of sight.

After the war, Chinatown was recovering from the difficult and scarring war years. It had earned a reputation as seedy, disreputable, and dangerous. During the years immediately after the war, Chinatown received much less attention than at any other time. As Hawai'i began to pivot toward postwar concerns, Chinatown languished. Buildings became more dilapidated. Now that there were fewer military personnel in the Islands, the number of visitors to the area declined, leaving Chinatown nearly abandoned by many. The booming postwar economy emphasized the difference between successful Chinese who moved away from Chinatown and those who remained and were less likely to have profited from the stronger economy. But while there might have been less overt attention paid to and celebration of Chinatown during this time, beneath the surface, processes were underway that would affect the long-term future of Chinatown. During the Cold War years, underground discourses were developing that shaped all lives in Hawai'i, as well as U.S. racial constructions and political, social, and environmental landscapes. The processes developing at the time related to an increased focus on making Hawai'i "modern," which began to shape the urban landscape, the construction of race in the United States, the rising influence of neoliberalism in the United States and across the world, the increasing importance of Asia to the United States and to the world at large, and new intersections of economies and states across national boundaries. These processes began to take hold after Hawai'i was made a state and grew more and more visible in the years afterward.

STATEHOOD AMID COLD WAR POLITICS

CHANGES IN HAWAI'I

In Hawai'i in the decades just after World War II, important shifts were occurring in both the economy and the racial politics that shaped all Island life. These came about as Hawai'i became a key outpost of U.S. military and economic strategy, thus changing the composition of the population. And as the sugar industry declined, tourism rose to become the dominant industry in Hawai'i's economy.

The sugar industry faced several challenges. The United States had passed laws in the 1930s that reduced Hawai'i's sugar quota and increased competition for sugar growers. The increasing production of beet sugar and other sugars in the continental United States also threatened Hawai'i's place in the industry.[1] In addition to outside threats, Hawai'i's sugar growers also had to deal with the increasing power of the labor movement in Hawai'i; a series of major strikes before the war increased pressure on growers to improve wages and conditions for plantation laborers. The perception of plantation workers' poor and unequal treatment during the war led to a major increase in the power of labor unions after the war, with membership in the International Longshore and Warehouse Union increasing thirty-fold after the war. The union led a strike in 1946 in which workers at thirty-three of the thirty-four largest sugar plantations worked together to demand change. The strike and the growing power of labor forced growers to concede to workers' demands. Hawai'i's laborers then became some of the highest paid agricultural workers in the United States; compensation was higher in Hawai'i than in areas such as Louisiana, the Caribbean, and the Philippines. Labor also played a large role in the changing political realm, helping to grow support for the Democratic Party: "In its active, unequivocal concern for openness, acceptance, and the development of opportunity . . . [the Democratic Party] . . . unleashed a pent-up energy and enthusiasm that underlay the process of change across the board."[2] All of these changes threatened the power, primacy, and future of Hawai'i's sugar industry[3] and changed the overall balance of power in the Islands.

Many assumptions about race and ethnicity had been shaken by events during the war. The complete lock on the economy and government that haole had had for nearly a century and the fact that most haole in Hawai'i were of the elite class had seemed to make the superiority of whiteness

STATEHOOD AMID COLD WAR POLITICS

indisputable and the lasting power of Hawai'i's racial hierarchy inevitable. But as we saw in chapter 3, the war brought other white people to Hawai'i, and the class diversity in this group shook the foundation of the connection between race and class that had stood for so long. Now, there were white people who worked at unskilled and low-skilled jobs and those who were in the military ranks, subject to the whims and the orders of those above them in class standing. Even the prostitutes who worked in Honolulu during the war contributed to this change; most prostitutes were white women, which underscored "how little white skin meant in the way of moral superiority or some sort of 'natural' right to order over the vast majority of Hawai'i's people of darker hues . . . [and] . . . made mockery of the whole racialist setup."[4] At the same time, Asians were moving into leadership and supervisory positions, adding to the upheaval of previous assumptions about race and ethnic hierarchies.

Perhaps the most obvious evidence of the shift in Hawai'i racial politics can be seen in the Hawai'i Democratic Revolution of 1954. In that year, Hawai'i-born Japanese and labor groups came together to upend the dominance of the Hawai'i Republican Party and thus haole political control in the Islands; in the territorial elections of 1954, Japanese moved into important political positions. How? One factor was the role of Hawai'i's Japanese Americans during World War II. They were under deep suspicion because Japan was the enemy of the United States, and many Americans were concerned that Japanese in the United States were loyal to Japan, not the United States. But Japanese Americans—in spite of their treatment during the war (particularly their incarceration)—enlisted in the military and joined the fight to defeat Japan and Germany. The famous 442nd Infantry Regiment (made up entirely of Japanese Americans, with a predominant contingent from Hawai'i) suffered enormous casualties, thereby proving they were loyal Americans. In Hawai'i, those Japanese soldiers returned as heroes. In the early 1950s, local Japanese, many now college graduates through funding from the GI Bill, joined coalitions that crossed race and class boundaries and entered local politics in significant numbers.

Chinese were also moving into positions of power and economic strength. These years saw the expansion of Chinese businesses that often began as small, family-run enterprises but were now financially strong and powerful. For example, David Chung Ai took over his family's business from his father, C. K. Ai and further expanded the City Mill hardware

STATEHOOD AMID COLD WAR POLITICS

business. And a family business founded by Lau Kun was expanded by his daughter, Joanna, and her husband into Foodland, one of the largest supermarket groups in Hawai'i.[5] Many Chinese-owned businesses blossomed at this time. The chapter 3 discussion of the rise of Chinese into the professions is key here, as more and more were earning both undergraduate and graduate degrees. Because of these advances in education and because of the occupational opportunities the war economy provided, the financial situation of Chinese saw drastic improvement. Between 1949 and 1959, the mean annual income of Chinese rose from $2,964 to $5,096.[6] That figure was higher than the mean annual income for any other ethnic group, including haole, though even the mean income of Japanese was higher than that of haole by 1959. These changes came about not only because Chinese and Japanese were acquiring higher-paying jobs and more assets but also because, after the war, haole no longer consisted of only the elite and wealthy but many others whose incomes were much lower.

After the war, as Chinese increased their buying power and found more acceptance, they continued to move to new neighborhoods. Upscale areas of the city saw an influx of Chinese residents between 1940 and 1950: the percentage of Chinese in the Pacific Heights area grew from 3.4 percent to 11.3 percent, and in lower Makiki Heights from 7 percent to 19.8 percent.[7] The change in Makiki Heights came about not through the purchase of existing homes but through the purchase of new tracts of land that had become available, as when a Territorial auction of land made thirty-four new lots available for purchase in 1951. Of the thirty-four successful buyers (out of the five hundred people who tried to buy), twenty-four (70.6 percent) were Chinese.[8] The percentage of Chinese in the high-value Makiki Heights neighborhood remains high today, where in 2010, they made up 31.6 percent of its residents.[9] The ability to buy land, often as house plots, was an important factor in Chinese economic success. It allowed them residential stability, access to previously unattainable neighborhoods, and investment opportunities. A Chinese student researcher, for example, describes her family's move from the Makiki area to Mānoa, a more upscale, predominantly haole neighborhood. She recounts her nervousness about the move and her inexperience interacting with haole. But she also writes of coming to understand that it was better for her parents to live among these new neighbors and how she herself "no longer ha[d] the feeling of being an outsider." And while this young woman came to value the opportunity to get to know and live among haole, she also points out that her younger sister "knows little about Chinese culture" nor is able to speak Chinese, which she attributes to her sister having "adopted [haole children's] ideas and standards."[10] Her family's story represents that of many others—moving to new neighborhoods with non-Chinese neighbors and losing ties to the Chinese community in the process.

During the postwar years, the Hawaiʻi economy experienced a major shift as it pivoted toward tourism as its major source of revenue. More and more tourists were coming to Hawaiʻi, which prompted both the local government and private businesses to focus on this part of the economy. However, these changes did not mean a complete upending of the economic structures that had been in place for the past century, as haole maintained economic dominance in the Islands. The "Big Five" (i.e., the sugar industry's most dominant companies), for example, reconfigured themselves to pursue profit through tourism but retained much of the power they had always had. By the 1960s, they had developed into multinational corporations,[11] investing in many industries in many places, thus mitigating the decline of the profitable and powerful sugar industry. While sugar continued to be a Big Five investment for some years, it soon became only one among many.

The military also played a role in the economic shift toward tourism, with the two economic pillars of the military and tourism working hand in hand. Hawaiʻi catered to military personnel during the war, including acting as a site for soldiers on R&R, and later the U.S. military presence helped to jumpstart tourism.[12] In addition, those who had spent time in Hawaiʻi during the war brought home stories of the Islands, increasing Hawaii's popularity among Americans looking for new vacation destinations. As plane travel increased and became more affordable, the number of visitors to Hawaiʻi grew, and the types of visitors expanded beyond the earlier groups of wealthy travelers to increasingly include more middle-class Americans. Former military airport runways began to be used for civilian aircraft, and during their stays, many tourists visited military sites, such as Pearl Harbor, where a memorial to those who had lost their lives was erected in 1962.[13] Local governments came to see tourism as a better investment than sugar and began to allocate more land and resources (such as water) to tourist properties, resort development, and housing. Labor, too, moved away from the plantations and into the tourist industry.

STATEHOOD AMID COLD WAR POLITICS

Hawai'i's increasing dependence on tourism and the military affected all aspects of the Territory. Land use, employment practices, water distribution, and environmental health were all influenced. Equally so were social aspects of Hawai'i society as the Islands began to see an increasing influx of visitors from other places, primarily the United States but later also from Japan. The heavy presence of the U.S. military meant priority for land use being given to military training and operations and brought about a changing demographic, as young people from all parts of the United States came to Hawai'i for their years of service. Hawai'i also began to expand the tourist industry, finding new ways to sell the Islands to potential visitors.

Along with these shifts in Hawai'i—and contributing to them—were changes in the relationship between Hawai'i and the United States. Key to these changes was the permanent presence of the U.S. military in the Islands. After the war, the military's involvement in Hawai'i's economy came to be seen as necessary and durable, and the presence of the military became deeply embedded in local society, even in peacetime. The military presence signaled the sheer power of the U.S. government in Hawai'i in the form of the development of more and larger bases, a more permanent footprint on all islands, and an increasing share of Hawai'i's economy. But it also reflected the ways that Hawai'i was seen as central to U.S. designs and missions in Asia. As Hickam Air Force Base's official website touts, "Hickam Air Field earned the official nickname 'America's Bridge Across the Pacific' for it's [sic] central role in heavy airlift of personnel and materiel in World War Two, the Korean War, and the Vietnam War."[14] The increased military presence made Hawai'i more dependent on the U.S. government as the military acquired more land and began to influence local government priorities in terms of economic investment and resource distribution. Hawai'i leaders were sometimes convinced, though sometimes not, that their best option was to align with U.S. government and military interests, especially because the military provided jobs and infrastructure support.[15] However aligned or resistant leaders were, Hawai'i's relationship with and dependency on the United States deepened in the years following the war.

THE UNITED STATES IN THE WORLD

The place of the United States in the world was also undergoing change following the war as the nation became a major player in world politics.

Of course, one of the dominant geopolitical narratives of these years was the Cold War and the tensions between the United States and the USSR. In the early years of the Cold War, when the threat of warfare was most acute, attention focused on competition between the United States and the USSR in military might and atomic power as both sides ramped up the arms race. But after those initial years, the attention of both powers turned to the Third World as each sought to convince countries in the Global South to align with them and sign on to their version of modernity and governance. Many believed that in this battle to gain popular support elsewhere, the balance of the world was at stake.

That many of these Third World countries were newly independent and developing a sense of what the future might hold for them was significant; amid these changes, the United States tasked itself with finding ways to convince new states in Africa, Latin America, and Asia to follow the American path. As the United States and the USSR competed for world dominance, America's reputation as a supporter of independence movements across the world came under new scrutiny. In its struggle for the "hearts and minds"[16] of previously colonized and mostly nonwhite peoples, America's own racial politics became a flex point. How could a country claim to support democracy, equality, and racial justice in other places when its own domestic practices involved vast racial inequalities and discriminatory practices and laws?

The Soviet Union spoke loudly and regularly about America's racial problems and how nonwhite people in the United States were treated. The United States was a racist state, the Soviets argued, so what did that say about democracy? Indeed, U.S. state officials were well aware how America's bad record on race politics might be seen by peoples in the Global South. With the civil rights movement underway, there were signs of coming change. But the United States faced substantial problems because of its racism.

U.S. state officials worked to counter the narrative of the country's racism and inequality: "The Cold War had turned racial equality into a national priority."[17] Race equality—or at least its appearance—became a part of the American agenda. U.S. promotional materials developed for Third World countries incorporated a variety of measures as evidence that the United States did believe in racial equality. It sent well-known non-white celebrities from African American and Asian American communities

STATEHOOD AMID COLD WAR POLITICS

on world tours to talk about the United States or demonstrate their talents and thus showcase American racial equality. The "jazz ambassadors"— including Dizzy Gillespie, Dave Brubeck, and Louis Armstrong—traveled the world and promoted U.S. rhetoric through their music. A number of Asian Americans were also sent abroad as "cultural ambassadors." Sammy Lee, an Olympic diving medalist in 1948 and 1953, who was a medical doctor and a member of the U.S. Army Medical Corps, traveled throughout Asia as an official sports ambassador to the region. Jade Snow Wong, the author of the memoir *Fifth Chinese Daughter*, also went on a tour of Asia; her story of success and her downplaying of racism supported the American message to Asian countries that the United States was a place of opportunity for all.[18] These exemplars were presented as "living testament[s] before the peoples of the world to equality of opportunity in America."[19]

The government also circulated statistics meant to convince nonwhite peoples of the Global South that the United States provided opportunities to all, no matter their race, ethnicity, gender, or socioeconomic class. These data highlighted the apparent success of Asians in the United States. The 1960 U.S. census showed that on average, by 1960, compared with white American men, Japanese American and Chinese American men had received more years of education, had a higher rate of labor force participation, and a higher percentage working in professional jobs;[20] they even had higher annual average incomes.

What was not publicized was that, once education was controlled for, Japanese and American men actually earned much lower salaries than their white peers, a gap that reflects the discrimination they faced in the labor force.[21] Another indicator that Asians in the United States were not the equals of white Americans came from housing, an area in which data on the racial integration and segregation of American neighborhoods provided contradictory evidence of just how accepted Asians were in the United States. On the one hand, more and more Chinese were leaving Chinatowns and moving into neighborhoods that had previously been all-white, indicating that there were places that were accepting of new Asian American neighbors. But there was no simple or widespread acceptance of racial integration at the time. First, while some neighborhoods tolerated Asians in their midst, others did not. There were many cases—some taken to court by Chinese Americans—in which Asians were barred from living

STATEHOOD AMID COLD WAR POLITICS

in all-white communities.[22] That was true in parts of California, where—long after explicit laws forbidding Chinese from living in certain areas were struck down—white residents effectively barred Chinese Americans from moving to their neighborhoods.[23] In addition, some places accepted Asian residents but continued to exclude Black residents. For example, after World War II, Chinese in Los Angeles "often flocked to restricted neighborhoods that welcomed Asians but not blacks."[24]

These fights over residence revealed several telling aspects of racial politics in the postwar United States. For one, what happened to Asian Americans was not necessarily indicative of the experience of other minority groups, particularly African Americans. There were times when all nonwhites were barred from certain neighborhoods but others when some Asian groups were tolerated because their behavior was interpreted as being "closer" to that of white people.[25] Here, again, we see the developing model-minority framework, with groups positioned differently along a continuum of white perceptions of their actions, reactions, and lives. But narratives of Asian American success also paper over the discriminatory and racist practices that had long kept Asians in segregated housing communities. The incarceration of Japanese citizens of the United States during the war is the most glaring evidence of how Asians in the United States were treated, but there is also much evidence from the time following the war. The story of "how succeeding generations of Asian Americans were starting to let go of old world ways and take up the social mores of mainstream society"[26] neglects and erases the reason Chinese lived in Chinatowns to begin with—in most cases, they were not allowed to live elsewhere. In addition, many Chinese were looking to move to houses outside Chinatown partly because they planned to have families, which is a reminder that it was only in 1943 that the Chinese Exclusion Act was lifted. Before that, immigration restrictions prevented many Chinese individuals from forming families. Thus, moving out of Chinatown was not a straightforward, positive story of Chinese becoming more "American" (read: white) but a more complicated one of important changes in domestic and international laws that led to changes in the demographics of Chinese communities and a gradual opening of some white communities to accepting some nonwhite neighbors.

There is further evidence that the Cold War era was not a time of an unequivocal increase in the acceptance of Asian Americans but rather one

STATEHOOD AMID COLD WAR POLITICS

that highlighted contradictory assumptions about Asians in the United States. While Asian Americans were lauded for their success and portrayed as representing the best that America had to offer the world, they were also viewed with deep suspicion, as "unassimilated aliens whose ties to their country of origin need to be monitored and regulated."[27] Asian Americans were assumed to be forever foreigners, forever tied to their countries of origin in a way that was not true of European immigrants and their descendants. This was particularly true of Chinese and Koreans in the United States—who were regularly accused of Communist affiliation—because of the involvement of China and Korea in Cold War politics. In the 1950s, federal officials put out an alarm that the United States was under threat from Communist Chinese spies who were entering the country illegally, thus justifying continued government surveillance of Chinese American communities.[28] Behind many worries over the potential Communist affiliation of U.S.-born Korean and Chinese Americans was an assumption that their loyalties would always lie with their "home" countries rather than the country of their birth. Many continued to view Asians in the United States as "foreign, subversive, suspect."[29]

HAWAI'I'S PLACE IN THE COLD WAR

Hawai'i came to play an outsized role in these domestic and global politics. Indeed, while Hawai'i was important as a U.S. military outpost and provided a strategic link to Asia, the Islands became even more valuable to the United States during the Cold War for other reasons. As the United States competed with the Soviet Union to gain allegiance from other countries, and as the Soviets drew attention to U.S. racial problems, Hawai'i was very useful to the U.S. state's goals and its attempt to develop a different discourse for and a new image of the United States. Hawai'i was touted as a "racial paradise" and an example of U.S. racial equality: "Unlike many parts of the mainland that called into question America's commitment to racial equality, Hawai'i appeared to present a ready-made model of interracial amity; it needed only to be exploited, not fostered through legislation or painful social change. . . . In short, Hawai'i's difference was turned into an instrument of American foreign policy."[30] Hawai'i's place in U.S. foreign policy was especially evident in discussions around statehood.

Debating Statehood

Discussions about whether Hawai'i should be made a U.S. state had been ongoing throughout the first half of the twentieth century, starting at least by the time of annexation in 1898. Hawai'i's petitions for statehood were rejected several times in the early decades of the twentieth century. Many of those discussions were centered on race and the small percentage of white people in the racial mix of Hawai'i's population. As early as annexation, concerns about potential statehood were being expressed. James Beauchamp Clark, a congressional representative from Missouri who would later become House Speaker, was one of many who publicly discussed the racial "problem" that Hawai'i presented. In 1898, on the floor of the House, he argued that the annexation of Hawai'i was dangerous, partly because it might subsequently lead to statehood. He described Native Hawaiians as "a lot of non-descript Asiatico-Polynesian ignoramuses." But he was more concerned about Asians and what it would mean to have Hawai'i representation in Congress: "How can we endure our shame when a Chinese Senator from Hawaii, with his pigtail hanging down his back, with his pagan joss in his hand, shall rise from his curule chair and in pigeon [*sic*] English proceed to chop logic with George Frisbie Hoar or Henry Cabot Lodge? O tempora! O mores!"[31] He wanted an alternative, some solution that would not "pollut[e] and weaken . . . our system of government by taking to our bosom a horde of Asiatic savages."[32]

Echoing the themes of those earlier debates, early postwar arguments around statehood included concerns about whether Hawai'i was truly American, whether the United States could endure the potential threat of such a large nonwhite population, and what other consequences statehood might have. To counter opposition to statehood, some pointed to how Hawai'i resembled other parts of the United States. For example, *Paradise of the Pacific*, an important tourist magazine that advertised Hawai'i to Americans, ran an article titled "Statehood for Hawaii's People" that argued that Hawai'i *was* American:

> Hawaii, in its urgent desire for immediate statehood, finds itself putting on two different faces for the eyes of the rest of the world. Like a married woman playing the part of a seductive mistress to her husband, Hawaii wants

STATEHOOD AMID COLD WAR POLITICS

to be known as an enchanted land with the exotic glamor of the 'foreign,' but also as a place that is as American as a hot dog at a drive-in.

The delightful fact is that both aspects of Hawaii are true. . . . This 'show case' of American democracy is peopled by men, women, and children whose ancestors came from divergent places yet who are as American as any fan who ever cheered for the Yankees or the Braves. . . . How these Americans of diverse origins work and play together as fellow Americans offers an example of living democracy unique in the eyes of the world. In this respect, Hawaii feels it has more to give than to gain as a result of statehood.[33]

But even though not all believed that Hawai'i posed a threat to the United States, such arguments that Hawai'i was similar to other parts of the country had not been effective. Clearly, Hawai'i was *not* like other places. Even though some 60 to 80 percent of Americans supported statehood for Hawai'i,[34] a vocal minority in Congress opposed it. Ambivalence about Hawai'i's place in the United States continued throughout the postwar years, when Hawai'i's difference—particularly its racial difference—was a central issue and raised questions about what it would mean to the future of the United States to admit a place where white people made up a minority of the population.[35] The nineteen Democratic senators who voted against the 1953 bill that would have given statehood to Alaska and Hawai'i were all from the Old South; their stance was a "last desperate, sometimes violent defense of racial segregation and white supremacy."[36]

Concerns were also raised about potential communist influence in the Territory, some of which came from the labor organizing and strikes that were taking place and some of which was connected to the ways that Korean Americans and Chinese Americans in the United States had been targeted as potential links to communist organizations in Asia. As mentioned, such targeting was often based in racist assumptions, as many American leaders assumed that all Asian Americans were more loyal to their Asian origins than to their American home.[37] This notion added a racialized component to the discussion of whether Hawai'i "deserved" statehood. Debates over statehood revealed not only American feelings about Hawai'i but also discourses of race and empire. Opponents showed deep distrust of Asian Americans and were concerned that white supremacy was losing its foundations.

STATEHOOD AMID COLD WAR POLITICS

Gradually, as the Cold War intensified and the United States grappled for ways to win over nonaligned nations, the statehood conversation shifted. Hawai'i's very difference and its racial makeup were seen as exactly the evidence the United States needed to project an image of its racial tolerance and inclusiveness. It was at this point that Hawai'i's racial composition—the very thing that had caused Hawai'i to be labeled dangerous—was reimagined as useful to U.S. state interests: its racial difference was now its strength. Here was a place where Chinese and Japanese had risen from the bottom of the social hierarchy to become powerful, that rise being evidence not only of their hard work but also of the tolerant society that would allow it.

Many in the U.S. government believed that statehood for Hawai'i would serve another useful purpose: a recasting of the nation's colonial history. During the Cold War era, the U.S. state supported the independence of many countries in the Global South, celebrating newfound breaks from colonial powers such as Britain and France. It maintained that stance even as it had also functioned as an imperial power itself in places such as Puerto Rico, the Philippines, and Guam. To be clear, U.S. arguments in favor of statehood were not for Hawai'i's independence but its incorporation into the United States—by doing so, the United States would appear tolerant and inclusive. It would also show that the United States could liberate less fortunate, less wealthy, less powerful areas by placing them under its tutelage and care. By advocating statehood for Hawai'i, the United States could thus veil its history as a colonial power in Hawai'i. Thus, while this narrative touted Hawai'i's great racial success, it also effectively kept Native Hawaiian claims to sovereignty or land out of sight; Hawaiians disappeared in this U.S. positioning, as their history, experiences, and claims would spoil the image of the United States as liberator and supporter of colonized peoples. Even the focus of the narrative—Asian Americans—carefully avoided the full history of Asians in the Islands: how they were stripped of citizenship at annexation, their inability to apply for citizenship until 1943 (Chinese), 1946 (Filipinos), or 1952 (Japanese), and the continued discrimination they endured in most aspects of their lives.

Making Hawai'i a state thus allowed the United States a way to assert its racial equality and avoid much of the evidence that contradicted that narrative. The United States silenced all discussion of Hawaiian sovereignty, instead positioning itself as a liberating force: "In contrast to the

STATEHOOD AMID COLD WAR POLITICS

Philippines's Cold War fate of decolonialization (or, rather, neocolonialism), Hawai'i's was incorporation. This approach emphasized America's modern and liberal embrace of diversity and inclusion, including discourses of multiculturalism and statehood deployed to mitigate accusations of US racial apartheid. As the more 'successful' colonial project, avoiding the expense and violence of an armed insurgency, Hawai'i was an ideal Cold War showcase that touted the rewards of US-style capitalism and military occupation. . . . Its inclusion in the union . . . legitimated the murky and contested origins of American occupation."[38]

Within Hawai'i, opinions on statehood varied. From a distance, it appeared that there was large support for statehood among residents. In 1959, a plebiscite asked residents whether they supported statehood; 90 percent of eligible voters cast a ballot, and they voted overwhelmingly in favor of statehood, at a margin of seventeen to one.[39] But a closer look at the support and opposition to statehood shows the ongoing racial politics in the Territory at the time. Haole elite believed that statehood was good for Hawai'i—and for themselves—because it meant closer ties to the United States, which would likely strengthen the economy; thus, they actively urged Congress to pass such a measure. Most Japanese and Chinese in Hawai'i also supported statehood, but their support was more complicated because of their recent history within U.S. jurisdiction. When Hawai'i was annexed to the United States in 1898, Asians lost their citizenship and voting rights, leaving most without citizenship to any state. Japanese and Chinese believed that statehood would give them U.S. citizenship. While they were aware of the poor treatment of Asians in the continental United States (until just a few years earlier, Asians born outside the country had not been allowed to become citizens, vote, or own land), Hawai'i's Asian communities thought statehood—and the rights to American citizenship it would give them—was the best opportunity for their future and were hopeful that statehood would give them a pathway to full acceptance into American political, economic, and social citizenship. But, notably, they were still looking for ways to prove themselves loyal Americans and deserving of full acceptance and believed that support for statehood signaled their patriotism. Native Hawaiians were opposed to statehood,[40] viewing the process as the last act in a series that had resulted in losing their land, their social standing, their power, and their country.

Over the next decade, Native Hawaiians would become increasingly vocal and active in their opposition to statehood and make more explicit what had been lost by their community. As Angela Krattinger states, "Statehood further absorbed the Hawaiian nation under the United States, making sovereignty and decolonization even further unimaginable."[41] The 1959 plebiscite was telling in this regard; voters were given a choice: did they support Hawai'i becoming a state, or did they want Hawai'i to remain a U.S. territory? Independence—the likely choice of most Hawaiians—was not on the ballot.[42]

For Hawai'i's leaders, statehood would mean that Hawai'i would be easier to sell as a tourist destination. With tourism growing rapidly, Hawai'i was becoming increasingly popular among Americans, and leaders in Hawai'i worked hard to strengthen the image of Hawai'i as a desirable vacation destination. This effort aligned with that of the United States to mark and celebrate its diverse ethnic population in ways that were safe, exotic, and marketable.

The rise of neoliberalism further shaped how Hawai'i—and racial diversity—were brought into the U.S. system: "As a set of theoretical principles legitimating political and economic restructuring in the interests of global capital, neoliberalism 'proposes that human well-being can best be advanced by liberating individual entrepreneurial freedoms and skills within an institutional framework characterized by strong private property rights, free markets, and free trade.'"[43] Hawai'i, with its new focus on tourism certainly met the requirement of free market offerings, and neoliberal perspectives began to dominate depictions of Hawai'i—those of American leaders and those within Hawai'i itself. But Hawai'i, with its "race problem," was also an early example of neoliberal multiculturalism, a framework for incorporating racial difference in to the neoliberal system. In these developing discourses, the achievements of Chinese and Japanese were central, and Native Hawaiians, and their loss of land and sovereignty, were further erased. Hawai'i itself was drawn as part of but apart from the United States in ways meant to entice interest in the Islands, but doing so also constructed it as different, always liminal, and reflecting a "useful foreignness."[44] Despite the significant difference in its geography and climate from that of the continental United States, it was Hawai'i's racial difference that was responsible for this construction, a construction that remains in use today.

STATEHOOD AMID COLD WAR POLITICS

CELEBRATING MULTICULTURAL HAWAI'I

In the discourses, arguments, and political actions in the years leading up to Hawai'i becoming a state in 1959, we can see that Hawai'i fit into—and reinforced—a neoliberal multicultural narrative, one that paints some groups as model minorities and disappears others. In America's careful reckoning and shaping of Hawai'i as a safe but different part of the United States, we see a foreshadowing of the racial politics that have shaped American society since.

Chinese and Japanese had long been seen as threatening to a white American nation. Japanese incarceration during World War II and the lengthy, often violent anti-Chinese movement in California were just two manifestations of this belief. How, then, could a territory like Hawai'i ever become a legitimate part of the United States? Hawai'i was not part of the continent, it was situated in the tropics, and 80 percent of its population was not white. Nevertheless, during the Cold War, many within the U.S. government came to recognize that Hawai'i was valuable to its military and state strategic interests. Many in Hawai'i also wanted inclusion in the United States. The solution to this seeming contradiction was to construct Asians in Hawai'i—and Hawai'i itself—as safe and nonthreatening.

This process involved constructing a narrative that made Asians in Hawai'i into model minorities. While the details of this model-minority discourse differed from that working in the continental United States, the Hawai'i version drew from that larger one and mimicked some of its key features. Asians in Hawai'i were described as hardworking and eager to get ahead by pursuing education and obtaining good jobs. They had risen from plantation laborers to successful business and community leaders. The daring exploits of Hawai'i's Japanese on the battlefields of World War II were seen as evidence of their Americanness: "Once marginalized and excluded from the American dream, Japanese American and Filipino American veterans enter into the body politic through military fraternity. Just as their militarized heroics are put on display in Hawai'i's military-tourist circuits, so too are their plantation labor pasts recycled for the tourist industry. . . . As good multicultural citizen-soldiers, their patriotism seals the permanence of Hawai'i's relationship to the United States in 1959."[45] Importantly, Hawai'i's model-minority framework fit into and supported neoliberal multiculturalism, a way to bring difference into neoliberal ideology.

STATEHOOD AMID COLD WAR POLITICS

A 1930 editorial in a major Hawai'i newspaper addressed the place of Chinese in the debate over race: "The Chinese citizen of Hawaii is the equal, physically, mentally, and morally of the citizens of any other ancestry. And their patriotism extends to all local endeavors, religious, welfare, sports, and drama. Hawaii is proud of its American citizens of Chinese ancestry. In this territory, one of the problems that has troubled the western world has been solved. There is no racial antagonism, but the most friendly feeling and communion among the citizens of Hawaii, of whatever ancestry."[46]

Reflecting this new framework of multicultural acceptance, the tourist magazine *Paradise of the Pacific* began to profile Chinese differently in its pages by the mid-twentieth century. Earlier, *Paradise* either downplayed the number of Chinese in the Islands or completely ignored their presence, as if by doing so it could sidestep the contentious issue of race in Hawai'i and thereby make the Islands more palatable to Americans.[47] But in the 1940s, the magazine shifted its approach. It had regularly run a column titled "American Families in Hawaii"; until the late 1940s, nearly all profiled families were haole, though occasionally a hapa–haole (Hawaiian–haole) family was featured. In 1947, the magazine broke new ground, running a profile of the Li family in which it highlighted the success of this Honolulu Chinese family of three doctors. The article pointed to how they had achieved success by "combining in their teachings the culture and moral virtues of China with the standards of the American way of life" and concluded that "the Li family symbolizes [the] blend of Chinese culture and American democracy."[48] In 1950, readers were introduced to the Herbert K. H. Lee family. Although Herbert's father was an immigrant from China, Herbert was now a senator in the Hawai'i legislature. He was well educated, a successful attorney, and had served as deputy attorney general for the Territory of Hawai'i. Herbert had an attractive, modern (read: Western) home (as readers could see in the photo spread), and an English name. "And what of the other brothers and sisters of this remarkable American-Chinese family?" the article asked. Herbert's brother, Dr. Richard Lee, was the director of the Hawai'i Board of Health, another was a statistician for the Hawaiian Pineapple Company, and another owned a successful flower business.[49] Such profiles were clearly meant to argue for the acceptance of Chinese as successful members of the community who had acquired the markers of white success—citizens to be admired, not feared.

It is important to recognize that alongside these stories of success, Chinese and Japanese continued to face discrimination and be seen as outsiders. Two student researchers who studied a local insurance firm provide an example. In this firm, all top positions were filled by haole. The researchers found that all haole respondents believed there was no discrimination in the firm, with one arguing, "If Orientals are not in the top positions in the company, it is because they would be unable to meet or entertain mainland business contacts. Some places these people could not take their visitors, and it would prove embarrassing for both the visitor and the host who is representing the company."[50] The Asian employees, on the other hand, insisted that discrimination against non-haole was widespread: "No matter what we do, no matter how long we stay here, we will never be able to become department heads. . . . Take R. C. for example. He came to work right after he graduated from McKinley [High School] and that was way back in the 20s. He started off as an office boy and now he probably knows more about automobile insurance than anyone in the office, including the officers and [department] heads. Back in '39, when Mr. ___ resigned, we all expected R. C. to get the job. But instead, Mr. ___ got it. After that, there were . . . two more resignations in the same [department] but still R. C. didn't get the job. After that, we realized that he would never get the job, no matter how hard he worked. We've all given up."[51] Another pointed out, "I think . . . they [the directors and officers] might not like the idea of an Oriental telling them what to do and what should be their insurance program."[52]

But even—or especially—amid such practices, Chinese and Japanese were depicted as desirable workers. Drawing on other elements of the larger model-minority framework, tourist publications, promotional materials, and arguments in Congress regularly pointed out that Chinese and Japanese did not make trouble—or even any noise, an assertion meant to highlight that they were not like African Americans who were involved in the ongoing civil rights movement. This model-minority rhetoric emphasized that Chinese and Japanese would work within the system and find a way to belong and to get ahead, rather than trying to change the system, for example, by protesting the discrimination they faced. The evidence for this notion includes the enormous sacrifices that Japanese Americans made in World War II—while so many were incarcerated at home—and the fact that Chinese had just put their heads down and carried on, finding success without looking for government handouts.

STATEHOOD AMID COLD WAR POLITICS

Along with and through the creation of Chinese as a model minority, Hawai'i itself was depicted as safe and nonthreatening, providing another argument for granting the Territory statehood. Here, it was not only that Chinese and Japanese immigrants and their descendants worked hard to succeed; the setting of Hawai'i also *allowed* them to succeed by creating opportunities for them. A speech by President John F. Kennedy in 1963 in which he held up Hawai'i as an example of racial harmony came of just such an argument.[53] In this depiction, Hawai'i was not simply like other places; rather, its racial difference was constructed as a strength, albeit it in small, careful amounts.

In its role as a tourist destination, Hawai'i was also promoted as deserving inclusion in the United States; visitors could get away from their ordinary lives and play in a tropical paradise, a place where there was no racial strife in spite of its diverse racial mix. It was just a little "oriental" or exotic but not enough to make it dangerous. *Paradise of the Pacific* thus enticed readers with headlines like "Slice of Orient Can Be Found in Hawaii"[54] and "Why Go to the Orient When We Have It Right Here?,"[55] which presented Hawai'i as an exotic but safe and accessible getaway. Even the Chinese community used these kinds of images; one editorial in the *Hawaii Chinese Journal* promoted Chinatown as a tourist draw, declaring "Here in Chinatown, merchants have a natural drawing card for tourists. Here is the Chinatown in the United States that takes tourists about as close to the Orient as most of them will ever get. Here is your atmosphere, of many races mingling in business, of strange goods, and exotic foods."[56] In these constructions, Hawai'i becomes attractively—and safely—different. The increase in travel as a newly available form of consumption plays an important role in this story; in it, Hawai'i was a marketable entity that was accessible to those looking to consume. As Vernadette Vicuña Gonzales has argued, "Tourism's amenability to delivering the values of consumer culture across borders made [Hawai'i] an ideal Cold War ambassador."[57]

These discourses all played into U.S. state goals during the Cold War. Hawai'i became the most visible example of U.S. racial harmony and opportunity, a site of both difference and acceptance. Importantly, and tellingly, these discourses are the basis of neoliberal multiculturalism, a framework in which difference is incorporated into a white-dominated system in careful, palatable ways. Not all difference is allowed easy entry into this system; rather, it is those who play by the rules—the rules of a white-dominated

STATEHOOD AMID COLD WAR POLITICS

system in which proper consumption is a key marker of success. Chinese and Japanese in Hawai'i fit well in this system, reinvigorating the "triumphant immigrant success story."[58] That this story fortified U.S. state Cold War arguments for world dominance is part of what made and continues to make Hawai'i valuable to the United States. It is not only a beautiful place to take a vacation but also one that, by its inclusion *in* the United States, reinforces U.S. rhetoric and U.S. justification for its powerful place in geopolitics. It was also used in narratives to convince countries in the Global South to align with the United States. Indeed, the U.S. decision to grant Hawai'i statehood came out of the country's Cold War goals and was as much connected to the U.S. role and design in global politics as to anything else. Importantly, the use of Hawaii in the narrative of U.S. racial tolerance and opportunity for all also allowed the United States to reframe its history of anti-Asian actions, including the recent incarceration of thousands of Japanese Americans; "Hawai'i could then be celebrated as a civil rights victory, a 'happy ending' and proof that America was amending its past. This narrative was particularly salient because it contrasted with the more pronounced racial disputes between white and black Americans."[59]

The very different place of Chinese and Native Hawaiians in these constructions of racial harmony is an indication of the depth—and limits—of such acceptance of difference, particularly in a settler colonial society like Hawai'i. While Hawai'i now included nonwhite individuals in its communities and its social, economic, and political structures, Hawai'i remained a white society—in the ways that the structure, the very bones, of the society were white and constructed from white-dominated (and Christian) frameworks.[60] Indeed, white influence was often as much about discourse and frameworks—for example, what counts as success—as any position in the state legislature. In the process of celebrating how a group like the Chinese could be successful in this system, what was being celebrated was the system itself, one that included only those groups that played by the (white) rules and worked to the advantage of the "whites in charge."

Importantly, the "avenues laid out for success and empowerment are paved over Native lands and sovereignty."[61] Indeed, during the same postwar years, Native Hawaiians lost out completely. Not only were their strengths and resources diminished by haole intrusion, but they were also not part of the foreign strategies of the U.S. state. Their story was one that named the United States as an empire that stole lands from indigenous peoples,

STATEHOOD AMID COLD WAR POLITICS

overthrew a legitimate state, and continued to oppress those people once it was firmly in charge. As in other settler colonial states, in Hawai'i, indigenous peoples and their history and struggles were erased. That story, of course, did not align with U.S. attempts to depict the United States as a liberating, accepting, and anti-racist force around the world.

THE ROLE OF CHINESE IN COLD WAR U.S. RACIAL POLITICS

The Cold War years were significant for Asians living in the United States and in Hawai'i. It was at this time that Chinese found a place in Hawai'i society. But, importantly, this society was organized around a settler colonial presence, and Chinese had not played the same colonial role as haole. Indeed, in 1848, at the time of the Māhele land division—when all land was privatized and Hawaiians lost the bulk of it—Chinese had not yet arrived in Hawai'i in substantial numbers. Nevertheless, Chinese and Japanese in Hawai'i did play a part in the settler colonial system and have ever since. Their roles relate to how they bought into the system, and we can see their increasing acceptance of the system in their success in the postwar years. Chinese had faced a lot of difficulties and discrimination as they worked to find a way into Hawai'i society, finding occupational niches and specialties that fit into the haole-dominated system. In the process of gaining acceptance in Hawai'i society, they came to align their fates with that of haole by believing in their system. To be clear: by the time they were leaving plantation work at the end of the nineteenth century, there was only one system to make their way into—that built and controlled by haole, which reflected Hawai'i's version of "deep and malleable whiteness."[62] It is important to keep in mind the absolute power over the Islands of those who established, ran, and controlled the sugar industry, their overwhelming, all-encompassing power in the Islands. Given that dominance, it is not really clear what else any outside group could have done under the circumstances. But Chinese did find a way to benefit from the settler colonial system. And they benefited from how haole treated the Native Hawaiian community.

Two of the most obvious examples of how Chinese benefited at the expense of Native Hawaiians occurred in the mid-twentieth century: land acquisition and statehood. In both, the Chinese were not initiators of the events, but we have seen how they benefited from them. Hawaiian land loss gave Chinese the opportunity to buy land and accumulate property

STATEHOOD AMID COLD WAR POLITICS

assets, an important element of their economic success. Their support of statehood might have been even more significant, in that it not only shored up the vote for statehood in the Islands but also reinforced a particular ideology. The support of Asians in Hawai'i for statehood provided ballast to arguments about the United States being racially tolerant. And their socioeconomic rise became an important talking point—for haole, for white Americans, and for Asians themselves—and became particularly important during Cold War struggles as the United States tried to sell itself as a country where all could succeed, no matter their race or ethnicity. In their support, Asians indicated their belief in the white system, a system of neoliberal multiculturalism. In the process of statehood, which involved the claim of Hawai'i's Asians being loyal citizens who had succeeded the American way, the story of the Hawaiians was ignored and buried. According to Sarah Miller-Davenport, "While Hawai'i's Asian population was celebrated because of how they might aid United States-Asia relations, Native Hawaiians, with no obvious racial role to play in the Cold War, were largely absent in the statehood debates."[63] Asian "statehood advocates, in holding up their rights to full U.S. citizenship, ignored the long-standing, competing rights claims of Native Hawaiians who sought not membership in the American union, but independence from it."[64]

It was not a coincidence that the narrative of Asian success and the erasure of Native Hawaiian history both became prominent in the postwar years; these stories underscored the usefulness of Hawai'i statehood for the U.S. state in its designs for world power and dominance. These stories have had long legacies. Out of these years came an argument that the United States provides opportunity for people of all backgrounds. In fact, neoliberal multiculturalism does allow for some difference in the white system. Nonwhite groups who behave themselves and follow the rules—and who are most likely to accept what Lani Guinier and Gerald Torres have called a "racial bribe"[65]—are given a place in the system, although one that is not equal to that of white people. What is considered acceptable behavior is rooted in consumption as a measure of success—having the right house, the right education, the right job. If you work hard, keep your head down, and do what is expected of you, then you will succeed—the American system will *allow* you to succeed. Chinese adopted this neoliberal ideology, frequently citing their successes—particularly their economic successes—in their argument for inclusion into the polity as early as 1898, at the time of annexation. And throughout the twentieth century, they continued to use their hard work and subsequent achievements—their rags-to-riches story—as evidence that they belonged and should be treated as equal to any other Hawai'i residents. We see these arguments in their protection of Chinatown as well, which became a visual representation of Chinese success in Hawai'i. This is, of course, the model-minority story: the story of success through hard work, proper consumption, and avoiding racial unrest. And one that pits the stereotyped model minority against groups who are *not* considered model minorities. It is not only Black people and their efforts in the civil rights movement that take on a more menacing character in such a framing. Native Hawaiians, too, become part of the nondeserving.[66]

Thus, in the Cold War years, we can see how Hawai'i was constructed—by both outsiders and those in Hawai'i—to support several existing and future discourses. Most immediately, Hawai'i became an important tool for growing American dominance in the world, particularly in Asia and the Pacific. Held up as a site of racial difference and harmony and equal opportunity for all, Hawai'i served to silence those who pointed to American racial disharmony and inequality and, in turn, acted as an enticement for countries to align with U.S. interests and against those of the Soviet Union.

But the legacy of these developments goes further. The discourse around immigrant success and racial opportunity bolsters an argument for multiculturalism that is pleasantly compatible with neoliberalism. In these racial and ethnic constructions, the seeds of a model-minority ideology are evident. We see this clearly in the relationship between Hawai'i and the United States, but the United States extends the model and its assertion of U.S. benevolence beyond U.S. borders. For example, as Cindy Cheng argues, the Museum of Modern Art's *Family of Man* exhibit in 1955 endorsed this vision of the United States. The exhibit, composed of five hundred photographs, emphasized that all cultures share many important things, like birth, death, love, and happiness. The message was that differences across the world are to be accepted and celebrated. The U.S. government sponsored a world tour of the exhibit, thus sending the message that the United States would lead the way through cultural and racial differences to a peaceful world. It is notable that the exhibit toured during the very years that the question of Hawai'i's statehood was being discussed.

STATEHOOD AMID COLD WAR POLITICS

As Cheng argues, "The early cold war years . . . saw the growing appeal of a multicultural vision that looked to bridge the social and political divisions by transcending the recognition of difference."[67] Hawai'i played a key role in supporting that vision.

Hawai'i became the fiftieth U.S. state in 1959. From that point forward, Hawai'i has navigated the tension of being different from the rest of the United States and yet a legitimate part of the nation. Race continues to play a role in these maneuvers. As we will see in the following chapter, Chinatown took on a new shape in the midst of changes in the Cold War rhetoric about race, difference, consumption, and empire—and in how Hawai'i could best position itself within the U.S. sphere. Hawai'i has worked to project itself as a tourist destination different from others, as a bridge to Asia and other points in the Pacific, as a trans-Pacific financial hub, and as an important U.S. military outpost. In the process, difference has become an important selling point for Hawai'i, but that difference has been carefully choreographed against a background of U.S. world dominance, a history of settler colonialism, and a global capitalist system in which consumption plays a central role. These discourses would lead to a reinvigorated Chinatown as Hawai'i's Chinese—and many others—worked to make the area a celebration of all that Hawai'i had to offer the United States.

Chapter Five

RECONSTRUCTING CHINATOWN
FOR A NEW ERA

Statehood in 1959 was a watershed event for Hawai'i but also one of many in a process that had been underway for decades. The provision of statehood meant that Hawai'i's (haole) leaders no longer needed to wheedle, cajole, argue for or position themselves in relation to Americans, at least in the way they had had to do for decades. Now, Hawai'i was part of the United States. But Hawai'i was not like other states, and the next decades would underscore Hawai'i's differences. The differences and similarities between Hawai'i and other states were clear in the changes that took place in and around Honolulu's Chinatown in the years after Hawai'i was granted statehood. During the next two decades, two processes were most important to Chinatown—to its size, character, meaning, and survival. The first was the process of massive urban renewal that was undertaken in the area. And the second was the process of Honolulu designating Chinatown a historic district in 1973, officially the Chinatown Historic District. In this chapter, I explore how those processes developed and their outcomes. As has been true throughout the history of Chinese in Hawai'i, urban renewal and historic designation took place against a larger background of the events of the 1960s and 1970s, which involved U.S. geopolitics, issues of race and ethnicity in the United States, the relationship between Hawai'i and the United States, and the changing racial, political, and economic climate in Hawai'i. Once again, these experiences underscore how place—the place of

RECONSTRUCTING CHINATOWN FOR A NEW ERA

Chinatown—is meaningful and how it is imbued with and influences the politics around it.

THE U.S. CONTEXT

Hawai'i's statehood came at a time of significant U.S. turmoil. One major tension that defined the United States at the time was around race. In the 1960s and 1970s, the U.S. civil rights movement was fully underway. People were in the streets fighting for change, the courts were busy addressing challenges to existing and new laws involving race, and ordinary people were witnessing these struggles in the streets and in public institutions such as courts, schools, or restaurants. The United States seemed poised to move away from its long history of racist laws and ready to enact new laws and systems that would open up American society to African Americans. Increasing attention was also being paid, and efforts were also being made, to address the needs of other groups who had been left out of America's polity. Native Americans and gay and lesbian people began to seek changes in their status as Americans. The women's movement grew increasingly vocal, organized, and effective as feminists pushed for gender equality. This was the time when Asians in the United States began to use "Asian American" to describe themselves, a term that originated in student activist groups in California and was meant to signal a new pan-Asian coalition that would stand together against racism and against U.S. empire building in Asia. Adding to the turmoil, during these decades the United States was deeply involved in a war in Southeast Asia which served as a highly visible marker of U.S. connections to and ambitions in Asia. It was also a widely unpopular war, and it, too, brought turmoil to the country's streets, schools, and courts as those opposed to the war made their stances known and sought to avoid and end the draft. With U.S. withdrawal from Vietnam in 1973 and the end of the war in 1975, thousands of refugees from Southeast Asia made their way to the United States, creating new populations of racial minorities that arose because of U.S. involvement in Asia. These efforts and changes did not happen without resistance. Many Americans felt their country was under siege, and some worried about what the future would look like and whether and how they would be included in the new America. The result was often violent attacks on those seeking change— from police, government, and school officials and from ordinary citizens.

RECONSTRUCTING CHINATOWN FOR A NEW ERA

The United States was also experiencing economic growth. The mean income of U.S. families increased by an average of 2.5 percent between 1950 and 1960. Both poorer and well-off families saw growth in their incomes, with families with incomes in the lowest quintile experiencing a growth of 3.7 percent and the richest families experiencing a growth of 2.2 percent. This was an era of a growing middle class. This widespread economic growth translated into more families and individuals having discretionary income that they might use to travel and take vacations. And this growth happened as air travel became more affordable, bringing Hawai'i closer to the continental United States in many ways.

IN HAWAI'I

Changes were also underway in Hawai'i. Perhaps most significant were the continuing changes in the long-standing racialized power structure. While haole remained in positions of power, other groups began moving into top economic and political positions. As we saw in chapter 4, the 1954 Democratic Revolution brought increasing numbers of Japanese into the state government and, especially after statehood, into federal positions. Chinese movement into powerful positions might have been less visible than that of Japanese, but if so, that was mostly because they were fewer in number. Hiram Fong, for example, became the first Chinese American and the first Asian American to serve as a U.S. senator; he served from 1959 until 1977. In many ways, Fong exemplified the growing success of Chinese in Hawai'i. He grew up in the Honolulu neighborhood of Kalihi, one of eleven children of a former sugar plantation worker who had migrated from China in the late nineteenth century. Fong attended public schools in Hawai'i and graduated from McKinley High School in 1924, where his story was shared by many other students, including Daniel Inouye, who would also rise from humble beginnings to become a U.S. Senator. From McKinley High School, Fong went on to the University of Hawai'i and in 1935 received a law degree from Harvard University before entering into a lifetime of political involvement and financial success.

After statehood, Native Hawaiians remained marginalized; Hawaiian communities were suffering some of the worst moments of their history as statehood seemed to remove any possibility of reclaiming their land.

RECONSTRUCTING CHINATOWN FOR A NEW ERA

The numbers of Hawaiians had declined to around eleven thousand,[1] and indicators in health, income, and other areas made clear that Native Hawaiians were positioned at the bottom of the new state's hierarchies, whether measured by wealth, poverty rates, educational attainment, health, or land ownership.[2] But this was also a time of regrouping and regathering for Hawaiians. The Hawaiian Renaissance, which started around 1970, drew from U.S. social movements demanding change in the social order. Efforts focused on a wide range of issues, from restoring Hawaiian culture, such as music and dance, to beginning a renewed effort to reclaim Hawaiian sovereignty. Recovering the Hawaiian language also became an important goal, and the community made renewed efforts to teach Hawaiian children their language. It was during this era that hula was reestablished as central to Hawaiian culture and Hawaiian navigation ways were restored through the construction and sailing of the Hōkūleʻa, a Polynesian canoe built to represent the wayfaring experiences of the earliest Hawaiians. But the central issue of the time was the recovery of land rights.

The increased visibility and vocalization of Native Hawaiians was connected to another important change in Hawaiʻi: the rise of tourism. Hawaiʻi had been attempting to increase tourism in the Islands for decades, but as the sugar industry declined, tourism received even more attention. Some key figures at the center of the industry became central to the development of tourism as many sugar corporations shifted their investments and land use from sugar production to tourism. The timing of sugar's decline was also important because it happened as tourism was on the rise across the world. Air travel became more affordable, making Hawaiʻi a more possible destination for many. Tourist numbers to Hawaiʻi grew between the end of World War II and 1960, but those numbers doubled between 1958 and 1960 and then grew even more rapidly. By 1970, Hawaiʻi saw 1.7 million tourists each year, a ten-fold increase since 1958, and that traffic brought more money into the state than did the U.S. military.[3] Numbers continued to climb, and by 2000, visitors outnumbered residents at a ratio of close to 6 to 1.[4] In the early years, the tourist market was made up mostly of Americans, but in the 1970s, tourism from Japan began to expand and in the 1980s, grew rapidly.[5] Thus, especially in the early years of the tourism boom, Hawaiʻi looked to the continental United States for visitors.

The shift of the economy to tourism affected all aspects of life in Hawai'i. The tourist industry soon employed a significant proportion of Hawai'i's workers, from service workers to investment entrepreneurs. The Islands began to shape themselves around this business, and, in the process, race was once again front and center.

In promoting itself as a desirable tourist destination, Hawai'i had to position itself to stand out from other destinations. Americans might be more inclined to go someplace much closer, like Florida, if they wanted to escape winter and find a bit of sun. Or perhaps it was Europe—with its combined foreignness and familiarity—that would draw tourists. The Caribbean was also a competing attraction, with its similar tropical seas and shores. Certainly, Hawai'i's physical beauty—with its blue oceans and magnificent mountains—was a strong draw. But Hawai'i also began to develop another way to attract tourists: advertising its multiculturalism. Hawai'i promoted itself as a safe nonwhite place, a place home to peoples of many ethnicities, where English was spoken, and a visitor could have Japanese food for lunch, Korean barbeque for dinner, and an American breakfast.

In this multicultural construction, difference shifted from being something to hide to being something to celebrate, and a way to mark and sell Hawai'i. Of course, it was not just difference but a particular version of difference. Hawai'i began to promote itself not just as a tropical paradise but also as a racial paradise, where people of many races and ethnicities lived together without rancor or tension. Here, racial capitalism—"the process of deriving social or economic value from the racial identity of another person"[6]—was at play. To sell racial difference, Hawai'i's tourist leaders needed—again—to make Hawai'i's nonwhite population appear safe, this time for white visitors (who, until Japanese tourist numbers started increasing in the 1970s, made up the bulk of tourists in Hawai'i). They did that by constructing Japanese and Chinese in Hawai'i as model minorities, which was an especially effective move at the time, given the civil rights activism in the United States. The discourse drew from the World War II and Cold War eras and counted on the tales brought home by soldiers who had been stationed in or passed through Hawai'i. At the same time, Native Hawaiians were represented in much tourist literature as entertaining and interesting—and nonthreatening; indeed, it was these portrayals of Hawaiians and the use of their culture by the tourist industry that helped galvanize Native Hawaiians to organize a stronger resistance to the ways the tourist industry (and others) used their culture, communities, and land.[7]

THE RELATIONSHIP BETWEEN HAWAI'I
AND THE UNITED STATES

The rise of tourism and its goals squared well with the continuing development of the relationship between Hawai'i and the continental United States. The U.S. military buildup in Hawai'i paralleled and supported tourism as tourism and militarism "jointly enable overlapping projects of colonialism, developmentalism, and neoliberalism."[8] The military presence can be seen as jumpstarting the tourist trade, partly in how Hawai'i was used as a site for troops' R&R in World War II; "tourist" expenditures by military personnel in 1945 far exceeded those of sugar or pineapple production.[9] After the war, the large military population meant there was a large population of mostly white Americans in Hawai'i helping to develop the industry.

The U.S. military also continued to focus on Asia, and Hawai'i continued to be an important outpost for maneuvers and wars. Japanese Americans—who were assumed to have language and cultural knowledge that would be useful in that context—were recruited to work in U.S.-occupied Japan after the war, and Japanese in Hawai'i were an obvious target for this recruitment.[10] The United States was still locked into a Cold War struggle with the Soviet Union and trying to encourage alignment with many countries in the Global South who had achieved independence from their colonizers. In addition, the United States was now in a full-out war in Vietnam. All the events, processes, and ideologies of the time meant that Hawai'i remained a key site for U.S. interests in Asia and the Pacific. Not only did the Vietnam War mean that troops passed through Hawai'i, but Hawai'i was also used as a simulated site for training soldiers on their way to fight in Southeast Asia.[11] With Hawai'i's terrain and its Asians and Pacific Islanders being used as stand-ins for Vietnam and enemy Vietnamese, this mock-village staging of war further inscribed Hawai'i's difference and foreignness.

American leaders' concerns about Hawai'i's "race problem" did not simply disappear after statehood. But it did take on new elements. Before statehood, attention was focused on whether a territory with an overwhelmingly nonwhite population could really be American. After statehood, the question turned to how Hawai'i might best serve the United States. In the search for answers, race was again central. Given its location, Hawai'i was touted as a connection to Asia, thus furthering U.S. interests there. That connection was partly about its location, midway between North America and Asia.

RECONSTRUCTING CHINATOWN FOR A NEW ERA

And it was also about how Hawai'i's Asian population made that connection seem natural. Once again, Hawai'i was considered part of, yet apart from, the United States, with its people "not quite" regular Americans. The use of Hawai'i and its citizens to prepare U.S. soldiers for war in Asia is just one example of how the United States positioned the Islands. In 1960, the U.S. Congress established the East-West Center to foster better relations across the Pacific Ocean. Congress and the U.S. Department of State argued that Hawai'i "offered special advantages for a national institution with an Asia Pacific focus that could not be duplicated anywhere else in the country."[12]

Hawai'i's leaders were also considering the relationship between Hawai'i and the United States and how Hawai'i might take advantage of its new standing. With its new status as a state, Hawai'i wanted to deepen connections with the United States and receive support for its goals. Even though—but also because—its social and economic landscapes differed from those of most parts of the United States, Hawai'i was able to capitalize on its relative position. It drew from American discourse, too, and increasingly positioned itself as a gateway to Asia. Even before statehood, Hawai'i's leaders touted its Asia connections. In 1952 in a communication with a U.S. Senate committee, the president of the Honolulu Chamber of Congress, Farrant Turner, argued, "We are very close to Asia and have good intelligence from the countries of the Far East as well as Southeast Asia."[13] Long after World War II ended, Hawai'i's leaders continued to welcome the military's use of the Islands as a valuable training ground, and supported increased military connections, seeing the economics of military presence as beneficial to the new state.[14] With U.S. involvement in wars in Korea and Vietnam, that military relationship deepened Hawai'i's position as a symbol of U.S. empire building and its special place in the American discourse of "racialized and gendered notions of benevolence, protection, and uplift."[15] In this way, Hawai'i continued to have an important role in the U.S. empire, but it was a different one from those of other places occupied by the United States. Of the territories "acquired" or stolen by the U.S. government in the late nineteenth century, including Guam, the Philippines, and Puerto Rico, only Hawai'i was fated for statehood.

Thus, as Hawai'i's relationship with the United States changed with statehood, the new state vied for more acceptance by Americans. Given its many differences from other U.S. states, that meant managing those differences and constructing them in ways that would not penalize Hawai'i and might even work to its benefit. Along with the militarization of Hawai'i, the Islands also had to wrestle with definitions of modernity, American, and, as we will see, urban, all amid the racialization of these discourses. Were there changes that Hawai'i should make to encourage Americans to consider Hawai'i a real part of the United States? All of the change Hawai'i was experiencing, as well as the debates over Hawai'i's inclusion in a new vision of the United States, influenced the changes that occurred in Chinatown after statehood.

URBAN RENEWAL COMES TO HONOLULU

Hawai'i engaged in many of the same postwar ideas and constructions that were occurring in the continental United States. There, as suburbanism and middle-class family values took hold as symbols of the new prosperous and powerful America, consumption increased. Questions about what to do about the deterioration of urban areas (especially after the "white flight" to the suburbs) were important in planning circles. Hawai'i, even as an outsider, witnessed these changes and began to participate in them. Hawai'i also began demonstrating its new status as a state through the erection of government buildings that would help claim its place in the United States. As in many places, consumption was at the core of many of Hawai'i's new urban projects. Ala Moana and Pearlridge, huge shopping mall complexes, were built in 1959 and 1972, respectively, drawing shoppers and reshaping the city in important ways. Honolulu was taking shape as a hub of finance, consumption, and tourism.

No process had more influence on Honolulu's Chinatown than the urban renewal program that swept through the United States during these years. Between 1949 and 1974, the federal government encouraged and funded a process in urban areas across the country that demolished old buildings and neighborhoods in the interest of remaking cities and getting rid of urban blight. Through funding and loans given to local governments, the federal government underwrote local urban redevelopment efforts. These moneys were attractive to areas that had seen declines in tax revenues from central urban areas as white people moved out of cities and into suburbs. Large highway construction projects were also underway.

Whatever the original intentions, by the 1960s, there was much criticism of the program, because of both the destruction of neighborhoods and communities and the lack of new affordable housing or, in some places, replacements for what had been razed. Originally, the program was meant to allow the construction of both business and residential areas, thus renewing and resettling urban areas in modernized settings. While federal money was available for razing buildings, local municipalities were responsible for rebuilding. Because municipalities were eager to grow their tax bases, they looked more favorably on making room for commercial businesses than for low- or middle-income housing. In most places, the urban renewal program ended up displacing poor and marginalized communities who were unable to afford to live in the newly created places. Lost, too, were small and family-owned businesses. The underlying argument for this process was that economic success—embodied in shiny, tall new buildings that housed big corporations and companies—encourages strength, modernity, and success.

By the 1970s, many communities had begun to mobilize against these kinds of changes, particularly nonwhite communities who had experienced the worst effects of urban renewal. African American and Puerto Rican communities were disrupted and displaced through gentrification and were often targeted for complete clearance. The growing civil rights movements of the era gave voice to the resistance of these groups and their increasingly marginalized presence and lives in urban areas. Partly because of their proximity to central downtown areas, urban renewal efforts around Chinatowns were often undertaken with a goal of replacing crowded areas of Chinatowns with public buildings that would revive the downtowns.[16] But across urban areas, "urban renewal aimed to preserve middle class whites' attachments to downtown, partly by expulsing poor minority neighborhoods."[17]

Along with many other cities in the United States, Honolulu sought and received federal money to redevelop its inner city, seeing in redevelopment a potential to increase the tax base of its downtown area. And early in the process were hints that the priority of urban renewal efforts would be economic potential rather than affordable housing and the likely harm that urban renewal would inflict on poorer communities. As one early redevelopment document made clear, "Land for multi-family structure use in this general district [a Chinatown area] does not command as high a price as does land for business use."[18] At least some in Hawai'i also had another goal for urban renewal: after the protracted struggle for statehood and the

RECONSTRUCTING CHINATOWN FOR A NEW ERA

depiction of Hawai'i as less "modern" than other places, perhaps a new profile for its capital city would lead to Hawai'i being accepted in Washington and in the United States as completely as any other state. In this process, Hawai'i drew from the established discourse of what makes a city modern and successful—in its looks, in who lives there, and in the central place that consumption holds.

Chinatown and nearby areas were key targets of Honolulu's urban renewal projects. These areas were close to the central business district and thus more visible and more valuable than some other areas. These areas had a number of poorly maintained residences and were neighborhoods of mostly poor and nonwhite residents, whose voices were not usually part of the public record.

Some hoped that the increasing tourist market might be able to revive Chinatown, to bring it out of the difficult war years, without it being destroyed. *Hawaii Chinese Weekly* published a plaintive editorial in 1959:

> For many years the people of the Chinese community and the Chinese Chamber of Commerce have talked about a 'new Chinatown.' They have tried to brighten the present one up . . . but with little success. With statehood, undoubtedly, before long, tourism will be Hawaii's leading industry. To share in this growth, Chinatown must be made appealing to the tourist. Now is the time for the community to stop talking and to begin its planning. The Chinese in Hawaii have in the past always been aggressors and leaders in all fields of endeavor. Are we to rest on our laurels or will we progress with the rest of Hawaii?[19]

But any such efforts were unsuccessful in the face of interest in urban renewal.

There had long been interest in improving the Chinatown area. Even in the 1930s, many argued for clearing what some considered the "slum areas" of Chinatown; parts of Chinatown had flooded in the huge storm of February 1935, leaving some streets under three to six feet of water.[20] But any such plans were delayed by the war. With newly available federal funding after the war, plans began anew. The newly created (and federally funded) Honolulu Redevelopment Agency (HRA) supervised a process in which the city and federal governments purchased "blighted" properties and relocated residents from those areas. The federal government provided two-thirds of the funding for these first stages. The land was then sold to private developers who would build new structures on the land, adhering to HRA guidelines.[21]

The first urban renewal work actually began in the early 1950s, before Hawai'i was a state, and focused on the peripheral areas of Chinatown. In the late 1950s, the HRA "planned to clear and redevelop about 182 acres between School and King Streets, and from Liliha to Queen Emma Streets. The area comprised almost one-third of Honolulu's urban core."[22] After much controversy over the design and function of the proposed project, the Queen Emma Project went ahead in 1962 and was completed in 1964 with three high-rise towers forming the new Queen Emma Gardens. For the first decades, the five hundred apartments were rented to moderate-income households, but in 1996, the buildings were converted to condominiums and sold at market value.[23]

That project kick-started the focus on "fixing" Chinatown and surrounding areas, with urban renewal projects taking an increasing toll on Chinatown as they moved closer to Chinatown's core. With each project, the shape and spirit of the area were further affected. The Kukui Project began deconstruction of seventy-five acres of urban blocks adjacent to Chinatown in the early 1960s. The site lay just north of Chinatown's core. Two important neighborhoods—Hell's Half Acre and Tin Can Alley—were involved. Before World War II, these areas contained "five chop suey houses, twenty-one cafes, eleven beer parlors, two poolrooms, two movie theaters, a toy store, dance hall, five jewelry stores, two meat markets, sixteen dry goods stores, one doctor and three liquor stores," as well as seventeen thousand residents (one-eighth of Honolulu's population) living in low-income housing.[24] After these areas were destroyed as part of urban renewal efforts, the city eventually built Kukui Gardens in 1970, housing low- and medium-income families in 389 units in twenty three-story buildings. It has remained as affordable housing and is now managed by EAH Housing (from its original name, the Ecumenical Association for Housing), a nonprofit corporation that develops and manages affordable rental properties. As part of the Kukui urban renewal project, Honolulu Tower was also built in 1982; a forty-one-story high-rise, its 396 apartments were and are sold at market value.[25]

An early construction project that literally overshadowed Chinatown was the Kukui Tower, a thirty-two-story apartment building with 308 units.

It was built in 1976 by private developers who worked with the city to provide affordable housing and is now operated by EAH Housing. Although Honolulu Tower and Kukui Tower were on the outskirts of Chinatown, their height meant they were visible throughout the area. A later project focused on the Aʻala area, at the Ewa end of Chinatown. Vineyard Boulevard, which ran just mauka (north) of Chinatown, was also expanded in the 1970s. The Pauahi Project, begun in the 1970s and completed in 1981, focused on a two-block area of Chinatown and received federal funding to raze the structures there. While some affordable housing was built after the area's destruction, it did not meet the needs of the displaced residents.

Each project contributed to the diminishment of Chinatown, and the changes brought about by urban renewal have haunted the area ever since. The justification of the projects was that these areas had been home to buildings that were "dilapidated" and "substandard." Indeed, the condition of buildings in these areas and in Chinatown more generally, was poor. But as was true in many other urban areas, the new development wiped out vibrant communities and left former residents with little future. As the activist Nancy Bannick argued, "The HRA destroyed a friendly neighborhood of old style plantation-like wooden houses. They called it substandard, but those owners had their gardens, their little shops, shrines, temples and ethnic societies."[26] A Chinese student researcher wrote about Hell's Half Acre, for example, as "the kind of environment which our family thrived in for over twenty years." She remembered her childhood in the area fondly, in spite of the difficulties her family faced: her mother was widowed and raising four children on her own without many resources. But the author countered the assumption that the area was terrible to grow up in, insisting that "our neighborhood was a good one . . . everyone was friendly with each other and enjoyed each other's company. . . . Living in such a neighborhood makes on[e] realize the feeling of friendship with one another." She describes receiving an eviction notice from the HRA as producing "the frantic hunt for a home."[27] Another student researcher who had lived in Chinatown for sixteen years concurred: "To residents in other parts of Honolulu," he wrote, "Chinatown is where much vice and crime are prevalent, the stamping ground of socially undesirable persons." But he argued that those assumptions were inaccurate: "Contrary to popular belief, Chinatown is not an area inhabited solely by indigents and undesirables. The economic status of the residents runs the gamut, from a relatively low point of the social scale, through the middle portion, up to the upper portion of the scale. . . . The social undesirables constitute merely a minority of the total inhabitants."[28] He pointed to the many social institutions—stores, language schools, clubs, clan and tong (organization) groups, business clubs, and benevolent societies—that anchored the community and made the area attractive to many. Nevertheless, the physical conditions of the area drew the greater attention of those interested in redeveloping the area. These conditions highlighted how badly served poorer communities were; most residents did not own their homes and were unable to get landlords to make necessary improvements, leading to further decline in the housing stock and neighborhood.

An example of such a community that was on the list of those threatened was "Old Vineyard" (OV) in the Vineyard Boulevard area. In 1973, the city proposed razing the community as part of the planned capital improvement projects. The government was looking to create "a historic, cultural, and scenic district." By clearing OV, the city could build a parking garage to service employees working in government buildings nearby. OV was composed of about sixty-two households, most living in apartments, and some small businesses near the central business district. Most residents were low income or living on a pension and renting their apartments, and most buildings were in good condition. Evictions of community residents would mean complete displacement because there was no housing similarly affordable in the area. "OV is truly an urban neighborhood where its people earn their living in construction, as carpenters, and cooks. Yet the community itself, with its many trees, well-tended gardens and walkways, and cleanliness, reflects a sense of pride in belonging." One resident explained, "All of us consider ourselves lucky to have found this place. Not only because it is affordable and convenient, but because we have good neighbors and a good neighborhood."[29] But the efforts to retain their community and support from outside groups were unsuccessful, and the neighborhood was razed within the year.

What was planned to replace these razed neighborhoods was as important as what was destroyed. In the place of the destroyed mixed-zone communities, which housed apartments, churches and temples, small family businesses, and schools, were plans to erect large multiblock high rises with rigid zoning laws.[30] This type of urban renewal underscores how Honolulu—and Chinatown—underwent massive changes as the image of

RECONSTRUCTING CHINATOWN FOR A NEW ERA

what a modern cityscape should look like took hold in Honolulu's planning offices.

Opposition to urban renewal projects grew. Some came from individual shop owners who saw value in staying in Chinatown. In 1977, one small shop owner explained his decision to stay in Chinatown: "I guess if I wanted a high-key business, I would have gone to the shopping center, uh, cause that's where everything is at. But I, what I created here in Chinatown was my shop, my . . . studio, our factory, our living, my living quarters. And I really like it. . . . I felt I needed to come back here, establish my business here, and in my own way try to save a little bit of old Honolulu that is dying so rapidly. . . . More people . . . [are] heading back this direction again . . . small business, uh, the almost mama-papa kinda store where . . . it's very important in this day and age, I think."[31]

Other opposition was more organized. A group called People Against Chinatown Evictions (PACE) focused its efforts on threatened evictions in the central Chinatown area. Using community meetings, petitions to the government, posters, and community organizing, it argued that any new urban renewal project in Chinatown would be disastrous for the residents of the area. They shone a light on who was living in Chinatown: mostly immigrants, retired former plantation workers, renters, and people living on low incomes. One of its publications spelled out what would be lost:

> Many of us are retired Filipino workers who worked on the sugar and pineapple plantations to help build Hawaii's economy. There are also families and other ethnic groups (Chinese, Korean, Japanese, Hawaiian etc.) who call Chinatown home. Courtyards and low rise buildings where we can socialize with our friends and neighbors is an important part of our lifestyle. We need places we can relax and talk story, have gatherings, let our children play, and keep animals. Gardens are a vital part of our lives since the fruits and vegetables we grow supplement our limited income and provide nutritious meals. We depend upon the many kinds of small businesses in Chinatown to meet our basic needs of food and clothing. Here all are within walking distance.[32]

PACE—through its publications, street actions, and legislative efforts—focused on the ways that Chinatown evictions and redevelopment were ultimately about making money for wealthy developers. Promises to build new low-income housing rarely materialized, and tenants were left without their communities and without affordable housing. PACE pointed out that federal funding and the desire to build higher-income properties on razed land were the fundamental motivating factors behind urban renewal. As one resident argued, "The costs of urban renewal and redevelopment in the old Chinatown areas . . . have been high for the thousands of residents and small businesses evicted. The rewards were minimal—after long delays, a few units of low-income housing. However the rewards for property owners and developers have been great: handsome rents in the new buildings and the wholesale removal of poor families and pensioners, whose presence in the neighborhood must detract from the classy image that developers . . . want to project."[33]

Having seen what happened with earlier projects, PACE and others were determined to put up all possible resistance to more urban renewal efforts in Chinatown. They demanded "decent housing, no relocation outside of the Chinatown area, affordable rents, and preservation of residents' lifestyles in Chinatown."[34] Through legal action, PACE was able to prevent some tenant evictions and force the building of affordable apartments in Chinatown.[35]

We can see the mixed results of the various efforts to resist urban renewal in what happened in the Pauahi Project, completed in 1981. This project also destroyed several blocks, but its version of redevelopment took on a different tenor and had a different goal from those of other renewal efforts. Initial plans were for the area to be razed and new high-rise apartment buildings to be built. But those plans changed. As the *Honolulu Advertiser* explained, "The theme now is low-rises and less obtrusive structures. These will blend with structures that will be retained."[36] A four-story low-rise apartment building, with priority given to low-income residents, would be erected instead. PACE's efforts were credited with this outcome, along with the strongly voiced desires of residents to maintain some of the old character of the neighborhood. But even so, much of the local flavor of the area was destroyed, and in people's memories of an establishment in the area, Tin Tin Chop Suey, we can see how redevelopment not only meant the end of communities, but also often resulted in severing ties across communities. Tin Tin Chop Suey was one of many chop suey restaurants serving inexpensive Chinese meals to Honolulu residents, including many from outside the Chinese community. As one restaurant reviewer described it, "Tin Tin Chop Suey [was] one of downtown's busiest late-night noodle shops when we had a downtown that was hoppin', before the days of urban renewal."[37]

RECONSTRUCTING CHINATOWN FOR A NEW ERA

The end of Tin Tin signaled another change from the old ways: how little restaurants, "just a hole in the wall,"[38] were a draw to the area and encouraged interactions between Chinatown residents and those from other areas who came to eat at their favorite places and "slurp down a bowl of saimin, won ton min, or sam see mein."[39]

To some extent, PACE's efforts (and those of Chinatown residents) received help from another group who in 1965 also began to work toward stopping development in Chinatown. One initiative of this group was to have Chinatown declared a national historical district. Although this group and PACE shared the goal of stopping redevelopment in Chinatown, in the different compositions we can see differences in strategies and goals, differences that would have ramifications down the road. PACE was begun as a grass-roots coalition of groups, including labor groups, that focused on the evictions of low-income residents and worked to protect the rights of those whose voices often went unheard. In their publications, they highlighted the stories of residents who would be displaced by urban renewal projects.[40]

The new group was made up of people with more power and visibility in Honolulu. They, too, were dismayed at the proposed urban renew projects and wanted to stop the destruction of Chinatown. By the time the group was formed, members had seen the destruction of the Kukui, A'ala, and Queen Emma districts as Honolulu embraced urban renewal. Chinatown's core was now in the city's sights, and the group was hoping to find a way to save the area from redevelopment. But their focus and their methods were different from those of PACE. They focused on buildings and architecture and worked from that perspective to stop urban renewal. Involved in these efforts were several prominent citizens, some connected to or sitting on key city committees, as well as the City Beautification Committee of the Honolulu Chamber of Commerce and the newly created State Historic Preservation Office. Prominent members used their status and connections to argue against upcoming HRA plans. For example, Nancy Bannick, a member of the City Beautification Committee, enlisted the help of architects and historians to gather information on the buildings and residents of Chinatown. She published a series of stories about the area in the *Honolulu Advertiser*, one of Hawai'i's major newspapers, which drew more attention to the city's plans and the likely results of redevelopment. Although her focus was preserving built structures, she did not ignore the area's community. In one article, she argued that the city's plans were "drawn with little regard for the existing character of the district, an area of first settlement for the city's immigrant groups, particularly the Chinese and Japanese. It is a place of small shops with living quarters above and behind, of many elderly people who go about in old-country dress and gossip in their native tongue, of shrines, temples, and ethnic societies which were founded by lonely minorities chiefly for mutual aid and a banding together but which over the years have become institutions for the perpetuation of socio-religious customs of the Asian peoples who have given Honolulu its rich and diverse culture."[41]

The work of Bannick and her committee led to the establishment of the Mayor's Historic Buildings Task Force in 1965, of which Bannick was made chair. On the committee were architects, archivists, planners, and community leaders. Students from the University of Hawai'i helped the task force with the work of identifying what makes a building historic and surveyed the city's old buildings to identity those that met the criteria. Because most buildings in Chinatown had been built after the 1900 fire, it was not their age that made them valuable. Rather, the task force argued, it was their place in the community. For that reason, the group (and its later incarnation, the Historic Hawai'i Foundation) worked to designate the area a historic district.

In 1971, the State Historic Preservation Office drafted a nomination to designate the whole of Chinatown a historic district, having it listed on both the Hawai'i Register of Historic Places and the National Register of Historic Places. Earlier urban renewal projects had reduced the footprint of Chinatown, and the goal was to preserve as much of what was left as possible. The boundaries ran along Beretania Street on the north (mauka) side to the harbor on the south (makai) side. The west (Ewa) boundary would be River Street, and Nu'uanu Street would be the east (Diamond Head) border.

Very few single buildings met the Hawai'i Register's definition of historic value, but as a district, Chinatown qualified. As a whole, it was "a cohesive collection of buildings in a defined geographic area that shared a common historical association."[42] It was "the most extensive area in Honolulu reflecting a contiguous architectural and historic character which recalls a sense of time and place. . . . Chinatown is one of the few areas of Honolulu which has maintained a sense of identity as

RECONSTRUCTING CHINATOWN FOR A NEW ERA

a community over the years."[43] As its application made clear, Chinatown was no longer strictly Chinese in terms of its residents or businesses. Indeed, by 1970, Chinese made up less than 20 percent of the residents; the largest proportion was Filipinos, who made up 47 percent. Chinatown's designation as a historic district underscored how Chinatown reflected "the full impact of the city's role as a center of attraction for many diverse races and cultures."[44] In its arguments, Bannick's committee pointed out that Chinese institutions still had a place in Chinatown: there were many Chinese businesses, Chinese societies (such as the Chinese Chamber of Commerce), two Chinese newspapers, and many Chinese restaurants. But these were only a part of the area. It also housed Filipino-owned businesses, such as pool halls, barber shops, and restaurants, and Japanese businesses, including a bookstore, newspaper, and a bank. Vegetable, fish, and meat markets attracted many who lived outside the area. The application emphasized the place of Chinatown in Honolulu: "In no other portion of either the city or the state is it possible for tourists and residents alike . . . to observe within such compact dimensions so much of Hawaii's varied peoples and cultures, both past and present."[45]

Honolulu's application was approved by the Hawai'i Register of Historic Places and then the National Register, and in 1973 Chinatown became the first historic district registered in Hawai'i. This status meant that the urban renewal program—and the federal funds connected to it—would not be able to demolish any more of Chinatown. In addition, building owners could apply for preservation grants and a 25 percent tax credit for restoring a building to its original condition.

The next steps in preservation involved deciding how to revitalize an area that had grown seedy and less central as a result of the urban renewal that had already occurred. A major influence on downtown Honolulu was the newly built Ala Moana Shopping Center, which siphoned off a lot of businesses and customers from the previously central shopping areas. As Bob Gerrell, one of the developers involved in the Chinatown area explained, "Ala Moana Center and Pearl City sucked the vitality out of downtown and Chinatown to the point where nobody cared. Seedier businesses moved in. Chinatown was at its low when we got involved in 1975–76."[46] Gerell eventually undertook the Maunakea Marketplace development, which brought small shops and stands selling vegetables, meats, and foodstuffs to the center of Chinatown. Harry Lee, the first urban renewal coordinator, and a resident of the area, also argued for the importance of these small shops, pointing out that early renewal efforts had displaced many families. The renewal projects "mean . . . uprooting businesses. . . . These small stores [are] where the older people have earned their living for so long, and to uproot them would be wiping out their whole livelihood."[47]

Chinatown's role in Hawai'i's growing tourist economy was also important and was promoted as a reason for investment in the area. For example, a 1968 report prepared by Victor Gruen Associates, an architectural firm that acted as a consultant to the City of Honolulu, outlined the goals and proposed process of the Chinatown revitalization, and argued that urban renewal could benefit the area by making it more attractive to tourists, drawing on Hawai'i's unique racial history and composition. They pointed to "the Island's historic (and unprecedented) role in the constructive reconciliation of racial diversity into a unified, dynamic, varied, and colorful urban complex," and they noted that Chinatown could highlight "Honolulu's emerging as the Capitol of the Pacific, the bridge between America and the Far East, the center of trade, exchange, and representation."[48] Some developers also saw tourist potential in a renewed Chinatown. Bob Gerrell agreed: "The biggest potential market should be the tourist industry. We see the uniqueness of Chinatown, the uniqueness of the architecture, the uniqueness of the individuals living and working in Chinatown as . . . generating a lot of interest on the part of tourists."[49]

But what tourists might be interested in would likely differ from what community members wanted or needed. Many argued that the goal for Chinatown's revitalization should be physical improvements without destroying the district or its spirit. And some wanted a return to the old ways. In an interview, Rudy Paccarro, an area councilor, spoke about what he hoped for:

> I'd like to remember Chinatown years ago even during the war and after the war, of the mingling of all kind of people. You know, where you can walk down where we had the little saimin wagon where the guy pushes the thing, he stops and you know, you go out to the movies, 'n you come out, you want eat saimin, you order, you stand on the side, you eat . . . and other things where you can have the chop suey you know, nice. There are so many things[;] I think many of us, when we think about Chinatown, we have this nostalgia, you know, of hey, why don't we bring the good day, the old days back again.[50]

RECONSTRUCTING CHINATOWN FOR A NEW ERA

Everyone wrestling with what to do with Chinatown had to deal with ongoing dilemmas, such as how to incorporate different needs and perspectives into the plans and how to deal with less savory elements of the area, such as prostitution and, later, drug dealing. Gradually, different real estate investors and developers began to work on different blocks within Chinatown, and revitalization got underway. One of the first buildings to be renovated was the Mendonca Block of Hotel Street. That project, completed in 1978, undertook renovation and restoration of the largest historic building in Chinatown and jumpstarted further historic renovations in Chinatown.[51] Renovations were often undertaken by people who were not part of the local community, often wealthy haole developers. But many others came from the same communities that had resided in Chinatown for decades, including several prominent and wealthy Chinese businesspeople. An early construction project, the See Dai Doo Society Building, was undertaken by the architects George K. C. Lee and Arthur K. C. Hee. The new building was part of the Queen Emma Development Project and was built to replace the society's earlier headquarters, which had been razed in earlier urban renewal efforts.[52]

All of this work—from the first efforts of the Historic Buildings Task Force onward—did indeed help save Chinatown from destruction through urban renewal and was vital to Chinatown's survival. However, most of these efforts focused on making Chinatown a profitable area. That focus has meant that the people who once lived in Chinatown—those whom PACE was trying to support—were usually left out. Low-income rentals bring in much less revenue, including tax revenue, than do up-scale stores and businesses. Chinatown's goals became aligned with the image of a modern American city, one that is based on consumption and where success is measured primarily by its revenue and tax base.

Bob Gerrell's involvement underscores the complicated history and priorities of Chinatown's revitalization. Gerrell was an important developer from the early days of Chinatown's designation as a historic district. By 1988, Gerrell and his partners had renovated or preserved nineteen properties in the Chinatown area.[53] In that way, he made a significant contribution to saving Chinatown and bringing new attention to the area. However, even though he played such a key role in Chinatown's survival, PACE organizers point to the fact that, in the process of his work, Gerrell probably evicted more Chinatown residents than had anyone else.[54] PACE, whose slogan was "People, not profits," linked not just urban renewal but also later redevelopment efforts—and the gentrification they signaled—to evictions and community displacements. They argued that many residents were evicted because developers received grants from the federal government, local tax breaks, and permission to use public lands for their projects. In the process of saving Chinatown, those involved leaned heavily on a script of success based on tax revenues and land value. There were also splits within the Chinese community itself, as those with more money and power were more supportive of redevelopment efforts than were the renters living in Chinatown.[55] While many involved in Chinatown's revitalization did consider its residents, the priority—for many non-Chinese and Chinese alike—was more often finding ways to get a monetary return on investment.

SITUATING THE PRESERVATION OF CHINATOWN IN HAWAI'I HISTORY AND POLITICS

The enormous changes that occurred during the 1960s and 1970s had a significant impact on Chinatown and its place and meaning in Honolulu. By the end of the 1970s, Honolulu, Hawai'i, and Chinatown looked much different from how they had at the beginning of the 1960s. Hawai'i had become the fiftieth state of the United States, presumably giving it new status and weight in national events and processes. Hawai'i had increasingly become known as a tourist destination, and more and different kinds of visitors arrived in the Islands daily. Hawai'i was undergoing a massive economic change, changing from a sugar economy into a tourism economy. It was still many of the same elite haole families and individuals who were at the center of the new economy, but tourism had a different impact on the Islands from that of sugar, especially because it meant that millions of people from outside Hawai'i would come to the Islands and see Hawai'i for themselves. The political arena now looked different, too, as Japanese Americans and other non-haole began to move into politics and haole exerted less power there. Native Hawaiians were increasingly vocal about the mistreatment they had endured and in seeking change.

The role of Chinatown had definitely shifted. By the 1950s, Chinese no longer made up most of the residential population of Chinatown. Most Chinese lived in other parts of the city and went to schools throughout the city. But Chinatown also remained an economic enclave for the city's

RECONSTRUCTING CHINATOWN FOR A NEW ERA

Chinese and a hub for Hawai'i's Chinese. While many Chinese were now involved in large-scale businesses and companies, many Chinese ran restaurants, stores, or social clubs in the district, and Chinese owned much of the local real estate. At the same time, most residents were Filipino, Hawaiian, or Vietnamese, and many small businesses in the district were owned and operated by individuals from these groups.

Through its work organizing residents and tenants, PACE was instrumental in keeping some low-income housing in the Chinatown area, and its work was not insignificant in the struggle to save Chinatown. But it was the developers—the Bob Gerrells—who dominated in setting the stage for the future of Chinatown. The process through which Chinatown was designated a historic district was significant both for Chinatown itself and for what historic designation signaled on a broader scale. It saved Chinatown from urban renewal efforts—but at a cost. To succeed, Chinatown had to fit into the larger societal calculation of what is worth saving: from what, for what purpose, and through what process. The revitalized Chinatown needed to be useful to all those involved. Chinatown's location near Honolulu's central business district and state capitol signaled its value. But the assessment of Chinatown's value is more complicated than simply the value of its land. One landlord who owned property in Chinatown at the time spoke of the frustrations that many there encountered:

> For a while, the government thought it had an answer with urban renewal. Now all of a sudden it's preservation, the direct opposite. It leaves us all in a quandary as to where Chinatown is going . . . our buildings are getting old. . . . But the cost of new construction is so high it just isn't feasible with these extra restrictions. . . . Urban renewal did destroy some valuable historic buildings and we don't want that. But it's a mistake to preserve all of Chinatown . . . we need some kind of redevelopment . . . I don't know. I have been criss-crossing Chinatown for thirty-eight years and I've tried to think for myself what should be done. I don't have an answer![56]

Chinatown embodies the powerful and sometimes contradictory narratives that have shaped Hawai'i's history, which is anchored in Hawai'i's connections to the history of the United States in Asia and the Pacific and the role of race in that history.

RECONSTRUCTING CHINATOWN FOR A NEW ERA

But commonly calculated value has also been part of Chinatown's history. The investors who worked to redevelop the area wanted to see returns on their investment, which meant that revenue-generating development was a priority. That decision resulted in less replacement of low-income housing for former area residents and more renovations for businesses. It may be that the focus on profit and investment, often at the expense of the area's communities, has contributed to the continuing struggles that Chinatown has faced in its attempts to find its footing and gain back its earlier vitality. The chop suey joints of old that were destroyed through urban renewal were more than restaurants; they were places where neighbors gathered and provided a reason for those from outside Chinatown to come to the area to eat, shop, and mix in the neighborhood.

In addition, in a place where tourism was becoming the dominant industry, Chinatown's racial difference was seen as a benefit. Hawai'i was trying to position itself as a destination that differed from other places. In its use of racial difference as a marketing tool, we can see how racial capitalism[57] was employed by the tourist industry. Chinatown's racial difference was highlighted in many tourist publications in the early decades of the renewed Chinatown post-statehood. It was during the postwar years that the Chinatown Narcissus Festival and Pageant had its origins. Originally, organizers saw the festival as a way to revitalize the area and "as a way to rebuild trade and [the] public image of Chinese in Hawaii."[58] As we will see in chapter 6, selling Chinatown as a tourist draw in that way continues today. The Narcissus Festival, for example, is held every year and has been described as a way "to preserve and showcase Chinese art and culture, while promoting local and international commerce."[59]

Chinatown also had important symbolic value. It was the physical manifestation of neoliberal multiculturalism, telling a story of Chinese immigrants who had arrived poor but over the years, and after generations of hard work, had succeeded and become locally powerful. Chinese were proud of their accomplishments, and Chinatown allowed them to celebrate those achievements. That story spoke to the ability of a group—any group, no matter the color of their skin—to achieve the American dream. In this way, Chinatown argued for an interpretation of Hawai'i as a racial paradise, a place that allowed nonwhite people to take their place as important community members. That possibility was important to Hawai'i's leaders who wanted Hawai'i to be seen as a model of racial harmony. And it represented an image that the United States wanted to project, of a country that valued racial equality so strongly that it would include in its borders a state in which most residents were not white.

Chinatown's proximity to the state capitol and to Honolulu's central business district has always been important. Although it might have been a liability at times, threatening to Chinatown's existence as many coveted such valuable land, with preservation, it remained where it was. And that permanency underscores the incorporation of the Chinese story into the Hawai'i story, and the Hawai'i story into the American story. Visitors to the state capitol or to the offices of large financial corporations would easily see this slice of Hawai'i, the history of Chinese in the Islands. Indeed, juxtaposing the state capitol with Chinatown is useful. Both were meant to make an impression, to show that Hawai'i could fit into the U.S. model but on its own terms. The capitol, built in 1969, is impressive for its unusual style; it is the only state capitol built in a modernist style. Unlike most state capitols, it does not mimic the U.S. Capitol in Washington, DC. Rather, its style combines elements of Western architectural traditions, particularly Bauhaus: "but like all other architectural imports to Hawai'i, Bauhaus was transformed into a uniquely Hawaiian style."[60] It is meant to be a modernist rendering of the Islands, reflecting a vision of Hawai'i as the place of volcanoes, the ocean, and palm trees. Its difference and modernity sent a deliberate message, as Governor John A. Burns made clear in his address at its opening: "It is by means of the striking architecture of this new structure that Hawaii cries out to the nations of the Pacific and of the world, this message: 'We are a free people. . . . We are an open society. . . . We welcome all visitors to our island home. . . . We welcome you! E Komo Mai! Come in! The house is yours!'"[61]

Chinatown, visible from the capitol building and just five city blocks away, helps to reinforce the narrative of Hawai'i as safely different from other places in the United States. It is American and reflects how Hawai'i and Honolulu have the requisite elements of Americanism, including economic success and urbanism. But it also proffers racial difference—safe and contained racial difference. Hawai'i and Honolulu present a visual story of what some might see as a model minority, a group who worked hard to achieve the American dream. And it reflects a model of neoliberal multiculturalism. In this narrative, we see how race is accommodated in the U.S. empire. A group like the Chinese are allowed in because they contribute to the model by consuming properly and by endorsing the talismans of a U.S. capitalist system and empire that purportedly allows minority groups a pathway to success. It is important that it was not only haole developers who imagined and implemented a revitalized Chinatown. Wealthy Chinese—many of whom came from humble immigrant backgrounds—also participated. That they could do so argued for the inclusion of nonwhite groups in successful enterprises and signaled their status as successful Americans. In this way, Chinatown complements the capitol building. Majestic, designed in a modern architectural style partly borrowed from Western models. But with a difference, one that reflects Hawaiʻi's unique history and incorporates elements special to Hawaiʻi, including its racial politics. Chinatown thus joins the state capitol in projecting a "part yet apart" image. And it is Chinatown in particular that embodies and demonstrates how race comes into empire.

However, Chinatown has not forged a clear pathway to acceptance, either full racial acceptance in the American system nor acceptance of all groups. Indeed, Chinatown illuminates the contradictions and difficulties of neoliberal multiculturalism. It is just as important to notice what is not reflected, celebrated, or even acknowledged here as what is. One missing element is alternative versions of success, which are easily overshadowed by the emphasis on consumption and a modernity that depends on economic success. But even more central to understanding Hawaiʻi's relationship with the United States is that the success of Chinese in Hawaiʻi disappears the story of Native Hawaiians and the destruction of their community, culture, and nation during the same years that Chinese found success. Chinatown not only reflects the many successes of Chinese since their arrival in Hawaiʻi in the mid-nineteenth century but also underscores that Hawaiʻi itself has been shaped by and into a particular version of success and modernity, one built on global capitalism and neoliberal multiculturalism.

Chapter Six

CHINATOWN TODAY

Confluence of Past and Present

Chinatown in Honolulu today bears the scars and successes of the history of Chinese in Hawai'i over the last 150 years. It is not surprising that it is unlike Chinatowns in other places. As Jesse Shircliff has argued, visitors and outsiders often see Chinatowns as interchangeable and decontextualized from their specific history and politics.[1] Local residents are more likely to understand the historical context of and the regional influences on the area and from those derive the meaning of Chinatown. Thus, Chinatown provides a useful lens for understanding the experience of Chinese in Hawai'i and the context and politics of their history. Some events have been shared by Chinese and Chinatowns in other locations. But Honolulu's unique history and location mean that many of the processes its Chinatown has experienced are specific to Hawai'i. In this way, we can see how race and place have come together in Hawai'i, for Chinese as well as for all other ethnic and racial groups, including haole, Japanese, and Native Hawaiians. Thus, Chinatown provides a window on and an interpretation not only of the Chinese story but also the story of race and empire in Hawai'i and the story of the relationship between Hawai'i and the United States. We see Hawai'i's unique politics in Chinatown's struggles in recent decades to define itself, in what is still present in Chinatown today, and in what is missing both physically and ideologically—in what story is being told and what stories are missing. When scrutinized, we see that Chinatown is a tangible, visual

CHINATOWN TODAY

representation of race in Hawai'i and of how racial constructions in Hawai'i have been entangled and shaped by Hawai'i's relationship with the United States—with its racial constructions and with its history of empire in Asia and the Pacific. In the narrative of Honolulu's Chinatown, we can see ideologies of neoliberal multiculturalism, U.S. racial history and practice, model-minority constructions, and the place of the United States as an empire with ties to Asia.

CHINATOWN TODAY

Today, Chinatown's struggles and contradictions dominate news about the area. The tenor of the narrative suggests that Chinatown has struggled to define itself or to be defined. Throughout the last decades of the twentieth and the early decades of the twenty-first centuries, Chinatown has remained dynamic, as if trying on one kind of presentation after another. After it takes on a new tone, the media announces that Chinatown had been "revived," only to have that new image recede and fade once the next has been taken on. In 1998, an article in the *Star Bulletin*, one of Honolulu's major newspapers, declared Chinatown "a city waiting to be reborn."[2] In 2006, an article in the same newspaper declared, "Chinatown at a crossroads."[3] And in 2017, *Honolulu Magazine* seemingly captured the ups and downs of Chinatown in recent years when it ran a lengthy article titled, "Chinatown's Latest Revival Is Putting It Back on the Map. But Will It Last?"[4] Despite the doubts and incorrect predictions of the past, the author argued, "To anyone who has lost count of the 'revival of Chinatown' stories of the past few decades, this one feels more real, less hyped." But in the years since, more such articles have wondered if and when Chinatown can be revived. Drawing on its history, one optimistic writer insisted that it will survive: "Chinatown is a plucky place that has always had resilience at its core, having in previous decades fought off fire, pestilence and misguided urban redevelopment initiatives that threatened its extinction. Despite the avalanche of recent bad news, Chinatown appears on the threshold of an upswing."[5]

Chinatown remains a geographically small but important part of Honolulu. It emerged from the efforts of the 1970s and 1980s into a new era. But it is not always clear what Chinatown should or wants to be. The destruction of large sections of Chinatown through urban renewal

CHINATOWN TODAY

and redevelopment have contributed to these uncertainties; as the city tried to mold it into a component of a modern city through urban renewal and development, and through efforts to resist those processes, the area began to take on a new character. Urban renewal and development projects led to communities being destroyed, with nothing really taking their place. Also contributing to Chinatown's mixed meanings have been the large social and economic changes that Hawai'i has experienced, changes that also affected the United States and Asia. This historical context can still be seen in the area today.

Another tension experienced as Chinatown tries to find its way is that it continues to mean different things to different people and different groups. That is true even for the locals who visit Chinatown regularly, as can be seen in how the area and activities there change throughout the course of most days. While it has been true since the early twentieth century that most Chinese residents in Honolulu do not live in the Chinatown area and that Chinese no longer make up the largest proportion of Chinatown residents, it is also true that many Chinatown residents are Chinese. At the time of the 2010 census, although Chinese made up only 4 percent of the state's total population, they made up 40 percent of the Chinatown census tract, 58.2 percent of the adjacent A'ala Park area, and 47.1 percent of the nearby Foster Garden area.[6] Chinatown today is clearly still connected to its historical roots. Even for Chinese who live away from Chinatown, the area's activities often draw them back, connecting them to the Chinese community.

Indeed, even as city officials remind people that Chinatown is not just about or for Hawai'i's Chinese, the area retains a decidedly Chinese character. Most streets have offices belonging to Chinese organizations, including social clubs, lion-dancing organizations, and family-name associations. The family-name associations no longer play the central role they did in early migrants' lives. But they continue to be centers for socializing. Elderly Chinese, some who live nearby but also others who regularly travel to Chinatown from other parts of the city continue to value their connection to the area. Its shops, services, and people are important parts of their lives, and they rely on Chinatown to find company or a quiet place to spend an afternoon. Leaders of Chinese organizations also want Chinatown to retain its importance to younger Chinese and use its clubs to bring younger Chinese residents into Chinatown to encourage them to develop and sustain a connection to the Chinese community and to their heritage. There are about a dozen lion-dancing organizations that teach dance and martial arts to a broad range of students. Not all students are Chinese, but the head of one such organization explained that he feels it is his obligation to connect students with the history of Chinese in Hawai'i: "[Chinese] culture is in a decline, in the sense that it gets kind of watered-down or lost, so we are always in this kind of struggle to educate . . . particularly in martial arts and Chinese lion dance. . . . It is important . . . that students learn an understanding of that history. . . . [I] . . . try to impart that history and get it out there. . . . So we try to bring it to the forefront a little bit. Even if it's just a little part of their [the students'] day or a little part of their week."[7]

Other organizations have similar goals of making connections among its members and "paying homage to Chinese culture here." The Honolulu Chinese Jaycees, which has a junior relationship to the Chinese Chamber of Commerce of Hawai'i, has a membership of more than sixty and supports many activities in and around Chinatown. It also has a service arm, providing aid to Honolulu and other communities during times of need. In this organization, we can see that Chinese networks reach outside Hawai'i; the organization has relationships with other Jaycees chapters in the continental United States and in Asia, including Taiwan and Hong Kong. Those connections provide local members with connections outside Hawai'i. As the local chapter officer explained, "A lot of these folks in our sister chapters, some of them are business owners, some of them are executives in businesses. By taking the opportunity, by taking the initiative to become more involved with our sister chapter relations, those are opportunities that we give to our members to capitalize on, to begin forging relationships with them too. So we don't actively try to pull strings or anything, but we definitely provide the opportunity and the spaces to network and to form the relationships organically."[8] But this organization also stresses the local foundation of the Honolulu Chinese Jaycees, with its roots in the local Chinese community as well as its ties to other local communities.

Chinatown is also the site of several important celebrations throughout the year. The Narcissus Festival and Pageant, which kicks off at Lunar New Year and runs events throughout the spring, is a long-running festival meant to draw both Chinese and others into Chinatown. It was established

CHINATOWN TODAY

in 1949 with the hope of helping to revive Chinatown and offer a way for the Chinese community to define itself rather than be defined by others.[9] As one founder explained, "Like all ethnic celebrations in Hawai'i, the Narcissus Festival was born in the need for identity survival. It was not so much a desire to impress or entertain others. A real need has to do with identity survival, a solidarity, a true sense of 'being' in a polyglot community."[10] That was seen as especially important for the many Chinese who lived outside Chinatown, as the festival gave them a connection to the area and to the community.[11] It never really lived up to the goal of reviving Chinatown, and in the following years, the festivals leaders tried to tweak it so that it might attract more participants to its events and more visitors to Chinatown. One such tweak was the introduction of the Narcissus Pageant, an erstwhile beauty pageant now promoted as a scholarship pageant. The festival's heyday was the 1950s and 1960s when it was routinely included in promotional tourism campaigns[12] and was well attended by tourists, locals, politicians, and community leaders from across the Islands and beyond. It continues today, although changes have been made along the way in terms of location, participants, and sponsors. The reach of the festival is also now much smaller, and fewer organizations participate in sponsoring and running it. But the festival is still important to the Chinese community. As its official sponsor, the Chinese Chamber of Commerce of Hawai'i, states, "The festival's purpose is to preserve and showcase Chinese art and culture, while promoting local and international commerce." Importantly, many festival events are no longer strictly Chinese but include elements of the wider society, such the hula and Hawaiian music used in its shows.[13]

One recent change in Chinatown is that Chinatown now includes connections to "greater China," incorporating connections and people from a wider geographical area than it has in the past, when most Chinese in Hawai'i traced their origins to southern China. Today, many merchants in Chinatown are ethnically Chinese but from Southeast Asia[14] and as likely to offer foods and other goods found in Vietnam as in China. There have also been some tensions around whether local institutions should be explicitly connected to the Republic of China (Taiwan) or the People's Republic of China, but Honolulu has avoided some of the most rancorous debates on this political issue.[15] Given that these tensions have engulfed other Chinatowns, and that Sun Yat-Sen, the father of the Republic of China, had deep roots in Hawai'i, that this has not become a more contentious issue is remarkable. In Honolulu, "Chinese" more easily encompasses a broad range of ethnic Chinese whose geographical roots run throughout Asia.

Along with the activities and businesses that are clearly marked Chinese are even more non-Chinese businesses and stores; Chinatown also continues to draw non-Chinese locals. Restaurants in Chinatown continue to provide lunch for those who work in the central business district, and restaurant patrons come from other parts of Honolulu to enjoy a wide variety of cuisines, including Chinese, Filipino, and French. Lines regularly form outside the Sing Cheong Yuan bakery, a traditional Chinese bakery, as customers wait their turn to order and take home pork hash, sui mai, shrimp har gao, or some of its many preserved and candied fruits. There are Filipino and Vietnamese restaurants. Many open markets are run by Filipino, local Japanese, and South Pacific Islanders, along with Chinese. Noodle factories and stores selling Chinese cooking ingredients and cookware are also a draw. These and the street stands and markets sell ingredients and implements used in Chinese cooking—such as bai cai, bean sprouts, mango, woks, and rice cookers—but they are as often bought by those cooking Filipino, Japanese, or what might be termed "local" food, nonspecific Asian or Pacific Islander food.

Vegetable, produce, and meat markets are a valued part of the area and draw a range of visitors to Chinatown. Locals—both Chinese and non-Chinese—go to Chinatown to buy ingredients that are not readily available in regular stores or that are much less expensive in Chinatown. For example, in Hawai'i, regular grocery stores carry Japanese-style soy sauce but have limited and sometimes no Chinese soy sauce. Chinatown offers a variety of brands and flavors. Fresh noodles are also more easily found in Chinatown than elsewhere in Honolulu. The lines outside the Sing Cheong Yuan bakery suggest that Chinatown's businesses are seen to offer items and services that are unavailable elsewhere in Honolulu, that are deemed superior to those offered outside Chinatown, or that are less expensive in Chinatown. And while Honolulu's many farmers' markets offer a wide variety of fresh produce, Chinatown is still able to offer rarer and often less expensive produce. Larger and smaller produce markets are found throughout Chinatown. The Yee Hop Market, first built in 1966, sells fish, meat, and vegetables. The O'ahu Market is even older, built in 1904, and is the last remaining open market building in Honolulu with stalls selling all manner of foodstuffs.[16]

CHINATOWN TODAY

Throughout its history, Chinatown has seen small stores, restaurants, and bars come and go. Gary Coover has chronicled the history of most buildings in Chinatown; one of the most striking things about this history is that buildings have been used for many purposes for needs that have changed over time. For example, the Wing Wo Tai Building on Nuʻuanu Street was originally built in 1917 to house the relocating Wing Wo Tai Chinese export company. The company originated in Hong Kong in 1845 and expanded to Hawaiʻi in 1877,[17] where it sold liquor and groceries, as well as items from China, such as furniture and silks, to both Chinese and non-Chinese customers. The original location suffered during the 1900 bubonic plague outbreak when the first case in Honolulu was that of a bookkeeper working for the company. The building was subsequently targeted by the Hawaiʻi Board of Health for fumigation and the destruction of most goods on the premises.[18] In its new location, the firm continued business from 1917 to 1955. After that, an office appliance company occupied the space until 1975. In 1977, the building underwent restoration under the new rules of historic preservation applied to the Chinatown Historic District. Between 1978 and 1985, it housed a sequence of various businesses including an oyster bar, another restaurant, and an architectural institute. It is now the headquarters of the Nature Conservancy. Most buildings in Chinatown have seen similar transformations, reflecting the many changes the area has experienced and highlighting how at different times, Chinatown has been focused on servicing the Chinese community, connected to the office workers in the nearby central business district, or attractive to outside customers.

Chinatown is thus a place for Chinese and non-Chinese. The way these groups come together—and just how Honolulu's Chinatown is situated *in* Hawaiʻi can be seen in the history of one of the area's iconic restaurants, the Char Hung Sut Restaurant, founded by Bat Moi Kam Mau in 1946. She had come to Hawaiʻi from China at the age of fifteen, following her Hawaiʻi-born Chinese husband, Harry Marn Sin Mau.[19] After working in canneries and dim sum restaurants, she opened the Char Hung Sut Restaurant. The well-known and locally loved restaurant became known for its manapua, half-moons, and pork hash. Each was derived from Chinese dim sum (bao, half-moons, and siu mai) but had been localized and made into something different from their Chinese beginnings. Manapua are bigger than Chinese bao, and the Hawaiʻi versions are often filled with a variety of fillings, from the traditional char siu to coconut to chicken curry. Similar to the incorporation of local elements into the Narcissus Festival, that a restaurant in Chinatown is known for its manapua—not its bao— underscores how Chinatown has absorbed its locality so that its food is as much the food of Hawai'i as it is of Chinese. Char Hung Sut closed in 2020, during the COVID-19 pandemic. For the thousands of Hawai'i residents who over the decades lined up to pick up a box of famous half-moons or manapua, this closure was testament to the struggles of Chinatown in recent years, especially during the pandemic.

Perhaps the biggest change in Chinatown has been the introduction of businesses meant to attract a new clientele to the area. Today, Chinatown is sometimes touted as a hip and cool place that appeals to young people of all ethnicities who patronize businesses that are not specifically Chinese but rather happen to be located in an area named Chinatown.[20] Those changes began when Pegge Hopper, a local artist, opened a studio in the area in 1982 and expanded it a few years later. Hopper's arrival was the first of several artists' studios and galleries that came to Chinatown. Along with these have come small boutiques selling unusual works and clothing and several upscale restaurants (which serve eclectic food, some Asian or Pacific Rim but much that is not; some advertise their food as "New American," for example). One new chef and owner explains what these new businesses have meant to the area: "This whole block was full of people who weren't normally in Chinatown coming at night taking notice of the neighborhood."[21] It is especially in the evenings that the more upscale, non-Chinese restaurants bring in patrons who otherwise might not consider visiting Chinatown.

While many have celebrated these new visitors to the area, there have also been tensions around the different kinds of businesses in Chinatown, with some Chinese store owners feeling that artists and other outsiders are trying to crowd out the old mom-and-pop stores.[22] A Chinatown leader worried that the influx of new businesses had "haolified" the area and argued that the galleries did not promote business on "the other side" of Chinatown.[23] One leader of a local Chinese organization talked about how "the whole feel of Chinatown" has changed, especially now that "there's a lot of businesses coming in that are not Chinese and [Chinatown] is relegated down to just one street, Maunakea Street."[24] New business owners face challenges partly because of these tensions. One owner of a prominent non-Chinese restaurant talked about the difficulty of breaking into the Chinatown community; it took a lot of time for him to develop a cooperative relationship with local suppliers, and he referred to the community as being "closed" to outsiders.[25] But he also described how one supplier came around and began to supply him with a much-needed staple for his restaurant. Although he still did not feel close with most Chinatown vendors and still felt they were wary in their dealings with him, he had begun to develop adequate working relationships. His and others' experiences point to continued differences in and uncertainties with regard to whom Chinatown is serving and how best to meet their needs.

Chinatown remains an area that garners attention, both good and bad. Recently, there has been much angst about how disreputable the area has become, scaring away potential customers or store and restaurant owners. That had been true for some time, but concerns have been exacerbated by the COVID-19 pandemic, as downtown patrons and workers are fewer in number and there seem to be more people experiencing homelessness. Scott Saiki, the House Speaker who represents part of downtown, elaborated, "It's depressing, it's empty[;] there are (fewer) restaurants, and certain areas are sketchy. . . . There was a time when you'd walk down the sidewalk at any time of the day and you would run into people you knew. You'd stop and talk[;] you met people for lunch. Downtown should be one of the most vibrant and intellectual areas of our state. But right now, it doesn't always appear that way."[26]

In recent years, there has also been controversy and discussion about the River of Life, a religious organization that for thirty-five years has provided services such as meals, food boxes, showers, social work support, and Christian counseling to people experiencing homelessness in Honolulu. As homelessness has increased across the Islands, criticism of the organization and its effect on Chinatown has grown, with many arguing that River of Life attracts people experiencing homelessness to the area, which has made Chinatown more dangerous, less clean, and less attractive to visitors. In February 2022, River of Life leaders and city officials agreed to move River of Life out of Chinatown and provide meals at smaller hubs throughout Oʻahu. That move does not address the processes that lead to homelessness in the first place, but merchants and others in Chinatown hope that the relocation of River of Life will give the area more opportunity to attract patrons to Chinatown's shops and restaurants.

CHINATOWN TODAY

Given the many uses of Chinatown, it is not unexpected that the meaning of Chinatown varies across groups and sometimes changes after Chinatown has been in the news, whether for good or bad reasons. Recent restaurant openings suggest that there continue to be major and positive changes occurring, and local government officials continue to say that "fixing" or "strengthening" Chinatown is a priority. But Chinatown is still considered dirty and dangerous by many. In the evenings, we can see a mix of people experiencing homelessness and upscale diners. How are continuing negative images and new positive ones reconciled?

Chinatown also has contradictory meanings for Hawai'i's Chinese. Even though the area remains a key site for local Chinese, Chinatown has likely lost its previous importance—as both a place of daily visits and as a refuge—as Chinese have become more and more deeply embedded in Hawai'i society and have come to yield more and more power across a variety of spheres. Chinese no longer need Chinatown to accomplish what they want to do; useful contacts, businesses, restaurants, and social activities are now spread across the city and the state and even farther afield. Along with many other changes in the last fifty years, the rise and spread of global capitalism has affected the place of many Chinatowns, including Honolulu's. Given the flexible nature and mobility of corporations, businesses are now less tethered to a particular place than in the past.[27] While contacts and mentorship are still important, those processes can happen outside Chinatown. Nevertheless, because place is still a part of these processes, especially because states have strong connections to corporations,[28] Chinatown remains important, just differently from in the past. As I will discuss, Chinatown's importance may now lie as much in its symbolic value than in the amenities and services that used to make its physical presence so key—and unique—in the lives of Chinese.

As Chinatown continues to try to reconcile the various meanings and uses of the area, and as it struggles to find its place and messaging among locals, many also see Chinatown as a potential tourist draw. But even though this attention should come as no surprise, given the importance of tourism to Hawai'i's economy, for tourists, Honolulu's Chinatown presents differently from other Chinatowns.

In many cities, Chinatowns and other marked ethnic spaces have been used to draw visitors and tourists to the city. As one scholar argues, "Local governments regard the utilization of culture for the purpose of city

CHINATOWN TODAY

marketing and image creation as a significant redevelopment marketing strategy."[29] This commodification of ethnicity[30] has grown with the rise of the consumer society, making diversity a selling point for a city or community. In this environment, both city officials and "ethnic entrepreneurs aim . . . to capitalise on the development [of consumerism] by refashioning their neighborhoods as urban spaces providing 'authentic experiences.'"[31] In some places, such as Amsterdam, Chinatowns have become "lightly themed shopping areas"[32] for tourists and have little to offer Chinese residents. Scholars disagree on the effects of ethnic tourism on the areas and consumers. Jan Lin focuses on the potential positive outcomes, arguing that "ethnic tourism exists for the benefit of ethnic insiders as well as touristic outsiders. Successful ethnic tourism and heritage preservation rely upon the efforts of a generative cluster of ethnic community leaders, business entrepreneurs, and institutional stakeholders including artists, historians, museum curators, restaurant owners, tourism promoters, and community based organizations. The staging of ethnic tourism in US cities promotes greater public consumption of ethnic foods, culture, and heritage for a general cultural audience as well [as] for ethnic audiences."[33]

But others have pointed out that such tourism does not always benefit the communities affected and that these communities do not always maintain control over the images or outcomes that result. For Hawai'i, with its long history of selling its lands and peoples to the tourist market— often in caricatured ways that are deeply harmful to various groups[34]— this is a key issue.

Although Honolulu's Chinatown draws Hawai'i's Chinese and other locals, it also looks for ways to put itself on tourists, maps. The description of Chinatown provided by the website of the Hawai'i Tourism Authority is worth quoting at length to understand how Chinatown is being marketed to visitors to Hawai'i. The piece first describes Chinatown as "a center for art and dining in Honolulu," thus providing no mention of Chinese history. It goes on to describe the area as follows: "Located on the western hem of Honolulu's financial district, Chinatown's historic buildings are home to a hodgepodge of shops, herbalists, lei makers, antique dealers, temples, bars and restaurants. By day, explore Chinatown's bustling markets like the Maunakea Marketplace or the O'ahu Market. Here you'll find exotic fruits, seafood and curiosities like the "thousand-year old egg," [and] incredible temples like the Izumo Taishakyo Mission Shrine and the Kuan

Yin Temple[, which] transport you to historic Japan and China."[35] But it doubles back on its non-Chinese elements:

> For foodies, Chinatown has become an epicenter of eclectic and hip new restaurants. The neighborhood's eclectic restaurants serve everything from dim sum (Chinese dumplings) to Eurasian, Vietnamese, Malaysian and even Cuban and French fare. And with a range of taste like this, it's no wonder that downtown Honolulu and Chinatown are up-and-coming culinary destinations.
>
> Chinatown is also the epicenter of Oʻahu's arts scene. Take the Chinatown art walk along and around Nuuanu and Bethel Street during the monthly First Friday festivities, the best time to experience all the area has to offer. In fact, Chinatown is a hot spot for Oʻahu nightlife. Home to the historic Hawaii Theatre for live music and shows, you can find some of Hawaiʻi's hottest underground bars, clubs and restaurants in the weathered lofts and buildings of urban Chinatown after dark.[36]

We can see in this official version of Chinatown the efforts to make it both a site of alluring cultural and racial difference and a place of urban entertainment. First Fridays, held on the first Friday of every month, are meant to bring new visitors—locals and tourists alike—into the area regularly. The First Friday site promotes the event as follows: "Chinatown is the place to be if you want to join the hip crowds at the many unique galleries, boutiques, cafes and restaurants that feature exciting art exhibits and free entertainment."[37] But not all paint a rosy picture of the area. A 2017 *Wall Street Journal* article described the area differently: "In years past, tourists—at least the wholesome variety—gave Chinatown a wide berth. Despite serving as a longtime hub for various Asian communities, the neighborhood has struggled to shake a seedy reputation that dates back to its mid-1800s inception. . . . A handful of new restaurants, bars and galleries [have opened], but at night, the same gritty Chinatown, where few rental cars dared to tread, held sway." However, it went on to claim that the area is a "must-see . . . with some of the best food, art, and shopping in the state."[38]

As part of Hawaiʻi's focus on tourism, but for locals, too, efforts are underway to make Chinatown more attractive to visitors. That includes upgrading and renovating old buildings in the area as well as building new spaces. An example is the recent work on the Wo Fat Building.

CHINATOWN TODAY

The building that housed the Wo Fat Restaurant has been one of the most visible in Chinatown for many decades. The current building was built in 1938, designed by the architect Y. T. Char, after its previous incarnations had burned down twice, in the 1886 and 1900 fires. It served as a restaurant until 2009; since then, it has housed small grocery stores but has fallen into disrepair.[39] But there are current plans—funded by a development firm from the continental United States—to renovate the building and install a new restaurant and a boutique hotel.

Despite such efforts, Honolulu's Chinatown is not the tourist lure that Chinatowns are in other places, such as Sydney or San Francisco. The reason likely has to do with the unique context of each Chinatown. The difference represented by Chinatowns is an important part of their tourist appeal, making "the space a permanent fixture of otherness in the cityscapes of the United States."[40] But Hawai'i encourages us to ask, "Otherness from what or whom?" In Hawai'i, with its unique racial and ethnic mix, Chinatown does not stand out as different in the same way it might in a city whose population is whiter. If visiting Chinatowns is typically about experiencing a bit of the exotic in the midst of a Westernized city, then in Honolulu, visitors are likely to assess all of Hawai'i as different enough from where they live that a visit to Chinatown is less necessary. In that way, the ethnic and cultural diversity across Hawai'i influences the meaning and attraction of Honolulu's Chinatown. From this perspective, Chinatown allows us to see more clearly how Hawai'i itself is regularly seen by tourists, other visitors, and Americans generally as a bit foreign, and not really American. Here, the absence of tourists in Chinatown reflects that Hawai'i itself has been constructed as different.

But we can also find evidence for other tourist views of Chinatown. Shircliff argues that visitors to Chinatowns often see them as generic, unconnected to a particular context.[41] In a thread on a popular travel website titled "Chinatown – Is It Worth a Stop?," we can see evidence of mixed attitudes about Honolulu's Chinatown, as well as continuing beliefs about Chinatowns more generally. One poster asks, "Is the ChinaTown [*sic*] here like the Chinatowns elsewhere full of violence or is it more calm?" Responses varied, with some pushing back on the assumption of violence: "I'm curious as to what violence you refer to. I've been to Chicago's Chinatown a few times and Chinatown in Manhattan plenty of times as well and never experienced any violence." Others point to the number of people experiencing homelessness in the area: "We . . . found it rundown, dirty and depressing with all the homeless people. It is not a tourist attraction like Chinatown in San Francisco or Sydney." Another response states, "Honolulu's Chinatown is small—somewhat authentic. However, if you come from San Francisco, Vancouver, Toronto, NYC, there's no real point in visiting Honolulu's Chinatown," reflecting the perceived interchangeability of Chinatowns that Shircliff writes about.[42]

"Strategic self-orientalizing"[43] is at play here, too. Even though it was not undertaken as vigorously as in other places like San Francisco, some have argued that Chinatown's Asian character is important. Some building renovations deliberately incorporated a Chinese style. The Lung Doo Building, rebuilt in 1965, used architectural features such as a round circular door and a rooftop pagoda to bring notice to the structure, which has housed the Lung Doo Benevolent Society (a charitable organization focused on the Chinese community) since then.[44]

In his support for designating Chinatown a historic district, Lawrence Halprin, an architect from the U.S. continent asked, "Where else in America can you wander around in a Chinatown as real, as lively, and authentic as this in Honolulu which [has] the same qualities, on a smaller scale of course, as a trip to Hong Kong?"[45] Chinese businesses and community leaders have also recognized that creating or maintaining symbols that distinguish the area might attract more visitors. Many festivals and street fair activities are designed not only to entertain or celebrate Chinese heritage but also to serve as markers of Chinese ethnicity for non-Chinese residents and visitors. Organizers work to bring in and welcome those participants as well. The 2023 Chinese New Year was loudly celebrated in Chinatown and was particularly meaningful because the COVID-19 pandemic had prevented its being held for the previous three years. Street closures, activities for visitors of all ages, food booths, lion dancing, and other activities were meant to draw participants from well beyond the Chinese community, allowing Chinese culture and Chinatown to be celebrated by Chinese and non-Chinese alike.

But another difference in Hawai'i is that the selling of ethnic and cultural difference takes place across the landscape, not only in limited ethnic areas as is true in other places. That means that we can see the performance of Chinese ethnicity in a variety of locales, which raises further questions about the value of Chinatown in maintaining community ties. The recent challenges of homelessness and safety suggest other questions: How should Chinatown be tied to the rest of Honolulu? Does a greater police presence make Chinatown seem safer or more dangerous? Keeping Chinatown looking and feeling safe, as well as accessible and relevant, continues to be important to all who value Chinatown.

INTERPRETING THE PLACE OF CHINATOWN TODAY

Given the changing meaning of Chinatown, its reduced importance to Chinese activity and even identity, as well as the reduced interest of non-Chinese in visiting, what are the meaning and place of Chinatown today? Chinatown's position, meaning, and future are all tied to its history—not only the history of Chinese in Hawai'i but also the history of Hawai'i itself, of race and ethnicity in Hawai'i and in the United States, of empire, of troubled and easy relationships with the United States and with the economy of Hawai'i, when it was built on sugar and now that it is built on tourism. Chinatown is the visual, tangible representation of all of these processes, of a Hawai'i that is entangled with a U.S. history of race and empire. Here, it is important to keep in mind arguments that place is not only shaped by but also shapes behavior and attitudes.[46]

First and foremost, Honolulu's Chinatown reminds all who visit or even consider the area about the distance Chinese have traveled. No longer are Chinese confined to a geographical area in the city. It offers an easy comparison to the early days, as well as a way to assess all that has happened in the lives of Chinese and the Chinese community in Hawai'i. These reminders can be heartening for all. Chinese can look back and see what their hard work, commitment to the future, and hardships endured have brought them. At a recent ceremony to dedicate an archway to be erected at the entry to Chinatown, city and business leaders noted the importance of the fourteen notable Chinese who are honored with this monument. One attendee, Central Pacific Bank Executive Vice Chair Catherine Ho, pointed out, "It is a significant reminder of exactly how much the original Chinese immigrants achieved after coming to Hawaii without much more than the clothes on their backs and the promise of a better life."[47] As Jan Lin explains, for older Chinese, an ethnic heritage site can "preserve and display the cultural legacy of racial-ethnic ancestry so that new generations can look back and comprehend with better insight the trajectory of their posterity."[48] Many Chinese efforts in and around Chinatown over the past decades, such as the new buildings or the Narcissus Festival, can be seen as "racial rearticulation"—a process in which "subordinates advance their cause by reinterpreting racist discourse—thereby rearticulating it into an empowering racial identity."[49] Chinatown is a physical showcase of that process. Indeed, many older Chinese in Hawai'i speak of Chinatown in exactly this way: as a link between the history and lives of the past and those of younger Chinese today.

It is also an area that reminds many of old-time Hawai'i. As we saw in chapter 5, preserving Chinatown was important as much for saving Hawai'i's old ways as for preserving Chinese history. Small shops, family businesses, open-air markets—these are not the usual elements of modern cities, and many in Hawai'i are glad to keep these old ways alive, at least in one small part of the city. In that way, Chinatown stands out partly for an increasingly rare connection to past ways. As one resident of the area exclaimed in 1977 about Chinatown's value, "We think that Chinatown should be preserved, and it's worth preserving! We think that people of Hawai'i will benefit by having this cultural, historic, and scenic district to remind them of what has happened here in Hawai'i."[50]

Those resonances are important. But they do not occur in a vacuum, and that is where the history of Hawai'i, of race and ethnicity, of settler colonialism, and of the United States comes into the picture. Celebrating how far Chinese have come emphasizes a particular ideology that insists that hard work is rewarded and no one is prevented from achieving success because of race or ethnicity. Importantly, this space celebrates the present in relation to a past of oppression and discrimination over which Hawai'i has triumphed. In that way, it reflects "a sense of coming to terms with the past and acceptance of a 'new' multicultural" present.[51] That brings us back to the work that Hawai'i—its racial history, and its purported racial harmony—does for American ideological stances of race and ethnicity. Chinatown in Honolulu also serves as a visible, available support of all that Hawai'i stands for and means, both to those in Hawai'i and to those who live in the wider United States. Jan Lin has argued that spaces like Chinatowns allow for the expansion of public history and memory, including previously unrecognized voices.[52] An argument can be made for such a contribution; but at the same time, Honolulu's Chinatown reminds us that any such addition will be mediated by and through

CHINATOWN TODAY

the dominant culture; we must ask on whose terms previously marginalized voices are included and whether, in the process, the overall narrative undergoes significant change.

One of the most important messages that Honolulu's Chinatown imparts is Chinese achievement—economic achievement. It is a geographical space, multiple city blocks in the center of the city, that showcases just how far Chinese have come. As we saw in the last chapter, its proximity to—within sight of—the state capitol district emphasizes its unique Hawai'i setting. That it is situated next to the central business district underscores the economic element of Chinatown, as one article promoting the area makes clear. It points out that downtown Honolulu and adjoining Chinatown "couldn't be more different in most respects. Downtown is mostly large, shiny, glass-and-steel high rises with lots of chain restaurants, stores, and wide streets. Chinatown, on the other hand, has narrow streets, low-rises, historic buildings with mom-and-pop stores and not a single chain merchant. What the two have in common, however, is business: making money."[53]

Some of the work that Honolulu's Chinatown does is complemented by and done through the meanings of Chinatowns across the world, where they are seen as places of past segregation, reflecting a time (and space) when Chinese were new arrivals and struggling for acceptance in their new homes. Today, in Honolulu, that history is highlighted—that prior space is now preserved—even though Chinese are now successful members of the Hawai'i community. Even the proximity to the shiny high rises in the central business district suggests the distance traveled. Indeed, proximity to the financial center of Honolulu serves to reinforce the argument of successful consumption, that Chinese have been able to take their place in the upper echelons of Hawai'i society. One measure of Chinese success in Hawai'i is their purchase of land whenever it was available for purchase. As we saw in chapters 2 and 3, land purchases, even small house plots, were a form of investment for individual Chinese. But they also signaled success to the wider world, providing tangible evidence that Chinese were increasingly part of a growing Hawai'i society. The purchase of land in the Chinatown area, in the center of the city, was even more of an investment, and even more visible a sign of the success of Chinese residents. Since the middle of the twentieth century, Chinese have been active in real estate in the area, purchasing land and buildings and establishing businesses or renting space to others. For example, not long after immigrating from China to Hawai'i in 1872, Yim Quon began to invest in land and businesses in Chinatown. Even the 1886 and 1900 fires did not deter him from these investments, and by some reports, he acquired several properties in the area.[54]

Indeed, the value of land in the Chinatown area is a reminder of how successful Chinese have been at establishing a footprint in Honolulu. That was true in the past and is also true today. Restrictions imposed by the historical area designation keep Chinatown's buildings at under four stories in height but nearby and certainly within sight of Chinatown strollers, are high-rise office buildings, many owned by successful Chinese. That some of these are Chinese-owned bank buildings also signals that proper consumption is valued and is seen as the pathway to success in the United States and in Hawai'i. Hawai'i National Bank's history is a good example of the visible evidence of the rise of Chinese from humble beginnings to financial success. It was established in 1960 in Chinatown by K. J. Luke and was the only bank with a national charter in Hawai'i at the time; it continues to be a major bank in the Islands today. The original bank building was next to a business owned by another successful Chinese businessperson, Ching Sing Wo who opened his furniture store, C. S. Wo in 1911, which has become the largest furniture dealer in Hawai'i.[55]

Some Chinese success stories have had even wider broadcast. Chinn Ho, a local Chinese businessperson, established Capital Investment Company in Chinatown at 47 North King and from there began to establish a large, far-flung financial empire that included a former planation in Wai'anae, investments in California, and ownership of a major Hawai'i newspaper. He even managed to break into one of the "Big Five" sugar dynasties, long dominated by haole families, to become a director of the Theo H. Davies company. Ho was often one of the first Asians to hold such powerful positions and has become a symbol of how Chinese overcame racial discrimination and rose to financial success in Hawai'i.

This kind of tangible evidence in the Chinatown area not only celebrates Chinese achievement but also argues for Hawai'i's racial tolerance. A message given by Hawai'i's senator, Daniel Inouye, in 1970 in support of the Narcissus Festival that year argues just that: "Colorful and exciting, the Narcissus Festival is more than just a week of celebration, it stands as a testament of a great American success story. Chinese culture has become delicately interwoven into the exotic fabric of our Hawaiian society, and we have become one, a Pacific people proud of our own individual heritage,

CHINATOWN TODAY

yet part of a greater community which faces the future with supreme confidence."[56]

Thus, it is not only Chinese who can be proud of their achievements but all people of Hawai'i, who can see themselves as part of a society that encourages and honors all people's success, no matter how humble the beginnings or what race or ethnicity.

That message fits squarely with the kind of ideology that has shaped Hawai'i and its economy since the beginning of its contact with the United States. The enormous success and power of the sugar industry, which was under near total control by a few haole families for nearly all of its existence, brought and established a particular model of success to Hawai'i. That model, in which a powerful, landowning group held the Islands' economy in its hands for nearly a century, an economy that bound Hawai'i's economy to that of the United States and of the world, meant that Hawai'i's system of norms, values, and rewards was based on a neoliberal model. Chinese came to mirror such success and adhere to that model through their successful rise into professional and business careers, through their residence in upscale neighborhoods, and through their economic success across various sectors of the economy. They were excluded from the upper tiers of society and economy in their early decades in Honolulu. In response, they built a system that was parallel to that of haole.

As we saw in chapter 3, Ruddy Tongg established an airline that became one of Hawai'i's two main airlines. His achievements speak to the prominence of Chinese in Hawai'i's economy. But for someone like Tongg, much of his individual success was built on the system of *huis*, a group of investors who worked together to achieve economic success. *Huis* were first used by immigrants in Hawai'i as part of the parallel system they created to combat the discrimination they faced from haole. Haole-controlled banks would not lend to Chinese, but *huis* allowed Chinese access to loans and cash that they could then use to invest. This system gave them access into and eventual dominance over various sectors of Hawai'i's economy. But notably, this pathway to financial success was not a contrast to the neoliberal haole system but a parallel system that propelled them into successful positions in the larger—haole-dominated—Hawai'i society.

Thus, it was within a particular model—one built by haole and modeled on an American framework—that Chinese and other immigrant groups achieved success in the Islands. While Hawai'i's racial composition was very different from that of other places, including the United States, we have seen that racial difference was incorporated into a version of Hawai'i that would be promoted as an example of U.S. racial tolerance during the Cold War era. By making racial difference safe and acceptable—always within a white-dominated framework—Hawai'i became a symbol of neoliberal multiculturalism.[57] Chinese success could be offered as a happy example of that framework working for nonwhite groups, too.

Indeed, Chinese success in Hawai'i fits snugly in the performance of those processes and ideology. Chinatown offers concrete evidence of the success of a neoliberal multicultural model and an assertion that it is the best model for the United States. Ethnic groups—the model minorities— who adhere to that model are the ones who find success and are held up as evidence of the U.S. society's tolerance of racial difference. As she recounts the success of Chinese in Kaua'i, a Hawai'i Chinese journalist proudly points to the legacy of Chinese in the Islands: "They accepted the social order as it existed without trying to reform it, relentlessly pursued their vision of its potentials and harvested brilliant success."[58]

Central to the neoliberal multicultural framework and to a group's societal acceptance is evidence of good consumption, which underscores that tolerance of racial difference does not necessarily mean a different version of success but rather an acceptance of the dominant group's version, one based on economic position, financial standing, and proper consumption.[59] In this way, Chinatown celebrates "good Asians" and signals who is accorded social citizenship in Hawai'i and in the United States. Today, Chinatown is no longer about the segregation that defined it in the past but about a future in which multiculturalism—an acknowledgment and appreciation of difference—is marked and celebrated.[60] In projecting Chinatown as an important ethnic space, and one that celebrates success, other Honolulu and O'ahu neighborhoods, such as Kalihi (Filipino), Nānākuli (Native Hawaiian), and Kūhiō Park (Samoan), are not celebrated or put on tourist maps. Those differences suggest that the acceptance of nonwhite groups is a limited and contingent appreciation, bestowed only upon those who reflect the dominant neoliberal ideology. As Olaf Kaltmeier argues, in "the postmodern urban cultural economy, ethnicity must sell in order to gain the right of recognition."[61] Thus, what is celebrated is a "permitted multiculturalism" or a "permitted ethnicity," one contingent on being consumable. In this way, a place like Chinatown simplifies those processes of inclusion and exclusion, and what is left is celebration. The absence of groups who may not present themselves as model minorities is not easily noticed.

Chinatown also hints at the important ties to Asia about which Hawai'i regularly boasts. Such ties include both those that have arisen from immigration from China to Hawai'i and current connections. Thus, Chinatown, Chinese, and Chinese business interests help to develop and maintain an assertion that Hawai'i is a valuable place—in itself and for the United States—because of its strong ties to Asia. Community leaders promote their ties to China as a contribution to Hawai'i, supporting trade missions to China, Taiwan, and Hong Kong and providing evidence that the community is "playing a significant role in globalizing Hawai'i and helping the establishment of the budding relationship between Hawai'i and China."[62] Through these activities, Hawai'i asserts its importance as part of a globalized world and as leading U.S. forays into Asia and the Pacific. China's investments—especially in commercial real estate and business investments—have not been as strong as those in other places, such as Sydney or California.[63] Indeed, one analyst sees the China wave as not "as fast or as large as we expected,"[64] attributing the low level of investment to the limited investment opportunities in Hawai'i, especially compared with other potential sites. Nevertheless, and in spite of the challenges Hawai'i poses to investors, including the high costs of land and labor, Hawai'i continues to position itself as an economic bridge to Asia.

That all of these shifts in Hawai'i's economy and society were happening in the shadow of—and as part of—U.S. empire building is hidden in the celebration of neoliberal multiculturalism. It is difficult to see the complete history of Chinese in Hawai'i from the available discourse told through buildings, districts, and brochures. It is difficult to discern from that evidence that Chinese navigated a landscape rooted in the relationship between Hawai'i and the United States. The large role of the U.S. military—in Hawai'i, the larger Pacific, and in Asia—is missing in this version of the story. Neither the racial politics of Hawai'i and the United States nor the use of Hawai'i by the United States to achieve its Cold War aims, as discussed in chapter 4, is readily apparent in the space of Chinatown today, and in fact seem deliberately avoided and absent. Rather, an alternative interpretation is represented: *because* of U.S. involvement and benevolence in Hawai'i, groups like Chinese were able to rise from poor beginnings to take their place as equals in society.

In addition, and key to an understanding of what Chinatown is and is not, is that its history—and its celebration—ignore important elements of the Hawai'i landscape. First, in celebrating Chinese achievement, there is an implicit argument that all minority groups—all ethnicities—have done equally well, having similarly followed a pathway from plantation to positions of success and power. But that perception belies the continuing inequality in Hawai'i. Filipinos, for example, are much less likely to have a college education than Chinese, have lower household and individual incomes, and are much less likely to have entered elite groups in business or government.[65] Samoans and Tongans have faced similar challenges to finding success in the face of discrimination and lack of opportunity in Hawai'i. Further, Chinatown not only does not acknowledge the history and experience of Hawaiians but actually erases their history, creating a silence around the crises that Hawaiians continue to face today. As is true of the Chinese community, the image of the Hawaiian community has been constructed to align with U.S. interests. Ignored and silenced during the Cold War, Native Hawaiians have since remain marginalized on their own land. The multicultural model to which neoliberalism adheres has no space for indigenous populations. If its underlying argument is that any group can succeed by following a white capitalist model, it cannot address the claims of indigenous peoples who are not interested in inclusion but looking for something else entirely. "Unlike other minoritized groups, the political project of Indigenous peoples is not one of inclusion, equality, or even equity (what does the equitable distribution of stolen land . . . look like?)[;] rather it is about decolonization, a political project that begins and ends with land and its return," say Sandy Grande and Lauren Anderson.[66] The neoliberal framework does not allow for inclusion or even recognition of indigenous claims. In this model, the very celebration of Chinese success because of "a nominally antiracist liberal state that [has] declared itself reformed of the racial violences of the earlier white supremacist state" helps to disappear the history of Native Hawaiians: "Ironically, the very act of claiming that racial and settler colonial dispossession and violence are entirely of the past is exactly the ideological structure through which settler colonialism replicates itself in the present."[67] Evidence that the success of groups like Chinese came about through the involvement of the United States with Hawai'i as it grew its empire is nowhere available in Chinatown.

CHINATOWN TODAY

The recent attention to the problems of Chinatown, such as violence and increasing homelessness, and a general sense that it is not an easy place to navigate indicates how disturbing these issues are to many. Vendors, restaurant owners, and business owners in the area worry about whether business will suffer because negative stories keep customers away. Potential visitors worry about how safe it is to travel, shop, and eat there. But concerns also go deeper. These issues reflect the difficulties that many in Hawai'i have in finding a foothold in the Islands, including struggles with mental health and poverty. For Honolulu more broadly, Chinatown's proximity to the central business and the capitol districts highlights the continuing struggles that Honolulu and Hawai'i face in providing all people a safe, healthy, and satisfying life. But the focus on Chinatown itself has further ramifications that connect to its special place in the Hawai'i landscape. For Chinese, negative images of the area seem to reflect on the ethnic group itself. If Chinatown represents how far Chinese have come from their early plantation days, how should they react when Chinatown is seen as dirty and dangerous? Here, David Wilson's argument of how "good" neighborhoods rely on "bad" ones for their meaning is relevant. He argues that Chicago's Chinatown stands out, and is viewed more positively, because it is *not* a poor ethnic "ghetto," like those that can be found in other parts of the city.[68] In that case, what does the negative image of Honolulu's Chinatown do to the argument that Chinese are immigrant success stories? And what happens to the argument that Chinatown serves as a visible symbol of how all races and ethnicities are welcomed into the Islands and the United States? The value—both material and symbolic—of Chinatown to many is clear from the increased resources the city has devoted to the area (e.g., police protection, infrastructure support, beautification efforts) and in how the area is discussed by local government officials, such as Mayor Rick Blangiardi's announcement that revitalizing Chinatown is a priority of his administration.[69]

PUTTING HONOLULU'S CHINATOWN IN COMPARATIVE PERSPECTIVE

Comparing Honolulu's Chinatown with other Chinatowns and other ethnic and social urban spaces illuminates the importance of context. Honolulu's Chinatown shares many of the worries, struggles, and successes that other neighborhoods have faced. But because of its unique context, its unique history and people, no other Chinatowns quite mirror Honolulu's.

As one of the largest, oldest, and most famous Chinatowns in North America, San Francisco's Chinatown stands out as a model of Chinese community with a long history. Indeed, as we have seen in earlier chapters, the Chinatowns of Honolulu and San Francisco have many similarities, especially historical ones. For both, a perceived threat of disease and infection shaped authorities' attention to the area. But today, the two Chinatowns are quite different from each other; for example, Honolulu's is much smaller in size and scope. The traffic through these Chinatowns is also quite different. In San Francisco, Chinatown draws Chinese from the area, who shop, visit, attend school, and do business in the district. But it is also a major tourist attraction for the city. After the San Francisco fire of 1906, Chinatown rebuilt in a style meant to enhance its appeal to white visitors. Prompted by an elite Chinese merchant in the area and building on white interests in Chinatown, local merchants and building owners (both Chinese and white) rebuilt in an exotic, "oriental style" of architecture designed to "attract tourists" and "boost business." "Hence," says Raymond Rast, "the Sing Chong Building at the northwest corner of California and Grant was distinguished by pagoda-like towers, upturned eaves, and a color scheme of bright red, green, and gold. Architects designing other buildings followed suit."[70] The new architecture was seen as more "authentic" and brought in more tourism, leading to the area becoming a major tourist attraction for the city. While Chinatown in Honolulu has done some "self-orientalizing," it has not been nearly as extensive as what is seen in San Francisco.

There are, of course, Chinatowns in other parts of the world where the majority of the population and many visitors are Asian, thus potentially muting interest in "self-orientalizing." In such places, if there is interest in bringing tourists to the area, organizers and tourist industry leaders must consider what the special attraction of a Chinese-dominated area is.[71] On the other hand, as may be true in Hawai'i, many visitors from outside Asia now experience difference from their own communities in the wider society and thus may not find Chinatown as attractively different, or as different from its surroundings, as they might in other cities. As we have seen, Chinatowns take on specific uses and meanings rooted in their local histories. For example, Singapore's Chinatown is seen as

CHINATOWN TODAY

a site of first settlement for Chinese immigrants and in that way makes distinctions between newer and more established generations of Chinese Singaporeans.[72]

In many U.S. cities, certain neighborhoods were also home to immigrants from Europe, becoming places that were symbols of immigrant settlement and that provided shelter to residents amid hostile social interactions. The differences between these areas and Chinatowns speak to the different experiences of Asian and white immigrants in the United States over the last centuries. Places like Little Italy in New York City provided newly arrived Italian immigrants with a safe haven where they could interact with others like themselves, where Italian rather than English was the usual language heard on the streets and in the shops, and where connections among neighbors and friends helped the newly arrived to adjust to their new home. Little Italy's importance to Italian Americans lessened as Italians moved into mainstream society, were educated in American schools, and were hired into American firms and businesses. Being Italian continued to be an important identity for later generations, but it was a chosen one, one that has involved participating in rituals and experiences that continue to be meaningful but that are no longer subject to prejudice or discrimination by others. Individuals from such groups often represent their ethnic ties symbolically rather than tangibly. Here, too, we can talk about safe difference, how ethnicity and ethnic experiences add spice and interesting elements to American life but without interrupting a larger American racial narrative.

Chinese Americans, with their obvious racial difference from other Americans, have not had the same choice in how they connect with their racial group because the presumptions and actions of others are often a determining factor in their place in society. Thus, if the importance of Chinatown to and its influence on the Chinese residents of a city lessens over time, that process is likely different from what white ethnic groups have experienced. The fates of the spaces of Chinese and white ethnic groups has also likely differed. In places like New York, for example, the original Chinatown in Manhattan has generated multiple outlying Chinatowns, such as those in Flushing, Queens, and Sunset Park in Brooklyn, as well as a number of smaller Chinese areas in the New York City area, such as those in Forest Hills and Elmhurst. That Chinatown has not disappeared but remains a vital place for Chinese and non-Chinese residents alike is significant, speaking to the continuing need for whatever Chinatown offers them: Chinese foods and ingredients, a place where Chinese is the spoken language—and a refuge from discrimination encountered elsewhere in the city. In most parts of the United States, Chinese continue to be seen as separate and, by many Americans, as forever foreign.

Other groups have clustered in neighborhoods, seeking a friendly or safe space for themselves. That those neighborhoods have diminished in importance also provides some lessons about Chinatown in Honolulu. For example, "gayborhoods" were established in U.S. cities like Washington, DC, and Chicago when being openly gay carried risks and dangers. In these areas, gay residents felt they could be themselves and avoided the discrimination they experienced in other parts of the city. But over the last decade or so, many of these neighborhoods have been changing for a number of reasons. As the U.S. population in general has come to accept gay people, as same-sex marriage is now legal across the country and is increasingly accepted, as the acceptance of gay people moving into other neighborhoods has increased, and as many gay people are now able to be open about their sexuality with their families, at work, and at churches, many have less need for a neighborhood of their own.[73] In addition, gayborhoods have often been located in areas with higher rents and real estate costs, making them expensive places to live for anyone.

It may be the trajectory of some gayborhoods, rather than those of other ethnic enclaves, that most mirrors that of Honolulu's Chinatown. Chinese in Hawai'i are now able to live across the Islands, they experience little overt discrimination against them because of their being ethnically Chinese, and Chinatown is often not considered an ideal place to raise a family. Such a process is less likely to occur in cities where Chinese Americans or Asian Americans more generally remain a minority. But in Hawai'i, where Asians, Hawaiians, and Pacific Islanders make up about three-quarters of the population, Chinese are able to move around the Islands without much attention. But what is lost with a decline in the importance of these neighborhoods, whether Chinatown or a gayborhood?

From this perspective, we can better appreciate that the designation of Honolulu's Chinatown as a historic district preserves something not as easily preserved in other places. Despite its nod to a static meaning of Chinese, historic preservation has also kept outside forces from completely overtaking the area. Its location near the central business district makes

CHINATOWN TODAY

Chinatown's land especially valuable and likely to be subject to massive high-rise construction if restrictions were removed. That Chinatown is a place not only for Chinese actually underscores my earlier argument that efforts to preserve Chinatown can also be interpreted as a resistance to a modern Western version of an urban landscape, as I discussed in chapter 5. Chinatown today, with its low-rise buildings and small family businesses, resists the flashy and upscale nature of most cities' central areas. It is an assertion that Hawai'i and Honolulu are different from other American cities and evidence, perhaps, that Hawai'i has held on to its version of the urban and of ethnicity differently from other places.

As Kay Anderson argues about Vancouver's Chinatown, the social geography of Honolulu's Chinatown is "the built and physical landscape [and] the transformation into material form of past and newly negotiated realities [and demonstrates that] landscapes are linked in circular relations to ideological formations, systems of power, and sets of social relations."[74] In the process of the enormous changes that have taken place in the United States and in its connections with Asia and the Pacific, the meaning of Chineseness has also changed. And with it the place and meaning of Chinatown. In the past, a vision of the United States as white and assumptions that the Chinese "were fundamentally and constitutionally different from other immigrant groups and from the general population"[75] kept Chinese outside the polity. Chinatown represented that foreignness, that exclusion. In recent years, Chinese have come to reflect the multicultural nature of the United States today. From that perspective, Chinatown represents an attention to multiculturalism, its otherness incorporated safely into a white society. It is a way to celebrate difference, but on particular terms—where race is a commodity, consumption is key, and success is financial success. We have also seen how the place of Hawai'i's Chinese and Chinatown is not just about racial dynamics in Hawai'i but also about the politics of the relationship between Hawai'i and the United States and U.S. empirical history, in which Hawai'i played a central role in creating a settler colonial society and aligning racial groups in a particular way. Chinatown pays tribute to a particular brand of inclusion, one that celebrates those who perform in the (white) American (capitalist) way and hides the history of white empire builders who stole Native Hawaiians' land—and country. While the United States has engaged in this history and these processes in many places, Hawai'i's history is also different from that of other places. Hawai'i's Chinatown is necessarily

CHINATOWN TODAY

different from other Chinatowns because of the differently racialized society around it. Chinatown is a result of the unique history of Hawai'i and of Chinese in Hawai'i, a living testament to the challenges Hawai'i has faced, seen (as have Asians in the United States more generally), as being apart from and a part of the United States.

LAST WORDS

This volume has argued that Chinatown is the physical manifestation and representation of the racial politics in Hawai'i and in the relationship between Hawai'i and the United States. These politics—including their history and meaning—reflect many of the ideologies, experiences, and goals of Hawai'i more generally. Chinatown "function[s] as [a] 'reality' that help[s] to infuse narrations of people, places and processes with meaning."[76] Central to this story is the way that race was brought into the U.S. empire. The history of Hawai'i, including but not limited to the experience of Chinese there, reflects the complicated process of racialized empire building. As Jodi Byrd has argued, to appreciate the complexities of that process, places like Hawai'i—with its many groups of settlers, who arrived with different resources and had different experiences and outcomes, argues for a wider lens than one that sees settler colonialism as only about settlers and natives.[77] In Hawai'i, all of its groups—Native Hawaiians, Chinese, Japanese, haole, and others—were part of the process of U.S. empire building. Chinatown allows us to see the place of Chinese, but Chinatown's place is best understood in the larger context of a racialized Hawai'i, the interconnected histories and experiences of its various communities, and the relationship between Hawai'i and the United States.

Thinking about whiteness in novel ways allows us to fully appreciate the influence of those larger processes. Michelle Christian has argued that the construction of race operates at the global level, a construction that emerged with modernity. She urges us to think about whiteness not as a thing but as a process, and thus beyond bodies, and makes a case for seeing the world as shaped by a "deep and malleable whiteness."[78] The power of whiteness comes from the "persistence of white domination globally, and in all national racial social systems, even those that are ostensibly without white bodies."[79] She explains, "As a process . . . whiteness embodies a structural position of historical global wealth accumulation and political economic power that reproduced itself through contemporary structural practice. Whiteness also embodies the discursive meanings to the characteristics of whiteness . . . as a form of symbolic value, morality, aesthetics and advancement."[80] That whiteness is deeply embedded in global capitalism and has structured all social systems—spatial arrangements, wealth, tastes, values, preferences, and family, among others—even in places whose populations are not predominantly white.

Hawai'i, with its complex and fluid racial politics, its settler colonial history, and its relationship to U.S. empire building, is an important site in which to consider this model. J. Kēhaulani Kauanui elaborates Christian's argument in addressing the role of colonialism in this global system: "Coloniality—the establishment of racialized and gendered socioeconomic and political hierarchies according to an invented Eurocentric standard is part of all forms of colonialization . . . and [has] determined the socioeconomic, racial and epistemological value systems of contemporary society, commonly called 'modern' society."[81] The experience of Chinese in the Islands reflects these processes, but the work of Kauanui and many others[82] reminds us that despite Hawai'i being a predominantly nonwhite society, all groups there have been affected by the power of this global system and the pervasive power of whiteness and that different groups have interacted with whiteness differently and thus experienced different outcomes.[83] The differences in how Chinese and Native Hawaiians negotiated this system are salient, reflecting elements of the cultural histories of each group, the role of each in the designs of the white authorities as they tightened their grip on Hawai'i and expanded the U.S. empire, and the ways groups caught in this web interacted with and influenced the others as they threaded their own pathway through the white system.

For example, Kauanui has traced the ways that Kānaka leaders, in the midst of haole takeover, acted in "paradoxical" ways by using the American (white, Western) system in their efforts to protect Hawaiian sovereignty. We might consider these leaders complicit in the processes of colonialization—through how they aided and enabled the imposition of Christian, capitalist ways that restructured Hawaiian society through acts such as the privatization of property (via the Māhele land division and the Kuleana Act) and the imposition of Christian marriage as the legitimate form of family. But Kauanui argues that these acts on the part of Hawaiian elites were carried out under great structural duress—"which undoubtedly shaped the entire range of their policy choices"[84]—and were actually instituted in an effort to fend off colonization and haole control.[85] Hawaiian leaders understood the need for Hawai'i to be seen as modern and civilized and that the metrics used to measure modernity were Western, white, and Christian. Yet, adopting nineteenth-century conventions that Hawaiian leaders hoped would allow Hawai'i to be accepted as a legitimate nation and keep takeover at bay "paradoxically [meant] . . . submitt[ing] to colonial logics."[86] Another example of Western influence on Hawaiian systems is how the basis of citizenship changed. For Hawaiians, it was allegiance that formed the basis of citizenship, but that changed in 1887 when the king was forced to sign the Bayonet Constitution. From that point on—following Western logics—race took on new importance and became the new basis of citizenship.[87] With the passage of that constitution, groups, including Chinese, were disenfranchised not because they were disloyal to the king and the kingdom but because of their race. Indeed, in what happened in Hawai'i, we see further support for Michelle Christian's argument that race emerged with modernity.

The experience of Chinese in Hawai'i was vastly different from that of Native Hawaiians, but they, too, were subject to the power, dominance, and influence of the deep and malleable whiteness that pervaded Hawai'i. They were outsiders to Hawai'i society, but—brought in primarily as laborers for plantation work—they were vital to haole plans for the economic development of the Islands. Marked as "unassimilable" by haole in Hawai'i and white Americans, Chinese pushed back and strove to find ways to be accepted by Hawai'i society, as we have seen throughout this volume. Most obviously, they used their resources to develop a parallel system. And many Chinese did indeed, forge a successful pathway into modern and modernizing Hawai'i. But, notably, and in contrast to Hawaiian strategies, most Chinese efforts aimed not at overthrowing or even resisting the haole-dominated system but rather at finding a pathway to inclusion in it. Thus, it is key that the distance that Chinese traveled from their early plantation origins reflects not only their own efforts but that those efforts were undertaken as part of a framework in which "whiteness remains the uncontested marker of cultural, economic, political, social, and symbolic capital and power."[88] The clearest evidence of Chinese success is their economic success, particularly their investment in real estate. In this, we see the shadow of the white American, capitalist, Christian, colonial influences that have been dominant in Hawai'i for the last two centuries. The Māhele land division of 1848(and the subsequent Kuleana Act of 1850) was not only "the single most critical dismemberment of Hawaiian society"[89] but as land was privatized and made available for sale, it also provided Chinese an important entry to success in Hawai'i; by buying land, they were able to establish and later expand their financial footprint in the Islands. Chinese entry into Hawai'i's economy—their development of entrepreneurial success—was also predicated on Hawai'i's connection to the global economy and the importance of global capitalism to U.S. empire building. Their perceived value and acceptance—as a nonwhite group—has been based on their proximity to capitalism,[90] and, as we have seen, their willingness and ability to consume properly. There is a certain irony that the strategies—particularly the privatization of land—used by Hawaiian leaders to navigate the difficult terrain of the threat of white dominance and takeover actually opened the door to Chinese success. Chinese history and their navigation of the haole-controlled social and economic realms of Hawai'i, then, allow us to see "how non-white bodies and spaces can symbolically and materially gain advantages of whiteness."[91] Chinese took advantage of what white colonializing efforts and empire building did in Hawai'i and, in the process, helped to reinscribe the very system that had kept Chinese themselves out for decades. Tracing Chinese experience highlights "the situated, actual events through which Asian settlers invest, and are invested, in US colonialism."[92]

The different strategies employed by the Native Hawaiian and Chinese communities underscore how the parameters of the system—the structural constraints—shape responses. As Kauanui argues about the ways Kānaka leaders enacted laws that were also, in the end, harmful to the community, "This is not to disregard the[ir] agency . . . but to account for the structural forces that shaped their adaptation and to assess the costs."[93] Indeed, there has been and continues to be resistance of many kinds to the dominant narratives. Resistance has included labor strikes on the plantations, the development of a "local" identity as oppositional to haole control[94]; the many Hawaiian actions against U.S. dominance and control[95]; legal challenges to discrimination faced by various groups, including Filipinos, in the hiring process for public jobs[96]; and even girls' resistance to white models in literature.[97] Despite the resistance by all nonwhite groups in Hawai'i against colonial dominance, the effectiveness of any such resistance must contend with the power of hegemony[98] and the fact that hegemony involves not just political and economic control but also its equally powerful influence on values, beliefs, social norms, and expectations. As we have seen, haole influenced even the possibility of cooperation and alliance between Native Hawaiians and Chinese in their efforts to sustain or expand their communities or to resist haole domination.

As we assess the meaning of Chinatown today, these historical processes must be part of our calculation. In recent decades, Chinese have come to reflect the multicultural nature of the United States today. Here, then, we see how otherness is brought safely into the (deep and malleable) whiteness of Hawai'i society. As discussed in earlier chapters, Chinese accepted the racial bribe offered by haole and became incorporated into the settler colonial system. In that process, we see that Chinese inclusion not only helped to sustain and strengthen the system but was actually a *part of* the settler colonial system. In how Chinese are now held up as a model of success, by both by haole and Chinese themselves, Chinese have thus played an important role. Their history points to how inclusion (of Chinese) or noninclusion (of Native Hawaiians) plays a role in the success not only of the group but of the very continuation of the system itself. In the process, "Asian settlers' shift from subjection to white settler colonialism into shareholders of that system [and] buoyed an 'illusion' of modern Hawai'i multiracial harmony."[99] In both cases, haole control was justified: in how Chinese needed guidance in assimilating into the white culture and how Native Hawaiians needed governing by a "more civilized" group to thrive or even survive.

Thus, Honolulu's Chinatown celebrates neoliberal multiculturalism and the successful inclusion of Chinese in that framework, providing evidence of Chinese as proper consumers and promotors of the global capitalist system. It celebrates "good Asians" and marks their achievements. According to Grace Kyungwon Hong, the model-minority discourse argues for a "narrative that 'Asians have been able to overcome the racist treatment and policies . . . to form a harmonious multiculturalism.'"[100] Bianca Kai Isaki reminds us that that process proceeds partly by "resetting the historical referent of Hawai'i's social formation to plantation-era in-migration of Asians, Portuguese, and Chicano laborers, as opposed to the 1893 Overthrow of the Hawaiian Kingdom."[101] That move, juxtaposing nonwhite immigrants with haole, works to construct an ongoing "settler community by, amongst other things, eliding . . . [the] history of settler complicity with Hawaiian dispossession."[102] In this way, Chinatown represents the "liberal moral allegory of nonwhite groups into the United States."[103] Chinatown underscores how an acceptable model of multiculturalism can be celebrated as a better outcome than either a racist all-white system or acknowledging indigenous claims to sovereignty. As Dean Itsuji Saranillio writes, "This representational strategy of working through racial difference, in other words, to use a multicultural non-White face as a means to further consolidate US settler and imperial hegemony, is itself the afterlife of Hawai'i's movement for statehood and its ideological function in post-war US empire building during the Cold War."[104]

That Hawai'i's is a white system does not mean Asians are exempt from an understanding and acknowledgment of how their strategies of resistance and for acceptance came at the expense of others and underscores their responsibility to work to resist and change it.[105] Indeed, it is incumbent upon those who are as successful as Chinese have been in Hawai'i to be agents of change. Understanding that settler colonialism is "a structure, not an event"[106] means that Hawai'i's colonialism is not simply of the past but is ongoing, and all in Hawai'i continue to play a role. Those, like the Chinese, who occupy powerful positions and have benefited from the colonial system must acknowledge that history and their role in it and work toward change.[107] In her analysis of two exhibits at the Bishop Museum in Honolulu representing the experiences of Asian Americans and Native Hawaiians, Lisa King has pointed out that rather than "creating parallel narratives of oppression in [an] effort to demonstrate how each community has suffered and overcome," it is more effective to acknowledge the interwoven histories of these groups in Hawai'i's history, to form alliances, and to "find . . . ways to dismantle the systems that created that oppression."[108] As Saranillio argues, "Placing Asian American and Native histories in conversation might create the conditions of possibility of using settler colonialism against itself, where social justice-oriented Asian Americans might conceptualize liberation in ways that are accountable to Native aims for decolonization."[109]

We see, then, that Chinatown speaks to the deep and strong white imprint even—or especially—on a place like Hawai'i, where white people have never been numerically dominant but have always played a dominant role in shaping the experiences, successes, and failures of all who reside there, as well as in Hawai'i's role in Asia and the Pacific. In Chinatown, we

CHINATOWN TODAY

see how place and race have come to play a role in the racialized ideology of the United States that has undergirded its empire. In the U.S. seizure and annexation of Hawai'i, in the use of Hawai'i to shore up American interests and exploits during and after the Cold War, and in the deepening effects of a neoliberal multicultural model that has spread throughout the world, the story of Chinese in Hawai'i illuminates the key role that Hawai'i has played in U.S. history and racial politics.

NOTES

NOTES ON TERMINOLOGY

1. Jonathan Okamura, "Why There Are No Asian Americans in Hawai'i: The Continuing Significance of Local Identity," in "The Political Economy of Hawai'i," ed. Ibrahim G. Aoude, special issue, *Social Process in Hawai'i* 35 (1994): 161–78.

INTRODUCTION: RACE AND PLACE IN THE EMPIRE

1. Nicholas Ordway and Michaelyn Chou, "Chinatown as Metaphor: Special Views of Chinese Land Ownership in Hawaii" (Paper presented at Lucky You Come Hawaii Conference, Honolulu, HI, July 18–21, 1988), 1.
2. Nayan Shah, *Contagious Divides: Epidemics and Race in San Francisco's Chinatown* (Berkeley: University of California Press, 2001), 129.
3. Michelle Christian and Assumpta Namaganda, "Good Mzungu? Whiteness and White Supremacy in Postcolonial Uganda," *Identities* 30, no. 2 (2023): 218.
4. Jan Lin, *The Power of Urban Ethnic Places: Cultural Heritage and Community Life* (New York: Routledge, 2011), 9.
5. Gregory Bourassa, "Neoliberal Multiculturalism and Productive Inclusion: Beyond the Politics of Fulfillment in Education," *Journal of Education Policy* 36, no. 2 (2021): 253.
6. David Wilson, "Making Historical Preservation in Chicago: Discourse and Spatiality in Neoliberal Times," *Space and Polity* 8, no. 1 (2004): 44.
7. Thomas Gieryn, "A Space for Place in Sociology," *Annual Review of Sociology* 26 (2000): 466.
8. Gieryn, "A Space for Place," 474.

INTRODUCTION

9. Herbert Gans, "Involuntary Segregation and the Ghetto: Disconnecting Process and Place," *City and Community* 7, no. 4 (2008): 353–57.

10. Yoonmee Chang, *Writing the Ghetto: Class, Authorship, and the Asian American Ethnic Enclave* (New Brunswick, NJ: Rutgers University Press, 2010), 2.

11. Anmol Chaddha and William J. Wilson, "Reconsidering the 'Ghetto,'" *City and Community* 7, no. 4 (2008): 384.

12. Kay Anderson, *Vancouver's Chinatown: Racial Discourse in Canada, 1875–1980* (Montreal, QC: McGill-Queen's University Press, 1991), 18.

13. Talja Blokland, "From Outside Looking In: A 'European' Perspective on the Ghetto," *City and Community* 7, no. 4 (2008): 375.

14. Jesse Shircliff, "Is Chinatown a Place or a Space? A Case Study of Chinatown Singapore," *Geoforum* 117 (2020): 225–33.

15. Ordway and Chou, "Chinatown as Metaphor," 1.

16. Anderson, *Vancouver's Chinatown*, 74ff.

17. Mitchell Duneier, *Ghetto: The Invention of a Place, the History of an Idea* (New York: Farrar, Straus and Giroux, 2016), 44.

18. Duneier, *Ghetto*, 45.

19. Fred Wong, "Chinese Cultural History in the American West Put in Spotlight by Forest Service, Partners," U.S. Department of Agriculture, April 7, 2016, https://www.usda.gov/media/blog/2016/04/07/chinese-cultural-history-american-west-put-spotlight-forest-service-partners; Robert G. Lee, *Orientals: Asian Americans in Popular Culture* (Philadelphia: Temple University Press, 1999), 56–82; 83–89; 91–105.

20. Beth Lew-Williams, *The Chinese Must Go: Violence, Exclusion, and the Making of the Alien in America* (Cambridge, MA: Harvard University Press, 2018), 1–13.

21. Anderson, *Vancouver's Chinatown*, 81.

22. Howard Markel and Alexandra Stern, "The Foreignness of Germs: The Persistent Association of Immigrants and Disease in American Society," *Milbank Quarterly* 80, no. 4 (2002): 757–88; Alan Kraut, "Plagues and Prejudices: Nativism's Construction of Disease in Nineteenth- and Twentieth-Century New York City," in *Hives of Sickness: Public Health and Epidemics in New York City*, ed. David Rosner (New Brunswick, NJ: Rutgers University Press, 1995), 65–90.

23. Markel and Stern, "*Foreignness of Germs*," 764.

24. Markel and Stern, "*Foreignness of Germs*," 764.

25. Roger Daniels, "'No Lamps Were Lit for Them': Angel Island and the Historiography of Asian Americans," *Journal of American Ethnic History* 17 (1997): 2–18.

26. Quoted in Yong Chen, *Chinese San Francisco, 1850–1943* (Palo Alto, CA: Stanford University Press, 2000), 147.

27. Shah, *Contagious Divides*, 74.

28. Chen, *Chinese San Francisco*, 98–99.

29. Barbara Berglund, *Making San Francisco American: Cultural Frontiers in the Urban West, 1846–1906* (Lawrence: University Press of Kansas, 2007), 98.

30. Berglund, *Making San Francisco American*, 100.

31. Anderson, *Vancouver's Chinatown*, 92.

32. John Kuo Wei Tchen, *New York Before Chinatown: Orientalism and the Shaping of American Culture, 1776–1882* (Baltimore, MD: Johns Hopkins University Press, 1999), 276–78.

INTRODUCTION

33. Amy Sueyoshi, *Discriminating Sex: White Leisure and the Making of the American "Oriental"* (Champaign: University of Illinois Press, 2018), 21–23.
34. Min Zhou, *Chinatown: The Socioeconomic Potential of an Urban Enclave* (Philadelphia: Temple University Press, 1992), 8–10; Volkan Aytar and Jan Rath, "Introduction: Ethnic Neighborhoods as Places of Leisure and Consumption," in *Selling Ethnic Neighborhoods: The Rise of Neighborhoods as Places of Consumption*, ed. Volkan Aytar and Jan Rath (London: Taylor and Francis, 2011), 1–15; Lin, *The Power of Urban Ethnic Places*, 27–31.
35. Kartik Naram, "'No Place Like Home': Racial Capitalism, Gentrification, and the Identity of Chinatown," *Asian American Policy Review* 27 (2017): 33–50.
36. Bernard P. Wong, "Introduction: Chinatowns Around the World," in *Chinatowns Around the World: Gilded Ghetto, Ethnopolis, and Cultural Diaspora*, ed. Bernard P. Wong and Chee-Beng Tan (Leiden: Brill, 2013), 1–18.
37. On San Francisco, see Chen, *Chinese San Francisco*, 58.
38. Chen, *Chinese San Francisco*, 61.
39. Chen, *Chinese San Francisco*, 47; see also Duneier, *Ghetto*, 217–30.
40. Shah, *Contagious Divides*, 209.
41. Mae Ngai, *The Lucky Ones: One Family and the Extraordinary Invention of Chinese America* (Princeton, NJ: Princeton University Press, 2012), 47–48.
42. Guenter Risse, "Translating Western Modernity: The First Chinese Hospital in America," *Bulletin of the History of Medicine* 85, no. 3 (2011): 413–47.
43. Risse, "Translating Western Modernity." The hospital was destroyed in the San Francisco earthquake and fire of 1906 and was not rebuilt until 1925.
44. Peter Kwong, *The New Chinatown* (New York: Hill and Wang, 1987), 81–123.
45. Bernard P. Wong, "Introduction: Chinatowns Around the World," 4.
46. Hsiang-shui Chen, *Chinatown No More: Taiwan Immigrants in Contemporary New York* (Ithaca, NY: Cornell University Press, 1992).
47. Timothy Fong, *The First Suburban Chinatown: The Remaking of Monterey Park, California* (Philadelphia: Temple University Press, 1994); Min Zhou, *Contemporary Chinese America: Immigration, Ethnicity, and Community Transformation* (Philadelphia: Temple University Press, 2009).
48. Zhou, *Contemporary Chinese America*, 82.
49. Zhou, *Contemporary Chinese America*.
50. Cindy I-fen Cheng, *Citizens of Asian America: Democracy and Race During the Cold War* (New York: NYU Press, 2013), 30–48.
51. Ching Lan Pang, "Gateways to the Urban Economy: Chinatowns in Antwerp and Brussels," in *Selling Ethnic Neighborhoods: The Rise of Neighborhoods as Places of Leisure and Consumption*, ed. Volkan Aytar and Jan Rath (London: Taylor and Francis, 2011), 52–67.
52. Rose Hum Lee, "The Decline of Chinatowns in the United States," *American Journal of Sociology* 54, no. 5 (1949): 422–32.
53. Domenic Vitello and Zoe Blickenderfer, "The Planned Destruction of China-towns in the United States and Canada Since c.1900," *Planning Perspectives* 35, no. 1 (2020): 143–68.
54. Vitello and Blickenderfer, "The Planned Destruction of Chinatowns."
55. Bonnie Tsui, *American Chinatown: A People's History of Five Neighborhoods* (New York: Free Press, 2010), 130–33.

INTRODUCTION

56. Lin, *The Power of Urban Ethnic Places*, 36; Pang, "Gateways to the Urban Economy", 52–67; Aytar and Rath, "Introduction," 1–15.
57. Naram, "'No Place Like Home,'" 4.
58. Aytar and Rath, "Introduction," 2.
59. Kay Anderson et al., *Chinatown Unbound: Trans-Asian Urbanism in the Age of China* (Lanham, MD: Rowman and Littlefield, 2019), 133.
60. Anderson, *Vancouver's Chinatown*, 176.
61. Greg Umbach and Dan Wishnoff, "Strategic Self-Orientalism: Urban Planning Policies and the Shaping of New York City's Chinatown, 1950–2005," *Journal of Planning History* 7, no. 3 (2008): 214–38.
62. Peter Li and Eva Xiaoling Li, "Vancouver Chinatown in Transition," in *Chinatowns Around the World: Gilded Ghetto, Ethnopolis, and Cultural Diaspora*, ed. Bernard P. Wong and Chee-Beng Tan (Leiden: Brill, 2013), 27.
63. Anderson et al., *Chinatown Unbound*, 1–14.
64. Anderson et al., *Chinatown Unbound*, 13.
65. Najia Aarim-Heriot, *Chinese Immigrants, African Americans, and Racial Anxiety in the United States, 1848–82* (Champaign: University of Illinois Press, 2003).
66. Gary Okihiro, *Margins and Mainstreams* (Seattle: University of Washington Press, 1994), 10.
67. Susan Craddock, "Embodying Place: Pathologizing Chinese and Chinatown in Nineteenth-Century San Francisco," *Antipode* 31, no. 4 (1999): 355.
68. Laura Eichelberger, "SARS and New York's Chinatown: The Politics of Risk and Blame During an Epidemic of Fear," *Social Science & Medicine* 65, no. 6 (2007): 1284–95.
69. Simeon Man, "Anti-Asian Violence and U.S. Imperialism," *Race & Class* 62, no. 2 (2020): 22–33.
70. Lisa S. H. Park, *Consuming Citizenship: Children of Asian Immigrant Entrepreneurs* (Palo Alto, CA: Stanford University Press, 2005), 4–9.
71. Okihiro, *Margins and Mainstreams*, 142–43.
72. Aytar and Rath, "Introduction," 2.
73. Anderson et al., *Chinatown Unbound*.
74. Aihwa Ong, *Flexible Citizenship: The Cultural Logics of Transnationality* (Durham, NC: Duke University Press, 1999), 16–24.
75. Anderson, *Vancouver's Chinatown*, 145.
76. Julia Katz, "The Politics of the Pipe: Opium Regulation and Protocolonial Governance in Nineteenth-Century Hawai'i" in *Imagining Asia in the Americas*, ed. Zelideth María Rivas and Debbie Lee-DiStefano (New Brunswick, NJ: Rutgers University Press, 2016), 109.
77. Li Jinzhao, "Constructing Chinese America in Hawai'i: The Narcissus Festival, Ethnic Identity, and Community Transformation, 1949–2005" (PhD diss., University of Hawai'i at Mānoa, 2005), 257–58.
78. Ordway and Chou, "Chinatown as Metaphor," 1.
79. Advertisement in *Paradise of the Pacific* 57, no. 3 (1945): 28.
80. Celeste Kay Moore, "Hawaii's Tourists," *Paradise of the Pacific* 59, no. 9 (1947): 18.
81. Thomas Kim, "Being Modern: The Circulation of Oriental Objects," *American Quarterly* 58, no. 2 (2006): 379–406; Rey Chow, "Have You Eaten Yet?" *Amerasia Journal* 31, no. 1 (2005):19–22.

1. SETTING THE STAGE

82. Ligaya Malones, "Bean-to-Bar Chocolate and Sailor Jerry Tats: An Insider's Guide to Honolulu's Chinatown," *New York Magazine*, May 3, 2018.
83. "A Local's Guide to Chinatown Honolulu: Restaurants, Bars & Shopping," Hello Jetlag, accessed August 28, 2023, https://hellojetlag.com/chinatown-honolulu/.
84. Tom Smith, "Hawaiian History and American History: Integration or Separation?" *American Nineteenth Century History* 20, no. 2 (2019): 161–82.
85. John R. Eperjesi, *The Imperialist Imaginary: Visions of Asia and the Pacific in American Culture* (Hanover, NH: Dartmouth College Press, 2005), 2–4; David A. Chang, *The World and All the Things Upon It: Native Hawaiian Geographies of Exploration* (Minneapolis: University of Minnesota Press, 2016), vii–xi.
86. Shah, *Contagious Divides*, 169.
87. Tchen, *New York Before Chinatown*, 263.
88. Tchen, *New York Before Chinatown*, 266.
89. Sue Fawn Chung, *In Pursuit of Gold: Chinese American Miners and Merchants in the American West* (Champaign: University of Illinois Press, 2011).
90. Pang, "Gateways to the Urban Economy."
91. Anderson et al., *Chinatown Unbound*, 108.
92. Gwenfread Allen, *Hawaii's War Years: 1941–1945* (Honolulu: University of Hawai'i Press, 1950), 230–34.
93. Beth Bailey and David Farber, *The First Strange Place: Race and Sex in World War II Hawaii* (Baltimore, MD: Johns Hopkins University Press, 1992).
94. Simeon Man, "Aloha, Vietnam: Race and Empire in Hawai'i's Vietnam War," *American Quarterly* 67, no. 4 (2015): 1085–1108.
95. John F. Kennedy, "Address in Honolulu Before the United States Conference of Mayors," American Presidency Project, June 9, 1963, https://www.presidency.ucsb.edu/documents/address-honolulu-before-the-united-states-conference-mayors.
96. Seth Archer, *Sharks Upon the Land: Colonialism, Indigenous Health, and Culture in Hawai'i, 1778–1855* (Cambridge: Cambridge University Press, 2018).
97. Christian and Namaganda, "Good Mzungu?," 220.
98. Patrick Wolfe, "Settler Colonialism and the Elimination of the Native," *Journal of Genocide Research* 8, no. 4 (2006): 387–409.
99. Lin, *The Power of Urban Ethnic Places*, 9.
100. Jonathan Y. Okamura, *Ethnicity and Inequality in Hawai'i* (Philadelphia: Temple University Press, 2008).
101. Jeff Chang, "Local Knowledge(s): Notes on Race Relations, Panethnicity, and History in Hawai'i," *Amerasia Journal* 22, no. 2 (1996): 1–29.
102. Gieryn, "A Space for Place," 482.

1. SETTING THE STAGE: CHINESE EXPERIENCE BEFORE 1900

1. Robert C. Schmitt, "Shifting Occupational and Class Structures: 1930–1966," in *Modern Hawaii: Perspectives on the Hawaiian Community*, ed. Andrew W. Lind (Honolulu: University of Hawai'i, Labor-Management Education Program, College of Business Administration, 1967), 27–40.
2. Julia Katz, "From Coolies to Colonials: Chinese Migrants in Hawai'i" (PhD diss., Rutgers University, 2018), 26.

1. SETTING THE STAGE

3. Clarence Glick, *Sojourners and Settlers: Chinese Migrants in Hawaii* (Honolulu: University of Hawai'i Press, 1980), 12.

4. Glick, *Sojourners and Settlers*, 12.

5. Jessie Lutz, "Chinese Emigrants, Indentured Workers, and Christianity in the West Indies, British Guiana and Hawaii," *Caribbean Studies* 37, no. 2 (2009): 133–54; author's interview with a descendant of these laborers.

6. Katz, "From Coolies to Colonials", 87; Steven Zuckerman, "Pake in Paradise: A Synthetic Study of Chinese Immigration to Hawaii," *Bulletin of the Institute of Ethnology Academia Sinica* 45 (1978): 39–80.

7. Although the word *coolie* was used in newspapers and some reports, the Chinese were not in fact coolies. The term can be interpreted merely as a translation of the Chinese for "hard work." Chinese laborers in Hawai'i indeed worked hard. But *coolie* has come to be a derogatory term that refers to indentured laborers, not proper workers, and its use in this sense was a way to construct Chinese as acting in ways that "civilized" white people would not.

8. Ronald Takaki, *Pau Hana: Plantation Life and Labor in Hawaii* (Honolulu: University of Hawai'i Press, 1983), 59, quoted in Karen W. F. Lee, "The Coming of the Chinese: The Early Immigrant Community in Hawaii" (PhD diss., University of Hawai'i, 1990), 107.

9. Takaki, *Pau Hana*, 58–60.

10. William Lee, *RHAS Transactions* 1, no. 3 (1852): 6, quoted in Colette Higgins, "Anti-Chinese Sentiments in Hawaii from 1852 to 1886," student paper for History 484 class, fall 1990, 2, Student Papers, Romanzo Adams Social Research Laboratory (RASRL), University of Hawai'i.

11. Zuckerman, "Pake in Paradise," 43–44.

12. Lee, "The Coming of the Chinese," 112.

13. Glick, *Sojourners and Settlers*, 66.

14. Katz, "From Coolies to Colonials," 116.

15. Katz, "From Coolies to Colonials," 116.

16. Julia Katz, "Ahuna and the Mo'o: Rethinking Chinese Success in Hawaiian Commercial Food Production," *Pacific Historical Review* 84, no. 4 (2017): 622.

17. Katz "From Coolies to Colonials," 49, 91; Davianna Pōmaika'i McGregor, *Na Kua'āina: Living Hawaiian Culture* (Honolulu: University of Hawai'i Press, 2007).

18. Katz, "Ahuna and the Mo'o," 601.

19. Katz, "Ahuna and the Mo'o," 619.

20. Katz, "Ahuna and the Mo'o," 600.

21. John Coulter and Chee-kwon Chun, "Chinese Rice Farmers in Hawaii," *University of Hawaii Bulletin* 16, no. 5 (1937): 18.

22. Coulter and Chun, "Chinese Rice Farmers," 54.

23. The details in this paragraph were drawn from Douglas Dai Lun Chong, *Ancestral Reflections: Hawaii's Early Chinese of Waipahu—An Ethnic Community Experience, 1885-1935* (Waipahu, HI: Waipahu Tsong Nyee Society, 1998), xii–xiv.

24. Carol MacLennan, *Sovereign Sugar: Industry and Environment in Hawai'i* (Honolulu: University of Hawai'i Press, 2014), 52.

25. Frank Damon, quoted in Chong, *Ancestral Reflections*, 14.

26. Chong, *Ancestral Reflections*, 99.

1. SETTING THE STAGE

27. Chong, *Ancestral Reflections*, 99.
28. Ping Kyau Minn, *Memoirs of the Third Son: Zane Kee Fook* (Honolulu: Hawaii Chinese History Center, 1978), 8–12.
29. Diane Mai Lin Mark, *Chinese in Kula: Reflections of a Farming Community in Old Hawaii* (Honolulu: Hawaii Chinese History Center, 1975).
30. Katz, "From Coolies to Colonials," 104.
31. Clarence Glick, "Residential Dispersion of Urban Chinese," *Social Process in Hawai'i* 2 (1936): 28–34.
32. Glick, *Sojourners and Settlers*, 128.
33. President of the Board of Education, 1886, quoted in Andrew W. Lind, *Hawaii: The Last of the Magic Isles* (Oxford: Oxford University Press, 1969), 56.
34. Carol Forster, "Chinese Entrepreneurs in Nineteenth Century Hawaii" (master's thesis, University of Alberta, 1995), 27.
35. Katz, "From Coolies to Colonials," 89.
36. Xu Huang, "The Schooling of the Children of Early Chinese Immigrants in Hawaii" (master's thesis, University of Hawai'i, 1989), 79; Sylvianne Fei-Ai Li, "A History of the Education of the Chinese in Hawaii" (master's thesis, Oberlin College, 1940), 2.
37. Li, "A History of the Education," 24.
38. Huang, "The Schooling of the Children," 82.
39. Quoted in Michelle Morgan, "Americanizing the Teachers: Identity, Citizenship, and the Teaching Corps in Hawai'i, 1900–1941," *Western Historical Quarterly* 45, no. 2 (2014): 147.
40. Maenette Kape'ahiokoalani Padeken Benham, "The Voice 'Less' Hawaiian: An Analysis of Educational Policymaking, 1820–1960," *Hawaiian Journal of History* 32 (1998): 132.
41. Li, "A History of the Education," 3.
42. Huang, "The Schooling of the Children," 110.
43. Huang, "The Schooling of the Children," 37.
44. Clif Stratton, *Education for Empire: American Schools, Race, and the Paths of Good Citizenship* (Berkeley: University of California Press, 2016), 87.
45. J. Kēhaulani Kauanui, *Paradoxes of Hawaiian Sovereignty: Land, Sex, and the Colonial Politics of State Nationalism* (Durham, NC: Duke University Press, 2018), 35, quoting Matsuda.
46. Kauanui, *Paradoxes*, 89, quoting Oliveira.
47. Katz, "Ahuna and the Mo'o," 606.
48. Kauanui, *Paradoxes*, 217, quoting Linnekin.
49. Glick, "Residential Dispersion," 25.
50. Edward Lydon, *The Anti-Chinese Movement in the Hawaiian Kingdom, 1852–1886* (San Francisco: R. and E. Research Associates, 1975), 7.
51. Reverend George L. Chaney, quoted in Paul Kimm-Chow Goo, "Building Hawaii's Prosperity," in *The Chinese of Hawaii* (Honolulu, HI: Overseas Penman Club, 1929), 16.
52. Fred K. Lam, "A Survey of the Chinese People in Hawaii Historically, Educationally, Commercially, Religiously, and Socially" (Third Conference of the Institute of Pacific Relations, Kyoto[?], October 31–November 8, 1929).

1. SETTING THE STAGE

53. Robert Man War Lee, "Vertical Mobility Among the Chinese in Hawaii" (master's thesis, University of Hawai'i, 1951), 17.
54. "Chinese store as a social institution," Student Papers, box 9, 1965, RASRL, University of Hawai'i.
55. Bung Chong Lee, "The Chinese Store as Social Institution," *Social Process in Hawaii* 2 (1936): 35–38.
56. "Life in a Chinese grocery store," Student Papers, box 7, 1964, RASRL, University of Hawai'i.
57. Lee, "Vertical Mobility," 20.
58. Lee, "Vertical Mobility," 17.
59. Susan Craddock, "Embodying Place: Pathologizing Chinese and Chinatown in Nineteenth-Century San Francisco," *Antipode* 31, no. 4 (1999): 353.
60. Katharine Coman, *The History of Contract Labor in the Hawaiian Islands* (New York: MacMillan, 1903; New York: Arno, 1978), 36. Citation refers to the Arno edition.
61. *Pacific Commercial Advertiser*, December 23, 1865, quoted in Lydon, *The Anti-Chinese Movement*, 26.
62. Craddock, "Embodying Place," 355.
63. "True Citizens Meeting," *Pacific Commercial Advertiser*, October 16, 1869.
64. Reply of Cabinet to Petition Regarding Chinese Restriction, 1889, quoted in T'ing Y'u Hsieh, "The Chinese in Hawaii," *Chinese Social and Political Science Review* (1930): 23.
65. Lydon, *The Anti-Chinese Movement*, 55.
66. Lydon, *The Anti-Chinese Movement*, 45–47.
67. John E. Reinecke, *Feigned Necessity: Hawaii's Attempt to Obtain Chinese Contract Labor, 1921-23* (San Francisco: Chinese Materials Center, Inc., 1979), 9.
68. H. P. Huang, 1989, cited in Forster, "Chinese Entrepreneurs," 6.
69. Katz, "From Coolies to Colonials," 43.
70. John Harden Connell, "The History of Chinese in Hawaii," *Mid-Pacific Magazine* 46, no. 5 (1933): 419–24.
71. Lydon, *The Anti-Chinese Movement*, 38.
72. Lydon, *The Anti-Chinese Movement*, 9.
73. Lydon, *The Anti-Chinese Movement*, 25.
74. Glick, *Sojourners and Settlers*, 29.
75. Z. Y. Squires, *The Planters' Mongolian Pets* (Honolulu, HI, 1884), 7–8, https://missionhouses.org/library-archives/.
76. Lydon, *The Anti-Chinese Movement*, 40.
77. *Pacific Commercial Advertiser*, November 6, 1869, 2, quoted in Shelton Jim On, "Chinese Immigration to Hawai'i, 1852–1898" (BA honors thesis, University of Hawai'i, 1972), 26.
78. *Pacific Commercial Advertiser*, May 27, 1876, quoted in Lydon, *The Anti-Chinese Movement*, 52.
79. Reverend George L. Chancey, *The Friend* 31, no 11 (1882): 115, quoted in Goo, "Building Hawaii's Prosperity," 16.
80. Derek Taira, "Making 'Womenly Women' or 'Servants of Civilization': Ida Pope and Native Hawaiian Female Education, 1894-1914," *Pacific Historical Review* 92, no.1 (2023): 37.

2. 1900 TO 1930: DESTRUCTION OF CHINATOWN

81. For a similar process in the continental United States, see Manu Karuka, *Tracks of Empire: Indigenous Nations, Chinese Workers, and the Transcontinental Railroad* (Berkeley: University of California Press, 2019), 82–91.
82. Katz, "From Coolies to Colonials," 49.
83. *Pacific Commercial Advertiser*, August 16, 1879, quoted in Lydon, *The Anti-Chinese Movement*, 61.
84. Lydon, *The Anti-Chinese Movement*, 27.
85. H. P. Huang, 1989, cited in Katz, "From Coolies to Colonials."
86. Quoted in Arlene Lum, "The Centenary Was *Not* a Time for Celebration," in *Sailing for the Sun: The Chinese in Hawaii 1789–1989*, ed. Arlene Lum (Honolulu, HI: Three Heroes, 1988), 119.
87. Quoted in Katz, "From Coolies to Colonials," 132.
88. Ho Fong, "The Hawaiian Anti-Asian Union," *Pacific Commercial Advertiser*, March 12, 1888, 3.
89. Yong Chen, *Chinese San Francisco, 1850–1943* (Palo Alto, CA: Stanford University Press, 2000).
90. Nayan Shah, *Contagious Divides: Epidemics and Race in San Francisco's Chinatown* (Berkeley: University of California Press, 2001), 167.
91. Ronald Takaki, "They Also Came: Chinese Women and the Migration to Hawaii" (paper presented at the Lucky You Come Hawaii Conference, Honolulu, HI, July 18–21, 1988).
92. George Anthony Peffer, *If They Don't Bring Their Women Here: Chinese Female Immigration Before Exclusion* (Champaign: University of Illinois Press, 1999), 9.
93. Frank Damon, "Home for the Homeless: A Plea for Chinese Females Immigration," *The Friend* 38, no. 11 (1881): 98.
94. Jessie Lutz, "Chinese Emigrants, Indentured Workers, and Christianity in the West Indies, British Guiana and Hawaii," *Caribbean Studies* 37, no. 2 (2009): 133–54.
95. Jim On, "Chinese Immigration," 17.
96. Peffer, *If They Don't Bring Their Women Here*, 19.
97. Takaki, "They Also Came," 20.

2. 1900 TO 1930: DESTRUCTION OF CHINATOWN AND THE (RE)BUILDING OF A CHINESE AMERICAN COMMUNITY

1. Willy Daniel Kaipo Kauai, "The Color of Nationality: Continuities and Discontinuities of Citizenship in Hawai'i" (PhD diss., University of Hawai'i, 2014), 152.
2. Robert C. Schmitt, *Demographic Statistics of Hawaii: 1778–1965* (Honolulu: University of Hawai'i Press, 1968), 120–21.
3. Edward Lydon, *The Anti-Chinese Movement in the Hawaiian Kingdom, 1852–1886* (San Francisco: R. and E. Research Associates, 1975), 8.
4. Carol MacLennan, *Sovereign Sugar: Industry and Environment in Hawai'i* (Honolulu: University of Hawai'i Press, 2014), 27.
5. Noel Kent, *Hawaii: Islands Under the Influence* (Honolulu: University of Hawai'i Press, 1993), 78.
6. Kent, *Hawaii*, 72.

2. 1900 TO 1930: DESTRUCTION OF CHINATOWN

7. Schmitt, *Demographic Statistics*, 70, 116.
8. Clarence Glick, "Residential Dispersion of Urban Chinese," *Social Process in Hawai'i* 2 (1936): 28–34.
9. Schmitt, *Demographic Statistics*, 120.
10. Glick, "Residential Dispersion," 25.
11. Eileen Tamura, *Americanization, Acculturation, and Ethnic Identity: The Nisei Generation in Hawaii* (Champaign: University of Illinois Press, 1994), 191, quoted in Qi Chen, "The Acculturation of Chinese Intellectuals in Hawaii: 1894–1959" (PhD diss., University of Hawai'i, 1997), 63.
12. Q. Chen, "The Acculturation of Chinese Intellectuals," 64.
13. Q. Chen, "The Acculturation of Chinese Intellectuals," 66.
14. Howard Markel and Alexandra Stern, "The Foreignness of Germs: The Persistent Association of Immigrants and Disease in American Society," *Milbank Quarterly* 80, no. 4 (2002): 757–88.
15. Alan Kraut, "Plagues and Prejudices: Nativism's Construction of Disease in Nineteenth- and Twentieth-Century New York City," in *Hives of Sickness: Public Health and Epidemics in New York City*, ed. David Rosner (New Brunswick, NJ: Rutgers University Press, 1995), 65–90.
16. Markel and Stern, "The Foreignness of Germs," 765.
17. Joan B. Trauner, "The Chinese as Medical Scapegoats in San Francisco, 1870–1905," *California History* 52, no. 1 (1978): 70–87.
18. Susan Craddock, "Embodying Place: Pathologizing Chinese and Chinatown in Nineteenth-Century San Francisco," *Antipode* 31, no. 4 (1999): 352.
19. Nayan Shah, *Contagious Divides: Epidemics and Race in San Francisco's Chinatown* (Berkeley: University of California Press, 2001), 47.
20. *San Francisco Municipal Report*, 1870, quoted in Craddock, "Embodying Place," 358.
21. Yong Chen, *Chinese San Francisco, 1850–1943* (Palo Alto, CA: Stanford University Press, 2000), 48.
22. Y. Chen, *Chinese San Francisco*, 60.
23. "The Public Health," *Pacific Commercial Advertiser*, September 29, 1885, quoted in Colette Higgins, "Anti-Chinese Sentiments in Hawaii from 1852 to 1886," student paper for History 484 class, fall 1990, 14–15, Student Papers, RASRL, University of Hawai'i.
24. Hawai'i Board of Health report, 1882, quoted in Lydon, *The Anti-Chinese Movement*, 55.
25. Lydon, *The Anti-Chinese Movement*, 55.
26. O. A. Bushnell, *The Gifts of Civilization: Germs and Genocide in Hawai'i* (Honolulu: University of Hawai'i Press, 1983), 147.
27. MacLennan, *Sovereign Sugar*, 25.
28. Lydon, *The Anti-Chinese Movement*, 54.
29. Glick, "Residential Dispersion," 31.
30. James Mohr, *Plague and Fire: Battling Black Death and the 1900 Burning of Honolulu's Chinatown* (Oxford: Oxford University Press, 2005), 59.
31. Myron Echenberg, "Plague in Paradise: Honolulu, 1899–1900," in *Plague Ports: The Global Urban Impact of Bubonic Plague, 1894–1901*, ed. Myron Echenberg (New York: NYU Press, 2007), 186.

2. 1900 TO 1930: DESTRUCTION OF CHINATOWN

32. C. B. Wood, "History of Medicine in Hawaii" (unpublished manuscript, May 1, 1926), 12, https://evols.library.manoa.hawaii.edu/bitstreams/69d290e5-e118-4640 -b718-7ccbd6de1e7b/download, quoted in Lana Iwamoto, "Plague and Fire of 1899–1900 in Honolulu," *Hawaii Historical Review* 2, no. 8 (1967): 380.
33. Craddock, "Embodying Place," 365.
34. Craddock, "Embodying Place," 355.
35. Shah, *Contagious Divides*, 102.
36. Shah, *Contagious Divides*, 75.
37. Katherine Coman, *The History of Contract Labor in the Hawaiian Islands* (New York: MacMillan, 1903; New York: Arno, 1978), 36. Citation refers to the Arno edition.
38. Lydon, *The Anti-Chinese Movement*, 55.
39. Mohr, *Plague and Fire*, 32.
40. Trauner, "The Chinese as Medical Scapegoats," 79; Charles Richter and John S. Emrich, "How Honolulu's Chinatown 'Went Up in Smoke,'" American Association of Immunologists, July 2020, https://www.aai.org/About/History/History -Articles-Keep-for-Hierarchy/How-Honolulu%E2%80%99s-Chinatown-Went-Up -in-Smoke-The-Fi.
41. Jennifer Thigpen, *Island Queens and Mission Wives: How Gender and Empire Remade Hawai'i's Pacific World* (Chapel Hill: University of North Carolina Press, 2014), 31–32.
42. Karen W. F. Lee, "The Coming of the Chinese: The Early Immigrant Community in Hawaii" (PhD diss., University of Hawai'i, 1990), 188.
43. Mohr, *Plague and Fire*, 32.
44. Mohr, *Plague and Fire*, 41.
45. Clarence Glick, *Sojourners and Settlers: Chinese Migrants in Hawaii* (Honolulu: University of Hawai'i Press, 1980), 208.
46. Mohr, *Plague and Fire*, 122.
47. Echenberg, "Plague in Paradise," 199.
48. Mohr, *Plague and Fire*, 107.
49. "A Great and Sore Distress," *The Friend*, 58, no. 2 (1900): 3.
50. Mohr, *Plague and Fire*, 126–28.
51. Richter and Emrich, "How Honolulu's Chinatown 'Went Up in Smoke.'"
52. Julia Katz, "From Coolies to Colonials: Chinese Migrants in Hawai'i" (PhD diss., Rutgers University, 2018), 168.
53. Glick, *Sojourners and Settlers*, 289.
54. Iwamoto, "Plague and Fire," 133.
55. Mohr, *Plague and Fire*, 183.
56. Q. Chen, *Acculturation of Chinese Intellectuals*, 101–3.
57. Mohr, *Plague and Fire*, 59.
58. Mohr, *Plague and Fire*, 191.
59. Glick, "Residential Dispersion," 25.
60. Andrew W. Lind, *Hawaii: The Last of the Magic Isles* (Oxford: Oxford University Press, 1969), 107.
61. Lind, *Hawaii*, 106.
62. Norman Westly, "Race Differences in Home Ownership in the Makiki Area," *Social Process in Hawaii* 18 (1954): 33–34.

2. 1900 TO 1930: DESTRUCTION OF CHINATOWN

63. Robert Schmitt, "Death, Disease, and Distance from Downtown," *Hawaii Medical Journal* 15, no. 2 (1955): 131–32.
64. Sylvianne Fei-Ai Li, "A History of the Education of the Chinese in Hawaii" (master's thesis, Oberlin College, 1940), 31.
65. Li, *A History of the Education*, 42.
66. Clif Stratton, *Education for Empire: American Schools, Race, and the Paths of Good Citizenship* (Berkeley: University of California Press, 2016), 94.
67. MacLennan, *Sovereign Sugar*, 195.
68. Li, *A History of the Education*, 43.
69. Xu Huang, "The Schooling of the Children of Early Chinese Immigrants in Hawaii" (master's thesis, University of Hawai'i, 1989), 80.
70. Huang, "The Schooling," 126
71. Katherine Cook, *U.S. Office of Education Bulletin*, 1935,54–55, quoted in Li, *A History of the Education*, 53.
72. Li, *A History of the Education*, 54.
73. J. Kēhaulani Kauanui, *Paradoxes of Hawaiian Sovereignty: Land, Sex, and the Colonial Politics of State Nationalism* (Durham, NC: Duke University Press, 2018), 10, 19–21, 116, 123–124.
74. Huang, "The Schooling," 90.
75. Glick, *Sojourners and Settlers*, 99 (table 3).
76. Glick, *Sojourners and Settlers*, 99 (table 3).
77. Robert Man War Lee, "Vertical Mobility Among the Chinese in Hawaii" (master's thesis, University of Hawai'i, 1951), 81.
78. Lydon, *The Anti-Chinese Movement*, 57.
79. Lee, "Vertical Mobility," 20.
80. Lee, "Vertical Mobility," 84, based on *Reports of the Treasurer to the Legislature, Territory of Hawai'i*, 1910–1936.
81. Lee, "Vertical Mobility," 22.
82. Lee, "Vertical Mobility," 23.
83. Q. Chen, *Acculturation of Chinese Intellectuals*, 358.
84. Lillian Awai Lum, "Biography of a 'Country' Club: The United Chinese Club of Kohala, Hawaii" (unpublished manuscript, 1990).
85. Lee, "Vertical Mobility," 64.
86. Leonard K. M. Wong, "Hawaii Chinese: The Americanization Movement" (master's thesis, University of Hawai'i at Mānoa, 1999), 76.
87. Ch'eng-K'un Cheng, "A Study of Chinese Assimilation in Hawaii," *Social Forces* 32, no. 2 (1953): 163–67.
88. Wong, "Hawaii Chinese," 46–49.
89. Quoted in Wong, "Hawaii Chinese," 10–11.
90. Wong, "Hawaii Chinese," viii.
91. Wong, "Hawaii Chinese," 33.
92. Wong, "Hawaii Chinese," 78.
93. Gary Okihiro, *Cane Fires: The Anti-Japanese Movement in Hawai'i, 1865–1945* (Philadelphia: Temple University Press, 1991), 189.
94. Lani Guinier and Gerald Torres, *The Miner's Canary: Enlisting Race, Resisting Power, Transforming Democracy* (Cambridge, MA: Harvard University Press, 2002), 225.

95. Guinier and Torres, *The Miner's Canary*, 225.
96. MacLennan, *Sovereign Sugar*, 253.
97. Kauanui, *Paradoxes*, 89; Julia Katz, "Ahuna and the Moʻo: Rethinking Chinese Success in Hawaiian Commercial Food Production," *Pacific Historical Review* 84, no. 4 (2017): 599–631.
98. Violet Lai, student paper for Soc 267 class, January 1938, 3, Student Papers, RASRL, University of Hawaiʻi.
99. San Moi Wong, "Bingham Tract Thru the Eyes of a Chinese," January 20, 1940, Student Papers, RASRL, University of Hawaiʻi.
100. Him Mark Lai, "The Chinese Community Press in Hawaiʻi," in "The Hawaiʻi Chinese," special issue, *Journal of the Chinese Historical Society of America* (2010): 95–103.
101. Okihiro, *Cane Fires*, 86.
102. Wong, "Hawaii Chinese," 36.
103. T. F. Farm, "What Have the Chinese Contributed to Hawaii," *Hawaii Chinese Journal* November 30, 1939, 4–5, quoted in Wong, "Hawaii Chinese," 37.
104. Gary Coover, *Honolulu Chinatown: 200 Years of Red Lanterns and Red Lights* (Honolulu, HI: Rollston, 2022), 169.
105. Coover, *Honolulu Chinatown*, 169.
106. Wong, "Hawaii Chinese," 38.
107. Q. Chen, *Acculturation of Chinese Intellectuals*, 358.
108. Y. Chen, *Chinese San Francisco*, 47.

3. THE 1930S THROUGH THE 1940s:
WORLD WAR II COMES TO HAWAIʻI

1. Clarence Glick, "Residential Dispersion of Urban Chinese," *Social Process in Hawaiʻi* 2 (1936): 28–34.
2. Beth Bailey and David Farber, *The First Strange Place: Race and Sex in World War II Hawaii* (Baltimore, MD: Johns Hopkins University Press, 1992), 33.
3. Daniel Immerwahr, *How to Hide an Empire: A History of the Greater United States* (London: Farrar, Straus and Giroux, 2019), 6.
4. Immerwahr, *How to Hide an Empire*, 6.
5. Franklin Odo, *No Sword to Bury: Japanese Americans in Hawaiʻi During World War II* (Philadelphia: Temple University Press, 2004), 3.
6. Andrew W. Lind, *Hawaii: The Last of the Magic Isles* (Oxford: Oxford University Press, 1969), 45.
7. Gary Okihiro, *Cane Fires: The Anti-Japanese Movement in Hawaiʻi, 1865–1945* (Philadelphia: Temple University Press, 1991), 129.
8. Harry Scheiber and Jane Scheiber, *Bayonets in Paradise: Martial Law in Hawaiʻi During World War II* (Honolulu: University of Hawaiʻi Press, 2016), 135.
9. Andrew W. Lind, "The Japanese in Hawaii Under War Conditions" (paper presented at the Eighth Conference of the Pacific Institute, Mont Tremblant, QC, December 1942), https://oac.cdlib.org/ark:/28722/bk001392v15/?brand=oac4.
10. Odo, *No Sword to Bury*, 149.

3. THE 1930S THROUGH THE 1940S

11. Lind, "The Japanese in Hawaii," 16.
12. Tom Coffman, *The Island Edge of America: A Political History of Hawai'i* (Honolulu: University of Hawai'i Press, 2003), 74.
13. Scheiber and Scheiber, *Bayonets in Paradise*, 31.
14. Yukiko Kimura, "Social Effects of Increased Income of Defense Workers of Oriental Ancestry in Hawaii," *Social Process in Hawaii* 7 (1941): 46–55.
15. Scheiber and Scheiber, *Bayonets in Paradise*, 123.
16. Melody M. Miyamoto Walters, *In Love and War: The World War II Courtship Letters of a Nisei Couple* (Norman: University of Oklahoma Press, 2015), 44.
17. Walters, *In Love and War*, 45.
18. Winifred Tom, "The Impact of War on Chinese Culture," *Social Process in Hawai'i* 8 (1943): 202.
19. Bailey and Farber, *The First Strange Place*, 35.
20. Bailey and Farber, *The First Strange Place*, 42.
21. Quoted in Bailey and Farber, *The First Strange Place*, epigraph.
22. Walters, *In Love and War*, 74.
23. Gwenfread Allen, *Hawaii's War Years: 1941–1945* (Honolulu: University of Hawai'i Press, 1950), 219.
24. Allen, *Hawaii's War Years*, 72.
25. Scheiber and Scheiber, *Bayonets in Paradise*, 120.
26. Scheiber and Scheiber, *Bayonets in Paradise*, 83–92.
27. Kimura, "Social Effects," 53.
28. Allen, *Hawaii's War Years*, 265.
29. Kyle Kajihiro, "Nation Under the Gun: Militarism and Resistance in Hawai'i," *Cultural Survival* 24, no. 1 (2010), https://www.culturalsurvival.org/publications /cultural-survival-quarterly/nation-under-gun-militarism-and-resistance-hawaii.
30. Kajihiro, "Nation Under the Gun."
31. Kajihiro, "Nation Under the Gun."
32. Glick, "Residential Dispersion," 27.
33. Allen, *Hawaii's War Years*, 246.
34. Bailey and Farber, *The First Strange Place*, 97.
35. Gary Coover, *Honolulu Chinatown: 200 Years of Red Lanterns and Red Lights* (Honolulu, HI: Rollston, 2022), 136.
36. Coover, *Honolulu Chinatown*, 139.
37. Coover, *Honolulu Chinatown*, 139.
38. Bailey and Farber, *The First Strange Place*, 107.
39. Thomas Gieryn, "A Space for Place in Sociology," *Annual Review of Sociology* 26 (2000): 463–96.
40. Daniel Kwok, "By History Remembered," in *Sailing for the Sun: The Chinese in Hawaii 1789–1989*, ed. Arlene Lum (Honolulu: Three Heroes, 1988), 22.
41. Xu Huang, "The Schooling of the Children of Early Chinese Immigrants in Hawaii," (master's thesis, University of Hawai'i, 1989), 93.
42. Eileen Tamura, *Americanization, Acculturation, and Ethnic Identity: The Nisei Generation in Hawaii* (Champaign: University of Illinois Press, 1994), 108 (figure 4).
43. Huang, "The Schooling of the Children," 127.
44. Eileen Tamura, "The Americanization Campaign and the Assimilation of the Nisei in Hawaii, 1920 to 1940" (PhD diss., University of Hawai'i, 1990), 449 (table 13).

3. THE 1930S THROUGH THE 1940S

45. Author's research interviews, CL, PJ.
46. Mindy Pennybacker, "The 'Haole Rich Kids' School: An Update," in *Punahou: The History and Promise of a School of the Islands*, ed. Nelson Foster (Honolulu, HI: Punahou School, 1991), 119–49.
47. Lind, *Hawaii*, 51 (table 5).
48. Robert Man War Lee, "Vertical Mobility Among the Chinese in Hawaii" (master's thesis, University of Hawai'i, June 1951), Appendix B.
49. Lind, *Hawaii*, 53.
50. Lind, *Hawaii*, 65.
51. Lee, "Vertical Mobility," 84. From 1936, data on bank deposits by racial or ethnic group were no longer collected.
52. Lee, "Vertical Mobility," 53.
53. Lee, "Vertical Mobility," 53.
54. Lind, *Hawaii*, 107.
55. Robert C. Schmitt, "Death, Disease, and Distance from Downtown," *Hawaii Medical Journal* 15, no. 2 (1955): 131–32.
56. Andrew W. Lind, *Hawaii's People*, 4th ed. (Honolulu: University of Hawaii Press, 1980), 68.
57. Nellie Lum, "Bingham Tract," student paper for Soc 151a class, March 23, 1950, Student Papers, box 18, file 36, RASRL, University of Hawai'i.
58. Lind, *Hawaii's People*, 69.
59. Lee, "Vertical Mobility," 47.
60. "1321 Alewa Drive/Hung Lum Chun Residence," Historic Hawai'i Foundation, March 3, 2014, https://historichawaii.org/2014/03/03/1321-alewa-drive-hung-lum-chun-residence/.
61. Lee, "Vertical Mobility," 47–51.
62. Lee, "Vertical Mobility," 59.
63. Lee, "Vertical Mobility," 61.
64. Lee, "Vertical Mobility," 61.
65. William Lee, "The Assimilation of the Chinese Members of the Class of 1928 of the University of Hawaii, Chiefly of Its Economic Aspect" student paper, 1935, 4; Student Papers, RASRL, University of Hawai'i.
66. Lee, "Vertical Mobility," 16.
67. Andrew W. Lind, "A Preliminary Study of Military Morale," *Social Process in Hawaii* 8 (1943): 15.
68. Betty Vellom, "Race Relations in Jobs," student paper, 1946, 6, Student Papers, RASRL, University of Hawai'i.
69. Lee, "Vertical Mobility," 20.
70. Wei Li et al., "How Ethnic Banks Matter: Banking and Community/Economic Development in Los Angeles," in *Landscapes of the Ethnic Economy*, ed. David H. Kaplan and Wei Li (Lanham: Rowman and Littlefield, 2004), 113–33.
71. Frank J. Taylor, "Labor Moves On in Hawaii," *Saturday Evening Post* 219, no. 52 (1947): 25.
72. Arthur Yuh-chao Yu, "A Study of Chinese Organizations in Hawaii with Special Reference to Assimilative Trends," student paper for American Studies 641 class, December 15, 1970, 12, Glick Papers, "Other Hawaiian," RASRL, University of Hawai'i.

3. THE 1930S THROUGH THE 1940S

73. Yu, "A study of Chinese Organizations," 12.
74. Mike Gordon, "Post-war Prejudice Gave Rise to Aloha 'The People's Airline,'" *Honolulu Advertiser*, April 8, 2008.
75. Gordon, "Post-war prejudice."
76. Vivian Sun, "Second Generation Chinese as Cultural Hybrids in the Territory of Hawaii," student paper, 1937, 11, Glick Papers, box 2, RASRL, University of Hawai'i.
77. Lawrence Fuchs, *Hawaii Pono: A Social History* (New York: Harcourt Brace Jovanovich, 1961), 433.
78. Fuchs, *Hawaii Pono*, 434.
79. Vellom, "Race Relations in Jobs," 8.
80. Andrew W. Lind, "Mounting the Occupational Ladder in Honolulu," student research lab report no. 4, 1957, Student Papers, RASRL, University of Hawai'i.
81. Taylor, "Labor Moves On," 25.
82. Lee, "Vertical Mobility," 31.
83. Clarence Glick, *Sojourners and Settlers: Chinese Migrants in Hawaii* (Honolulu: University of Hawai'i Press, 1980), 115; *Polk's Directory of Honolulu*, 1940, 1949, University of Hawai'i at Mānoa Library, Hawaiian and Pacific Collections; Population: Hawaii: fifteenth census of the United States 1930 (Washington, DC: U.S. Government Printing Office, 1931), 48.
84. Hawai'i State Archives.
85. Hawai'i State Archives.
86. Richard K. C. Lee, "The Educated Class: One Man's Journey," in *Sailing for the Sun: The Chinese in Hawaii 1789-1989*, ed. Arlene Lum (Honolulu: Three Heroes, 1988), 149-65.
87. Julia Katz, "From Coolies to Colonials: Chinese Migrants in Hawai'i" (PhD diss., Rutgers University, 2018), 132.
88. Qi Chen, "The Acculturation of Chinese Intellectuals in Hawaii: 1894-1959" (PhD diss., University of Hawai'i, 1997), 319; Leonard K. M. Wong, "Hawaii Chinese: The Americanization Movement" (master's thesis, University of Hawai'i at Mānoa, 1999), 75-77.
89. Okihiro, *Cane Fires*, 37, 83.
90. Jonathan Y. Okamura, "Race Relations in Hawai'i During World War II: The Noninternment of Japanese Americans," in *The Japanese American Historical Experience in Hawai'i*, ed. Jonathan Y. Okamura (Dubuque, IA: Kendall Hunt, 2001), 67-90.
91. Coffman, *The Island Edge of America*, 24.
92. Yong Chen, *Chinese San Francisco, 1850-1943* (Palo Alto, CA: Stanford University Press, 2000), 258.
93. Quoted in Clif Stratton, *Education for Empire: American Schools, Race, and the Paths of Good Citizenship* (Berkeley: University of California Press, 2016), 106.
94. Madeline Hsu, *The Good Immigrants: How the Yellow Peril Became the Model Minority* (Princeton, NJ: Princeton University Press, 2015), 98.
95. Hsu, *The Good Immigrants*, 98.
96. Arthur Turner, "Racial Discrimination in Employment in Hawaii," student paper, 1949, 1, Student Papers, RASRL, University of Hawai'i.
97. Lind, "Mounting the Occupational Ladder."
98. Minto Hannus, "Interracial Relationships in Hawaii," student paper for Soc 257 class, 1949, Student Papers, RASRL, University of Hawai'i.

99. Eleanor Ai Chang, student paper for Soc 257 class, n.d., Glick Papers, box 9, RASRL, University of Hawai'i; Betty Au, "A Personal Account of Race Relations," student paper for Soc 257 class, 1946, Student Papers, RASRL, University of Hawai'i, 2.
100. Turner, "Racial Discrimination," 6.
101. Odo, *No Sword to Bury*, 6.
102. Lani Guinier and Gerald Torres, *The Miner's Canary: Enlisting Race, Resisting Power, Transforming Democracy* (Cambridge, MA: Harvard University Press, 2002), 225.

4. STATEHOOD AMID COLD WAR POLITICS

1. Noel Kent, *Hawaii: Islands Under the Influence* (Honolulu: University of Hawai'i Press, 1993), 106–7.
2. Tom Coffman, *The Island Edge of America: A Political History of Hawai'i* (Honolulu: University of Hawai'i Press, 2003), 153.
3. Edward Beechert, *Working in Hawaii: A Labor History* (Honolulu: University of Hawaii Press, 1985), 314–22.
4. Beth Bailey and David Farber, *The First Strange Place: Race and Sex in World War II Hawai'i* (Baltimore, MD: Johns Hopkins University Press, 1992), 120.
5. Yau Sing Leong, "From Kwangtung to the Plantations, Farm Stores and Beyond," in *Sailing for the Sun: The Chinese in Hawaii 1789–1989*, ed. Arlene Lum (Honolulu: Three Heroes, 1988), 72–95.
6. Andrew W. Lind, *Hawaii: The Last of the Magic Isles* (Oxford: Oxford University Press, 1969), 65.
7. Robert Man War Lee, "Vertical Mobility Among the Chinese in Hawaii" (master's thesis, University of Hawai'i, June 1951), 51.
8. "Makiki Ridge Lots Auctioned by Territory," *Honolulu Star Bulletin*, February 1, 1951, 4, quoted in Lee, "Vertical Mobility," 51.
9. State of Hawai'i, *Chinese Population by County, Island and Census Tract in the State of Hawaii: 2010* (Honolulu: Hawaii State Data Center, 2012), 10, https://files .hawaii.gov/dbedt/census/Census_2010/SF1/HSDC2010-8_Chinese.pdf.
10. "New Neighborhood, New Outlook," student paper, April 15, 1963, 6–7. Student Papers, box 7, folder 15, RASRL, University of Hawai'i.
11. Kent, *Hawaii*, 112.
12. Vernadette Vicuña Gonzalez, *Securing Paradise: Tourism and Militarism in Hawai'i and the Philippines* (Durham, NC: Duke University Press, 2013), 13.
13. Gonzalez, *Securing Paradise*, 13–14.
14. "Hickam AFB, HI History," Hickam AFB, HI, accessed November 26, 2023, https:// www.hickamafbhousing.com/history.
15. Christina Jedra, "Is It Time for Hawaii to Renegotiate Its Relationship with the Military?," *Honolulu Civil Beat*, May 23, 2022, https://www.civilbeat.org/2022/05 /is-it-time-for-hawaii-to-renegotiate-its-relationship-with-the-military/.
16. Jason C. Parker, *Hearts, Minds, Voices: US Cold War Public Diplomacy and the Formation of the Third World* (Oxford: Oxford University Press, 2016), 3.
17. Cindy I-fen Cheng, *Citizens of Asian America: Democracy and Race During the Cold War* (New York: NYU Press, 2013), 12.
18. Cheng, *Citizens of Asian America*, 96–97.

4. STATEHOOD AMID COLD WAR POLITICS

19. "Dr. Sammy Lee, Olympic Champion and Goodwill Ambassador," National Museum of American Diplomacy, accessed November 26, 2023, https://diplomacy.state.gov/u-s-diplomacy-stories/dr-sammy-lee-olympic-champion-and-goodwill-ambassador/.
20. Harriet Orcutt Duleep and Seth G. Sanders, *The Economic Status of Asian Americans Before and After the Civil Rights Act*, IZA Discussion Paper No. 6639 (Bonn: Institute for the Study of Labor, 2012), 3–5, http://dx.doi.org/10.2139/ssrn.2089668.
21. Duleep and Sanders, *The Economic Status of Asian Americans*, 3–5.
22. Cheng, *Citizens of Asian America*, 22–31.
23. Charlotte Brooks, *Alien Neighbors, Foreign Friends: Asian Americans, Housing, and the Transformation of Urban California* (Chicago: University of Chicago Press, 2009), 176–82.
24. Cheng, *Citizens of Asian America*, 42.
25. Cheng, *Citizens of Asian America*, 42–43.
26. Cheng, *Citizens of Asian America*, 58.
27. Cheng, *Citizens of Asian America*, 4.
28. Ellen Wu, *The Color of Success: Asian Americans and the Origins of the Model Minority* (Princeton, NJ: Princeton University Press, 2015), 113–14.
29. Michael Omi, "The Unbearable Whiteness of Being: The Contemporary Racialization of Japanese/Asian Americans," in *Trans-Pacific Japanese American Studies: Conversations on Race and Racializations*, ed. Yasuko Takezawa and Gary Y. Okihiro (Honolulu: University of Hawai'i Press, 2016), 50.
30. Sarah Miller-Davenport, *Gateway State: Hawai'i and the Cultural Transformation of Empire* (Princeton, NJ: Princeton University Press, 2019), 5–6.
31. "1898: Birth of an Overseas Empire," History, Art & Archives, United States House of Representatives, accessed November 26, 2023, https://history.house.gov/Exhibitions-and-Publications/APA/Historical-Essays/Exclusion-and-Empire/1898/.
32. "Hawaii," History, Art & Archives, United States House of Representatives, accessed November 26, 2023, https://history.house.gov/Exhibitions-and-Publications/APA/Historical-Essays/Exclusion-and-Empire/Hawaii/.
33. "Statehood for Hawaii's People," *Paradise of the Pacific* 71, no. 1 (1959): 11–14.
34. Roger Bell, *Last Among Equals: Hawaiian Statehood and American Politics* (Honolulu: University of Hawai'i Press, 1984), 253.
35. Bell, *Last Among Equals*, 149–52.
36. Coffman, *The Island Edge of America*, 155; see also Bell, *Last Among Equals*, 155.
37. Wu, *The Color of Success*, 111–14.
38. Gonzalez, *Securing Paradise*, 32.
39. Miller-Davenport, *Gateway State*, 46.
40. Bell, *Last Among Equals*, 257–58.
41. Angela Krattinger, "Hawai'i's Cold War: American Empire and the Fiftieth State" (PhD diss., University of Hawai'i at Mānoa, 2013), 32.
42. Miller-Davenport, *Gateway State*, 46; Krattinger, Hawai'i's Cold War," 46.
43. Helen Jun, *Race for Citizenship: Black Orientalism and Asian Uplift from Preemancipation to Neoliberal America* (New York: NYU Press, 2011), 125.
44. Miller-Davenport, *Gateway State*, 5.
45. Gonzalez, *Securing Paradise*, 34.
46. Editorial: Chinese-American Citizens, *Honolulu Advertiser*, February 28, 1930.

5. RECONSTRUCTING CHINATOWN FOR A NEW ERA

47. Nancy E. Riley, "Race Into the Empire: The "Chinese Problem" in Hawai'i" (unpublished manuscript, n.d.).
48. "American Families in Hawaii," *Paradise of the Pacific* 59, no. 1 (1947): 5–8.
49. George Wilkins, "The Herbert Lees," *Paradise of the Pacific* 62, no. 1 (1950): 3.
50. Evelyn Yama and Margaret Zimmerman, "Race Relations in a Hawaiian Business Firm," student paper for Soc 256 class, February 1952, 8, Student Papers, RASRL, University of Hawai'i.
51. Yama and Zimmerman, "Race Relations," 3.
52. Yama and Zimmerman, "Race Relations," 4.
53. John F. Kennedy, "Address in Honolulu Before the United States Conference of Mayors," American Presidency Project, June 9, 1963, https://www.presidency.ucsb.edu/documents/address-honolulu-before-the-united-states-conference-mayors.
54. *Paradise of the Pacific* 61, no. 4 (1949): 26.
55. *Paradise of the Pacific* 61, no. 5 (1949): 23.
56. "Your Part in a Million Dollar Venture," *Hawaii Chinese Journal*, October 6, 1949, quoted in Jinzhao Li, "Constructing Chinese America in Hawai'i: The Narcissus Festival, Ethnic Identity, and Community Transformation, 1949–2005" (PhD diss., University of Hawai'i at Mānoa, 2005), 98.
57. Gonzalez, *Securing Paradise*, 6.
58. Miller-Davenport, *Gateway State*, 200; see also Haunani-Kay Trask, "Settlers of Color and 'Immigrant' Hegemony: Locals in Hawai'i," *Amerasia Journal* 26, no. 2 (2000): 1–24.
59. Krattinger, "Hawai'i's Cold War," 70.
60. Michelle Christian, "A Global Critical Race and Racism Framework: Racial Entanglements and Deep and Malleable Whiteness," *Sociology of Race and Ethnicity* 5, no. 2 (2019): 169–85.
61. Dean I. Saranillio, "Why Asian Settler Colonialism Matters: A Thought Piece on Critiques, Debates and Indigenous Difference," *Settler Colonial Studies* 3, nos. 3–4 (2013): 286.
62. Christian, "A Global Critical Race and Racism Framework," 170.
63. Miller-Davenport, *Gateway State*, 48.
64. Miller-Davenport, *Gateway State*, 44–45.
65. Lani Guinier and Gerald Torres, *The Miner's Canary: Enlisting Race, Resisting Power, Transforming Democracy* (Cambridge, MA: Harvard University Press, 2002), 225.
66. Trask, "Settlers of Color," 4.
67. Cheng, *Citizens of Asian America*, 194.

5. RECONSTRUCTING CHINATOWN FOR A NEW ERA

1. Robert C. Schmitt, "How Many Hawaiians?," *Journal of the Polynesian Society* 76, no. 4 (1967): 467–76.
2. Bradley E. Hope and Janette Harbottle Hope, "Native Hawaiian Health in Hawaii: Historical Highlights," in "Hawaii," special issue, *Californian Journal of Health Promotion* 1, no. S1 (2003): 1–9; see also Seth Archer, *Sharks Upon the Land: Colonialism, Indigenous Health, and Culture in Hawai'i, 1778–1855* (Cambridge: Cambridge University Press, 2018), 2–3.

5. RECONSTRUCTING CHINATOWN FOR A NEW ERA

3. Sarah Miller-Davenport, *Gateway State: Hawai'i and the Cultural Transformation of Empire* (Princeton, NJ: Princeton University Press, 2019), 122.

4. Miller-Davenport, *Gateway State*, 122.

5. James Mak, *Developing a Dream Destination: Tourism and Tourism Policy Planning in Hawai'i* (Honolulu: University of Hawai'i Press, 2008), 21.

6. Kartik Naram, "'No Place Like Home': Racial Capitalism, Gentrification, and the Identity of Chinatown," *Asian American Policy Review* 27 (2017): 33–50.

7. Mililani Trask and Haunani Kay Trask, "The Aloha Industry: For Hawaiian Women, Tourism Is Not a Neutral Industry," *Cultural Survival* 16, no. 4 (1992), https://www.culturalsurvival.org/publications/cultural-survival-quarterly/aloha -industry-hawaiian-women-tourism-not-neutral-industry.

8. Vernadette Vicuña Gonzalez, *Securing Paradise: Tourism and Militarism in Hawai'i and the Philippines* (Durham, NC: Duke University Press, 2013), 8.

9. Jinzhao Li, "Constructing Chinese America in Hawai'i: The Narcissus Festival, Ethnic Identity, and Community Transformation, 1949–2005" (PhD diss., University of Hawai'i at Mānoa, 2005), 87.

10. Eiichiro Azuma, "Brokering Race, Culture, and Citizenship: Japanese Americans in Occupied Japan and Postwar National Inclusion," *Journal of American-East Asian Relations* 16, no. 3 (2009): 183–211.

11. Simeon Man, "Aloha, Vietnam: Race and Empire in Hawai'i's Vietnam War," *American Quarterly* 67, no.4 (2015): 1085–1108.

12. "About EWC: Origins," East-West Center, accessed November 26, 2023, https://www.eastwestcenter.org/about-ewc/origins.

13. Quoted in Man, "Aloha, Vietnam," 1108.

14. Man, "Aloha, Vietnam," 1087.

15. Man, "Aloha, Vietnam," 1086.

16. Domenic Vitello and Zoe Blickenderfer, "The Planned Destruction of Chinatowns in the United States and Canada Since c.1900," *Planning Perspectives* 35, no.1 (2020): 143–68.

17. Vitello and Blickenderfer, "The Planned Destruction of Chinatowns," 153.

18. "An Urban Renewal Program for the City and County of Honolulu," Honolulu Redevelopment Agency, 1955, https://babel.hathitrust.org/cgi/pt?id=uiug.30112076 135331&view=1up&seq=2&skin=2021.

19. *Hawaii Chinese Weekly*, July 24, 1959, quoted in Li, "Constructing Chinese America in Hawai'i," 99.

20. Tom Oyasato and Ronald Ozaki, "The Slums and Blighted areas of Honolulu," student paper for Soc 255 class, 1950, 1. Student Papers, RASRL, University of Hawai'i.

21. Historic Building Task Force, "Will Chinatown Survive?" (unpublished manuscript, 1966), 4. University of Hawai'i at Mānoa Library, Hawaiian and Pacific Collections.

22. Ian Lind, "A'ala and Its Surrounding Areas, 1958," essay accompanying Francis Haar, *Disappearing Honolulu*, exhibit, University of Hawai'i, John Young Museum, 2019, https://hawaii.edu/art/francis-haar-disappearing-honolulu/.

23. James W. Foster, "Queen Emma Gardens: The Making of a Landmark," Queen Emma Gardens Community Website, accessed November 26, 2023, https://www .queenemmagardens.com/post/read-about-the-history-of-queen-emma-gardens.

5. RECONSTRUCTING CHINATOWN FOR A NEW ERA

24. Quoted in Bob Sigall, "Remembering Honolulu's Hell's Half Acre and Tin Can Alley of the 1880s–1960s," *Honolulu Star Advertiser*, March 18, 2022, https://historichawaii.org/2022/03/23/remembering-honolulus-hells-half-acre-and-tin-can-alley-of-the-1880s-1960s/.

25. Gary Coover, *Honolulu Chinatown: 200 Years of Red Lanterns and Red Lights* (Honolulu, HI: Rollston, 2022), 123.

26. Nancy Bannick, Scott Cheever, and David Cheever, *A Close Call: Saving Honolulu's Chinatown* (Honolulu: Little Percent, 2005), 13.

27. "Chinese Family in Honolulu's Slum," student paper, 1963, 7 Student Papers, box 7, folder 17, RASRL, University of Hawai'i.

28. Bernard Yim, "Chinese as a Stable Group in Chinatown," student paper, 1950, 3 Student Papers, RASRL, University of Hawai'i.

29. Gail Miyasaki, "Old Vineyard," *Hawaii Hochi*, 48, no. 115 (May 11, 1973), 4–6.

30. Bannick, Cheever, and Cheever, *A Close Call*, 13.

31. "Voices of Chinatown," video transcript, 1977, Uncatalogued Papers, RASRL, University of Hawai'i.

32. John Kelly, "People Against Chinatown Eviction," PACE pamphlet, 1974, University of Hawai'i at Mānoa Library Digital Image Collections, accessed July 15, 2022, https://digital.library.manoa.hawaii.edu/items/show/31281.

33. Sonja Cookman, *Remembering Chinatown: Examining Eviction Struggles in Hawaii's Chinatown in the 1970s-80s* (Honolulu: Hawai'i People's Fund, 2016), 4, https://www.hawaiipeoplesfund.org/wp-content/uploads/2019/03/REMEMBERING-CHINATOWN.pdf.

34. Wayson Chow, "Wayson Chow," in *Autobiography of Protest in Hawai'i*, ed. Robert H. Mast and Anne B. Mast (Honolulu: University of Hawai'i Press, 1996), 43.

35. Chow, "Wayson Chow," 44.

36. Gerald Kato, "Look at Chinatown: Shifts in Approach," *Honolulu Advertiser*, September 3, 1979.

37. Nadine Kam, "The Weekly Eater: How Wun Is True to Tin Tin Legacy," *Honolulu Star-Bulletin*, December 19, 1996.

38. Kam, "The Weekly Eater."

39. Arnold Hiura, *Kau Kau: Cuisine and Culture of the Hawaiian Islands* (Honolulu: Watermark, 2009), 118.

40. Cookman, *Remembering Chinatown*, 10–14.

41. Bannick, Cheever, and Cheever, *A Close Call*, 24.

42. Bannick, Cheever, and Cheever, *A Close Call*, 38.

43. "Chinatown Historic District (Honolulu)," National Park Service, accessed November 26, 2023, https://www.nps.gov/places/chinatown-historic-district-honolulu.htm.

44. "Chinatown Historical District, Nomination Form," National Register of Historic Places, application to U.S. Department of the Interior, National Park Service, 1972.

45. "Chinatown Historical District, Nomination Form."

46. Bannick, Cheever, and Cheever, *A Close Call*, 41.

47. "Voices of Chinatown."

48. Victor Gruen Associates, *Report of the Studies and Recommendations for a Program of Revitalization of the Central Business District of Downtown Honolulu* (Honolulu: Victor Gruen Associates, Inc., 1968), 12.

49. Bob Gerrell, quoted in "Voices of Chinatown."
50. "Voices of Chinatown."
51. Coover, *Honolulu Chinatown*, 155.
52. "See Dao Doo Society Building: Kukui and Fort Streets, Chinatown," Hawai'i Modernism Library, accessed November 26, 2023, http://www.docomomo-hi.org/items/show/1122.
53. Coover, *Honolulu Chinatown*, 58.
54. *Tenants on the Move*, video, University of Hawai'i Department of Ethnic Studies in conjunction with Information Technology Services, 2001.
55. Li, "Constructing Chinese America in Hawai'i," 95.
56. Hei Wai Wong, quoted in "Voices of Chinatown."
57. Nancy Leong, "Racial Capitalism," *Harvard Law Review* 126, no. 8 (2013): 2153–54.
58. "Narcissus Festival," Chinese Chamber of Commerce of Hawaii, accessed November 26, 2023, https://www.chinesechamber.com/narcissus-festival.
59. "Narcissus Festival."
60. "#32 Story Map Capital Historic District – Hawai'i State Capitol Building," Historic Hawai'i Foundation, accessed November 26, 2023, https://historichawaii.org/portfolio-items/statecapitolbuilding/.
61. "#32 Story Map Capital Historic District."

6. CHINATOWN TODAY: CONFLUENCE OF PAST AND PRESENT

1. Jesse Shircliff, "Is Chinatown a Place or a Space? A Case Study of Chinatown Singapore," *Geoforum* 117 (2020): 225–33.
2. Peter Wagner, "A City Waiting to Be Reborn," *Honolulu Star Bulletin*, September 29, 1998.
3. Dan Martin, "Chinatown at a Crossroads," *Honolulu Star Bulletin*, June 18, 2006, https://archives.starbulletin.com/2006/06/18/news/story03.html.
4. Don Wallace, "Chinatown's Latest Revival Is Putting It Back On the Map. But Will It Last?," *Honolulu Magazine*, February 24, 2017, https://www.honolulumagazine.com/chinatowns-latest-revival-is-putting-it-back-on-the-map-but-will-it-last/.
5. Kirstin Downey, "Is Honolulu's Chinatown on the Brink of a Turnaround?" *Honolulu Civil Beat*, June 19, 2022, https://www.civilbeat.org/2022/06/is-honolulus-chinatown-on-the-brink-of-a-turnaround/.
6. State of Hawai'i, *Chinese Population by County, Island and Census Tract in the State of Hawaii: 2010* (Honolulu: Hawaii State Data Center, 2012), 9–15, https://files.hawaii.gov/dbedt/census/Census_2010/SF1/HSDC2010-8_Chinese.pdf.
7. Author's research interview, LD.
8. Author's research interview, JC.
9. Jinzhao Li, "Constructing Chinese America in Hawai'i: The Narcissus Festival, Ethnic Identity, and Community Transformation, 1949–2005" (PhD diss., University of Hawai'i at Mānoa, 2005), 81.
10. Larry Ing, quoted in Li, "Constructing Chinese America in Hawai'i," 112.
11. Li, "Constructing Chinese America in Hawai'i," 148.
12. Li, "Constructing Chinese America in Hawai'i," 128.

6. CHINATOWN TODAY

13. Li, "Constructing Chinese America in Hawai'i," 64.
14. Li, "Constructing Chinese America in Hawai'i," 245.
15. Li, "Constructing Chinese America in Hawai'i," 209.
16. Gary Coover, *Honolulu Chinatown: 200 Years of Red Lanterns and Red Lights* (Honolulu, HI: Rollston, 2022), 257.
17. "Wing Wo Tai & Co. Building," HiChinatown.com, accessed November 27, 2023, http://hichinatown.com/architecture/wing-wo-tai.
18. "Wing Wo Tai & Co. Building."
19. Helen Altonn, "Tireless Work Led to Big, Tasty Manapuas," *Honolulu Star Bulletin*, April 20, 2003.
20. On similar processes in other Chinatowns, see Volkan Aytar and Jan Rath, "Introduction: Ethnic Neighborhoods as Places of Leisure and Consumption," in *Selling Ethnic Neighborhoods: The Rise of Neighborhoods as Places of Consumption*, ed. Volkan Aytar and Jan Rath (London: Taylor and Francis, 2011), 1–15; Kartik Naram, " 'No Place Like Home': Racial Capitalism, Gentrification, and the Identity of Chinatown," *Asian American Policy Review* 27 (2017): 33–50.
21. Lizbeth Scordo, "Why You Shouldn't Leave Honolulu Without Visiting Chinatown," *Thrillist*, September 3, 2019, https://www.thrillist.com/eat/honolulu/best-restaurants-chinatown-honolulu-hawaii.
22. Author's research interview RB.
23. Author's research interview.
24. Author's research interview, LD.
25. Author's research interview.
26. Catherine Fox, "Downtown Honolulu Used to Be So Vibrant. What Happened?," *Honolulu Civil Beat*, October 7, 2022.
27. David Harvey, *A Brief History of Neoliberalism* (Oxford: Oxford University Press, 2005), 72–73; Aihwa Ong, *Flexible Citizenship: The Cultural Logics of Transnationality* (Durham, NC: Duke University Press, 1999), 3–4.
28. Ong, *Flexible Citizenship*, 6–7.
29. Olaf Kaltmeier, "Introduction: Selling EthniCity," in *Selling EthniCity: Urban Cultural Politics in the Americas*, ed. Olaf Kaltmeier (Farnham, UK: Ashgate, 2011), 2.
30. Aytar and Jan Rath, "Introduction,"1.
31. Aytar and Jan Rath, "Introduction," 8.
32. Jan Rath, et al., "Chinatown 2.0: The Difficult Flowering of an Ethnically Themed Shopping Area," *Journal of Ethnic and Migration Studies* 44, no.1 (2018): 83.
33. Jan Lin, *The Power of Urban Ethnic Places: Cultural Heritage and Community Life* (New York: Routledge, 2011), 57.
34. Haunani-Kay Trask, "Tourism and the Prostitution of Hawaiian Culture," *Cultural Survival* 24, no. 1 (2000), https://www.culturalsurvival.org/publications/cultural-survival-quarterly/tourism-and-prostitution-hawaiian-culture; Vernadette Vicuña Gonzalez, *Securing Paradise: Tourism and Militarism in Hawai'i and the Philippines* (Durham, NC: Duke University Press, 2013), 127–28; Jane Desmond, *Staging Tourism: Bodies on Display from Waikiki to Sea World* (Chicago: University of Chicago Press, 2001) 98–121.
35. "Chinatown," Hawai'i Tourism Authority, accessed November 27, 2023, https://www.gohawaii.com/islands/oahu/regions/honolulu/Chinatown.
36. "Chinatown."

6. CHINATOWN TODAY

37. "About First Friday," FirstFridayHawaii.com, accessed November 27, 2023, https://www.firstfridayhawaii.com/d/d/aboutfirstfriday.html.
38. Martha Cheng, "Honolulu's Newly Hip Chinatown: A Traveler's Guide," *Wall Street Journal*, March 15, 2017, https://www.wsj.com/articles/honolulus-newly-hip-chinatown-a-travelers-guide-1489595294.
39. "Chinatown Historic District (Honolulu)," National Park Service, accessed November 27, 2023, https://www.nps.gov/places/chinatown-historic-district-honolulu.htm.
40. Selma Siew Li Bidlingmaier, "Spaces of Alterity and Temporal Permanence: The Case of San Francisco's and New York's Chinatown," in *Selling EthniCity: Urban Cultural Politics in the Americas*, ed. Olaf Kaltmeier (Farnham, UK: Ashgate, 2011), 277.
41. Shircliff, "Is Chinatown a place or a space?," 225.
42. "Chinatown – Is It Worth a Stop?," TripAdvisor, accessed November 27, 2023, https://www.tripadvisor.com/ShowTopic-g60982-i38-k8402151-Chinatown_is_it_worth_a_stop-Honolulu_Oahu_Hawaii.html.
43. Greg Umbach and Dan Wishnoff, "Strategic Self-Orientalism: Urban Planning Policies and the Shaping of New York City's Chinatown, 1950–2005," *Journal of Planning History* 7, no. 3 (2008): 214–38.
44. Coover, *Honolulu Chinatown*, 182; Cynthia Ning, *Lung Doo Benevolent Society* (Honolulu: University of Hawai'i, 2008), https://scholarspace.manoa.hawaii.edu/collections/b3467ae9-f1e1-4191-a22b-6232df14f134.
45. Historic Building Task Force, "Will Chinatown Survive?" (unpublished manuscript, 1966), 1, University of Hawai'i at Mānoa Library, Hawaiian and Pacific Collections.
46. Thomas Gieryn, "A Space for Place in Sociology," *Annual Review of Sociology* 26 (2000): 463–96.
47. "Building an Archway for One of the Oldest Chinatowns in the United States," HonoluluChinatown.org, accessed November 27, 2023, http://honoluluchinatown.org;Hawaii Happenings (March 2, 2022). http://www.dingdingtv.com/?p=87828
48. Lin, *The Power of Urban Ethnic Places*, 9.
49. Li, "Constructing Chinese America in Hawai'i," 52, quoting Lon Kurashige.
50. "Voices of Chinatown," video transcript, 1977, Uncatalogued Papers, RASRL, University of Hawai'i.
51. Roshi Naidoo, "Never Mind the Buzzwords: 'Race,' Heritage and the Liberal Agenda," in *The Politics of Heritage: The Legacies of Race*, ed. Jo Littler and Roshi Naidoo (London: Taylor and Francis, 2005), 36.
52. Lin, *The Power of Urban Ethnic Places*, 24–26.
53. David Cheever, "What's Up with Today's Downtown/Chinatown?" *Honolulu Weekly* 20, no. 49 (2010), https://evols.library.manoa.hawaii.edu/items/cc3d2dc6-f607-437e-b8bb-bc602721e6c2/full.
54. Application for the Yim Quon building to be added to the National Register of Historic Places, Historic Hawai'i Foundation 2018, 15–17, https://historichawaii.org/download/yim-quon-building-honolulu/.
55. Coover, *Honolulu Chinatown*, 227.
56. *Twenty-First Narcissus Festival Souvenir Annual*, 1970, quoted in Li, "Constructing Chinese America in Hawai'i," 192.

6. CHINATOWN TODAY

57. Jonathan Y. Okamura, "The Illusion of Paradise: Privileging Multiculturalism in Hawai'i," in *Making Majorities: Constituting the Nation in Japan, Korea, China, Malaysia, Fiji, Turkey, and the United States*, ed. Dru C. Gladney (Palo Alto, CA: Stanford University Press, 1998), 264–85.

58. Ah Jook Ku, "Kauai's Chinese," in *Sailing for the Sun: The Chinese in Hawaii 1789–1989*, ed. Arlene Lum (Honolulu: Three Heroes, 1988), 60.

59. Lisa S. H. Park, *Consuming Citizenship: Children of Asian Immigrant Entrepreneurs* (Palo Alto, CA: Stanford University Press, 2005), 6–15; on this process among Japanese in Hawai'i, see Shiho Imai, *Creating the Nisei Market: Race and Citizenship in Hawai'i's Japanese American Consumer Culture* (Honolulu: University of Hawai'i Press, 2010), 93–105.

60. Lin, *The Power of Urban Ethnic Places*, 10.

61. Kaltmeier, "Introduction," 15.

62. Li, "Constructing Chinese America in Hawai'i," 246.

63. Ilima Loomis, "Hawai'i's China Wave Smaller Than Expected," *Hawai'i Business Magazine*, July 13, 2018, https://www.hawaiibusiness.com/hawaiis-china-wave/; Kay Anderson et al., *Chinatown Unbound: Trans-Asian Urbanism in the Age of China* (Lanham, MD: Rowman and Littlefield, 2019), 72.

64. Loomis, "Hawai'i's China Wave."

65. Jonathan Y. Okamura and Amy Abagyani, "*Pamantasan*: Filipino American Higher Education," in *Filipino Americans: Transformation and Identity*, ed. M. P. P. Root, 183–197 (Thousand Oaks, CA: Sage, 1997), 186.

66. Sandy Grande and Lauren Anderson, "Un-settling Multicultural Erasures," *Multicultural Perspectives* 19, no. 3 (2017): 139.

67. Grace Kyungwon Hong, "Speculative Surplus: Asian American Racialization and the Neoliberal Shift," *Social Text* 36, no. 2 (2018): 112.

68. David Wilson, "Making Historical Preservation in Chicago: Discourse and Spatiality in Neoliberal Times," *Space and Polity* 8, no. 1 (2004), 43–59.

69. Downey, "Is Honolulu's Chinatown on the Brink?"

70. Raymond W. Rast, "The Cultural Politics of Tourism in San Francisco's Chinatown, 1882–1917," *Pacific Historical Review* 76, no. 1 (2007): 29–60.

71. Joan Henderson, "Attracting Tourists to Singapore's Chinatown: A Case Study in Conservation and Promotion," *Tourism Management* 21, no. 5 (2000): 525–34; Shircliff, "Is Chinatown a Place or a Space?"

72. Sylvia Ang, "The 'New Chinatown': The Racialization of Newly Arrived Chinese Migrants in Singapore," *Journal of Ethnic and Migration Studies* 44, no. 7 (2018): 1177–94.

73. Amin Ghaziani, *There Goes the Gayborhood?* (Princeton, NJ: Princeton University Press, 2014), 99.

74. Kay Anderson, *Vancouver's Chinatown: Racial Discourse in Canada, 1875–1980* (Montreal, QC: McGill-Queen's University Press, 1991), 28.

75. Anderson, *Vancouver's Chinatown*, 37.

76. Wilson, "Making Historical Preservation in Chicago," 44.

77. Jodi A. Byrd, "Arriving on a Different Shore: US Empire and Its Horizons," *College Literature* 41, no. 1 (2014): 174–81; see also Dean Itsuji Saranillio, *Unsustainable Empire: Alternative Histories of Hawai'i Statehood* (Durham, NC: Duke University Press, 2018), 1–13.

6. CHINATOWN TODAY

78. Michelle Christian, "A Global Critical Race and Racism Framework: Racial Entanglements and Deep and Malleable Whiteness," *Sociology of Race and Ethnicity* 5, no. 2 (2019): 169–85.
79. Christian, "A Global Critical Race and Racism Framework," 179.
80. Christian, "A Global Critical Race and Racism Framework," 179.
81. J. Kēhaulani Kauanui, *Paradoxes of Hawaiian Sovereignty: Land, Sex, and the Colonial Politics of State Nationalism* (Durham, NC: Duke University Press, 2018), 18.
82. Saranillio, *Unsustainable Empire*; Julia Katz, "From Coolies to Colonials: Chinese Migrants in Hawai'i" (PhD diss., Rutgers University, 2018); Jonathan Y. Okamura, *Ethnicity and Inequality in Hawai'i* (Philadelphia: Temple University Press, 2008).
83. Jodi A. Byrd, "Arriving on a Different Shore," 174–81; Bianca Kai Isaki, "Asian Settler Colonialism's Histories," in *The Routledge Handbook of Asian American Studies*, ed. Cindy I. Cheng (London: Routledge, 2017), 142–53.
84. Kauanui, *Paradoxes*, 17.
85. See also Tom Smith, "Hawaiian History and American History: Integration or Separation?," *American Nineteenth Century History* 20, no. 2 (2019): 161–82; Noenoe Silva, *Aloha Betrayed: Native Hawaiian Resistance to American Colonialism* (Durham, NC: Duke University Press, 2004).
86. Kauanui, *Paradoxes*, 97.
87. Willy Daniel Kaipo Kauai, "The Color of Nationality: Continuities and Discontinuities of Citizenship in Hawai'i" (PhD diss., University of Hawai'i, 2014), 21–23.
88. Christian, "A Global Critical Race and Racism Framework," 179.
89. Jonathan Kay Kamakawiwo'ole Osorio, *Dismembering Lāhui: A History of the Hawaiian Nation to 1887* (Honolulu: University of Hawai'i Press, 2002), 44, cited in Kauanui, *Paradoxes*, 84.
90. Saranillio, *Unsustainable Empire*, 42.
91. Christian, "A Global Critical Race and Racism Framework," 179.
92. Isaki, "Asian Settler Colonialism's Histories."
93. Kauanui, *Paradoxes*, 97.
94. Jeff Chang, "Local Knowledge(s): Notes on Race Relations, Panethnicity, and History in Hawai'i," *Amerasia Journal* 22, no. 2 (1996): 1–29.
95. Silva, *Aloha Betrayed*.
96. Mari J. Matsuda, "Voices of America: Accent, Antidiscrimination Law, and a Jurisprudence for the Last Reconstruction," *Yale Law Journal* 100, no. 5 (1991): 1329–1407; Sheila Forman, "Filipino Participation in Civil Rights Policies and Practices in Hawai'i," *Social Process in Hawai'i* 33 (1991): 1–11.
97. Donna J. Grace and Anna Lee Puanani Lum, "'We Don't Want No Haole Buttholes in Our Stories': Local Girls Reading the Baby-Sitters Club Books in Hawai'i," *Curriculum Inquiry* 31, no. 4 (2001): 421–52.
98. T. J. Jackson Lears, "The Concept of Cultural Hegemony: Problems and Possibilities," *American Historical Review* 90, no. 3 (1985): 567–93.
99. Isaki, "Asian Settler Colonialism's Histories."
100. Hong, "Speculative Surplus," 112.
101. Isaki, "Asian Settler Colonialism's Histories."
102. Saranillio, *Unsustainable Empire*, 6.

6. CHINATOWN TODAY

103. Dean Itsuji Saranillio, "Colliding Histories: Hawai'i Statehood at the Intersection of Asians 'Ineligible to Citizenship' and Hawaiians 'Unfit for Self-Government,'" *Journal of Asian American Studies* 13, no. 3 (2010): 286.

104. Dean Itsuji Saranillio, "Why Asian Settler Colonialism Matters: A Thought Piece on Critiques, Debates and Indigenous Difference," *Settler Colonial Studies* 3, nos. 3–4 (2013): 281.

105. Saranillio, *Unsustainable Empire*, 18.

106. Patrick Wolfe, "Settler Colonialism and the Elimination of the Native," *Journal of Genocide Research* 8, no. 4 (2006): 388.

107. On this point, see Jonathan Y. Okamura, "Japanese American Settler Colonial Power in Hawai'i," in *Japanese American Ethnicity, Identity and Power in Hawai'i* (self-pub., 2023), 205–6, https://scholarspace.manoa.hawaii.edu/items/8f3a3802-07d9-4f4e-a136-8cfc31d225fa; Eiko Kosasa, "Ideological Images: US Nationalism in Japanese Settler Photographs," *Amerasia Journal* 26, no. 2 (2000): 66–99.

108. Lisa King, "Competition, Complicity, and (Potential) Alliance: Native Hawaiian and Asian Immigrant Narratives at the Bishop Museum," *College Literature* 41, no.1 (2014): 47.

109. Saranillio, "Why Asian Settler Colonialism Matters," 282.

BIBLIOGRAPHY

"#32 Story Map Capital Historic District—Hawai'i State Capitol Building." Historic Hawai'i Foundation. https://historichawaii.org/portfolio-items/statecapitolbuilding/.

"1321 Alewa Drive/Hung Lum Chun Residence." Historic Hawai'i Foundation, March 3, 2014. https://historichawaii.org/2014/03/03/1321-alewa-drive-hung-lum-chun-residence/.

"1898: Birth of an Overseas Empire." History, Art & Archives, United States House of Representatives. https://history.house.gov/Exhibitions-and-Publications/APA/Historical-Essays/Exclusion-and-Empire/1898/.

Aarim-Heriot, Najia. *Chinese Immigrants, African Americans, and Racial Anxiety in the United States, 1848–1882.* Champaign: University of Illinois Press, 2003.

"About EWC: Origins." East-West Center. https://www.eastwestcenter.org/about-ewc/origins.

"About First Friday." FirstFridayHawaii.com. https://www.firstfridayhawaii.com/d/d/aboutfirstfriday.html.

Allen, Gwenfread. *Hawaii's War Years: 1941–1945.* Honolulu: University of Hawai'i Press, 1950.

Altonn, Helen. "Tireless Work Led to Big, Tasty Manapuas." *Honolulu Star Bulletin,* April 20, 2003.

"American Families in Hawaii." *Paradise of the Pacific* 59, no. 1 (1947): 5–8.

"An Urban Renewal Program for the City and County of Honolulu." Honolulu Redevelopment Agency, 1955. https://babel.hathitrust.org/cgi/pt?id=uiug.30112076135331&view=1up&seq=2&skin=2021.

Anderson, Kay. *Vancouver's Chinatown: Racial Discourse in Canada, 1875–1980.* Montreal, QC: McGill-Queen's University Press, 1991.

Anderson, Kay, Ien Ang, Andrea Del Bono, Donald McNeill, and Alexandra Wong. *Chinatown Unbound: Trans-Asian Urbanism in the Age of China.* Lanham, MD: Rowman and Littlefield, 2019.

BIBLIOGRAPHY

Ang, Sylvia. "The 'New Chinatown': The Racialization of Newly Arrived Chinese Migrants in Singapore." *Journal of Ethnic and Migration Studies* 44, no. 7 (2018): 1177–94.

Application for Yim Quon Building to be added to the National Register of Historic Places. Historic Hawai'i Foundation, 2018. https://historichawaii.org/download/yim-quon-building-honolulu/.

Archer, Seth. *Sharks Upon the Land: Colonialism, Indigenous Health, and Culture in Hawai'i, 1778–1855.* Cambridge: Cambridge University Press, 2018.

Au, Betty. "A Personal Account of Race Relations." Student paper for Soc 257 class, 1946. Student Papers, Romanzo Adams Social Research Laboratory (RASRL), University of Hawai'i.

Aytar, Volkan, and Jan Rath. "Introduction: Ethnic Neighbourhoods as Places of Leisure and Consumption." In *Selling Ethnic Neighborhoods: The Rise of Neighborhoods as Places of Leisure and Consumption*, ed. Aytar Volkan and Jan Rath, 1–15. London: Taylor and Francis, 2011.

Azuma, Eiichiro. "Brokering Race, Culture, and Citizenship: Japanese Americans in Occupied Japan and Postwar National Inclusion." *Journal of American-East Asian Relations* 16, no. 3 (2009): 183–211.

Bailey, Beth, and David Farber. *The First Strange Place: Race and Sex in World War II Hawai'i.* Baltimore, MD: Johns Hopkins University Press,1992.

Bannick, Nancy, Scott Cheever, and David Cheever. *A Close Call: Saving Honolulu's Chinatown.* Honolulu, HI: Little Percent, 2005.

Beechert, Edward. *Working in Hawaii: A Labor History.* Honolulu: University of Hawai'i Press, 1985.

Bell, Roger. *Last Among Equals: Hawaiian Statehood and American Politics.* Honolulu: University of Hawai'i Press, 1984.

Benham, Maenette Kape'ahiokoalani Padeken. "The Voice 'Less' Hawaiian: An Analysis of Educational Policymaking, 1820–1960." *Hawaiian Journal of History* 32 (1998): 121–40.

Berglund, Barbara. *Making San Francisco American: Cultural Frontiers in the Urban West, 1846–1906.* Lawrence: University Press of Kansas, 2007.

Bidlingmaier, Selma Siew Li. "Spaces of Alterity and Temporal Permanence: The Case of San Francisco's and New York's Chinatowns." In *Selling EthniCity: Urban Cultural Politics in the Americas*, ed. Olaf Kaltmeier, 275–85. Farnham, UK: Ashgate, 2011.

Blokland, Talja. "From Outside Looking In: A 'European' Perspective on the Ghetto." *City and Community* 7, no. 4 (2008): 372–77.

Bourassa, Gregory. "Neoliberal Multiculturalism and Productive Inclusion: Beyond the Politics of Fulfillment in Education." *Journal of Education Policy* 36, no. 2 (2021): 253–78.

Brooks, Charlotte. *Alien Neighbors, Foreign Friends: Asian Americans, Housing, and the Transformation of Urban California.* Chicago: University of Chicago Press, 2009.

Bushnell, O. A. *The Gifts of Civilization: Germs and Genocide in Hawai'i.* Honolulu: University of Hawai'i Press, 1983.

Byrd, Jodi A. "Arriving on a Different Shore: US Empire at Its Horizons." *College Literature* 41, no. 1 (2014): 174–81.

Chaddha, Anmol, and William J. Wilson. "Reconsidering the 'Ghetto.'" *City and Community* 7, no. 4 (2008): 384–88.

BIBLIOGRAPHY

Chambers-Letson, Joshua. *A Race So Different: Performance and Law in Asian America.* New York: NYU Press, 2013.

Chang, David A. *The World and All the Things Upon It: Native Hawaiian Geographies of Exploration.* Minneapolis: University of Minnesota Press, 2016.

Chang, Eleanor Ai. Student paper for Soc 257 class, n.d. Glick Papers, box 9, RASRL, University of Hawai'i.

Chang, Jeff. "Local Knowledge(s): Notes on Race Relations, Panethnicity, and History in Hawai'i." *Amerasia Journal* 22, no. 2 (1996): 1–29.

Chang, William Bun Chang. "The Myth of Chinese Success in Hawaii." *Hawaii Pono Journal* 1, no. 4 (1971): 59–76.

Chang, Yoonmee. *Writing the Ghetto: Class, Authorship, and the Asian American Ethnic Enclave.* New Brunswick, NJ: Rutgers University Press, 2010.

Cheever, David. "What's Up with Today's Downtown/Chinatown?" *Honolulu Weekly* 20, no. 49 (2010). https://evols.library.manoa.hawaii.edu/items/cc3d2dc6-f607-437e -b8bb-bc602721e6c2/full.

Chen, Hsiang-shui. *Chinatown No More: Taiwan Immigrants in Contemporary New York.* Ithaca, NY: Cornell University Press, 1992.

Chen, Qi. "The Acculturation of Chinese Intellectuals in Hawaii: 1894–1959." PhD diss., University of Hawai'i, 1997.

Chen, Yong. *Chinese San Francisco, 1850–1943.* Palo Alto, CA: Stanford University Press, 2000.

Cheng, Ch'eng-K'un. "A Study of Chinese Assimilation in Hawaii." *Social Forces* 32, no. 2 (1953): 163–67.

Cheng, Cindy I-fen. *Citizens of Asian America: Democracy and Race during the Cold War.* New York: NYU Press, 2013.

Cheng, Martha. "Honolulu's Newly Hip Chinatown: A Traveler's Guide." *Wall Street Journal*, March 15, 2017. https://www.wsj.com/articles/honolulus-newly-hip-chinatown -a-travelers-guide-1489595294.

"Chinatown." Hawai'i Tourism Authority. https://www.gohawaii.com/islands/oahu /regions/honolulu/Chinatown.

"Chinatown Historic District (Honolulu)," National Park Service, https://www.nps.gov /places/chinatown-historic-district-honolulu.htm.

"Chinese Family in Honolulu's Slum." Student paper. Student Papers (1963), box 7, folder 17, RASRL, University of Hawai'i.

Chong, Douglas Dai Lun. *Ancestral Reflections: Hawaii's Early Chinese of Waipahu— An Ethnic Community Experience, 1885–1935.* Waipahu, HI: Waipahu Tsong Nyee Society, 1998.

Chong-Gossard, J. H. Kim On. *The Chong Family History: A Monumental Work.* Ka'a'awa, HI: Chong Hee, 1992.

Chow, Rey. "Have You Eaten Yet?" *Amerasia Journal* 31, no. 1 (2005):19–22.

Chow, Wayson. "Wayson Chow." In *Autobiography of Protest in Hawai'i*, ed. Robert H. Mast and Anne B. Mast, 42–49. Honolulu: University of Hawai'i Press, 1996.

Christian, Michelle. "A Global Critical Race and Racism Framework: Racial Entanglements and Deep and Malleable Whiteness." *Sociology of Race and Ethnicity* 5, no. 2 (2019): 169–85.

Christian, Michelle, and Assumpta Namaganda. "Good Mzungu? Whiteness and White Supremacy in Postcolonial Uganda." *Identities* 30, no. 2 (2023): 217–36.

BIBLIOGRAPHY

Chung, Sue Fawn. *In Pursuit of Gold: Chinese American Miners and Merchants in the American West*. Champaign: University of Illinois Press, 2011.

Coffman, Tom. *How Hawai'i Changed America*. Honolulu, HI: Epicenter, 2014.

——. *The Island Edge of America: A Political History of Hawai'i*. Honolulu: University of Hawai'i Press, 2003.

Coman, Katherine. *The History of Contract Labor in the Hawaiian Islands*. New York: Arno, 1978. First published 1903 by MacMillan.

Connell, John Harden. "The History of Chinese in Hawaii." *Mid-Pacific Magazine* 46, no. 5 (1933): 419–24.

Cook, Katherine H. *Public Education in Hawaii*. Bulletin 10. Washington, DC: U.S. Department of the Interior, Office of Education, 1935.

Cookman, Sonja. *Remembering Chinatown: Examining Eviction Struggles in Hawaii's Chinatown in the 1970s-80s*. Honolulu: Hawaii's People's Fund, 2016. https://www.hawaiipeoplesfund.org/wp-content/uploads/2019/03/REMEMBERING-CHINATOWN.pdf.

Coover, Gary. *Honolulu Chinatown: 200 Years of Red Lanterns and Red Lights*. Honolulu, HI: Rollston, 2022.

Coulter, John, and Chee-kwon Chun. "Chinese Rice Farmers in Hawaii." *University of Hawai'i Bulletin* 16, no. 5 (1937).

Craddock, Susan. "Embodying Place: Pathologizing Chinese and Chinatown in Nineteenth-Century San Francisco." *Antipode* 31, no. 4 (1999): 351–71.

Damon, Frank. "Home for the Homeless: A Plea for Chinese Females Immigration." *The Friend* 38, no. 11 (1881): 98.

Daniels, Roger. "'No Lamps Were Lit for Them': Angel Island and the Historiography of Asian Americans." *Journal of American Ethnic History* 17 (1997): 2–18.

Delaney, David. 2002. "The Space That Race Makes." *Professional Geographer* 54, no. 1: 6–14.

Desmond, Jane. *Staging Tourism: Bodies on Display from Waikiki to Sea World*. Chicago: University of Chicago Press, 2001.

Downey, Kirstin. "Is Honolulu's Chinatown on the Brink of a Turnaround?" *Honolulu Civil Beat*, June 19, 2022. https://www.civilbeat.org/2022/06/is-honolulus-chinatown-on-the-brink-of-a-turnaround/.

"Dr. Sammy Lee, Olympic Champion and Goodwill Ambassador." National Museum of American Diplomacy. https://diplomacy.state.gov/u-s-diplomacy-stories/dr-sammy-lee-olympic-champion-and-goodwill-ambassador/.

Duleep, Harriet Orcutt, and Seth G. Sanders. *The Economic Status of Asian Americans Before and After the Civil Rights Act*. IZA Discussion Paper No. 6639. Bonn: Institute for the Study of Labor, 2012. http://dx.doi.org/10.2139/ssrn.2089668.

Duneier, Mitchell. *Ghetto: The Invention of a Place, the History of an Idea*. New York: Farrar, Straus and Giroux, 2016.

Echenberg, Myron. "Plague in Paradise: Honolulu, 1899–1900." in *Plague Ports: The Global Urban Impact of Bubonic Plague, 1894–1901*, ed. Myron Echenberg, 185–212. New York: NYU Press, 2007.

Editorial. *Honolulu Advertiser*, February 28, 1930.

Eichelberger, Laura. "SARS and New York's Chinatown: The Politics of Risk and Blame During an Epidemic of Fear." *Social Science & Medicine* 65, no. 6 (2007): 1284–95.

BIBLIOGRAPHY

Eng, Marietta, and Rosalind Mau. *Hawai'i's Shining Star: Mun Lun School*. Honolulu, HI: Mo Hock Ke Lock Bo, 2011.

Eperjesi, John R. *The Imperialist Imaginary: Visions of Asia and the Pacific in American Culture*. Hanover, NH: Dartmouth College Press, 2005.

Farber, David, and Beth Bailey. "The Fighting Man as Tourist: The Politics of Tourist Culture in Hawaii During World War II." *Pacific Historical Review* 65, no. 4 (1996): 641–60.

Fong, Ho. "The Hawaiian Anti-Asian Union." *Pacific Commercial Advertiser*, March 12, 1888.

Fong, Timothy. *The First Suburban Chinatown: The Remaking of Monterey Park, California*. Philadelphia: Temple University Press, 1994.

Forman, Sheila. "Filipino Participation in Civil Rights Policies and Practices in Hawai'i." *Social Process in Hawai'i* 33 (1991): 1–11.

Forster, Carol. "Chinese Entrepreneurs in Nineteenth Century Hawaii." Master's thesis, University of Alberta, 1995.

Foster, James W. "Queen Emma Gardens: The Making of a Landmark." Queen Emma Gardens Community Website. https://www.queenemmagardens.com/post/read-about-the-history-of-queen-emma-gardens.

Fox, Catherine. "Downtown Honolulu Used to Be So Vibrant. What Happened?" *Honolulu Civil Beat*, October 7, 2022.

Fuchs, Lawrence. *Hawaii Pono: A Social History*. New York: Harcourt Brace Jovanovich, 1961.

Gans, Herbert. "Involuntary Segregation and the Ghetto: Disconnecting Process and Place." *City and Community* 7, no. 4 (2008): 353–57.

Ghaziani, Amin. *There Goes the Gayborhood?* Princeton, NJ: Princeton University Press, 2014.

Gieryn, Thomas. "A Space for Place in Sociology." *Annual Review of Sociology* 26 (2000): 463–96.

Glick, Clarence. "Residential Dispersion of Urban Chinese." *Social Process in Hawai'i* 2 (1936): 28–34.

——. *Sojourners and Settlers: Chinese Migrants in Hawaii*. Honolulu: University of Hawai'i Press, 1980.

Gonzalez, Vernadette Vicuña. *Securing Paradise: Tourism and Militarism in Hawai'i and the Philippines*. Durham, NC: Duke University Press, 2013.

Goo, Paul Kimm-Chow. "Building Hawaii's Prosperity." In *The Chinese of Hawaii*. Honolulu, HI: Overseas Penman Club, 1929.

Gordon, Mike. "Post-war Prejudice Gave Rise to Aloha 'The People's Airline.'" *Honolulu Advertiser*, April 8, 2008.

Grace, Donna J., and Anna Lee Puanani Lum. "'We Don't Want No Haole Buttholes in Our Stories': Local Girls Reading the Baby-Sitters Club Books in Hawai'i." *Curriculum Inquiry* 31, no. 4 (2001): 421–52.

Grande, Sandy, and Lauren Anderson. "Un-settling multicultural erasures." *Multicultural Perspectives* 19, no. 3 (2017): 139–42.

"A Great and Sore Distress." *The Friend* 58, no. 2 (1900).

Guinier, Lani, and Gerald Torres. *The Miner's Canary: Enlisting Race, Resisting Power, Transforming Democracy*. Cambridge, MA: Harvard University Press, 2002.

Hannus, Minto. "Interracial Relationships in Hawaii." Student paper for Soc 257 class, 1949. Student Papers, RASRL, University of Hawai'i.

BIBLIOGRAPHY

Harvey, David. *A Brief History of Neoliberalism*. Oxford: Oxford University Press, 2005.

"Hawaii." History, Art & Archives, United States House of Representativeshttps://history.house.gov/Exhibitions-and-Publications/APA/Historical-Essays/Exclusion-and-Empire/Hawaii/.

Henderson, Joan. "Attracting Tourists to Singapore's Chinatown: A Case Study in Conservation and Promotion." *Tourism Management* 21, no. 5 (2000): 525–34.

"Hickam AFB, HI History." Hickam AFB, HI. https://www.hickamafbhousing.com/history.

Higgins, Colette. "Anti-Chinese Sentiments in Hawaii from 1852–1886." Student paper for History 484 class, fall 1990. Student Papers, RASRL, University of Hawaiʻi.

Historic Building Task Force. "Will Chinatown Survive?" Unpublished manuscript, 1966. University of Hawaiʻi at Mānoa Library, Hawaiian and Pacific Collections.

Hiura, Arnold. *Kau Kau: Cuisine and Culture of the Hawaiian Islands*. Honolulu: Watermark, 2009.

Hong, Grace Kyungwon. "Speculative Surplus: Asian American Racialization and the Neoliberal Shift." *Social Text* 36, no.2 (2018): 107–22.

Hope, Bradley, and Janette Hope. "Native Hawaiian Health in Hawaii: Historical Highlights." In "Hawaii," special issue, *Californian Journal of Health Promotion* 1, no. S1 (2003): 1–9.

Hsieh, T'ing Y'u. "The Chinese in Hawaii." *Chinese Social and Political Science Review* (1930): 13–40.

Hsu, Madeline. *The Good Immigrants: How the Yellow Peril became the Model Minority*. Princeton, NJ: Princeton University Press, 2015.

Huang, Hsiao-ping. "Chinese Merchant Background and Experience Under the Monarchy." PhD diss., University of Hawaiʻi, 1989.

Huang, Xu. "The Schooling of the Children of Early Chinese Immigrants in Hawaii." Master's thesis, University of Hawaiʻi, 1989.

Imai, Shiho. *Creating the Nisei Market: Race and Citizenship in Hawaiʻi Japanese American Consumer Culture*. Honolulu: University of Hawaiʻi Press, 2010.

Immerwahr, Daniel. *How to Hide an Empire: A History of the Greater United States*. London: Farrar, Straus and Giroux, 2019.

Isaki, Bianca Kai. "Asian Settler Colonialism's Histories." In *The Routledge Handbook of Asian American Studies*, ed. Cindy I. Cheng, 142–53. London: Routledge, 2017.

Iwamoto, Lana. "Plague and Fire of 1899–1900 in Honolulu." *Hawaii Historical Review* 2, no. 8 (1967): 379–91.

Jedra, Christina. "Is It Time for Hawaii to Renegotiate Its Relationship with the Military?" *Honolulu Civil Beat*, May 23, 2022. https://www.civilbeat.org/2022/05/is-it-time-for-hawaii-to-renegotiate-its-relationship-with-the-military/.

Jim On, Shelton. "Chinese Immigration to Hawaiʻi, 1852–1898." BA honors thesis, University of Hawaiʻi, 1972.

Jun, Helen. *Race for Citizenship: Black Orientalism and Asian Uplift from Pre-emancipation to Neoliberal America*. New York: NYU Press, 2011.

Kajihiro, Kyle. "Nation Under the Gun: Militarism and Resistance in Hawaiʻi." *Cultural Survival* 24, no. 1 (2000). https://www.culturalsurvival.org/publications/cultural-survival-quarterly/nation-under-gun-militarism-and-resistance-hawaii.

BIBLIOGRAPHY

Kaltmeier, Olaf. "Introduction: Selling EthniCity." In *Selling EthniCity: Urban Cultural Politics in the Americas*, ed. Olaf Kaltmeier, 1–19. Farnham, UK: Ashgate, 2011.

Kam, Nadine. "The Weekly Eater: How Wun Is True to Tin Tin Legacy." *Honolulu Star-Bulletin*, December 19, 1996.

Kaneshiro, Kiyoshi. "Assimilation in a Slum Area of Honolulu." *Social Process in Hawaii* 4 (1938): 16–27.

Kaplan, Amy. "Manifest Domesticity." *American Literature* 70, no. 3 (1998): 581–606.

Kaplan, David, and Wei Li, eds. *Landscapes of the Ethnic Economy*. Lanham, MD: Rowman and Littlefield, 2006.

Karuka, Manu. *Tracks of Empire: Indigenous Nations, Chinese Workers, and the Transcontinental Railroad*. Berkeley: University of California Press, 2019.

Kato, Gerald. "Look at Chinatown: Shifts in Approach." *Honolulu Advertiser*, September 3, 1979.

Katz, Julia. "Ahuna and the Moʻo: Rethinking Chinese Success in Hawaiian Commercial Food Production." *Pacific Historical Review* 84, no. 4 (2017): 599–631.

——. "From Coolies to Colonials: Chinese Migrants in Hawaiʻi." PhD diss., Rutgers University, 2018.

——. "The Politics of the Pipe: Opium Regulation and Protocolonial Governance in Nineteenth-Century Hawaiʻi." In *Imagining Asia in the Americas*, ed. Zelideth María Rivas and Debbie Lee-DiStefano, 104–32. New Brunswick, NJ: Rutgers University Press, 2016.

Kauai, Willy Daniel Kaipo. "The Color of Nationality: Continuities and Discontinuities of Citizenship in Hawaiʻi." PhD diss., University of Hawaiʻi, 2014.

Kauanui, J. Kēhaulani. *Paradoxes of Hawaiian Sovereignty: Land, Sex, and the Colonial Politics of State Nationalism*. Durham, NC: Duke University Press, 2018.

Kelly, John. "People Against Chinatown Eviction." PACE pamphlet, 1974. University of Hawaiʻi at Mānoa Library Digital Image Collections, accessed July 15, 2022. https://digital.library.manoa.hawaii.edu/items/show/31281.

Kennedy, John F. "Address in Honolulu Before the United States Conference of Mayors." American Presidency Project, June 9, 1963. https://www.presidency.ucsb.edu/documents/address-honolulu-before-the-united-states-conference-mayors.

Kent, Noel. *Hawaii: Islands Under the Influence*. Honolulu: University of Hawaiʻi Press, 1993.

Kim, Heidi. *Illegal Immigrants/Model Minorities: The Cold War of Chinese American Narrative*. Philadelphia: Temple University Press, 2021.

Kim, Thomas. "Being Modern: The Circulation of Oriental Objects." *American Quarterly* 58, no. 2 (2006): 379–406.

Kimura, Yukiko. "Social Effects of Increased Income of Defense Workers of Oriental Ancestry in Hawaii." *Social Process in Hawaii* 7 (1941): 46–55.

King, Lisa. "Competition, Complicity, and (Potential) Alliance: Native Hawaiian and Asian Immigrant Narratives at the Bishop Museum." *College Literature* 41, no. 1 (2014): 43–65.

Klein, Christina. *Cold War Orientalism*. Berkeley: University of California Press, 2003.

Kosasa, Eiko. "Ideological Images: US Nationalism in Japanese Settler Photographs." *Amerasia Journal* 26, no. 2 (2000): 66–99.

BIBLIOGRAPHY

Kosta, Ervin. "The Power of Urban Ethnic Places: Cultural Heritage and Community Life—By Jan Lin." *International Journal of Urban & Regional Research* 37, no. 4 (2013): 1496–97.

Krattinger, Angela. "Hawai'i's Cold War: American Empire and the Fiftieth State." PhD diss., University of Hawai'i at Mānoa, 2013.

Kraut, Alan. "Plagues and Prejudices: Nativism's Construction of Disease in Nineteenth- and Twentieth-Century New York City." In *Hives of Sickness: Public Health and Epidemics in NYC*, ed. David Rosner, 65–90. New Brunswick, NJ: Rutgers University Press, 1995.

Ku, Ah Jook. "Kauai's Chinese." In *Sailing for the Sun: The Chinese in Hawaii 1789–1989*, ed. Arlene Lum, 46–61. Honolulu: Three Heroes, 1988.

Kwok, Daniel. 1988. "By History Remembered." In *Sailing for the Sun: The Chinese in Hawaii 1789–1989*, ed. Arleene Lum, 8–23. Honolulu: Three Heroes, 1988.

Kwong, Peter. *The New Chinatown*. New York: Hill and Wong, 1987.

"Labor Strikes." Hawai'i Digital Newspaper Project. https://sites.google.com/a/hawaii.edu/ndnp-hawaii/Home/subject-and-topic-guides/labor-strikes.

Labrador, Roderick. *Building Filipino Hawai'i*. Champaign: University of Illinois Press, 2015.

Lai, Him Mark. "The Chinese Community Press in Hawai'i." In "The Hawai'i Chinese," special issue, *Journal of the Chinese Historical Society of America* (2010): 95–103.

Lai, Violet. Student paper for Soc 267 class, January 1938, 3. Student Papers, RASRL, University of Hawai'i.

Lam, Fred K. "A Survey of the Chinese People in Hawaii Historically, Educationally, Commercially, Religiously, and Socially." Third Conference of the Institute of Pacific Relations, Kyoto[?], 1929.

Lears, T. J. Jackson. "The Concept of Cultural Hegemony: Problems and Possibilities," *American Historical Review* 90, no. 3 (1985): 567–93.

Lee, Bung Chong. "The Chinese Store as Social Institution." *Social Process in Hawaii* 2 (1936): 35–38.

Lee, Karen W. F. "The Coming of the Chinese: The Early Immigrant Community in Hawaii." PhD diss., University of Hawai'i, 1990.

Lee, Richard K. C. "The Educated Class: One Man's Journey." In *Sailing for the Sun: The Chinese in Hawaii 1789–1989*, ed. Arlene Lum, 149–65. Honolulu, HI: Three Heroes, 1988.

Lee, Robert G. *Orientals: Asian Americans in Popular Culture*. Philadelphia: Temple University Press, 1999.

Lee, Robert Man War. "Vertical Mobility Among the Chinese in Hawaii." Master's thesis, University of Hawai'i, 1951.

Lee, Robert Man War, ed. *The Chinese in Hawaii: A Historical Sketch*. Honolulu: Advertiser Publishing, 1961.

Lee, Rose Hum. "The Decline of Chinatowns in the United States." *American Journal of Sociology* 54, no. 5 (1949): 422–32.

Lee, William. "The Assimilation of the Chinese Members of the Class of 1928 of the University of Hawaii, Chiefly of Its Economic Aspect." Student paper, 1935. Student Papers, RASRL, University of Hawai'i.

Leong, Karen J. *The China Mystique*. Berkeley: University of California Press, 2005.

Leong, Nancy. "Racial Capitalism." *Harvard Law Review* 126, no. 8 (2013): 2153–54.

BIBLIOGRAPHY

Leong, Yau Sing. "From Kwangtung to the Plantations, Farm Stores and Beyond." In *Sailing for the Sun: The Chinese in Hawaii 1789–1989*, ed. Arlene Lum, 72–95. Honolulu: Three Heroes, 1988.

Lew-Williams, Beth. *The Chinese Must Go: Violence, Exclusion, and the Making of the Alien in America*. Cambridge, MA: Harvard University Press, 2018.

Li, Jinzhao. "Constructing Chinese America in Hawai'i: The Narcissus Festival, Ethnic Identity, and Community Transformation, 1949–2005." PhD diss., University of Hawai'i at Mānoa, 2005.

Li, Ling Ai. *Life Is for a Long Time: A Chinese Hawaiian Memoir*. New York: Hastings House, 1972.

Li, Peter, and Eva Xiaoling Li. "Vancouver Chinatown in Transition." In *Chinatowns Around the World: Gilded Ghetto, Ethnopolis, and Cultural Diaspora*, ed. Bernard P. Wong and Chee-Beng Tan, 19–34. Leiden: Brill, 2013.

Li, Sylvianne Fei-Ai. "A History of the Education of the Chinese in Hawaii." Master's thesis, Oberlin College, 1940.

Li, Wei, et al. "How Ethnic Banks Matter: Banking and Community/Economic Development in Los Angeles." In *Landscapes of the Ethnic Economy*, ed. David H. Kaplan and Wei Li, 113–33. Lanham, MD: Rowman and Littlefield, 2004.

Lin, Jan. *The Power of Urban Ethnic Places: Cultural Heritage and Community Life*. New York: Routledge, 2011.

Lind, Andrew W. *Hawaii: The Last of the Magic Isles*. Oxford: Oxford University Press, 1969.

——. *Hawaii's People*. Honolulu: University of Hawai'i Press, 1955.

——. *Hawaii's People*, 4th ed. Honolulu: University of Hawai'i Press, 1980.

——. "The Japanese in Hawaii Under War Conditions." Paper presented at the Eighth Conference of the Pacific Institute, Mont Tremblant, QC, December 1942. https://oac.cdlib.org/ark:/28722/bk001392v15/?brand=oac4.

——. "Mounting the Occupational Ladder in Honolulu." Student research lab report no. 4, 1957. Student Papers, RASRL, University of Hawai'i.

——. "A Preliminary Study of Military Morale." *Social Process in Hawaii* 8 (1943): 5–17.

Lind, Ian. "'A'ala and Its Surrounding Areas, 1958." Essay accompanying Francis Haar, *Disappearing Honolulu*. Exhibit, University of Hawai'i, John Young Museum, 2019. https://hawaii.edu/art/francis-haar-disappearing-honolulu/.

Loomis, Ilima. "Hawai'i's China's Wave Smaller Than Expected." *Hawai'i Business Magazine*, July 13, 2018. https://www.hawaiibusiness.com/hawaiis-china-wave/.

"The Lost Decade of the Middle Class: Fewer, Poorer, Gloomier." Pew Research Center, August 22, 2012. https://www.pewresearch.org/social-trends/2012/08/22/the-lost-decade-of-the-middle-class/#chapter-1-overview.

Low, Setha. *Spatializing Culture: The Ethnography of Space and Place*. London: Routledge, 2016.

Lum, Arlene. "The Centenary Was *Not* a Time for Celebration." In *Sailing for the Sun: The Chinese in Hawaii 1789–1989*, ed. Arelene Lum, 110–29. Honolulu, HI: Three Heroes, 1988.

Lum, Lillian Awai. "Biography of a 'Country' Club: The United Chinese Club of Kohala, Hawaii." Unpublished manuscript, 1990.

Lum, Nellie. "Bingham Tract." Student paper for Soc 151a class, March 23, 1950. Student Papers, box 18, file 36, RASRL, University of Hawai'i.

BIBLIOGRAPHY

Lutz, Jessie. "Chinese Emigrants, Indentured Workers, and Christianity in the West Indies, British Guiana and Hawaii." *Caribbean Studies* 37, no. 2 (2009): 133–54.

Lydon, Edward. *The Anti-Chinese Movement in the Hawaiian Kingdom, 1852–1886.* San Francisco: R. and E. Research Associates, 1975.

MacLennan, Carol. *Sovereign Sugar: Industry and Environment in Hawai'i.* Honolulu: University of Hawai'i Press, 2014.

Mak, James. *Developing a Dream Destination: Tourism and Tourism Policy Planning in Hawai'i.* Honolulu: University of Hawai'i Press, 2008.

Malones, Ligaya. "Bean-to-Bar Chocolate and Sailor Jerry Tats: An Insider's Guide to Honolulu's Chinatown." *New York Magazine,* May 3, 2018.

Man, Simeon. "Aloha, Vietnam: Race and Empire in Hawai'i's Vietnam War." *American Quarterly* 67, no. 4 (2015): 1085–1108.

——. "Anti-Asian Violence and U.S. Imperialism." *Race & Class* 62, no. 2 (2020): 22–33.

Mark, Diane Mai Lin. *Chinese in Kula: Reflections of a Farming Community in Old Hawaii.* Honolulu: Hawaii Chinese History Center, 1975.

Markel, Howard, and Alexandra Stern. "The Foreignness of Germs: The Persistent Association of Immigrants and Disease in American Society." *Milbank Quarterly* 80, no. 4 (2002): 757–88.

Martin, Dan. "Chinatown at a Crossroads." *Honolulu Star Bulletin,* June 18, 2006. https://archives.starbulletin.com/2006/06/18/news/story03.html.

Matsuda, Mari J. "Voices of America: Accent, Antidiscrimination Law, and a Jurisprudence for the Last Reconstruction." *Yale Law Journal* 100, no. 5 (1991): 1329–1407.

McGregor, Davianna Pomaika'i. *Na Kua'aina: Living Hawaiian Culture.* Honolulu: University of Hawai'i Press, 2007.

Miller-Davenport, Sarah. *Gateway State: Hawai'i and the Cultural Transformation of Empire.* Princeton, NJ: Princeton University Press, 2019.

——. "'A Montage of Minorities:' Hawai'i Tourism and the Commodification of Racial Tolerance, 1959–1978." *Historical Journal* 60, no. 2 (2017): 817–42.

Minn, Ping Kyau. *Memoirs of the Third Son: Zane Kee Fook.* Honolulu: Hawaii Chinese History Center, 1978.

Mohr, James. *Plague and Fire: Battling Black Death and the 1900 Burning of Honolulu's Chinatown.* Oxford: Oxford University Press, 2005.

Morgan, Michelle. "Americanizing the Teachers: Identity, Citizenship, and the Teaching Corps in Hawai'i, 1900–1941." *Western Historical Quarterly* 45, no. 2 (2014): 147–67.

Naidoo, Roshi. "Never Mind the Buzzwords: 'Race,' Heritage and the Liberal Agenda." In *The Politics of Heritage: The Legacies of Race,* ed. Jo Littler and Roshi Naidoo, 32–43. London: Taylor and Francis, 2005.

Naram, Kartik. "'No Place Like Home': Racial Capitalism, Gentrification, and the Identity of Chinatown." *Asian American Policy Review* 27 (2017): 33–50.

"New Neighborhood, New Outlook." Student paper, April 15, 1963. Student Papers, box 7, folder 15, RASRL, University of Hawai'i.

Ngai, Mae. *The Lucky Ones: One Family and the Extraordinary Invention of Chinese America.* Princeton, NJ: Princeton University Press, 2012.

Ning, Cynthia. *Lung Doo Benevolent Society.* Honolulu: University of Hawai'i, 2008. https://scholarspace.manoa.hawaii.edu/collections/b3467ae9-f1e1-4191-a22b-6232df14f134.

Nordyke, Eleanor, and Richard K. C. Lee. "The Chinese in Hawai'i: A Historical and Demographic Perspective." *Hawaiian Journal of History* 23 (1989): 196–216.

BIBLIOGRAPHY

Odo, Franklin. *No Sword to Bury: Japanese Americans in Hawai'i During World War II.* Philadelphia: Temple University Press, 2004.

Okamura, Jonathan Y. *Ethnicity and Inequality in Hawai'i.* Philadelphia: Temple University Press, 2008.

——. "Filipino American Ethnicity, Education and Diaspora in Hawai'i." Unpublished manuscript, 2021. https://scholarspace.manoa.hawaii.edu/items/1cc7f425-186d-47dd-a4ea-0ce258527b7f.

——. *From Race to Ethnicity: Interpreting Japanese American Experiences in Hawai'i.* Honolulu: University of Hawai'i Press, 2014.

——. "The Illusion of Paradise: Privileging Multiculturalism in Hawai'i." In *Making Majorities: Constituting the Nation in Japan, Korea, China, Malaysia, Fiji, Turkey, and the United States,* ed. Dru C. Gladney, 264–85. Palo Alto, CA: Stanford University Press, 1998.

——. "Japanese American Settler Colonial Power in Hawai'i." In *Japanese American Ethnicity, Identity and Power in Hawai'i,* 188–217. Self-published, 2023. https://scholarspace.manoa.hawaii.edu/items/8f3a3802-07d9-4f4e-a136-8cfc31d225fa.

——. "Race Relations in Hawai'i During World War II: The Non-internment of Japanese Americans." In *The Japanese American Historical Experience in Hawai'i,* ed. Jonathan Okamura, 67–90. Dubuque, IA: Kendall Hunt, 2001.

——. "Why There Are No Asian Americans in Hawai'i: The Continuing Significance of Local Identity." In "The Political Economy of Hawai'i," ed. Ibrahim G. Aoude, special issue, *Social Process in Hawai'i* 35 (1994): 161–78.

Okamura, Jonathan and Amy Abagyani. *Pamantasan*: Filipino American Higher Education. In *Filipino Americans: Transformation and Identity,* ed. M. P. P. Root, 183–197. Thousand Oaks, CA: Sage, 1997.

Okihiro, Gary. *Cane Fires: The Anti-Japanese Movement in Hawai'i, 1865–1945.* Philadelphia: Temple University Press, 1991.

——. *Margins and Mainstreams.* Seattle: University of Washington Press, 1994.

Omi, Michael. "The Unbearable Whiteness of Being: The Contemporary Racialization of Japanese/Asian Americans." In *Trans-Pacific Japanese American Studies: Conversations on Race and Racializations,* ed. Yasuko Takezawa and Gary Y. Okihiro, 39–59. Honolulu: University of Hawai'i Press, 2016.

Ong, Aihwa. *Flexible Citizenship: The Cultural Logics of Transnationality.* Durham, NC: Duke University Press, 1999.

Ordway, Nicholas, and Michaelyn Chou. "Chinatown as metaphor: special views of Chinese Land Ownership in Hawaii." Paper presented at Lucky You Come Hawaii Conference, Honolulu, HI, 1988.

Osorio, Jonathan Kay Kamakawiwo'ole. *Dismembering Lāhui: A History of the Hawaiian Nation to 1887.* Honolulu: University of Hawai'i Press, 2002.

Oyasato, Tom, and Ronald Ozaki. "The Slums and Blighted Areas of Honolulu." Student paper for Soc 255 class, 1950. Student Papers, RASRL, University of Hawai'i.

Pang, Ching Lan. "Gateways to the Urban Economy: Chinatowns in Antwerp and Brussels." In *Selling Ethnic Neighborhoods: The Rise of Neighborhoods as Places of Leisure and Consumption,* ed. Volkan Aytar and Jan Rath, 52–67. London: Taylor and Francis, 2011.

Park, Lisa S. H. *Consuming Citizenship: Children of Asian Immigrant Entrepreneurs.* Palo Alto, CA: Stanford University Press, 2005.

BIBLIOGRAPHY

Parker, Jason C. *Hearts, Minds, Voices: US Cold War Public Diplomacy and the Formation of the Third World*. Oxford: Oxford University Press, 2016.

Peffer, George Anthony. *If They Don't Bring Their Women Here: Chinese Female Immigration Before Exclusion*. Champaign: University of Illinois Press, 1999.

Pennybacker, Mindy. "The 'Haole Rich Kids' School: An Update." In *Punahou: The History and Promise of a School of the Islands*, ed. Nelson Foster, 119–49. Honolulu, HI: Punahou School, 1991.

Polk's Directory of Honolulu, 1940, 1949. University of Hawai'i at Mānoa Library, Hawaiian and Pacific Collections.

Rast, Raymond W. "The Cultural Politics of Tourism in San Francisco's Chinatown, 1882–1917." *Pacific Historical Review* 76, no. 1 (2007): 29–60.

Rath, Jan, Annemarie Bodaar, Thomas Wagemaakers, and Pui Yan Wu. "Chinatown 2.0: The Difficult Flowering of an Ethnically Themed Shopping Area." *Journal of Ethnic and Migration Studies* 44, no. 1 (2018): 81–98.

Reinecke, John E. *Feigned Necessity: Hawaii's Attempt to Obtain Chinese Contract Labor, 1921–23*. San Francisco: Chinese Materials Center, Inc., 1979.

Richter, Charles, and John S. Emrich. "How Honolulu's Chinatown 'Went Up in Smoke.'" American Association of Immunologists, July 2020. https://www.aai .org/About/History/History-Articles-Keep-for-Hierarchy/How-Honolulu%E2%80 %99s-Chinatown-Went-Up-in-Smoke-The-Fi.

Riley, Nancy E. "Race Into the Empire: The 'Chinese Problem' in Hawai'i." Unpublished manuscript, n.d.

Risse, Guenter. "Translating Western Modernity: The First Chinese Hospital in America." *Bulletin of the History of Medicine* 85, no. 3 (2011): 413–47.

Saranillio, Dean Itsuji. "Colliding Histories: Hawai'i Statehood at the Intersection of Asians 'Ineligible to Citizenship' and Hawaiians 'Unfit for Self-Government.'" *Journal of Asian American Studies* 13, no. 3 (2010): 283–309.

——. *Unsustainable Empire: Alternative Histories of Hawai'i Statehood*. Durham, NC: Duke University Press, 2018.

——. "Why Asian Settler Colonialism Matters: A Thought Piece on Critiques, Debates and Indigenous Difference." *Settler Colonial Studies* 3, nos. 3–4 (2013): 280–94.

Scheiber, Harry, and Jane Scheiber. *Bayonets in Paradise: Martial Law in Hawai'i During World War II*. Honolulu: University of Hawai'i Press, 2016.

Schmitt, Robert. "Death, Disease, and Distance from Downtown." *Hawaii Medical Journal* 15, no. 2 (1955): 131–32.

——. *Demographic Statistics of Hawaii: 1778–1965*. Honolulu: University of Hawai'i Press, 1968.

——. "How Many Hawaiians?" *Journal of the Polynesian Society* 76, no. 4 (1967): 467–76.

——. "Shifting Occupational and Class Structures: 1930–1966." In *Modern Hawaii: Perspectives on the Hawaiian Community*, ed. Andrew W. Lind, 27–40. Honolulu: University of Hawai'i, Labor-Management Education Program, College of Business Administration, 1967.

Scordo, Lizbeth. "Why You Shouldn't Leave Honolulu Without Visiting Chinatown." *Thrillist*, September 3, 2019. https://www.thrillist.com/eat/honolulu/best-restaurants -chinatown-honolulu-hawaii.

BIBLIOGRAPHY

Shah, Nayan. *Contagious Divides: Epidemics and Race in San Francisco's Chinatown*. Berkeley: University of California Press, 2001.

——. "Public Health and the Mapping of Chinatown." In *Asian American Studies Now: A Critical Reader*, ed. Jean Yu-wen Shen Wu and Thomas C. Chen, 168–92. New Brunswick, NJ: Rutgers University Press, 2010.

Shircliff, Jesse. "Is Chinatown a Place or a Space? A Case Study of Chinatown Singapore." *Geoforum* 117 (2020): 225–33.

Sigall, Bob. "Remembering Honolulu's Hell's Half Acre and Tin Can Alley of the 1880s–1960s." *Honolulu Star Advertiser*, March 18, 2022. https://historichawaii .org/2022/03/23/remembering-honolulus-hells-half-acre-and-tin-can-alley-of-the -1880s-1960s/.

Silva, Noenoe. *Aloha Betrayed: Native Hawaiian Resistance to American Colonialism*. Durham, NC: Duke University Press, 2004.

Smith, Tom. "Hawaiian History and American History: Integration or Separation?" *American Nineteenth Century History* 20, no. 2 (2019): 161–82.

Squires, Z. Y. *The Planters' Mongolian Pets*. Honolulu, HI, 1884. https://missionhouses .org/library-archives/.

State of Hawai'i. *Chinese Population by County, Island and Census Tract in the State of Hawaii: 2010*. Honolulu: Hawaii State Data Center, 2012, https://files.hawaii.gov /dbedt/census/Census_2010/SF1/HSDC2010-8_Chinese.pdf.

"Statehood for Hawaii's People." *Paradise of the Pacific* 71, no. 1 (1959): 11–14.

Stratton, Clif. *Education for Empire: American Schools, Race, and the Paths of Good Citizenship*. Berkeley: University of California Press, 2016.

Sueyoshi, Amy. *Discriminating Sex: White Leisure and the Making of the American "Oriental."* Champaign: University of Illinois Press, 2018.

Sun, Vivian. "Second Generation Chinese as Cultural Hybrids in the Territory Of Hawaii." Student paper, 1937, 11. Glick Papers, box 2, RASRL, University of Hawai'i.

Taira, Derek. "Making 'Womenly Women' or 'Servants of Civilization': Ida Pope and Native Hawaiian Female Education, 1894–1914." *Pacific Historical Review* 92, no. 1 (2023): 30–61.

Takaki, Ronald. *Pau Hana: Plantation Life and Labor in Hawaii*. Honolulu: University of Hawai'i Press, 1983.

——. "They Also Came: Chinese Women and the Migration to Hawaii." Paper presented at the Lucky You Come Hawai'i Conference, Honolulu, HI, July 18–21, 1988.

Tamura, Eileen. *Americanization, Acculturation, and Ethnic Identity: The Nisei Generation in Hawaii*. Champaign: University of Illinois Press, 1994.

——. "The Americanization Campaign and the Assimilation of the Nisei in Hawaii, 1920 to 1940." PhD diss., University of Hawai'i, 1990.

Taylor, Frank J. "Labor Moves On in Hawaii." *Saturday Evening Post* 219, no. 52 (1947): 24–25, 99–101.

Tchen, John Kuo Wei. *New York Before Chinatown: Orientalism and the Shaping of American Culture, 1776–1882*. Baltimore, MD: Johns Hopkins University Press, 1999.

Tenants on the Move. Video. University of Hawai'i Department of Ethnic Studies in conjunction with Information Technology Services, 2001.

Terzano, Kathryn. "Commodification of Transitioning Ethnic Enclaves." *Behavioral Sciences* 4 (2014): 341–51.

BIBLIOGRAPHY

Thigpen, Jennifer. *Island Queens and Mission Wives: How Gender and Empire Remade Hawaiʻi's Pacific World*. Chapel Hill: University of North Carolina Press, 2014.

Tom, Henry, Linda Furushima, and Paula Yano, eds. *A Hundred Years: McKinley High School, 1865–1965*. Honolulu, HI: McKinley High School Press, 1965[?].

Tom, Winifred. "The Impact of War on Chinese Culture." *Social Process in Hawaiʻi* 8 (1943):199–202.

Trask, Haunani-Kay. "Settlers of Color and 'Immigrant' Hegemony: Locals in Hawaiʻi." *Amerasia Journal* 26, no. 2 (2000): 1–24.

——. "Tourism and the Prostitution of Hawaiian Culture." *Cultural Survival* 24, no. 1 (2000). https://www.culturalsurvival.org/publications/cultural-survival-quarterly/tourism -and-prostitution-hawaiian-culture.

Trask, Mililani, and Haunani Kay Trask. "The Aloha Industry: For Hawaiian Women, Tourism Is Not a Neutral Industry." *Cultural Survival* 16, no. 4 (1992). https:// www.culturalsurvival.org/publications/cultural-survival-quarterly/aloha-industry -hawaiian-women-tourism-not-neutral-industry.

Trauner, Joan B. "The Chinese as Medical Scapegoats in San Francisco, 1870–1905." *California History* 52, no. 1 (1978): 70–87.

"True Citizens Meeting." *Pacific Commercial Advertiser*, October 16, 1869.

Tsui, Bonnie. *American Chinatown: A People's History of Five Neighborhoods*. New York: Free Press, 2010.

Turner, Arthur. "Racial Discrimination in Employment in Hawaii." Student paper, 1949. Student Papers, RASRL, University of Hawaiʻi.

Umbach, Greg, and Dan Wishnoff. "Strategic Self-Orientalism: Urban Planning Policies and the Shaping of New York City's Chinatown, 1950–2005." *Journal of Planning History* 7, no. 3 2008: 214–38.

Vellom, Betty. "Race Relations in Jobs." Student paper, 1946. Student Papers, RASRL, University of Hawaiʻi.

Victor Gruen Associates. *Report of the Studies and Recommendations for a Program of Revitalization of the Central Business District of Downtown Honolulu*. Honolulu: Victor Gruen Associates, Inc., 1968.

Vitello, Domenic, and Zoe Blickenderfer. "The Planned Destruction of Chinatowns in the United States and Canada Since c.1900." *Planning Perspectives* 35, no. 1 (2020): 143–68.

"Voices of Chinatown." Video transcript, 1977. Uncatalogued Papers, RASRL, University of Hawaiʻi.

Wagner, Peter. "A City Waiting to Be Reborn." *Honolulu Star Bulletin*, September 29, 1998.

Wallace, Don. "Chinatown's Latest Revival Is Putting It Back On the Map. But Will It Last?" *Honolulu Magazine*, February 24, 2017. https://www.honolulumagazine.com /chinatowns-latest-revival-is-putting-it-back-on-the-map-but-will-it-last/.

Walters, Melody M. Miyamoto. *In Love and War: The World War II Courtship Letters of a Nisei Couple*. Norman: University of Oklahoma Press, 2015.

Westly, Norman. "Race Differences in Home Ownership in the Makiki Area." *Social Process in Hawaii* 18 (1954): 33–34.

Wilkins, George. "The Herbert Lees." *Paradise of the Pacific* 62, no. 1 (1950): 3–5.

Wilson, David. "Making Historical Preservation in Chicago: Discourse and Spatiality in Neoliberal Times." *Space and Polity* 8, no. 1 (2004): 43–59.

BIBLIOGRAPHY

"Wing Wo Tai & Co. Building." HiChinatown.com. http://hichinatown.com/architecture /wing-wo-tai.

Wolfe, Patrick. "Settler Colonialism and the Elimination of the Native." *Journal of Genocide Research* 8, no. 4 (2006): 387–409.

Wong, Bernard P. "Introduction: Chinatowns Around the World." In *Chinatowns Around the World: Gilded Ghetto, Ethnopolis, and Cultural Diaspora*, ed. Bernard P. Wong and Chee-Beng Tan, 1–18. Leiden: Brill, 2013.

Wong, Edlie. *Racial Reconstruction: Black Inclusion, Chinese Exclusion, and the Fictions of Citizenship*. New York: NYU Press, 2015.

Wong, Fred. "Chinese Cultural History in the American West Put in Spotlight by Forest Service, Partners." U.S. Department of Agriculture, April 7, 2016. https:// www.usda.gov/media/blog/2016/04/07/chinese-cultural-history-american-west -put-spotlight-forest-service-partners.

Wong, K. Scott. *Americans First: Chinese Americans and the Second World War*. Cambridge, MA: Harvard University Press, 2005.

Wong, K. Scott, and Sucheng Chan, eds. *Claiming America: Constructing Chinese American identities During the Exclusion Era*. Philadelphia: Temple University Press, 1998.

Wong, Leonard K. M. "Hawaii Chinese: The Americanization Movement." Master's thesis, University of Hawai'i at Mānoa, 1999.

Wong, San Moi. "Bingham Tract Thru the Eyes of a Chinese," January 20, 1940. Student Papers, RASRL, University of Hawai'i.

Wood, C. B. "History of Medicine in Hawaii." Unpublished manuscript, May 1, 1926. https://evols.library.manoa.hawaii.edu/bitstreams/69d290e5-e118-4640-b718 -7ccbd6de1e7b/download.

Wu, Ellen. *The Color of Success: Asian Americans and the Origins of the Model Minority*. Princeton, NJ: Princeton University Press, 2015.

Yama, Evelyn, and Margaret Zimmerman. "Race Relations in a Hawaiian Business Firm." Student paper for Soc 256 class, February 1952. Student Papers, RASRL, University of Hawai'i.

Yamamura, Douglas, and Raymond Sakumoto. "Residential Segregation in Honolulu." *Social Process in Hawaii* 8 (1954): 35–47.

Yim, Bernard. "Chinese as a Stable Group in Chinatown." Student paper, 1950. Student Papers, RASRL, University of Hawai'i.

Yoshihara, Mari. *Embracing the East: White Women and American Orientalism*. Oxford: Oxford University Press, 2003.

Yu, Arthur Yuh-chao. "A Study of Chinese Organizations in Hawaii with Special Reference to Assimilative Trends," student paper for American Studies 641 class, December 15, 1970. Glick Papers, "Other Hawaiian," RASRL, University of Hawai'i.

Zhou, Min. *Chinatown: The Socioeconomic Potential of an Urban Enclave*. Philadelphia: Temple University Press, 1992.

——. *Contemporary Chinese America: Immigration, Ethnicity, and Community Transformation*. Philadelphia: Temple University Press, 2009.

Zuckerman, Steven. "Pake in Paradise: A Synthetic Study of Chinese Immigration to Hawaii." *Bulletin of the Institute of Ethnology Academia Sinica* 45 (1978): 39–80.

BIBLIOGRAPHY

ARCHIVES

Hawaii Chinese History Center
Hawai'i Medical Library Archives, Queen's Medical Centre
Hawai'i State Archives
Hawaiian Mission Children's Society Library Archives
Romanzo Adams Social Research Laboratory Archives, University of Hawai'i Libraries
University of Hawai'i at Mānoa Library, Hawaiian and Pacific Collections
William Smith Papers and Files, University of Hawai'i Libraries

INDEX

Aʻala Park, 187
African Americans, 21, 28, 142, 144; civil rights movement, 36, 133, 153, 161, 164, 168; urban renewal and, 168
agricultural labor, 93, 137
Ai, C. K., 138
Ai, David Chung, 138
air travel, 140, 163
Ala Moana (shopping mall complex), 167, 177
Alaska, 147
Ālewa Heights, 118
Alien Land Act (1913), 12
aliens, Chinese Americans as, 4, 12, 17–20, 60, 68, 145
Allen, Gwenfread, 112
Aloha Airlines, 122
American-born Japanese. *See* nisei
American-Chinese Club, 121
Americanism, 183
Americanization, 92, 96, 100, 108, 119
American Security Bank, 121
Amsterdam, 195
Anderson, Kay, 9, 16, 20, 211
Anderson, Lauren, 206

annexation of Hawaiʻi, 30, 44, 64–66, 73–74, 146
anti-Chinese discrimination and restrictions, 45, 59–64
anti-Chinese legislation, 17
anti-Chinese sentiments, 35, 55, 60, 62–63, 74; public health and, 76–81
anti-Chinese stereotypes, 60
anti-Japanese sentiments, 74, 104, 128
Antwerp, Belgium, 25
architecture, of state capitol, 183
Armstrong, Louis, 143
Asia and Pacific Collections at Hamilton Library, at University of Hawaiʻi, 34
"Asian American," as term, ix, 161
assets: financial, 116; property, 156–57
assimilation, 81, 96
Australia, 16, 19, 25, 197, 205
Autumn Festival, 16
Aytar, Volkan, 19

"bad" Asians, 32, 96, 114, 128, 134; model minority and, 73, 120; rhetoric beginnings around, 62
Bailey, Beth, 27, 112, 130

INDEX

banks, 56; American Security Bank, 121; Central Pacific Bank, 199; Chinese American Bank, 57, 121; Hawai'i National Bank, 202; Liberty Bank, 121
Bannick, Nancy, 171, 175–77
Basel missionaries, 39
Bauhaus, 183
Bayonet Constitution, 74, 214
Belgium, 25
Berglund, Barbara, 10
Big Five, 140
Bingham Tract, 89, 98, 117, 119
Bishop Museum, 217
Black Point, 117
Blangiardi, Rick, 207
blight, urban, 167
Board of Health (BOH), 35–36, 79, 80, 83–86, 126, 152, 191
Bourassa, Gregory, 5
Britain, 148
British Columbia, 20, 211; Vancouver, 9, 15
Brooklyn, New York, 209
Brubeck, Dave, 143
Brussels, Belgium, 25
bubonic plague epidemic, 35, 81–86, 118, 125
building conditions, in Chinatown, 78, 87, 117, 136, 169, 171–72, 181
Bureau of Labor, 131
Burns, John A., 183
Bushnell, O. A., 79
Byrd, Jodi, 212

cafeteria, school, 92
California, 91, 205; anti-Chinese sentiment in, 35; Los Angeles, 82, 144; Supreme Court, 12. *See also* San Francisco, California
Canada, 9, 15, 211
capital, 41–43, 50, 127; accumulation, 54; cultural, 23; global, 150, 214
Capital Investment Company, 202
capitalism, 53; global, 194, 215; neoliberal, 29; racial, 16, 19, 164, 182
Capitol: U.S., 183; Hawai'i state, 181, 183–84
Caribbean, the, 137, 164

Caucasians, 55, 110
Central Business District, 2, 32, 55, 79, 169, 181, 183–84
Central Pacific Bank, 199
Chaddha, Anmol, 7
change-makers, Chinese as, 17–20
Char, Y. T., 197
Char Hung Sut Restaurant, 191–92
Chen, Yong, 11
Cheng, Cindy, 142, 143, 144, 145, 158–59
Chicago, Illinois, 210
children: education of, 47, 48, 51–53, 90–93, 114–15
Chinatown: establishment and growth of, 55–59; historical constructions of, 8–12; as places of consumption, 14–17; today, 12–17, 186–207. *See also specific topics*
Chinatown Historic District, 26, 160, 175–78, 181, 198, 202, 210
"Chinatown – Is It Worth a Stop?" (travel website), 197
"Chinatown's Latest Revival Is Putting It Back on the Map. But Will It Last?" (article), 175–77, 186
Chinese American Bank, 57, 121
Chinese Chamber of Commerce, 188, 189
Chinese Civic Association, 121
Chinese Exclusion Act (1882), 12, 45, 65, 67, 74, 99, 129, 144
Chinese Hollywood, 89, 117
Chinese New Year, 198
"Chinese quarters," 8, 55
Chinese Student Alliance, 94
Ching, Hung Wo, 122
cholera, 79, 82, 83
Christian, Michelle, 212–14
Christianity, 10, 31, 52–53, 83, 92, 129, 155, 213–14
Christian marriage, 213
Chun, Elsie, 118
Chun, Hung Lum, 118
Chun, Quon, 118
citizenship, 127, 148, 214; social, 4, 18
City Beautification Committee, 175
City Mill hardware business, 138–39

INDEX

civil rights movement, 36, 133, 153, 161, 164, 168

Clark, James Beauchamp, 146

class: differences, 72; diversity, 138; "preferred classes," 116; working, 69. *See also* middle class

Club Hubba Hubba, 112–13

Cold War, 3, 31, 36, 133–36, 164–65, 204, 206; Hawai'i's place in, 145–50; multiculturalism and, 29, 151–56; racial politics in, 156–59; statehood debated in, 28, 146–50; United States in the world, 141–45

colonialism, 217; white, 45, 63, 66. *See also* settler colonialism

coloniality, 63, 213

commodification, of ethnicity, 195

Communism, 145

community centers, 56

Congress, U.S., 67, 99, 129, 146, 147, 149, 153, 166

Constitution of the Hawaiian Kingdom (Bayonet Constitution), 74

consumerism, 15, 195

consumption, 14–17, 18, 21–23, 32 154, 157, 158, 159, 167, 169, 201, 202, 204; racialized, 4, 155; linked to neoliberalism, 204

contemporary Pacific food, 2

contracts, labor, 20, 40, 59, 61

controlled burnings, for plague, 85

coolies, 224n7

Coover, Gary, 191

COVID-19 pandemic, 18, 192–93, 198

C. Q. Yee Hop, 118

C. S. Wo Chinatown, 101, 202

cultural ambassadors, 143

cultural capital, 23

data, secondary, 34

Davies, Theo H., 202

"deep and malleable whiteness" (Michelle Christian), 156, 212–13

Democratic Party, 137

Democratic Revolution (1954), 138, 162

dentistry, 124–26

Department of State, U.S., 166

"deserving" minority, 72, 127, 149

difference, 33–34; in class, 72; racial, 31, 77, 80, 135, 150, 182–83

Dillingham, Walter, 99

discrimination, racial, 11, 122, 123, 131–32, 148, 153, 206, 215 ; against Chinese, 8, 11, 20, 31, 37, 38, 59–64, 65, 69, 71, 76, 86, 94-5, 96, 101, 120; against Japanese 100, 105, 107–8, 130, 133, 143; against Filipinos, 131; future success and, 731

disease, 57–59; bubonic plague epidemic, 35, 81–86, 118, 125; gem theory of, 77, 124; haoles and, 49, 57–58, 84–85; public health and, 76–81; racialization of, 82; rats spreading, 82; screening, 9

Doll Face (film), 113

domestic servants, 55, 60, 93

EAH Housing, 171

East-West Center, 166

East–West divide, 26

economic growth, 123, 162

economic ladder, climbing, 49–53

economy: parallel, 121–22; racialized, 75; shifting, 123

education, 47, 48, 93; Japanese language schools, 106; medical training, 125–26; public schools, 90–92, *91*, 102, 106, 114–15, 126. *See also* schooling

elderly Chinese, 187

Elks Club, 121

Emmons, Delos, 107

empire (U.S.), 3, 199; American debates about, 147–48; Asian Americans against, 161; neoliberal multiculturalism and, 4; role in Hawai'i, 4–5, 26, 130, 133, 147, 155, 159, 166, 183–84, 212

empire building, 2–3, 4, 26, 136, 161, 166, 212

enclave, ethnic, 6–8

enfranchisement, Chinese exclusion from, 65, 74, 149

England Standard Schools, 114, 115

English language, "proper," 114–15

ethnic businesses, 15–16

ethnic enclave, 6–8

ethnic heritage sites, 199

INDEX

ethnicity, commodification of, 195
ethnic tourism, 195
ethnoburbs, 13
eugenics, 77
exoticism, 19, 31, 100

families, 69–70, 90; Christian marriage and, 213; Japanese, 128
Family of Man exhibit (1955), 158
Farber, David, 27, 112, 130
Farm, T. F., 96
Fat, Li Khai, 125
female migrants, 67–69
Fifth Chinese Daughter (Wong, J.), 143
Filipinos, 32, 37, 75, 103, 123, 131, 206, 215
financial assets, 116
fire: of 1900, 70, 71–73, 81–88; of San Francisco, 208
First Fridays, 196
first-generation immigrants, 52, 116, 124, 125
fish market, 1
Florida, 164
Flushing, Queens, 209
Fong, Hiram, 162
Fong, Ho, 65
foodstuffs, 2, 190
foreignness, 10–11
foreign policy, 145
Fort Shafter, 74
Foster Garden, 187
442nd Infantry Regiment, 138
France, 148
free-trade agreements, 64
Friend, The (newspaper), 62, 85
Fuchs, Lawrence, 122

gardens: Foster Garden, 187; Kukui Gardens, 170; market, 54
"gayborhoods," 210
Gentlemen's Agreement, 74
gentrification, 168, 180
Germany, 138
germ theory of disease, 77, 124
Gerrell, Bob, 177–79, 181
ghetto, 6–8
ghettoization, 7

GI Bill, 138
Gibson, Walter Murray, 59–60
Gieryn, Thomas, 6
Gillespie, Dizzy, 143
global capitalism, 194, 215
global politics, 75
Global South, 135, 142, 143, 148, 165
Gonzales, Vernadette Vicuña, 154
"good" Asians, 32, 113, 127–28, 132, 134, 204, 216; Americanization and, 96; model minority and, 73, 120; rhetoric beginnings around, 62
Gordon, Mike, 122
Grande, Sandy, 206
Great Depression, 119
"greater China," 189
Guam, 26, 148, 166
Guangdong Province, 11
Guinier, Lani, 97, 157

Hakka Chinese, 68, 95
Hakka Chinese Christians, 39
Hamilton Library, at University of Hawai'i, 34
haole, 20, 49, 72, 88, 95, 131, 156; Americanization and, 96, 119; anti-Chinese actions, 38, 45, 59–60, 61, 76, 93; decline in power of, 135; discrimination by, 31; disease and, 49, 57–58, 79, 84–85; education and, 91; efforts to discourage Native Hawaiian-Chinese interaction, 43, 61, 62–64; first settlers, 73–75; home ownership of, 119; income earned by, 116, 139; increasing control of Hawai'i by, 29–30, 47, 54, 73–75; Japanese Americans and, 106; Japanese-Chinese hostility and, 99; land ownership of, 89–90, 118; land rights and, 54; Native Hawaiians and, 42, 63–65; as owners of sugar plantations, 39, 46, 61; perceived privilege of, 120–21; rice industry and, 45; schools and, 52, 114–15; statehood opinions of, 149. *See also* whites
Harvard University, 162
Hawai'i. *See specific topics*
Hawaiian Airlines, 122

INDEX

Hawaiian Pineapple Company, 152
Hawaiian Renaissance (1970s), 163
Hawai'i Board of Health, 79, 80, 126, 152, 191
Hawai'i Chinese History Center, 35
Hawaii Chinese Journal, 96
Hawaii Chinese Weekly (newspaper), 169
Hawai'i Defense Volunteers, 108
Hawai'i National Bank, 202
Hawai'i Register of Historic Places, 176–77
Hawai'i State Archives, 35
Hawaii State Register of Historic Places, 118
Hee, Arthur K. C., 179
hegemony, 216
Hell's Half Acre, 170–71
Heong, Kong Tai, 125
Hickam Air Force Base, 141
high-rise apartment buildings, 174
Historic Buildings Task Force, 179
historic designation, 160, 176–77
Historic Hawai'i Foundation, 176
historic properties, 118–19
Ho, Catherine, 199
Ho, Chinn, 202
Hōkūle'a, 163
hole-hole, 40
holiday celebrations, 16
homelessness, 2, 193, 198, 199, 207
home values, 119
Hong, Grace Kyungwon, 216
Hong Kong, 188, 205
Honolulu. *See specific topics*
Honolulu Advertiser (newspaper), 174, 175
Honolulu Chamber of Commerce, 85, 166, 175
Honolulu Chinese Jaycees, 188
Honolulu Magazine, 186
Honolulu Redevelopment Agency (HRA), 169–70
Honolulu Tower, 170–71
Honolulu Trust Company, 121
Hope, Bob, 113
Hopper, Pegge, 192
Hotel Street, 112, 179
HRA. *See* Honolulu Redevelopment Agency

huis, 203
Hung Lum Chun Residence, 118

identity, "local," 215
Illinois, 210
Immerwahr, Daniel, 105
immigration, 64, 99; anti-Chinese legislation around, 17; earl years of, 8; germ theory of disease and, 77; law, 13, 45, 61, 67, 74; opinions on, 60; restrictions on, 44, 81, 144; women and, 68–69
imperialism, American, 35
incarceration, of Japanese Americans, 106, 138, 144, 151, 155
incomes: low-income housing, 170, 173, 181; mean, 162; median annual, 119; rise in, 116
individualism, 92, 98, 110
Inouye, Daniel, 202
interethnic relations, 97–100, 107
International Longshore and Warehouse Union, 137
interracial relations, 97–100; Hawaiian-Chinese relations, 41–44; Japanese-Chinese relations, 97–100
Isaki, Bianca Kai, 216
Italian Americans, 209
Izumo Taishakyo Mission Shrine, 195

Japan, 27, 36, 60, 99, 103, 105; as enemy nation, 104; Gentlemen's Agreement and, 74; Manchuria and, 98
Japanese Americans, 29, 37, 98–99, 123–24, 127, 132, 165; anti-Japanese sentiments, 74, 104, 128; families of, 128; incarceration of, 106, 138, 144, 151, 155; nisei, 99, 106, 107; during World War II, 138, 153
Japanese language schools, 52, 106

Kaho'olawe, 103, 111
Kaimuki, 89
Kajihiro, Kyle, 111
Kalākaua (king), 74
Kalihi, 162
Kaltmeier, Olaf, 204
Kānaka, 30, 42, 213, 215

INDEX

Katz, Julia, 20, 42, 43, 63, 75, 86
Kaua'i, 204
Kauanui, J. Kēhaulani, 53, 54, 213, 214, 215
Kaumakapili Church, 61
Kee Fook, Zane, 47
Kennedy, Jacqueline, 101
Kennedy, John F., 29, 154
Kent, Noel, 75
King, Lisa, 217
Kingdom of Hawai'i, 35, 37, 49, 64–65, 74
King's Cabinet, 74
Kohala plantation, 39
Korea, 60
Korean Americans, 147
Korean War, 27
Krattinger, Angela, 150
Kuan Yin Temple, 195–96
Kukui Gardens, 170
Kukui Project, 170
Kukui Tower, 170–71
Kuleana Act (1850), 54, 89, 213, 215
Kun, Joanna, 139
Kun, Lau, 139

labor: agricultural, 93, 137; contracts,
40; shortage, 110; strikes, 128–29, 137;
sugar industry, 2–3; unskilled, 38.
See also plantations
land, 53; acquisition of, 116–18, 156;
Māhele land division (1848), 54, 89,
118, 156, 213, 215; ownership, 54, 74, 75;
privatization of, 54, 89, 117; purchases,
201; rights, 30, 54, 163; value of, 202
language: Japanese language schools, 52,
106, 108; "proper" English, 114–15;
recovering, 163; Chinese language
schools 22, 52, 108
law: Alien Land Act (1913), 12; anti-
Chinese legislation, 17; Chinese
Exclusion Act (1882), 12, 45, 65, 67, 74,
99, 129, 144; immigration, 13, 45, 61,
67, 74; Kuleana Act (1850), 54, 89, 213,
215; martial, 105, 108, 110; Page Act
(1875), 67
Lee, George K. C., 179
Lee, Harry, 177–78
Lee, Herbert K. H., 152

Lee, Karen, 40
Lee, Richard K. C., 126, 152
Lee, Robert Man War, 122
Lee, Sammy, 143
lei shops, 1
leprosy, 58, 79
Li, Eva Xiaoling, 15
Li, Khan Fai, 118
Li, Min Hin, 118
Li, Minnie, 118
Li, Peter, 15
Li, Tai Heong Kong, 118
Liberty Bank, 121
Lin, Jan, 31, 195, 199, 200
lion-dancing organizations, 187–88
Little Italy, New York City, 209
"local" identity, 215
Los Angeles, California, 82, 144
Louisiana, 137
low-income housing, 170, 173, 181
Luke, K. J., 202
Lunar New Year, 188
lunchtime, business during, 1
Lung Doo Benevolent Society, 198
Lung Doo Building, 198

Māhele, 98; land division (1848), 54, 89,
118, 156, 213, 215
mai pake. See leprosy
Makiki Heights, 90, 139
manapua, 191–92
Manhattan, New York, 209
Mānoa Valley, 64, 117–18, 139
marginalized groups, 136
market gardens, 54
marriage: Christian, 213; same-sex, 210;
Hawaiian-Chinese, 42, 69
martial law, 105, 108, 110
Mau, Bat Moi Kam, 190–91
Mau, Harry Marn Sin, 191
Maunakea Marketplace, 177, 195
Mayor's Historic Buildings Task Force, 176
McKinley High School, 91, 92, 162
mean incomes, 162
median annual incomes, 119
medical training, 125–26
medicine, 124–26

INDEX

Mendonca Block, 179
methodology, 34–35
Mexicans, 10
middle class, 37–38, 71, 75, 81, 102, 106, 162; movement into, 114–26; rise of, 88–96
Mid-Pacific Institute, 47
military, 103, 140–42, 165, 166
Miller-Davenport, Sarah, 145, 150, 155, 157
Mills Institute, 47
missionaries, 39, 51, 52, 68, 75, 83, 92
mobility: socioeconomic, 123; upward, 116
model minority, 4, 17–21, 28–34, 65, 158; early construction of, 126–30; "good" and "bad" Asians and, 73, 120; neoliberal multiculturalism and, 151
modernity, 30, 167, 212, 214
Mohr, James, 80
Moloka'i, 58
Monterey Park, California, 13
Mormons, 10
multicultural acceptance, 97, 152
multiculturalism, 5, 32, 136, 151–56, 206; advertising, 164. *See also* neoliberal multiculturalism
Mun Lun School, 2, 22
Museum of Modern Art, 158

Narcissus Festival and Pageant, 182, 188, 189, 192, 200, 202
National Guard, 111
National Register of Historic Places, 176–77
Native Americans, 10
Native Hawaiians: cooperation with Chinese, 41–44; decline of communities, 29, 44, 46, 58, 97, 184; loss of land, 53, 54, 98, 111, 211; missing in Cold War rhetoric, 136, 148, 150, 155, 157; opposition to Chinese, 50, 58, 60–61, 64, 72, 97; opposition to statehood, 149, 150, 157
Nature Conservancy, 191
Navy, U.S., 105
neighborhood segregation, 7, 8, 80, 131, 143

neoliberal capitalism, 29
neoliberalism, 150
neoliberal multiculturalism, 36, 154, 157, 182, 184, 204–5, 216; model minority and, 151; racial capitalism and, 19; racial difference and, 150; success and, 4
New Year celebration, 16, 22, 188–89, 198
New York, 13, 209
New York Post, 129
New York Times, 9
nisei (American-born Japanese), 99, 106, 107
"not-deserving" minority, 72

O'ahu, 41, 45, 105
Oahu Country Club, 94
O'ahu Market, 190, 195
O'ahu Sugar Plantation, 46
Okihiro, Gary, 18
Old Vineyard (OV), 172
Orientalism, 15
Outrigger Canoe Club, 94, 121
OV. *See* Old Vineyard

Paccarro, Rudy, 178
PACE. *See* People Against Chinatown Evictions
Pacific Club, 94
Pacific Commercial Advertiser, 58–59, 64–66
Pacific Heights, 117
Pacific Islanders, 28, 165, 210
Page Act (1875), 67
Pang, Ching Lan, 25
Paradise of the Pacific (magazine), 22, 23, 146–47, 152, 154
parallel economy, 121–22
paternalism, 63
Pauahi Project, 171, 174
Pearl Harbor, 27, 36, 74, 103–6, 130, 133, 140
Pearl Harbor Shipyard, 107
Pearlridge (shopping mall complex), 167
People Against Chinatown Evictions (PACE), 173–75, 179, 181; slogan ("People, not profits"), 180

INDEX

People's Republic of China, 189
per capita savings, 93
"permitted multiculturalism," 204
Philippines, 26, 60, 137, 148, 166
Pidgin English, 96, 114
pineapple plantations, 39
place, 160–61; defining, 6–8; racial meaning and, 113
plague, bubonic, 35, 81–86, 118, 125
plane travel, 140, 163
plantations, 99; laborers, 37; labor shortage and, 110; leaving, 40–41; rice, 44–47; work declining on, 41–49; work in, 2, 39–41
politics: global, 75; racial, 3, 5, 26–28, 32, 36, 70, 138, 144, 156–59
Pope, Ida, 63
population: Black, 28; decline, 42, 45, 123; growth, 76; urban, 47
"preferred classes," 116
preservation, of Chinatown, 180–84
private schools, 92, 115
privatization of land, 30, 54, 89, 98, 117, 213, 215
produce, 1, 190
"proper" English, 114–15
property assets, 156–57
prostitutes, 23, 67–68, 103, 112–13, 138, 179
public health, 9, 35–36, 58–59, 76–88, 124–26
public schools, 90–92, 91, 102, 106, 114–15, 126
public services, lack of, 79
Puerto Ricans, 131, 168
Puerto Rico, 148, 166
Punahou School, 115, 120
Punti Chinese, 95

quarantines, for plague, 84
Queen Emma Development Project, 179
Queen Emma Project, 170
Queens, New York, 13, 209
Quon, Yim, 202

race, as social construction, 80
race equality, 142

racial bribe, 97, 132, 157
racial capitalism, 16, 19, 164, 182
racial categorization, 20
racial construction, 3
racial difference, 31, 77, 80, 135, 150, 182–83
racial discrimination, 11
racial diversity, 19
racial harmony, 29, 154, 155, 182
racial inequality, 53
racialization, 7, 83; of disease, 82; of social processes, 132
racialized economy, 75
racial landscape, 38
racial meaning, 113
racial plurality, 4
racial politics, 5, 26–27, 32, 36, 138, 144, 156–59; Cold War and, 28; settler colonialism and, 3, 34
racial tolerance, 31, 204
racism, 62, 67, 131, 133
Rast, Raymond, 208
Rath, Jan, 19
rats, disease spread by, 82
rebuilding, after fire, 87–88
reciprocity, 98
Reciprocity Treaty (1875), 64
redevelopment, 86, 167–68, 173–75, 180, 187
red-light district, 23, 112, 113
refugee camps, 87
Republican Party, 138
Republic of China, 189
retail businesses, 56
revitalization, 178–79
rice, 44–47
rights: civil rights movement, 36, 133, 153, 161, 164, 168; land, 30, 54, 163; voting, 74
River of Life, 193
Romanzo Adams Social Research Laboratory, 34
Roosevelt, Franklin, 105
Royal Hawaiian Agricultural Society, 41
rural enterprises, 30, 41–43
rural Hawai'i, plantation work in, 41–4
Russia. See Soviet Union

INDEX

Saiki, Scott, 193
salaried workers, 116
same-sex marriage, 210
Samoans, 206
Sam Yap Company, 11
San Francisco, California, 8–12, 24, 57, 76–78, 82, 129, 197–98; comparisons, 67–70; fire (1906), 208
San Francisco Chinese Times, 129
sanitation, 77, 87
Saranillio, Dean Itsuji, 216, 217
SARS epidemic (2003), 18
savings, per capita, 93
schooling, 47; Japanese language, 106; public, 90–92, *91*
School of Public Health at University of Hawai'i, 126
secondary data, 34
second-generation immigrants, 99, 128
See Dai Doo Society Building, 179
segregation, 7, 8, 18; of neighborhoods, 131
self-orientalizing, 198, 208
service businesses, 15
settler colonialism, 26, 29, 32, 38, 66, 70, 206, 211; model minority and, 4; racial politics and, 3, 34; sites of cooperation for, 43; as structure, 217
sex ratio, 68
Shah, Nayan, 2, 9, 12, 65, 68, 80, 81
Shaheen, George, 22
Shircliff, Jesse, 185, 197
Sinatra, Frank, 100–101
Singapore, 208
Sing Cheong Yuan bakery, 190
smallpox, 79, 82
Smith's Union Bar, 112
social change, 26
social citizenship, 4, 18
social geography, 211
socialization, 53; in public schools, 92
social ladder, climbing, 49–53
social organizations, 94, 121
social processes, racialization of, 132
socioeconomic mobility, 49–53, 71, 115–16, 123, 131

Soviet Union (USSR), 28, 133, 135, 142, 158, 165
space, 6–8
Star Bulletin (newspaper), 186
state capitol, 183, 184, 201
State Historic Preservation Office, 175, 176
statehood, 28, 136, 156–60, 165; debating, 146–50; opinions on, 149; racial politics and, 36
"Statehood for Hawaii's People," 146
stereotypes, 96; anti-Chinese, 60
strategic self-orientalizing, 198, 208
strikes, labor, 128–29, 137
student activist groups, 161
success, 32, 152–53, 157; discrimination and, 73; hard work bringing, 127; markers of, 155; neoliberal multiculturalism and, 4; reasons for, 120–24
Sueyoshi, Amy, 10–11
sugar industry, 35, 39, 45–46, 135, 137, 140, 180; decline of, 163; labor, 2–3; oligarchy, 75
Sunset Park, Brooklyn, 209
Sun Yat-Sen, 189
Supreme Court, California, 12
Switzerland, 39
Sydney, Australia, 16, 19, 25, 197, 205

Taiwan, 188, 189, 205
Tantalus, 118
taro, 42, 45–46, 75
Third World, 28, 142
Tin Can Alley, 170
Tin Tin Chop Suey, 174–75
tolerance, racial, 31, 204
Tongans, 206
Tongg, Ruddy, 122, 203
Torres, Gerald, 157
tourism, 26, 135, 154, 163–65, 180–82, 192, 196; ethnic, 195; military and, 140; statehood and, 150; strategic self-orientalizing and, 198, 208; urban renewal and, 169, 178
tourists, white, 10
transnationalism, 16, 25
Trans-Pacific Airlines, 122

INDEX

Tung Wah Dispensary, 12
Turner, Farrant, 166

United Club of Kohala, 94
United States (U.S.), 32, 160; annexation
of Hawai'i to, 30, 44, 64–66, 73–74,
146; anti-Chinese sentiment and,
63; Capitol, 183; Congress, 166; consumption in, 18; context of, 161–62;
Department of State, 166; disease in,
77, 81; disease screening in, 9; empire
building, 2–3, 4, 26, 136, 161, 166, 212;
foreign policy of, 145; ghettoes in,
7; Global South and, 155; Hawai'i as
valuable to, 27; health in, 76; labor
action in, 129; Navy, 105; Pearl Harbor
and, 27, 36, 74, 103–6, 130, 133, 140;
racial construction in, 3; racial difference for, 31, 147; racial harmony in,
29; racial politics in, 4, 5, 36, 156–59;
racism in, 26; Reciprocity Treaty in,
64; rice and, 45; segregation in, 8;
sugar and, 137; white America, 10; as
white nation, 17; in the world, 141–45.
See also specific topics
University of Hawai'i, 56, 91, 98, 114, 120,
162, 176; Asia and Pacific Collections
at Hamilton Library at, 34
unskilled labor, 38
Upper Nu'uanu Valley, 117
upward mobility, 116
urban blight, 167
urban population, Honolulu, 47, 48
urban renewal, 160, 167–80, 186
U.S. *See* United States
U.S. Army Medical Corps, 143
USSR. *See* Soviet Union

value, of land, 202
Vancouver, British Columbia, Chinatown
in, 9, 15, 211
Victor Gruen Associates, 178
Vietnam War, 27, 161, 165
Vineyard Boulevard, 171, 172
violence, 64, 67
voting rights, 74, 106, 149

Waipahu, 45, 46
Wall Street Journal, 196
War Department, 107
Washington, D.C., 183, 210
Western/American ideology, 3, 53, 97,
200, 203
Wheeler Army Airfield, 74
white/whiteness, 3, 30, 137–38, 212–14;
white colonialism, 45, 63, 66;
white flight, 167; white settlers, 38;
white supremacy, 3, 4, 147; working
class, 69
whites, 10, 17, 29, 60, 109, 138, 151; in
British Columbia, 20; constitution
by, 73; cultural capital for, 23; forced
segregation by, 11; Japanese Americans
and, 105–6; middle-class norms of, 81;
in Monterey Park, 13; in Waipahu, 45.
See also haole
Wilson, David, 6, 7, 207
Wing Wo Tai Building, 191
Wo, Ching Sing, 101, 202
Wo Fat Building, 196–97
Wo Fat Restaurant, 100–101, 197
Wolfe, Patrick, 31
women, 42, 67; immigration and,
68–69; as prostitutes, 113; and work,
110
women's movement, 161
Wong, Jade Snow, 143
Wong, Leonard, 101
working class, white, 49, 58, 67, 69, 104,
116
World War II, 27, 29, 36, 71, 99–100, 102–4,
112–13; buildup to, 105–11; Japanese
Americans during, 138, 153; Japanese
incarceration during, 151; legacies of,
130–34; model minority construction
in, 126–30; movement into middle
class in, 114–26; opportunities from,
30; prostitution and, 23

Yee Hop Market, 190
yellow peril, 17, 18, 81

Zane, Choy, 94